The
URANTIA
DIARIES
of Harold and Martha Sherman

VOLUME ONE: 1898-1942

Compiled, Transcribed and Edited by
SASKIA PRAAMSMA and MATTHEW BLOCK

SQUARE
CIRCLES
PUBLISHING

THE URANTIA DIARIES
of HAROLD and MARTHA SHERMAN
Volume One: 1898-1942
Compiled, Transcribed and Edited by
Saskia Praamsma and Matthew Block

Cover photos: [LEFT] Harold and Martha on the balcony of their
apartment on Riverside Drive in New York, circa 1940; [RIGHT]
Harry Loose in his front yard in Monterey Park, California,
mid-April 1941 [SHERMAN FAMILY PRIVATE COLLECTION].

Cover and interior: Syrp & Co.

ISBN: 978-0-9967165-9-8

Published by Square Circles Publishing
www.SquareCirclesPublishing.com

To go back to my letters again, I am told specifically that they must be "safely kept." I am hopeful that, as you suggest, some use may be made of them for the benefit of such humanity as could understand, by you putting them in some way into book form. I do not know. I do know, however, that the whole world is due very shortly for a great spiritual revival and attempt at understanding, and I do know that the great book, "The Book of Urantia," should be out in the next year-and-a-half to two years. And please remember when reading it and I am not here anymore, that although I had nothing to do with the writing of it, I have had other things to do with it for now over thirty-five years.

—*Harry Loose to Harold Sherman, March 10, 1941*

CONTENTS

INTRODUCTION

The years from approximately 1924 to 1955, in which the evolving manuscript of the Urantia Book was shared with a small group in Chicago called the Forum, is an intriguing period in the history of the Urantia Book and its readership. Only one source of extensive and detailed information about this period has come to light: the diaries and letters of Forumites Harold and Martha Sherman. During their stay in Chicago, from 1942 to 1947, the Shermans recorded what was said and done at every Forum meeting they attended. They also recorded their conversations with their Forumite friends and acquaintances outside Forum meetings. Their diligent documenting resulted in close to two thousand pages of eyewitness accounts which portray Forum life with unmatched vividness and immediacy.

What makes their story especially piquant is that Harold was a controversial figure. Outspokenly critical of some of the plans of Forum leaders Dr. William S. Sadler and his son Bill, Harold was accused by Dr. Sadler of disrupting the superhumanly authorized running of the Forum. Sadler allowed the Shermans to continue to attend Forum meetings, but they became estranged from the Sadlers and kept aloof from most of the Forumites. Feeling unjustly blamed, the Shermans wrote sharp, critical reports of the ensuing Forum activities, which contrast with the vague, rosy accounts of the Forum given decades later by non-Forumites.

In this and succeeding volumes of *The Urantia Diaries of Harold and Martha Sherman*, we present the Shermans' Urantia-related experiences, as reported by themselves in their letters and diaries.

Harold Morrow Sherman (1898-1987) was born in Traverse City, Michigan, into a middle-class family. He had a multi-faceted career. Starting out as a newspaper reporter and advertising copywriter, he went on to publish hundreds of short stories for boys and dozens of juvenile books. He also wrote six novels, two Broadway plays and two Hollywood screenplays. Deeply idealistic and feeling himself psychically gifted, he authored several bestselling books in the ESP and self-realization fields, some of which are still in print. Early in life he sensed that he had a mission to perform for humanity, a mission somehow connected to his writing, a mission he tried earnestly to discover and actualize as he continued to write.

Harold's wife, Martha Bain Sherman (1898-1998), was also born and raised in Traverse City. She trained as a nurse but devoted her life to caring for Harold and their two daughters. She was Harold's confidante and sounding board, sharing his occult and parapsychological interests and collaborating on many of his projects.

Eight years after the Shermans left Chicago, the Urantia Book was first published. It was, according to unverified stories, the outcome of a mysterious series of events that began when two Chicago physicians, William S. Sadler and his wife Lena K. Sadler, met a man who transmitted messages from higher sources in his sleep.

Alluding to the phenomenon in his 1929 book, *The Mind at Mischief*, Sadler said that the initial encounter occurred in the summer of 1911. He wrote that, in the ensuing eighteen years, he had been "present at probably 250 of the night sessions, many of which have been attended by a stenographer who made voluminous notes," in which various superhuman personalities spoke through the sleeping man. In an unpublished essay written in 1960, Sadler explained that the communications described the nature of God, the structure and administration of the universe, angelic realms and beings, the afterlife, and other inhabited planets. He said that a "contact commission," consisting of those who were present when the man transmitted messages, was formed. Its members were the Sadlers, Lena's sister Anna, and Anna's husband, Wilfred C. Kellogg. Later, the Sadlers' son Bill and their friend Emma L. Christensen joined.

Sadler told the Shermans and other Forumites that he invited other physicians and the magician Howard Thurston to observe the sleeping man, but the existence of this man has never been substantiated. No supporting documentation—Sadler's medical records of the man, the stenographer's notes of the sessions, or the man's own handwritten communications—has ever surfaced.

In 1923 Sadler formed a weekly discussion group at his home/office—the Forum—made up of his and his wife's patients and friends. In 1924 he shared with them some of the mysterious communications and told them that the superhuman beings were willing to answer their philosophical, cosmological and religious questions in connection with a comprehensive revelation they were preparing. Those in the Forum who were interested submitted hundreds of questions, via the contact commission, which led to the appearance of a bulky handwritten manuscript addressing many of those questions, in late 1924. The Forum became a closed, secret group whose function was to listen to and comment on the developing manuscript, and to submit further questions.

By the mid 1930s the higher beings had transmitted a prodigious document of 196 papers, including a highly detailed account of the life and teachings of Jesus. In 1942, the year the Shermans arrived, Sadler announced that the Forum's function as a question-asking body was terminated. The Forum members still met weekly to listen to Sadler, his son or other Forumites read out and comment on the manuscript.

"The Book of Urantia," as it was then called, was intended to be published and, as it spread, prove itself to be a major revelation of truth from celestial beings to our world. The superhumans were to give permission for printing when the time was right; until then, the group was to prepare the book for publication and raise money for the plates.

One of the early Forumites, who plays a pivotal role in this series of volumes, was a Chicago policeman and detective named Harry J. Loose. One evening in July 1921, when Loose was in Marion, Indiana, giving a Chautauqua lecture on crime, he was interviewed by Harold Sherman, then a young newspaper reporter. During their brief meeting, Loose dazzled Sherman with his apparent telepathic abilities and mentioned that he, Loose, would be dropping out of sight while on a "mission." In a letter to Sherman a few weeks later, Loose intimated that Sherman himself was "fitted to a mission of tremendous good and importance to the world." Soon afterward, Harold and his family moved to New York where Harold became a successful writer and radio personality, as well as a noted ESP experimenter. In February 1941, he felt impelled to track down Harry Loose and learned that he was living in retirement in Monterey Park, a suburb of Los Angeles, California.

The two men began a correspondence in which Loose explained that he and Sherman had a bond spanning many lifetimes, that the two belonged to a special order of beings who incarnated on Earth periodically to perform important missions. He also imparted much information derived from the Urantia material.

Enticed and inspired by Loose's repeated assertions that a great mission lay in store for him, Harold was anxious to see his mentor again face to face. His desire was realized in May 1941, when a screenwriting assignment brought him to Hollywood. As the men became better acquainted, Harold learned of Loose's connection to Dr. Sadler and the Urantia phenomenon. He also realized that Sadler was a cousin of an old friend of his and Martha's from Marion, Indiana, Josephine Davis, and it was through her that the Shermans were introduced to Sadler and accepted as Forum members during a brief trip to Sadler's home in Chicago in August 1941.

Even though they had still not seen or read the Urantia text, the couple were so impressed with what they'd heard from Harry Loose that they made plans to move to Chicago to pursue a full-time study of the new teachings as soon as Harold's screenwriting project was finished. Harold and Sadler also maintained a correspondence in which Harold expressed his ideas about the important role he believed he was destined to play in dramatizing aspects of the revelation to capture public attention.

This volume of *The Urantia Diaries* contains the correspondence Sherman had with Loose, Sadler, Sir Hubert Wilkins and others about the Urantia phenomenon before the Shermans arrived in Chicago in May 1942 and began attending the Forum and keeping the diaries. These letters are just as interesting historically as the diaries, giving a glimpse of how the knowledge of the Urantia text was diffused in these years.

BIOGRAPHICAL NOTES
ON WILLIAM S. SADLER
AND HARRY J. LOOSE

The Shermans' Urantia experience was largely conditioned by two fellow Midwesterners from the previous generation: Harry J. Loose and William S. Sadler. Loose introduced Harold to the Urantia revelation, assuring him of the great role he was to play in its presentation to the world; Sadler welcomed Harold into the fold as a favored Forumite but soon clashed with him, turned most of the Forumites against him and effectively stymied his Urantia ambitions. Following is a brief biographical sketch of each man.

WILLIAM SAMUEL SADLER, SR. (1875-1969) was born in Spencer, Indiana, and schooled at home in nearby Wabash and in Crawfordsville, Indiana. Embracing Seventh-day Adventism as a child (his parents, Samuel Cavins and Sarah Izzabelle Wilson Sadler, were already adherents), in 1889 he moved to Battle Creek, Michigan, where he worked at the Battle Creek Sanitarium and attended Battle Creek College, both SDA institutions. After working for fellow SDA members Dr. John Harvey Kellogg and his brother Will K. Kellogg, selling breakfast cereal and other vegetarian products to grocery stores, in 1893 Sadler was sent to Chicago by Dr. Kellogg, to help manage the SDA medical mission in Chicago. The purpose of the mission was to rehabilitate and Christianize slum dwellers. There he founded and co-edited *The Life Boat* magazine, which reported on the mission's activities. He also attended classes at Chicago's Moody Bible Institute.

In 1897 Sadler married Dr. Kellogg's half-niece, Lena Celestia Kellogg. Their first child died as an infant in 1900. A year later, the Sadlers were sent by Kellogg to establish a new medical mission in

San Francisco, and William became an elder (ordained minister) of the SDA Church. That same year both William and Lena enrolled at Cooper Medical College in San Francisco. In 1903 William became caught in a church policy dispute between the SDA leader and prophet, Ellen G. White, and Dr. Kellogg, and at White's request the Sadlers returned to Battle Creek, where they resumed their medical educations at the SDA's American Medical Missionary College.

Graduating in 1906, they moved to La Grange, Illinois, a suburb of Chicago, to work at the SDA-run Hinsdale Sanitarium. In 1907 their son, William Samuel Sadler, Jr., was born. About this time they founded The Chicago Institute of Physiologic Therapeutics, which administered treatments similar to those of Dr. Kellogg. Sadler also became a professor of physiologic therapeutics at the Post Graduate Medical School of Chicago.

From 1907 to about 1923, the Sadlers also lectured on the Chautauqua-Redpath circuit [*Ed. Note:* see footnote on p. 35], on such subjects as preventive medicine and slum conditions. Shortly after 1913 the Sadlers ended their involvement with the Seventh-day Adventist church, moving from La Grange to Chicago.

In about 1920 Sadler became senior attending surgeon at Chicago's Columbus Hospital. Sometime in the 1930s he began calling himself a psychiatrist, becoming a consultant in psychiatry at the same hospital. He lectured in pastoral psychiatry at the Presbyterian Theological Seminary (later called the McCormick Theological Seminary) in Chicago from about 1930 to 1956.

Active in the popularization of physical and mental hygiene, Sadler wrote dozens of articles for such magazines as *Ladies' Home Journal* and *The American Magazine*. He also wrote over thirty books, many of which, it has recently been discovered, were heavily derived from books by other authors. (See The Sadler Project on www.urantiabooksources.com for studies tracing Sadler's use of sources in several of his books.) His best-known works were *The Mind at Mischief: Tricks and Deceptions of the Subconscious and How to Cope with Them* (1929) and the textbook, *Theory and Practice of Psychiatry* (1936).

Outliving his wife by some thirty years, Sadler played a leading role in forming the Urantia Foundation and the Urantia Brotherhood and in publishing the Urantia Book. He died in 1969, without ever publicly identifying himself with the Urantia phenomenon.

* * *

Harry Jacob Loose was born in Springfield, Illinois, in 1880. In a letter to Harold Sherman dated April 30, 1941, Loose says: "I was born September 13, 1869. I will be 71 years old this coming September 13." Yet his *Chicago Daily News* obituary of November 22, 1943, states that he was 63 when he died, making 1880 the year of his birth. His gravestone in El Monte, California, likewise gives his birth year as 1880.

He was appointed to the Illinois State Police in 1901, served four years, and became a Chicago police officer in 1906. He worked for six years in the Juvenile Protection League at Jane Addams' famed Hull House. In 1914 he was chief investigator for the City Crime Commission, and he operated his own detective agency for several years. In 1928 he began work as head of the security staff at the *Chicago Daily News,* retiring in 1934 and leaving Chicago for California.

Loose authored one book, *The Shamus: A Real Detective's Story* (1920), which was described in a promotional notice as a "true tale of Thiefdom and an expose of the real system of crime."

Precisely when Loose become involved with William S. Sadler and the Urantia phenomenon is unknown. Loose certainly knew Sadler as early as 1917, because in a letter in February of that year, Sadler recommended Loose to the president of the International Lyceum Bureau (Sadler's Chautauqua-Redpath booking agency) as a man of "splendid ideals, lofty principles, and high moral character." Perhaps thanks to Sadler's recommendation, Loose traveled the Chautauqua-Redpath circuit, from about 1918 to 1923, lecturing several times a week every summer on the causes, prevention and nature of crime. At the same time, the Sadlers toured the circuit with presentations on health topics.

At some point previously, probably in the mid 1910s, Loose became a patient of Sadler's. The Shermans' diary entry of August 7, 1942 records Sadler's recollection of the circumstances:

> Dr. Sadler [said] that Harry . . . had come to him as a patient being nervously upset over attempts of his buddies in the police department to frame him. Harry was a man of great physical powers but had been shot through the abdomen and had had a serious operation some time before, which had no doubt contributed to his nervous condition. Dr. Sadler stated that it required several years for Harry Loose to be straightened out. . . .

Referring to the early days when he was investigating this phenomenon [of the sleeping man], Dr. Sadler said he called in several physicians as observers and also the well-known magician Thurston in an attempt to get some plausible explanation of what was occurring. These men were as confounded as Dr. Sadler. It was during this time that Harry J. Loose came to him as a patient and was introduced to this phenomenon by Dr. Sadler. When asked a point-blank question as to whether Harry Loose had actually witnessed the human instrument through whom the phenomena was being performed, Dr. Sadler declared he could not answer. . . . He did say, however, that Harry Loose often reassured Dr. Lena by saying, "Don't worry about the chief. He'll come around. He'll believe in this," indicating that Harry was "sold" on what was happening long before Dr. Sadler himself became convinced.

The Forum was organized in 1923, and Loose was probably among the first members. His wife, Emily, and daughter Josephine joined in 1931. The Looses remained in Chicago studying the Urantia material until 1934. Loose and the Shermans corresponded from 1941 until his death in November 1943.

One puzzling feature of Loose's letters to Sherman is his referencing of more than a score of passages from "The Life and Teachings of Jesus," a portion of the Urantia manuscript which, according to Sadler and others directly involved, did not appear until 1935 or 1936. If Loose left Chicago in 1934, how was he able to reference so many specific passages? The likely answer (although we have found no evidence for it) is that he returned to Chicago one or more times between 1936 and 1941 and was permitted to read the new Urantia material, and while reading made copious notes.

Another puzzling feature is Loose's deliberately cryptic references to these Urantia passages in his early letters and his mixing them together with his other esoteric ideas and occupations. For instance, in his letter of February 17, 1941, Loose tells Sherman that the writings from which the passages were gleaned "are safe in a 'Shangri-La' sort of a place. You will visit there some day too. From the written records there, which I have seen—how different is the truth, how much more fully informative than our own present Bible . . ." In the same

making,he taught the younger children to read by the use of that prayer written
with charcoal on a smooth board oh the wall of the carpenter shop---and it was
this prayer that they all used in the home life. Pardon the repitition but it i
so worth repeating. This is the true and accurate way in which we acquired the
Prayer". In the same line of thought,I will tell you that the now generally acc
pictures and personality expressed therein of Joshua are wrong badly.He was a m
medium height,judged by present day standards,but full fleshed,virile and power
With titian shoulder long hair that curled and a reddish short beard and small
mustache----large brown eyes that were very expressive and full of life. There w
nothing weak nor effeminate about him. He was all man. Please know that this
Intelligence,Joshua ben Joseph,was only one of many of an Order whose sole offi
was,and is,the introduction of Man to the Great Intelligence. At a certain peri
in the growth and developement of Life on these new worlds,whose making conti
goes on,comes a time when Man searches for God and the "why" and mystery of Li
After a long period of Man's groping in the darkness for the answer,and at the
proper time,comes one of the fully spiritual Order to which Joshua belonged. On
each young world,the proocedure is the same. No individual Intelligence,a membe
this Order,could answer the need. There are a great number. It is one of the w
proceeding from growth. The appearance of Joshua ben Joseph here was his 7th a
last presentation in this step of progress and growth. He was the "Son of God"
You,too,are a Son of God. Read your Bible.Nazereth was the cross roads of seve
busy caravan routes. Joshua became a caravan conductor,after some years back
old carpenter shop. He had the responsibility for the safety of the caravan,th
employees and animals and their loads of freight and the"mail"---written messa
to be delivered in the towns through which the caravan passed---he was also re
sible for the passengers that,for safety,accompanied it,and the paid guard & e
He met a very rich Persian who travelled as a passenger on one of these routes
man had a son of 16 years that accompanied him. For some years,Joshua travelle
this man as tutor to the son. He visited Rome and much of the then known world
the company of this man and his son. I could write on and on. I could tell you
Abner. He was a disciple of John before the coming of "the Christ". But after
Christ" came,Abner became His disciple. He was one of the seventy two discipl
that were sent out to carry the message to far places and establish Churches.
(See your Bible) And Abner did establish and build a Church in Philladelphia
Perea---accross the Gallilean Sea---and this Church remained there for 800 years
the passing of Joshua. It was finally distroyed---burned---and levelled to the
by the Arabs. Abner did not agree with James,the boother of Joshua,who became
of the new Church in Jerusalem or with Paul ,who became head of the new Churc
Antioch,because of their concessions to the religous cults of the day to help
converts and because they tried to make a religeon of Joshua and his life and
instead of what Joshua taught. However,Abner left his own writings of his expe
oes and they were not destroyed. It was to Abner's Church in the little town o
Philladelphia that Lazarus fled in fear of the Pharisees after being raised fr
dead by Joshua and who labored there with Abner. O I could go on and on and on
But I must get on with my letter. I am still leading you gently. I would like
take just these few lines though to become a bit personal and remark that you
be tremendously intreigued when you are introduced to real advanced telepathy.
will use it frivilously somewhat at first---just as I did. We are all the same.
would like to see you in the flesh---right here on this dimension---and talk wi
but I am in doubt as to whether it will ever occur. It would be better not. I
idea,too,that such a meeting would be a bit dissapointing to you to see me---me
a tired old man,in wrinkled clothes,like many of those that you see on the par
benches when you pass. Except that I could perhaps,permissably, talk to you o
of intrest to us both. I am old. Older than you think.I have been in service
long period and am tired. I know that my virility is leaving me slowly though
been well preserved. In the very natural course of human events,I will be re
in the not far distant future. It does not seem in accord that I should go on
the next dimension without leaving some younger,stronger,more virile mortal

A sample page from a Harry Loose letter.

letter Loose claims to have attended a meeting of a Dr. Mitchell in which the doctor testified to having encountered a poltergeist. Loose then verifies the existence of ghosts and poltergeists, contradicting the Urantia teachings. Moreover, a Google search of Loose's story of Dr. Mitchell shows that it was copied from a then recently published book. In his later letters Loose shared messages and other information he claimed to have received from higher sources, which he also copied from books.

Why did Loose engage in these obfuscations and misrepresentations, including telling Sherman that he was born in 1869 and not 1880? Apparently, Loose at first didn't expect to meet Sherman; when Sherman expressed his desire to meet him, he gave various reasons why such a meeting should not and would not take place. But the two men did meet and Sherman treasured their growing relationship, although he was perplexed occasionally by some of Loose's words and actions.

Editors' Note

This and the following volumes of *The Urantia Diaries of Harold and Martha Sherman* are a comprehensive revision of the five-volume *The Sherman Diaries*, which was published between 2002 and 2008 by Square Circles Publishing.

In this series we have omitted Harold's business-related correspondence, keeping the focus squarely on the Shermans' Urantia-related activities. We included such letters in the previous series to show that Harold carried on his Forum involvement in the midst of a strenuous and varied career. For this series we have substituted the business-related letters with footnotes or bridges, when necessary, informing the reader about the course of his various projects during the Forum years.

After the first series was published we found more letters from Harry Loose and have added them here. We have also been able to date his undated letters with certainty, thanks to having retrieved the original postmarked envelopes. On the back of each envelope Martha had summarized the contents of the particular letter, which made it easy to identify which letter belonged to which envelope.

In the first series we opted to make Loose's letters more readable by editing their punctuation, moving sentences, deleting repeated passages and inserting paragraph divisions. In the new volumes we are presenting the letters in their original, unedited form although we have let the paragraph divisions stand. We have also refrained from editing Harold Sherman's letters for this series, leaving his idiosyncratic punctuation and capitalization styles intact.

Acknowledgments

We wish to thank the following people for the help or information they have given us:

The late Martin Gardner, who announced the existence of the diaries in his 1995 book, *Urantia: The Great Cult Mystery*, and said they'd be made available at the University of Central Arkansas, in Conway, in January 2000.

Our friends John Bunker and Karen Pressler, who traveled to the UCA as soon as the diaries were released and copied them for us. More recently they helped us fill in gaps in the Sherman-Wilkins correspondence with letters they found in the Sir Hubert Wilkins papers at the Ohio State University Byrd Polar Research Center in Columbus, Ohio.

Mary Sherman Kobiella and Marcia Sherman Lynch, the daughters of Harold and Martha Sherman, who allowed us to include the Harry Loose letters as well as the Ara messages, both of which were still in their private possession when this project began. They also gave us permission to quote from Harold Sherman's published works. Both Mary and Marcia were gracious hostesses on numerous occasions when Saskia, alone or with Matthew, visited them at their respective homes in Arkansas. They gave freely of their time, sharing memories and photographs, and have since become lasting friends of ours.

The staff at the Archives and Special Collections at the University of Central Arkansas, especially Jimmy Bryant, David E. Bowie, Jr., Betty Osborn, Cynthia Frase, Artency Davis, Michelle Strouse, Sarah Langford and Aryn Denette, for helping us locate various materials.

Saskia Praamsma
Matthew Block
Lage Vuursche, the Netherlands
October 2016

Part 1

The Early Years

1.

TRAVERSE CITY

This and the following four chapters are made up of passages from some of Harold Sherman's books in which he tells his own story. The title of the book follows each excerpt.

I owe an everlasting debt to my father, Thomas H. Sherman, who left this life on March 1, 1921. I was twenty-two at the time, just commencing to formulate my concepts of what life was all about and to decide what part I wanted religion to play in it. . . .

In [his time], Dad would perhaps have been labeled a free thinker. He believed profoundly in an Infinite Intelligence that could not be contained or confined in any man-made creed or any religion—an Intelligence that could be worshipped in all nature, in all forms of life, in earth and sky and water—everything within and without man testifying to His presence as well as His greatness.

There were few people in the little town of Traverse City, Michigan, who were prepared or interested at that time to discuss these subjects with Dad, so he must have experienced a degree of loneliness in this area of his life. He was well read and spent many evenings at home in the company of books of the world's great thinkers. He was a lover of Shakespeare. Not having had much opportunity for schooling, he could truly be said to have been self-educated. He possessed an inner wisdom and an understanding of human nature which I have since come to realize was all too rare.

My mother, Alcinda Morrow Sherman, was a lifelong Methodist. Her father, Joseph Morrow, had served as a Methodist minister, although he had retired in later years, unable in conscience to continue preaching the orthodox doctrines. My father was happy for Mother to continue her activities in the Methodist Church, but he usually preferred to remain home with his readings during Sunday mornings. When he went to church, he preferred the Congregational faith, having left the Catholic Church, his family's religion, when he was nine years of age.

When I was a young boy of Sunday School age, Dad saw to it that I was not compelled to go to church. He had told Mother in his quiet, nonarguable way that he did not want his three boys to be indoctrinated in any faith; that he wished them to reach the age of accountability open-minded so they could decide for themselves what concepts of God and what philosophy of life felt right for them. This bestowal of freedom of thought, I came to realize, was Dad's greatest, most priceless gift to me. . . .

My youth was lived in the tranquil, uneventful, crystal radio-set days when one of my greatest thrills was the nights I was able to bring in WGY, Schenectady. It was so far away, and the outside world and what was going on there seldom occupied my thoughts. I couldn't care less what happened to anyone outside my own hometown. Life was peaceful and happy; I was in the womb of self-content. The First World War hadn't happened yet. Boys seldom left their places of birth. Many followed traditionally in their fathers' footsteps, and girls hadn't begun to seek careers beside the long-accepted one of wife and mother. If you wanted to smoke before you were out of knee pants, you had to roll your own with corn silk and take some secret puffs in the alley with the gang or behind the barn or an outhouse. When it came to drink, you had to be just as secretive; and while there was petting, the advertised risk of picking up a social disease or getting a girl pregnant was often enough to keep a fellow reasonably "straight." The "wages of sin" were preached at you from every side and you weren't permitted to forget the reality of hell and the promise of heaven. Automobiles—gas buggies—were just starting to corrupt the countryside by offering a freedom of travel that put distance between those who might stand guard over personal conduct and public morals.

We listened to lecturers who invaded our provincial area on rare occasions. Our most enlightening experience was when we annually went to see the Lyman Howe motion picture of distant scenes and peoples in foreign countries, with Lyman Howe, himself, standing beside the silent movie screen, doing his own narration and creating his own sound effects. *Bang!* There went a rear tire on the Tin Lizzie! *Pow! Pow!* Just see that old Wild West and those Injuns bite the dust!

[*How to Take Yourself Apart and Put Yourself Together Again*, 1970]

It was a few minutes after noon, October 6, 1914. I was about to bicycle back to high school on the other side of town when the premonition hit me. I saw that my younger brother, Edward, age eleven, had climbed the tree in our front yard, between the sidewalk and the street, and I had a fleeting vision of his falling and getting seriously hurt. My impulse at the moment was to stop and call him down and make him promise not to climb that tree again.

I reached in my pocket and took out a nickel with the thought that if I offered this to him, it would be added inducement for him to keep such a promise, although Edward was such a truthful little fellow, I knew whatever he promised would be done.

But a nickel meant more to a boy in those days than it does now. I juggled the coin in my hand and decided I was worrying about something that wouldn't happen; so I shoved it back in my pocket and dismissed my feeling of apprehension as I rode off to school, waving Edward goodbye.

Three hours later, as I rounded the corner onto our street, a block from home, I heard screams of pain and saw neighbors carrying my brother into our house. He had come home from nearby Boardman Grade School and gone up the tree again, but a rotten limb had broken off. He had been precipitated to the cement sidewalk, breaking both arms so badly that bones came through the flesh.

Mother and Dad were not home—only Margaret, our live-in maid. My parents had gone out for a ride on Grand Traverse Bay with our cousin Rob Price in his home-built yacht and would not be back until after dark.

As Edward was placed in my parents' downstairs bedroom, his pitifully broken arms resting on two pillows, he looked up at me as I came in and said, "Oh, Harold—see—I can't ever draw again!" Edward had artistic ability far beyond his years—an intelligence and perception, for that matter, far in advance of his age. All of us in the family had recognized this. I am sure that by his very nature and sunny disposition he was the most beloved of us three boys, for I had another younger brother, Arthur.

Our family physician, Dr. Martin, soon arrived, took quick note of the gravity of the situation, turned to me and said he would need help. The dining room table was cleared, and Edward was carried and laid upon it. Then Dr. Martin applied chloroform and started the grim business of setting the fractures, while I held Edward's body secure and handed the doctor whatever implements he needed. It was an ordeal that burns into my consciousness to this day, and all through the operation, the thought kept repeating, "This wouldn't have happened if you'd given Edward that nickel and made him promise . . . this wouldn't have happened! . . ."

Yes—I had been warned—something had told me about this impending tragedy. I had had my chance to prevent it, and I had somehow failed. How could I ever forgive myself? Had a nickel possibly meant more to me than my brother's life? Why had I talked myself out of speaking to Edward—which might have kept him from falling?

Finally, the two broken arms were set, as best as Dr. Martin could repair them, even though crudely, because it was difficult to straighten out the arms and stretch the protruding bones back into position with the facilities then available.

Leaving Margaret to care for the still anesthetized Edward, I jumped on my bicycle and raced the five blocks down to the Wequetong Club on the bay front where Cousin Rob kept his boat, and ran out on the dock and searched the waters for sight of the returning yacht. But, though I saw the familiar Marion Island, some eight miles away in the setting sun, there was no trace of a boat. Somewhere beyond and behind this island were my parents, enjoying this outing, all unmindful of the tragedy to which they would be returning.

Here I was, a boy of sixteen, alone on the beach, with only the rhythmic sounds of waves breaking on the shore, as dusk was dimming the landscape and the pink was leaving the sky. The gathering darkness seemed to add to the desolation I felt in my heart. Why did this have to happen? If there was an all-merciful, all-loving God, as I had been taught, how could He have permitted my innocent little brother, who had brought such joy and brightness to all his life had touched, suffer such an injury?

Up to this time, I had not been confronted with such questions. But now it was all so frighteningly impersonal; the world suddenly seemed so cold and cruel and unfeeling, and God so very far away.

Word had spread of my brother's fall from the tree, and Mr. Curtis, a neighbor who also had a yacht, took off to try to find the Rob Price boat and signal to him to hurry back. It seemed an eternity before I spotted the boat lights, and even longer before the boat docked and I was able to tell my anguished parents what had happened.

"I felt something was wrong," said Dad. "I couldn't explain it. I've been feeling uneasy for the past few hours."

Edward had returned to consciousness when we got back. Mother and Dad wondered, would this have happened had they not gone on the trip? If Mother had been home, might Edward have found something else to do, besides climbing trees? Who could ever know?

Within forty-eight hours infection had set in and the dread tetanus had developed. It was a losing, extremely painful fight, borne so heroically by Edward. On the sixth day, we knew his time for passing was near, and Edward knew it too. He called us all to him and singled us out, one by one, as he puckered his fevered lips and said, "Kiss you . . . kiss you! . . ."

Then, suddenly, as his eyesight failed, he said, "I can't see you— can you see me?" And when we assured him that we could, his vision then seemed to see things beyond our mortal eyesight, for he spoke of Mother's mother, Grandmother Morrow, and Mother's sister, our Aunt Flora, who were on a train coming from Indiana—and he seemed to be with them. At the last, he lifted his broken arms and reached out, saying in a musical voice, with a glow in his face, "You . . . you! . . ."

Let's hope that Edward was really looking into the Next World. Let's hope that, as we now have increasing evidence, there are such beings as guardian angels—or former mortals, relatives and friends— who are able to be in attendance upon us as we are making the change called Death. Let's hope that whatever Edward was seeing, which so lighted his dear face in those last few moments, on October 13, 1914, were not hallucinations. Based on the knowledge that has come to me since that tragic time, I prefer to believe that as Edward's spirit was leaving his pain-wracked body, he was being introduced to a greater life to come.

At his funeral, the minister said, "We can't understand why such a tragedy should befall one of God's children. Many who knew Edward Sherman have said that he was too good for this life and that they were sure God, in His wisdom, had needed him in Heaven and had called him home."

This statement stirred up a furious rebellion in me. I thought, if God had had anything to do with my brother falling from a tree, suffering those injuries and almost unbearable pain, only to die—cutting short such a promising young life—then He was not the kind of God I could worship. He was more a sadistic fiend than a loving Father, and I would damn such an idea of God the rest of my life if I was to burn in hell for it!

I was tortured enough by the thought that I had been given a foreknowledge of this happening and had done nothing about it. Had my brother's life depended upon my heeding this warning? Why did so many things occur that seemingly could have been prevented if someone had said or done something differently? Perhaps in the lives of all people, there have been deeds and misdeeds for which they have suffered deep regret and remorse and which, once committed, could not be recalled or atoned. This hardly made the bearing any easier.

Gradually, there came to me the realization that the universe is ruled by laws of Cause and Effect. These laws play no favorites. As a consequence, no God had decreed that my brother or anyone should get injured and die. In Edward's case, he had climbed the tree of his own free will, had reached up and gotten hold of a rotten limb, which had broken under the stress and strain, leading to his fall. It was now clear to me that there is Cause and Effect behind everything that happens, however small and seemingly insignificant. Nothing happens by chance. Our unthinkably great Creator has established laws for all life to follow. Obedience or disobedience of these laws, however knowingly, willfully, or blindly, determines whether or not they operate for or against us.

Through this shocking experience, the boy in me became a man. I was never again to look on life as an existence of all sweetness and light. Nor was I blindly and trustingly to accept religion as having all the answers.

[*How to Know What to Believe*, 1976]

The death of his son Edward was a loss from which Dad never recovered. . . . Following Edward's death, Dad prepared a study in a spare bedroom upstairs and would disappear into it following din-ner. Mother probably knew what he was working on, but Dad said nothing to me about it until his project was well advanced. Then, one night, he came downstairs with a manuscript in his hands, and a bit shyly, almost self-consciously, he announced to me that he had been writing a book. I had always been aware that Dad had a deep philo-sophic side to his life, about which he seldom spoke. . . .

Rather than trying to describe to me the nature of the book he had been writing, Dad handed me a sheet of paper containing his preface. He sat quietly, eyeing me as I read it. Now, reading this pref-ace again after all these years, with his published book, *Immortal Optimism*,[1] in my hands, I find myself as deeply moved today as I was then. . . . In the preface he said he "hoped that this memorandum might be of some comfort and help to members of my family and friends when I will no longer be with them." Then, in closing: "I do not like to hear the word God used often, although it seems necessary, because the greatest mistake we make is our minds' finite conception of such an infinite power and intelligence, and the word, therefore, can have little real meaning to us."

In this book he had compiled his lifetime thoughts and observa-tions, as well as selected thoughts of the great world thinkers. There is a universality in Dad's words, and what he had to say in his modest little book touches the deepest longings of the human soul. Under the heading of "Helpful and Hopeful Thoughts," my father wrote, "Why do we hope or expect that the finite mind of man, while bound in by material things and the physical senses, should comprehend the mind or plans of Infinite God? God's ways are not our ways, neither are His thoughts our thoughts. We should be content to advance a step at a time, knowing that each glimpse we catch of an eternal truth only teaches us to trust that future revelations will 'lead us into all truth.'"

[*How to Take Yourself Apart and Put Yourself Together Again*, 1971; *How to Know What to Believe*, 1976]

I was in my room on the second floor of our family home in the year 1915. This room faced west. The sun was setting, it was growing dark. I was at my typewriter, and I got up as I had done hundreds of times before, to turn on the electric light. As I reached for the switch,

---

[1] Thomas H. Sherman, *Immortal Optimism* (Traverse City, Mich.: Record Eagle Press, 1915).

a voice in my inner ear—not a voice that I heard externally—said, "Don't turn on the light!"

This was such an unexpected and such an eerie command that I hesitated, wondering why I should get such an impression. Unable to go against this impulse, I returned to my desk and typed for perhaps ten minutes longer, till it grew so dark that I just had to turn on the light.

But once more, as I fixed my attention on the electric light bulb, with my hand on the switch, the voice within repeated its warning: "Don't turn on the light!"

At almost the same instant, someone ran up to the porch downstairs and began banging the door and ringing the bell. I went downstairs without turning on the light and was confronted by a linesman, who said, "Don't turn on the light! There's a high voltage wire down across your line outside!"

Young man that I was, I realized that in some way I could not explain, as I had concentrated on the act of turning on the light, I had tuned in on the mind of the linesman. In the past ten minutes he had been running to several homes to warn people not to turn on their lights, and in that period of time, his emotionalized thoughts had reached my own mind, in advance of his physical arrival!

The evidence was too specific for this happening to be attributed to chance or coincidence. If, I reasoned, I have been able to pick up this thought impression, it proves that thought transference is not only possible, but that one should be able to repeat it at will, once sufficient knowledge of the processes involved is gained.

This realization started me on what became a lifetime quest—an unceasing desire to discover all I could concerning the mysteries of the mind and to bring mind power under conscious control or direction.

I first went to the library to see what literature I could unearth that might throw light on what had happened to me. But, in those early days, there was little of an authoritative nature. I did, however, come upon one remarkable book which still stands up today as a classic in its field. It was Thomson Hudson's *The Law of Psychic Phenomena*.[2] This man's knowledge of the functioning of mind and the nature of the subconscious was far ahead of his time. Because dependable, demonstrable knowledge of these extra-sensory faculties was so gen-

---

[2] Thomson Jay Hudson, *The Law of Psychic Phenomena* (Chicago: A. C. McClurg & Co., 1905).

erally lacking, I decided that I would have to make a guinea pig of myself, so to speak, and do my own research and experimenting.

When I read extracts from the book by Thomson Hudson to a high-school friend named Homer, and told him of my experience with the electric light linesman, he volunteered to try telepathy with me. Since Hudson had stated that it was easier to transmit a thought to a person when he was asleep and the conscious mind at rest, Homer suggested, "Why don't you try to send me a thought some night while I'm asleep, and wake me up at a certain time? I happen to be a sound sleeper and I seldom wake up for anything."

This simple experiment appealed to me but I told Homer I would not attempt it immediately because I felt he would be anticipating it too strongly and this might interfere with possible results. Homer said he would forget about it until and if something happened. He lived on the other side of town from me, and while we attended the same school, I did not see him again until after the experiment was tried.

On the third night following our agreement, I sat in my bedroom about ten o'clock at night, at a time when Homer had said he was usually at home and asleep. I could look out the window at the night sky and see the face of the clock on the courthouse dome two blocks away. Before me, on my lap, was a copy of the High School Annual, turned to a page which showed Homer's photograph. I felt, somehow, that if I could be aided in visualizing Homer's features in my mind's eye while I addressed him vocally as well as mentally, this would assist me in the transmission. This was solely my idea. I looked at Homer's picture till I could shut my eyes and see his image in my mind's eye. Then, fixing my attention upon him, I spoke, putting all the feeling I could behind my words:

"Homer, this is Harold. You are going to awaken exactly at two o'clock this morning and think of me as you hear the town clock striking two!"

I kept on repeating this statement for about fifteen minutes, sometimes opening my eyes and gazing out the window at the town clock and picturing the hands pointing to two a.m., and then closing my eyes and retaining in my mind this visualized image which I then *willed* to Homer.

I felt myself to be under quite an emotional strain, as though some energy was going out from me and was not being received. These are feelings difficult to describe. It was almost as though I had made contact with Homer's subconscious mind and had been repulsed. This caused me to try even harder to get through to him.

All of a sudden there came over me a feeling of great mental relief, as though the message I had been sending had finally found lodgment in Homer's mind. Instantly, I discontinued the attempted transmission and went to bed and to sleep.

The next morning, I was awakened at seven o'clock by the ringing of the telephone and sensed instantly who it was.

"Hello, Homer! Did it work?" I greeted.

"Did it work?" said Homer excitedly. "What time did you try to wake me up?"

"Just as the town clock was striking two!" I said.

"That's it!" cried Homer. "But don't ever do it again! I came to, wide awake. I could feel your presence in the room and it seemed like you had touched me on the forehead. I heard the town clock strike; it was uncanny. I had to get up and turn on the light before I could get rid of the feeling that you were right there with me! . . . Gosh! There's something to this all right—but it's too scary for me!" If Homer was startled by this experience, I was equally so. As I tried to think through what had happened, it raised a number of questions.

Since I had concentrated on Homer shortly after ten p.m., he must have received my thoughts at that time. Had I then performed what might be termed "post-telepathic suggestion," which caused Homer to be awakened at the time designated?

I, myself, had slept through the striking of the town clock. Had my subconscious mind at the appointed time, however, taken some action which aroused Homer? Had some energy gone out from me at the two o'clock hour which had given Homer the impression that I had actually touched him and might even be present in his room? I knew nothing about astral projection in those days or I might have speculated, from Homer's report, on the possibility that I had left my physical body and paid him a visit, without any conscious awareness of such a happening! Whatever the correct explanation may have been, there was absolutely no question as to the success of the experiment.

Radio was just coming into wide usage and this led me to wonder whether a "mental ether" existed in which thought waves traveled somewhat akin to radio waves. Was there a vast network of minds with which each human creature was identified on subconscious levels? And was each individual actually, without realizing it, a transmitter and a receiver? Were telepathy valid, then it appeared that myriad thoughts were being exchanged between minds at all times; and that people were being influenced, one way or another, usually without any conscious awareness of it or any developed ability to identify the different sources of this influence.

A whole new world of mental possibilities opened up before me, as frightening as it was thrilling. I could see great dangers as well as great benefits to be derived through development of these higher powers of mind. I reflected that every invention of man, depending upon how it was used, could result in either good or evil. However, the fact that destructive use might be made of any of man's creations had not kept him from creating.

[*How to Make ESP Work for You*, 1964]

As a youth in Traverse City Harold excelled in basketball, tennis and baseball. Too light for the football team, he satisfied his passion for the game by writing up reports for the local paper. His writing talent was recognized when he won a state prize for his essay, "The Settlement and Development of Traverse City," with local admirers predicting that he would go far as a writer. In 1916 a basketball injury brought on an attack of appendicitis. He was treated at the Battle Creek Sanitarium.[3]

The Battle Creek Sanitarium was a Seventh-day Adventist institution. While I was there, I was exposed to this religion, and I recall an "end of the world" prediction, when many Adventists sold their homes and possessions and gathered on a hilltop to await the coming of Christ.[4]

---

[3] Founded in 1866, the "San" pioneered in dietetic and hygienic treatments. Dr. John Harvey Kellogg was its medical superintendent, and his brother, William Keith (W. K.) Kellogg, first produced the cornflake there. While in their teens, William S. Sadler and his future wife, Lena C. Kellogg, worked at the San as hospital attendants.

[4] In the early 1840s William Miller, a Baptist preacher in New England, heralded the second advent of Christ, predicting that Jesus would return to earth on October 22, 1844. When Christ did not appear, thousands of Miller's followers left in disillusionment. Those who remained concluded that the date had been correct but that it referred to the beginning of the final judgment in heaven rather than the second coming of Christ on earth. The small remnant of New England "Adventists" grew and soon joined with believers in Battle Creek, Michigan, to form the Seventh-day Adventist Church in 1863. Among the church's early leaders was Ellen G. White who, Adventists believed, enjoyed God's special guidance as she wrote her counsels to the growing body of believers. William S. Sadler, Lena K. Sadler, Wilfred C. Kellogg and Anna B. Kellogg were raised in the Seventh-day Adventist faith.

When He didn't come, many of the followers were disillusioned and turned on their spiritual prophets and leaders. I sympathized with my Adventist friends who were severely shaken by this false prophecy and disappointed that the world had not ended.

I had assigned to me a most unusual male nurse by the name of David Quin. One night the commissary next to the hospital building caught fire and burned to the ground. I could see the reflection on the ceiling of my room, and there was great excitement in the corridor outside as some patients were moved for safety.

I did not fear but wished David Quin was on duty and could lift me out of bed and carry me to the window so I could see the conflagration. Less than an hour later, David appeared and performed this act. He had been awakened in his room across the city of Battle Creek, had received my mental call, and had dressed hastily and hurried to the sanitarium. As he sat me on the window sill, he smiled and said, "This is what you wanted, wasn't it?"

Surprised at his action, I asked him, "How did you know that this was what I wanted?"

"I have a way of knowing these things," David said, quietly. He then told me he was awakened from a sound sleep with the feeling that I was calling him. He knew instantly that I was in trouble of some kind, so he threw on some clothes, hurried out and caught a street car for the sanitarium. As he neared the hospital, he saw the flames and smoke and knew why I was summoning him. "But I did not sense what you actually wanted me to do," said David, "until I entered the room."

In the days that followed, I learned much about this unusual man. He predicted that many people would develop telepathic abil-

Harold in his military uniform, 1918 [Sherman Family Private Collection]

ity in time. I told him I already had had experiences in my own life which had convinced me of the truth of telepathy.

[*How to Make ESP Work for You*, 1964]

Harold remained at the "San" for almost a year, employed in various capacities as he regained his health. At twenty he left there with the title of "Assistant Efficiency Expert."

Rejected for active military service because of his recent operation, Harold found work as a secretary in the Detroit YMCA but was unable to receive a transfer overseas as he had hoped. Learning that the University of Michigan at Ann Arbor was offering classes in aviation, he enrolled there and received his military training in the Students Army Training Corps. He also studied journalism. With the signing of the Armistice, Harold left the university, finding the instruction too standardized.

The war over, I returned to Traverse City. I had kept in touch with David Quin, and many of his letters revealed that he had an amazing knowledge of my thoughts and feelings and experiences. Later, David left the sanitarium on tour with a wealthy patient in the Catskill Mountains in New York. In due time we lost contact with each other and my letters began to be returned, marked "no forwarding address." I often thought of David and wondered what had happened to him, but his close friends at the sanitarium, Isobel Macheracker and Victor Bjork, also had lost contact.

On the night of January 19, 1919, I had the first of a series of never-to-be forgotten experiences.

Awakening suddenly around one in the morning, I found myself temporarily paralyzed, unable to move a muscle. The room was in semidarkness with objects dimly outlined by the night light from the hall. Leaning over me, with his face expressive of great yearning, was David Quin! His lips were moving but no sound was coming forth. I was so shocked at the sight of him, momentarily unable to move, that I thought I must be having some kind of realistic nightmare, and tried mightily to free myself. As I regained control of my body and sat up in bed, the form of David Quin faded from view.

Quite unnerved, I wondered if David, wherever he might be, was sick or in trouble of some kind, and had been trying to reach me mentally. I finally decided that this had been a new type of dream experience, perhaps activated by long absence of any word from him and my concern over it. I even told myself that my apparent sighting of him had been a vivid hallucination and that this had really taken place inside my mind as a part of the dream.

But the next night, at approximately the same time, this experience was repeated. And I knew then that this phenomenon was occurring external to me—that there actually was a *presence* in my bedroom, and that this presence bore every resemblance to David Quin! I composed myself as much as possible and strained to hear what he was trying to say to me. I could see his face above me, with its intensely earnest expression, and I saw his lips moving as before, but there wasn't a sound. I reached up my hand toward him and spoke his name, "David!" But again, as had happened the first time, his form began to dissolve and disappeared from view.

I was certain now that David had been visiting me and endeavoring to communicate. I got up and turned on the light and wrote him a letter, telling him of my experience, together with my feeling that he was ill or in some kind of difficulty, and begging him to get in touch with me. When morning came, I told my parents of the unusual night adventures I had been having. I then mailed the letter to David's last known address.

There was no reason at all for me to have anticipated a third experience of this nature, but this is exactly what happened. Once more I was awakened, and there was David Quin, life-sized, beside me, lips moving, striving so hard to tell me something. And yet, not a sound. I extended both arms toward him and cried aloud, "David! David!" As I was about to touch him, with an expression of profound longing which I can still see in my mind's eye, his features began to melt into the darkness of the room.

There was a poignant feeling of finality associated with this disappearance. I tried to hold him there by sheer mental power, somehow feeling that I had failed him—that I should have been able to sense whatever message he had been trying so hard, these three nights, to communicate. But his form continued to dissolve, leaving me with the saddened conviction that I never would see him again in this life.

Three weeks passed. The letter I had addressed to David Quin was returned. Then, late one afternoon in February, I came home to find two letters in the same mail—one from Victor Bjork and the other from Miss Macheracker. Both letters had been written to tell me of David Quin's death on the night of January 21, in Brooklyn's Long Island College Hospital. He had been East on a case and had been caught in the influenza epidemic. His illness developed into double pneumonia. He died after having been in a coma for three days!

But the most startling point of this information was a statement made by Miss Macheracker. "It's strange," she wrote, "but on each of the three nights prior to David's passing, he appeared at my bedside. I knew he was in trouble and was calling to me, and I would have gone to him at once if I had only known where he was."

Here was confirming evidence of my own experience! Proof it had not been a dream! Miss Macheracker, three hundred miles away in Battle Creek, and I up in Traverse had had identical experiences! Allowing for the difference in time between Brooklyn and our locations in Michigan, David had passed away early in the morning of January 21, at almost precisely the moment we apparently had seen him on the third successive night!

[*How to Make ESP Work for You,* 1964]

It hurts me yet today to recount this poignant experience which again had to do with my father. I can still hear him saying, "Harold, you've been home from the service six weeks now. Don't you think it's about time you looked for a job—and found something you want to do in life?"

"I don't feel like going to work yet," I retorted. "Besides, I don't know *what* I want to do." Like many young men of that day, I had returned from service in World War I disturbed and unsettled in my mind. I had no desire to battle for my place in the world. What was the rush, anyway? Why was Dad pushing me? It was almost as though he no longer wanted me at home. Up to this time, my relations with Dad had been extremely close. He owned and operated a men's clothing store, a business in which I had not the slightest interest, but Dad had never tried to suggest that I plan to follow in his footsteps.

One night when he came home from the store and saw me lounging on the front porch, Dad said, "Still doing nothing?"

"That's right!" I rejoined.

"Have you been thinking about what you might like?" he asked.

"Yes, but there's nothing in this town that appeals to me," I answered.

Dad looked at me for a long moment, and then said, "Well, I guess, if that's the case, you'll have to leave town to find what *does* ap-

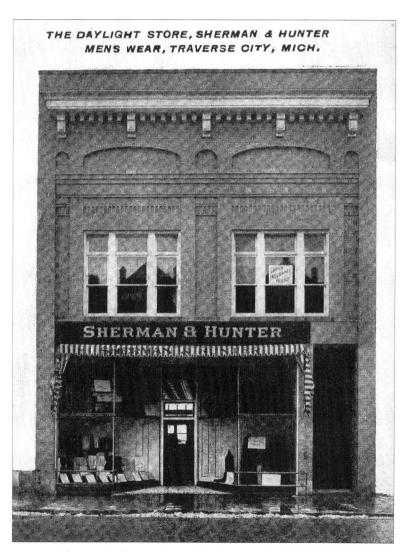

Thomas H. Sherman's men's clothing store in Traverse City
[Sherman Family Private Collection].

peal." A slap in the face could not have hurt me as much. So—now it was out. Dad was really trying to get rid of me.

"All right," I snapped. "I'll get out! I'll go to Detroit and get work with Henry Ford."

"That's a good idea," said Dad in his typically quiet way. "When would you like to go?"

"Tomorrow morning!" I blazed. "The six o'clock train."

Mother cried. She said I didn't have to go that soon, that Dad hadn't meant it that way.

When I rose before sunrise and went downstairs with my bag, I found Mother and Dad already up, and Mother had set a hot meal on the table. There were freshly baked breakfast rolls made only for special occasions. But I steeled myself against any show of feeling. We ate in almost complete silence. I could see that Mother was close to tears.

Dad had his eyes on the time and said, "We'd better get started. We've just time to walk it."

The Pere Marquette railroad station was about ten blocks away. I got up and grabbed my suitcase and headed for the door. On the porch I turned back as Mother reached her arms up to embrace and kiss me. "Goodbye, dear," she said, and handed me a small packet. "A little something to eat on the train."

I took it with a mumbled "thanks" and started down the steps. Dad reached for my bag. "I can carry it," I said. "You don't need to go to the station. I can make it all right."

"I think I'll come along anyway," said Dad.

At the corner, however, as we were about to turn out of sight of the old home, I looked back. There in the distance was the little figure of my mother. She raised her apron and waved it. Then I saw her turn and go into the house, the apron raised to her eyes.

"Oh, well," I thought, "when Dad sees how Mother is taking it, maybe he'll regret his words."

We walked the long ten blocks past familiar scenes I was so soon to leave behind. When we got to the station, Dad hurried into the depot ahead of me and bought my ticket. The train was already in the station. It was five minutes to six.

"Here you are," said Dad, and stuffed the ticket in my pocket. Then he handed me a ten-dollar bill.

"No, thanks," I said, pushing it away. "Keep your money—I don't need it."

The train whistle sounded. I picked up my bag and got ready to mount the steps onto the platform of the rear coach.

"Goodbye, Dad."

It was a quick handshake, and my jaws, I know, were set tight with resolve not to show any feeling.

"Goodbye, Harold," said Dad. "Write and keep Mother and me informed. If we can help. . . ."

I didn't answer. I was up the steps and into the coach, where I savagely shoved my suitcase in an overhead rack and dropped down in a seat.

Came the final whistle, the air brakes wheezed, and the train, with a jerk, started to move. All of a sudden, I was hit with a shock reaction. The panorama of my life flashed before me, and I saw in that instant all the sacrifices a loving mother and dad had gladly made so that my two brothers and myself might have the education and experiences they felt would be of benefit and pleasure to us. A great surge of homesickness and remorse came over me and I jumped up and rushed out onto the rear platform of the train, my eyes seeking out my father.

And there he was, walking along a sidewalk beside the tracks.

"Dad! Hi, Dad!" I called, and waved.

But he did not hear me; he did not see me. His head was bowed, and I could tell that Dad was doing something I had never seen him do through all the experiences our family had endured. He was *sobbing*.

"Dad!" I cried, with the train picking up speed. "Oh, Dad!"

But, no, he never raised his head. After all these years as I recall this scene, my eyes dim with tears. How I wish I could have relived this experience! How I wish I could have realized, as I did later, that Dad had felt called upon to do what is perhaps one of the most difficult things any parent can ever feel compelled to do. He had to force me, as gently but as persistently as possible, to get out on my own.

[*How to Take Yourself Apart and Put Yourself Together Again,* 1971]

2

DETROIT

In Detroit, Harold roomed with his mother's sister, Aunt May, and found work at the Ford Motor Company, first as a machinist and then as an assistant production superintendent in the triple-gear department. While working at Ford in the daytime, he signed up for a two-year course in writing advertising copy, sponsored by the Detroit Adcraft Club, which included classes in Applied Psychology presented by Harriet McCollum.[1]

During this time Harold became reacquainted with Martha Bain, a girl from his home town of Traverse City, who was then studying nursing at Detroit's Grace Hospital. They had been classmates since kindergarten and graduated from high school together. Starting off as "pals," their relationship deepened as Harold confided his hopes and ambitions to Martha—or "Marty," as he called her then—in frequent letters that he wrote between Saturday visits. Referring to his recent appendicitis, on August 28, 1919, he wrote:

> . . . Oh—Marty—if God will only give me *half* a chance to accomplish the *many* things I've dreamed about—hoped for—WORKED for, and STOOD for—before I enter the Great Beyond! What an opportunity there is now for REAL SERVICE to the world in every field of endeavor! I want to live to the fullest—that I may devote my life to something WORTHWHILE.

---

[1] Harriet McCollum (1874-1948) was a psychology and health lecturer whose 1932 book, *What Makes a Master?*, was a bestseller.

I care for no reward save the happiness my works might bring to *others*. Sometimes—a feeling creeps over me that I may be denied that chance for which I have *prayed*—and another sphere seems to beckon strongly. But—there is so much to do HERE! Surely there is need of many willing hearts to accept ready missions, and these should be spared to the world for a longer period. . . .

Of his love for Martha, he wrote on September 21:

. . . So you see—I had loved you for a long, long time—but I tried to keep this love as one would for a sister—keeping a brotherly, protective interest in your affairs . . . I do not know of a dull moment in all the years of our association together. We certainly have been PALS in the deepest, highest sense. How keenly have we understood each other—and how considerate we have been—one of the other! There has not been one moment of discord—our interest and our ideals have been, for the most part, so nearly allied. Oh—it was a glorious dream with me—that some day I might claim you—for my wife. . . . Think it over, Marty. Do you love me? Be *sure*. If you do—and can give me that love which I need so at this time—nothing within reason will be impossible for either of us. . . .

October 14 he wrote of their future together:

Oh, there are so many things I want to say; so many plans I'd like to unfold; such a host of dreams to be revealed! Where shall I begin? I love you, Marty, so *madly* that I feel the sense of separation even in the same city! I cannot express the *calm* and *peace* that comes to me when I am with you. It is a sort of realization that I am ALL together—that you are a vital part of ME and I— of YOU. . . . I look forward to years when I may have come into "my own" and when YOU will be my true HELPMATE in the good tasks I hope to perform. . . . I do not talk idly when I say that I expect to accomplish big things within the next ten years. Where there is a WILL there is a WAY—a pretty true axiom! I do not think of you as a mere housewife—as many men come to regard their wives—but as an ACTIVE CO-PARTNER in everything that I do—or *hope* to do. I'll need you by my side; your counsel; your encouragement; your help—in thousands of delightfully different ways. We'll live the same lovely PAL-LIKE life and my successes will be *yours* as well. . . .

Martha Bain in 1917 [SHERMAN FAMILY PRIVATE COLLECTION].

Envisioning his mission in life, Harold wrote on December 2:

There appears to be an ETERNAL URGE driving me on toward some yet mysterious but no less definite goal. I do not doubt but what *my* TIME will come when those good things I desire will be made POSSIBLE of achievement, but Marty—it's *so hard* to wait! I want to get busy *now*—to make a beginning—that I may approach their attainment, accomplish my purposes. I believe that "a man's true wealth is the amount of GOOD he does in the world." Marty—before we finish this life we are going to be MILLIONAIRES—in this respect! "Help thy brother's boat across and lo! thine own has reached the shore!" There is so VERY MUCH to be done—so many "brothers" to be *helped!* Our happiness will lie in bringing *others* happiness. Could you be content with doing this, sweetheart—and nothing more? . . . "The glory of life is to LOVE, not to be loved; to GIVE not to get; to SERVE, not to be served!" Let us do *all three* in abundance and attract unto ourselves the real glory of existence. . . .

Harold's feelings were reciprocated, as illustrated in Martha's letter to him of December 3, 1919:

. . . Do you remember that you said that you would like to have me write you just what my heart was saying?—to write the thoughts just as they passed thru my mind? If I did, it would simply be "I love you" from beginning to end. . . . It's fun to dream about the future and to imagine how wonderful everything will be, but *that* will never bring it to us. I must remember that it was not yesterday nor will it be tomorrow that counts, but just today. Today is all that we ever have with us, for the past does not matter and the future is never ours till it becomes today. Can you feel the kiss I am sending?

* * *

In the summer of 1920 I had an out-of-body experience. I was then employed by the Ford Motor Company in Detroit, Michigan, and often played tennis on the Ford recreation tennis courts. One day, I developed a water blister on a toe on my right foot. It broke open and became badly infected and swollen, requiring a lancing operation.

My family physician, Dr. Garner, decided to take care of me in his office. He called in a dentist to administer chloroform, with a nurse in attendance. My foot was prepared and I was stretched out on a table, with a cloth over my face through which I inhaled the drops of chloroform. Nothing happened for a few minutes, and then, suddenly, I had a dizzy, whirling sensation.

It was frightening. I tried to speak but found I could not talk or move a muscle. I heard the doctor say that I was "under," but I had not lost my feeling and sought desperately to make some move or sound which would indicate that I was still conscious. I felt a stab of pain as Dr. Garner applied the knife, and then there seemed to be an explosion in my brain, and I blacked out.

The next thing I knew, I was in the air above my body, looking down upon the operation, and seeing and hearing what was going on. Beside me, in the atmosphere, was my brother, Edward, who had died some six years before at the age of eleven. He had a happy expression on his face, as though he was glad to see me. I thought I must be having a vivid dream but now I saw that the dentist, who had been administering the chloroform, was greatly concerned. The nurse had reported to him that she felt no pulse. The cloth was removed from my face and efforts begun to revive me. I felt a curious sense of detachment as I viewed this scene, and was somewhat dazed and confused.

Then Edward took my arm, indicating that I was to leave with him. A shocking realization hit me. *I must be dead!* I pulled away from Edward, hearing myself say to him, "No, Edward, I can't go with you. Mother and Dad don't know anything about this. I'm not ready. I can't die now!" As I said this, my thoughts went to my parents in Traverse City, and I blacked out. The next awareness I had was of walking down Main Street in the business section of Traverse City. I was headed for the Sherman & Hunter Company, my father's men's clothing store. I passed a number of people on the street who paid no attention to me.

Entering the store, I walked the length of it to my father's bookkeeping office in the rear, passing Mr. Hunter, his partner, who did not notice me. Everything about me seemed natural and physical. I found my father in one of his familiar poses, working over the books. His back was turned to me. I stepped up and placed my hand on his shoulder, and spoke one word: "Dad!"

He did not move. I spoke again and took a position where he might see me, but got no response. This gave me a shock. My body form seemed real but I was making no impression upon those around me. Once more I called, and this time Dad looked up, unseeing, pushed back his chair, and got up, walking straight past me to the window, where he stood looking out over the waters of Grand Traverse Bay.

I thought of Mother and our home on Webster Street. Again there was a blackout, and I found myself inside our home, walking toward the kitchen where Mother was preparing a meal. I said, "Mother, this is Harold. I'm home!" She turned to get something and started directly toward me, but she did not see me. It dawned upon me that I must be in an entirely different body form. I must, somehow, return to my physical body.

The instant this decision was made, I had a swift, traveling sensation, followed by still another blackout. Now I was in some dark place, gasping for breath, and hearing a jumble of voices. There were cold, wet cloths on my face and someone was rubbing my wrists and someone else was putting pressure on my chest. I moaned, and I heard Dr. Garner say, "He's coming to!"

It was a full hour before I felt myself to be "all there," but I astounded Dr. Garner when I recited in detail what had taken place, that I knew I had been given an overdose of chloroform, that my heart had almost stopped, and that they had made frenzied efforts to resuscitate me. When I told him I had seen my brother, Edward, and had visited my parents in Traverse City, some three hundred miles away, he could only shake his head.

"Since you knew what took place while we were working on you, and even heard our conversation when we thought you were unconscious," said Dr. Garner, "who am I to say that you did not have these other experiences that you have reported?"

[*How to Make ESP Work for You*, 1964]

Harold and Martha were married on September 26, 1920, in Traverse City, Harold wearing a slipper on the injured foot.

After their honeymoon, Harold, having been placed on the disabled list, returned to work at the Ford Motor Company, going to Detroit ahead of his bride. Intending to look for an apartment of their own after Martha joined him in a few months, he continued to board with his Aunt May.

In late October he attended an appearance of spiritualist medium John Slater, at Orchestra Hall. By request, Harold and hundreds of others had sent up questions in advance, in sealed envelopes. Harold had written:

Harold and Martha on their wedding day with their parents
[SHERMAN FAMILY PRIVATE COLLECTION].

I feel that I need a college education to fit me to perform my mission in life—which mission has not been made clear to me as yet. It seems that the mission will be something for great good in the world and far-reaching. Can you see what it is; if I am being assisted on the spirit plane toward this end; and if my preparation for the performing of this mission will be amply taken care of, step by step?

I would like to get in touch with my brother, E.J.S., my two friends, D.H.Q. [David H. Quin] and V.J.B., as well as my cousin A.M.B. [Ashton M. Baldwin].

He described what happened next in a letter to his aunt and uncle, Dr. Mahlon ("Uncle Doc") and Flora Baldwin, who lived in Marion, Indiana:

... But John Slater never picked up my letter at all. As in the case of many, he said (passing from one influence to another): "Out of the world of spirit there comes to me an elderly, white-haired gentleman. I am impressed with his great spiritual power and quiet composure. He calls for Harold M. Sherman." I arose at mention of my name (there was an audience of 1,500 people—capacity house—and I was fortunate enough to be in the front row where I could see and hear everything very plainly). "This gentleman is your mother's father, your grandfather on your mother's side. He says to tell you to go ahead in your plans of a college course; that you will be able to accomplish what you desire in due time, and that those on the spirit plane are interested in your achievements." ... The messages came with unceasing rapidity and with faultless narration as to fact. Slater described scenes and events—past, present, future—apparently seeing them as distinctly as we are conscious of the things about us. ...

During this session, Harold was told that he would be leaving Detroit in three months for another city where he would start preparing for his life work. Soon afterward, just before the Christmas holidays, Ford Motor Company shut down for inventory and laid off its employees. Harold took this opportunity to introduce Martha to his mother's relatives—including Aunt Flora and Uncle Doc—in Marion.

3

MARION

Doc Baldwin, one of the pioneer physicians of central Indiana, who had served since the horse and buggy days, was a "progressive thinker," interested in exploring anything new in medicine, science, and philosophy. My Aunt Flora was equally interested. The loss of their soldier son, Ashton, in the First World War—a young doctor who had planned to be in business with his father—had been a great shock to them both, especially Aunt Flora. As a consequence, Uncle Doc had encouraged her to explore the possibility of communicating with Ashton through spirit mediums.

Chesterfield,[1] the famous Spiritualist camp, was only forty miles from Marion, and Aunt Flora had visited mediums there a number of times. When Martha and I arrived and the Baldwins learned of some experiences we had had, and that Martha and I had been privately practicing telepathy, Aunt Flora brought out a planchette and asked us to put our hands on it—to see if the board would move about and write messages.

We soon discovered that Martha could operate the planchette by herself, and then, with a little experimenting, that she could simply hold a pencil in her hand and do what is called "automatic writing."

---

[1] Home of the Indiana Association of Spiritualists. Founded in 1891, it has grown from tents and small buildings into a sprawling camp of lodges, cottages, and meeting halls for Spiritualists and mediums.

Very shortly, Ashton, whom Martha had never met, seemed to manifest, signing his initials "A.B." and encircling them as he had done in all his medical books, which greatly excited and impressed the Baldwins. This led to early morning sessions after breakfast, before Uncle Doc would go to the office. During these sessions, the Baldwins talked back and forth to Ashton as though he was physically present.

One morning, Ashton announced that a way was being opened up for "Harold to get a job as a reporter on the *Marion Chronicle*, the afternoon paper, so that he can remain in Marion and prepare for his life work in writing." Ashton urged his father to drop by the *Chronicle* office on his way to work, and to "speak to publisher George Lindsay about Harold." This Uncle Doc did and phoned shortly, telling me to get down to the *Chronicle* office at once and see editor Louis Spilman[2]—that their lead reporter had just wired his resignation to take effect immediately as he had accepted a position on the *Indianapolis Star*.

Thus, through this "spirit message" received through Martha, I was given a life-changing message. Martha and I returned to Detroit just long enough to sever connections with Ford and to pack our things for residence in the town where my mother had been born. Within two weeks we were back from Detroit and established as residents of Marion. Then, and only then, did we suddenly recall the prediction that had been made to me by John Slater that afternoon in Orchestra Hall, when he had said that "a way was being prepared" for me to leave Detroit, within three months, and to locate in another city where I would take up a new job, which would start me upon my life work.

The tie-up between this prediction and the manner in which this job was made known to me was almost too amazing to be believed. Certainly, after what had happened, we could not write this off as mere coincidence. It seemed to suggest that there really are intelligences in another dimension who, if not actually our friends and loved ones, nevertheless maintain an interest in, as well as possess a knowledge of, our activities and aspirations.

Once established as a reporter on the *Marion Chronicle*, my new job took my attention day and night. I had to attend and report many

---

[2] Louis and Emily Spilman went on to become lifelong friends of the Shermans.

civic meetings and other community events as well as my regular assignments, but Martha and I set aside time almost every night to continue our exploration of spirit communication with the Baldwins through Martha's automatic writing. This was done in evening time after Doc Baldwin's office hours, and it was seldom that Ashton did not seem to be present.

One night, Ashton startled us by stating that my father—his Uncle Tom—was suffering from a brain tumor and he would soon be coming over to "the Other Side." This was a shock; we had known my father had not been well, had been suffering from severe headaches, but had not realized they might be a sign of a serious affliction.

A warning type of dream had come to me in November, 1920, two months after I was married and had left my home town to reside in Detroit. My father, who with my mother had attended the wedding, was apparently in excellent health. And yet, one night, I had the following startling dream:

I seemed to be back, with Martha, in the family home in Traverse City. It was night and we were in the kitchen with the light on. Mother and Dad appeared to be out for the evening. I heard a key in the lock of the front door and knew they were returning. I left Martha in the kitchen and hurried through the house to greet them. But before I could reach the door, it opened and Mother stepped in, with Dad about to follow. Just at that moment, there was a short circuit and all the lights went out. Almost simultaneously, Mother started crying hysterically, "Oh, Harold . . . Harold! Tom is gone! . . . Tom is gone!" I found myself groping through the darkness to my mother's side and putting my arm around her to comfort her. She, however, was inconsolable, and continued to repeat: "Tom is gone!" The feeling came over me that Dad had disappeared in the darkness—that he was, indeed, gone—and I awakened, my face wet with tears, to tell Martha of this dream, and the conviction it had given me that my father did not have long to live.

There was no evidence, however, of any physical decline until some weeks later when Mother wrote us that Dad was having violent headaches and was complaining of impaired vision. I urged Dad to come to Detroit so that he might be examined by specialists. There it was determined that he had developed a tumor in the brain, on the pituitary gland. . . .

In a private talk I had with Dad, he expressed doubt as to his survival, and said he would not want to continue to live if his mind or his body were to be permanently crippled. . . . I told him of the unusual psychic experiences we were having in Marion, and which we were trying to evaluate. He listened with quiet interest and little comment. I then ventured to remark, on sudden impulse, that there was one way I felt he could establish proof of his own continuing identity, and that would be to return and write the signature of his business firm, Sherman & Hunter Co. Dad had been a Spencerian penman and wrote a fine hand. He had originated a way of writing the name of his men's clothing company without taking pen from paper, and doing it with so many flourishes that no forger in the Traverse City area ever had attempted to duplicate it in the passing of bad checks. Dad smiled at my suggestion and said, "I guess I am the only one who could do this."

He grew progressively worse and went to the Battle Creek Sanitarium in February, 1921, where an exploratory operation was performed. Martha, Mother and I were placed in a room directly across the hall from Dad's. I sat and held his hand during a three-hour operation wherein the surgeon went up through his nose in an effort to reach the tumor. The tumor was found to be inoperable. Shortly following the operation, Dad lapsed into a coma. . . . The second night I awakened in early morning from a fitful nap after our round-the-clock vigil, with a feeling that a drastic change was taking place. . . . The doctors had been summoned to remove radium placed through [Dad's] nose. They arrived shortly, bringing with them a floodlight which they set up beside the bed. There was a surgeon and two interns. Mother stood on one side of the bed and Martha and I on the other, behind the doctors. It was a tense moment because it seemed that each breath my father drew might be his last.

Suddenly, as one of the interns seized the floodlight to move it closer as an aid to the surgeon, he tripped over the cord. There was a short-circuit and the room was plunged into darkness. Now, my dream had become reality! I heard my mother cry out the very words I had heard in the dream some months before: "Oh, Harold . . . Harold! Tom is gone! . . . Tom is gone!" Repeating what I had done in the dream, I felt my way in the darkness to Mother's side and did what I could to reassure her. But Dad was gone, not long after.

Martha and I returned to Marion after the funeral, but it was some weeks before we felt settled enough to sit down and try to make contact with Ashton again. When we did, it seemed as though he had been standing by, anxious and eager to communicate. He told us that he had my father with him and that Uncle Tom, as Ashton called him, had been busy adapting himself to his new existence. He said that when Dad became stronger, he would try to write through Martha, but he was just interested in observing for the time being.

Finally came a day when, in faltering handwriting, through Martha's hand and arm, came the written words, "This is Dad." It was somewhat suggestive of his own penmanship. . . . After some time, when Dad seemed to gain greater command of writing, he wrote "test," and then, in an attempt to prove his identity, he wrote the words "Sherman" and "Hunter" over and over, and then, in a sudden burst, wrote the complete firm signature, which Martha had never seen!

For some months we continued the automatic writing sessions, keeping careful records. Our regular communicators remained Ashton and Dad. We asked them, occasionally, about other relatives and friends, and they gave us information concerning them. One time I specifically asked Dad about my brother Edward. . . . To my question, Dad reported that Edward had gone on to a higher dimension and was actively engaged in work there.

We were deeply impressed at this significant phenomenon. One night, however, Martha started going into a trance as some strange influence started to take over. This alarmed me as I had quite a time calling her back to consciousness, and I decided this was running too great a risk. As a consequence, we brought an end to our automatic writing experience and have never resumed since. I felt then—and I still feel—we should never surrender our free will to any outside influence.

[*How to Make ESP Work for You*, 1964; *How to Know What to Believe*, 1976]

There was one memorable séance held in the home of the Dr. Merrill Davises[3] in Marion. The materializing medium, Minnie Reichart, put on a demonstration in which a trumpet was used. Louis and Emily Spilman, together with Martha and I and the Davises, were present.

Louis had been an aviator in the First World War, and suddenly the trumpet took off at great speed in the darkened room, emitting

---

[3] Josephine (Mrs. Merrill) Davis was a cousin of Dr. William S. Sadler.

an airplane motor sound, while a voice cried out identifying itself by name as a former flying companion of Spilman's, who had crashed in flames. The trumpet illustrated the experience by nose-diving to the floor, its phosphorescent band showing throughout. Everyone present was stunned, especially Louis, who testified to the veracity of name and incident.

Several so-called spirit forms materialized, life-sized, and one figure, that of a woman, borrowed a handkerchief from Louis and explained as well as demonstrated how it could be built upon by ecto-plasmic substance. She increased its size to table cloth dimensions by fluttering it in front of the sitters, before seemingly dematerializing it and returning the original handkerchief to its owner.

These psychic-phenomena adventures caused much wonder-ment and speculation as to how many of these experiences were gen-uine—and intensified our desire to solve these mind mysteries if at all possible. . . .

Martha and I have sat in on quite a number of séances since, and found many to have been fraudulent. . . .

[*How to Know What to Believe*, 1976]

As recounted earlier, I had some boyhood psychic experiences that proved to me that telepathy is a fact, and which caused me, after mar-riage, to try to develop these higher powers in collaboration with Martha. We achieved sufficient results to make us yearn for someone who could give us authoritative information on these mysteries of the mind.

There is an old mystical saying: "When the pupil is ready, the teacher appears." This seemed to have been borne out in our case because in July, 1921, while serving as newspaper reporter on the *Marion Chronicle*, I was assigned to cover the Redpath Chautauqua Program[4] and to review the lecture on "Crime and Criminology" by the Chicago policeman and detective, Harry J. Loose.

There was nothing in what he said on the platform to indicate that Mr. Loose possessed any unusual psychic powers, but when I felt strongly impelled to call at his hotel that evening and seek a per-

---

[4] The Redpath-Chautauqua programs featured lectures and discussions on literary, scientific and moral topics. They took place in rural and small-town America from the 1870s to the Second World War. Drs. William and Lena Sadler were popular lecturers on the Redpath-Chautauqua circuit.

Harry Loose's Chautauqua lecture circuit brochure
[Special Collections Department, University of Iowa Libraries].

sonal interview with him, he astounded me by calling me by name and stating that he had known he was to meet me at this time for the past three weeks! He then explained that a highly spiritual woman, ninety-six years of age, who resided near Boston, had given him the equivalent of a college education while he slept at night; and that she was attracting young people to him on this lecture trip who had a potential for psychic development, and who needed encouragement. He said she could "tune in" on the minds of such people as she mentally surveyed the towns he was to be in—and transmit to the ones she wanted him to meet the impulse to seek him out. According to Harry, he had been waiting in his room for me to appear!

There followed three of the most remarkable and inspiring hours I have ever experienced on this planet, during which Harry told me more about myself than I had been aware. He predicted that I would go to New York City in two years or so in pursuit of a writing career; that if I kept up my interest in the higher powers of mind, we would likely meet again in this life; but that it might be as long as twenty years, because he had a "mission" to perform and would be dropping out of sight for a time after his lecture tour was completed.

At midnight Harry asked me to excuse him for the next half hour as he always communicated with Mrs. Loose from twelve to twelve-thirty. He said he would receive for the first fifteen minutes and send the last fifteen; that "Mother Loose," as he called her, opened his mail in Chicago and would make a list of other matters he needed to know about. As he received information, he would make a note of it and take care of what commanded his attention.

Harry had been stretched on his bed in his BVDs when I came in, this hot July night, and had drawn up a chair, on which I was now seated, beside the bed, as though expecting company. I sat watching him, fascinated, as he lay on his back, commencing to draw deep breaths, eyes closed. Occasionally, during the first fifteen minutes, he would raise up and make some notes on a pad that he had placed on the bedside table. After a time he pushed the pad away and remained unmoving. Finally, almost exactly at twelve-thirty, he opened his eyes, smiled at me, and said, "I have been permitted to let you see this little telepathic practice of mine. You and your Martha should be able to do this in time—if you continue to work at it." (We have never become this accomplished, but we have accurately sensed each other's thoughts for years.)

When I left the presence of this most unusual man that night, deeply moved, I could hardly wait to get home and report to Martha. As he shook my hand in a clasp that conveyed a feeling of indescribable warmth and assurance, Harry's last words had been, "Harold, your development is all up to you. Up to now, your mind has been filled with wonderment and doubts. You and Martha have been asking yourselves, could these higher powers of mind really exist? Could it be mostly imagination or hallucination or wishful thinking? What can you really believe or accept as the truth? It's a long journey and you'll have many disillusionments, but when you may be assailed with doubts, perhaps you will remember this night and take new heart. Goodbye until we meet again!"

[*How to Know What to Believe*, 1976]

The following paragraph as well as the narrative on p. 40 are drawn from Martha Sherman's essay, "How It Began," written in 1992 at the request of Martin Gardner, who was writing Urantia: the Great Cult Mystery:[5]

Although we had quietly kept the incident [of Harold's first meeting with Harry Loose] absolutely to ourselves, Harold did suggest in a July 25, 1921, letter to his mother, living in Traverse City, that when the Redpath made its circuit in that city, she might find the lecture by Mr. Harry J. Loose of great interest, that he had personally met Mr. Loose and to please identify herself to him if she attended. In the letter Harold enclosed a written message for Harry Loose:

> 924 S. McClure St.,
> Marion, Ind.
> July 25, 1921

Dear Friend:

The happy thought came to me that you would be in my home town, Thursday afternoon, August 11, and I took this method to reach you through sending a sealed letter to my mother and brother with instructions for either one of them to give it to you personally.

It is hardly needful for me to state that I *did feel* as you foretold directly after my departure from you. It is also prob-

[5] Martin Gardner, *Urantia: The Great Cult Mystery* (Amherst, NY: Prometheus, 1995).

ably within your knowledge that my nervous system is getting "toned down" and my rest is better of nights. I have taken my weight and shall keep watch of this detail.

Sunday afternoon I had the impression that there were other minds present and an overpowering sense of sleepishness came over me—so much so that I lay down upon the couch and almost immediately lost consciousness. I came to sometime later with the feeling that I had been in communication with these minds but could not bring back any conscious recollection of the experience.

As for the receptive mood at ten o'clock each night. I have not been in a position to try this out yet for the reason that the Chautauqua program has kept me out until a later hour. I am confident that I may get consciously in touch with your thoughts after a little practice of receptivity. If acquainted with the difference in time, I think that success might attend my efforts to send you thoughts in return. However, I know that I have received benefit subconsciously from your thoughts already.

Someone has said, "It is possible to change your fate but not your destiny," and I know that my destiny has prepared me most wonderfully for that which is just now beyond the horizon. The remarkable force which caused me to hunt you out when every material agency seemed against such a meeting—causes me to marvel at psychic unfoldment and guidance. Yet, I was told by those beyond that I would come in contact with an influence soon which would be the connecting link between my life work and spiritual and mental development.

I am led to repeat my wonderment at how short a time it took us to "find things in common," and the depths of understanding at which we conversed during our first meeting. My wife is as delighted as I in what the future may hold in store, knowing of my high ambitions.

It had seemed—until the Light came—that my lot might be doomed to a spiritual struggle weighed down by material means. As I had expressed the thought to you—a few who catch glimpses of the real nature of life and aspire to develop so as to be of great service to the world, are sometimes kept from doing so by force of circumstances which take up a great share of their time and energies. Yet, men of the world and wealth would gamble fifty thousand dollars on the outcome of a horse race and think nothing of it. These same men would not gamble fifty cents on the outcome of a human soul with a vision to develop so as to perform a big work for humanity.

It is cheering and encouraging to a young man to realize that there are minds who might be interested in his progress. Given an opportunity to develop under proper guidance, favored by my early years, I should be able to go far in the ordinary span that is allotted humans here.

I have arranged my vacation so that I will have a week in September or October and I am taking a week now. If word should arrive in these later months I will be able to act upon it.

It is impossible for me to say how much I appreciate what you are doing for me. There is a joy in my soul which has not been there before because I had gone about my preparations and study with the faith that the "way would open up some day" for me to get the higher development fitting me for a mission that I felt would be far reaching. Now I have a sense that the opportunity is very near the dawning. The rewards of RIGHT LIVING are *infinite*. . . .

My thoughts turn to you often and I am looking forward with much anticipation to a further meeting later. I shall be pleased to hear from you at any time or to entertain you in my home. As you have said, "There are very few people fitted to do this kind of work or who have the type of minds ready for greater development at this time." That is why it is such a privilege to have met one of the few.

With the best of wishes and regards, I am,
Sincerely yours,

P.S. Where will it be possible to reach you after September 1?

After the lecture, Mother Sherman, who enjoyed meeting people, went up on the platform and was chatting happily with Harry Loose when Harry suddenly excused himself, stepped over to the edge, and held out his hand to one of a small group of boys waiting there.

"Hello, Arthur," he said. "You don't look a bit like your brother." This was an experience that Arthur never forgot.

About two weeks later we received a handwritten letter from Harry Loose, with cryptic greeting and signature, in which he again indicated his intimate knowledge of Harold, his personality and habits, which letter we treasured carefully:

WHITING HOTEL
TRAVERSE CITY, MICHIGAN

August 11, 1921

Accept the drowsiness and sleep whenever it comes to you. Much that you know not of yet is accomplished while you sleep. You have been holding too tense. You must practice and achieve being able at will to relax all mental tension—then only are you receptive and then only can you be reached and taught. There has been some confusion, too—thought of heart—stomach—food. This must stop. Your own mentality, so expressed, is so powerful that nothing can enter in when you deny it entrance. Your physical condition must improve to carry the weight of the mind that now so overbalances the body. This must be built up by every possible means—the added weight and physical strength *must* come—you are so powerful mentally—that if you deny it I am afraid my promise of added weight may fail.

I cannot convey to you the importance of this physical condition emphatically enough—so much of your future depends absolutely on this. No matter how important some things may now appear to you remember there are greater things in prospect and your biggest and best thought should be toward getting the physical health and strength needed as background for much work ahead of you—things *big* to you now will seem *puny* after a little time, if you will but follow what is told you.

You are fitted to a mission of tremendous good and importance to the world—what it is I know not myself yet—but much, if not all, hangs on building up your physical body. Once "the way" is shown you, you will have great burdens to carry and must be physically balanced with that great mind of yours.

Your wife has only thought of you and your well-being—consult with her—in some things her way is much the best—she sees things physical better than you at the present. Exercise lightly—not too much—eat much and of what the wife advises. Sleep all you possibly can.

I have been with you several times but cannot make you *see* as yet—your mentality is too great for me to overcome in its strength and present innocence as yet. Suggestions have been given you—yes—I can really write no more—words on paper are futile things to convey sometimes, and in this you *must read between the lines.* Try to do as I have indicated—much depends on it. In another year, if all goes well, writing on paper won't be necessary for communication.

I may tell you that your "place" is far above mine—the plane is some degrees higher. Wish I could say more. You may write me in care of the Bureau at Kimball Bldg., Chicago, the first week in Sept. Will not be able to say anything till then in re coming down to Marion for a second visit—probably Oct. would be best for me if I can come. Would much like to talk to you then—I *might* by then be able to give you some *good news* though much will depend on yourself—all will really.

May I thank you for your letter. Could talk to you of some of its contents but can't write—you understand. Little Mother and brother were *fine* when I met them here today.

* * *

After working at the Chronicle *for about a year, Harold decided that he had gained all he needed from newspaper experience and resigned to join the Moss Advertising Agency, headquartered in Marion. There he spent a year handling local accounts. He also began writing plays and stories. One of his plays,* Home Town Follies, *became a local hit. In 1923, after selling his first juvenile story, "The Hidden Battle," to* Boys' Life, *the official publication of the Boy Scouts of America, Harold left the advertising business to become a freelance writer.*

4

New York

To be nearer the literary markets, the Shermans decided to move to New York City. They sold their furniture and other valuables, and on April 7, 1924, with $500 in his pocket (which included $75 from the sale of his second story, on young married life), Harold left Marion on a train bound for New York. Martha and their three-year-old daughter, Mary, went to Traverse City to stay with Martha's parents until Harold could get himself established and send for them. Entering the city entirely without connections, he found himself a room at the Bristol Hotel.

* * *

It had been my plan to secure a position as an advertising copywriter with one of the big ad agencies to support me, and to carry on my sports writing on the side, until I could establish sufficient reputation and income to switch over.

To assure my getting such a position, I had taken a number of letters from local merchants highly endorsing my advertising-writing abilities, which I was certain would profoundly impress the big advertising agency executives and make them realize what a "find" they were getting in me.

My first disillusionment came when they hardly glanced at these letters but asked me rather coldly, "What New York experience have you had?" When I confessed "none," that I had just come to New York from the small town of Marion, the stock reply was, "Sorry—not interested."

My visit to magazine editors proved almost as fruitless. It meant little or nothing to them that I had sold a story to *Boys' Life*. They would be glad to consider any stories I would care to submit but I was offered only mild encouragement. . . .

In my cheap hotel room [one] night, taking stock of the few dollars that I had brought with me to New York, and realizing how short a time I could stay if I could not get a job or sell another story, I wondered if I shouldn't put aside my pride, admit a mistake in having come to New York with so little ability and knowledge to compete against already established writers, and go back home until I was more ready.

During the next few days I was on the verge of making another decision which, in the light of later developments, would have been a wrong one—a decision to rescind my earlier decision, to give up my dream of achieving success in New York, and return to a place and a position which would afford me security, even though little opportunity for advancement. The temptation is always great when the "going is tough" to renege, to give up your plan, relinquish your objective— to play safe.

In my case, after prayerful consideration, I sat up all night and wrote a basketball story, and took it down to the editors of *Boys' Life*. They bought it—and they kept on buying my sport stories, giving me the benefit of their editorial advice. This provided me with eating and rent money. A few weeks later, I answered an ad in the paper for associate editor of a textile magazine, *Carpet & Rug News*, and Hank Price, a publisher who had come from the Midwest himself, said, "I don't want a man with New York experience. I just want a man who can do the job!"

So, now I had a weekly paying position and enough of an income to bring Martha and Mary to New York to share a walk-up apartment with me. Our New York residence lasted seventeen years!

[*How to Foresee and Control Your Future*, 1970]

Harold confided to Hank Price that he wanted to develop as a fiction writer, and Price agreed to let him write fiction on the paper's time, once his day's duties were done. Harold's stories soon appeared regularly in Boys' Life *and other publications, including* The American Boy, Youth's Companion, Top Notch, *and* Open Road. *He published his* Boys' Life *stories under three names: his own name for sports stories; "Thomas H. Baldwin" for humorous stories; and "Edward J. Morrow" for mystery and adventure yarns. Between 1924 and 1933 he wrote over three hundred short stories.*

While continuing to work for the Edward Lyman Bill Company (the publisher of Carpet & Rug News*), Harold wrote his first full-length book, a novelization of the 1926 motion picture,* One Minute to Play, *starring football star Red Grange. He finished the book in fifteen days, to coincide with the film's release.*

One Minute to Play *was a great success with men and boys throughout the United States, and Grossett & Dunlap, the book's publisher, received demands for follow-up sport books. Harold wrote over thirty sport and adventure books, including seven books in the "All American Sport Series," published by the Goldsmith Publishing Company, which sold in hundred-thousand lots. In 1933 he produced the* Tahara *series, four mystery and adventure stories about a boy mystic from India, also published by Goldsmith. With new Sherman novels appearing at the rate of six to ten a year, nearly every boy in America was familiar with his name and his writing. One adventure novel,* Cameron MacBain, Backwoodsman, *was jointly written with Hawthorne Daniel, a former editor of* Boys' Life *who became a close friend of the Shermans.*

Harold also wrote over twenty plays and produced sketches for radio. His one-set symbolic peace play, Not Until, *a biting attack on international conditions, was broadcast over WGBS in New York on Armistice Night, 1926. Its Communism-versus-Democracy theme emphasized that "not until fear and hate and greed and lust for power were removed from the heart of the individual could lasting peace ever come to the world."*

In 1927 the Edward Lyman Bill Company offered Harold the editorship of a new magazine, with a substantial steady paycheck. The offer was tempting, but Harold decided, after talking it over with Martha, that he would rather live on short rations a few years longer and stick to his fiction and playwriting. At Harold's suggestion, Louis Spilman, the editor who had employed him in Marion, was hired to fill the position Harold had turned down.

Louis shared my interest in the psychic world, and when he learned of an amazing mentalist by the name of Jacques Romano,[1] who had

---

[1] Jacques Romano (1864-1962) frequently appeared on radio programs such as "Strange As It Seems" and "Mysteries of the Mind." *The Jacques Romano Story*, by Berthold Eric Schwarz, M.D. (New York: University Books, 1968), relates a number of Harold Sherman's experiences with Romano.

entertained the Lyman Bills at the Bonnie Briar Club in Larchmont, New York, he arranged for me to meet him.

We found Romano all that had been claimed for him. He used card tricks as a means of setting the stage for genuine telepathy, working himself up into such a state of sensitivity that he was able to go around a circle of people whom he had never met before and tell them of past experiences they had had with astounding degrees of accuracy.

Romano had been traveling sales manager for the Eastman Kodak Company for years but had been researching the remedial value of different herbs and had developed some iodine solutions that could be taken internally, and which the old drug manufacturing firm of Eimer & Amend had purchased, setting up a laboratory for Romano to work with his preparations. Romano, in the course of his studies, had acquired one of the finest libraries of long-out-of-print books on herbs that had been effective in the treatment of different illnesses.

During the years that followed, Martha and I had Romano as a guest in our apartment in Manhattan easily over a hundred times, each time with different friends and acquaintances whom Romano had never met—and who were highly skeptical of Romano's reported telepathic powers. Invariably, all were amazed and convinced, and our get-togethers seldom broke up until around one or two in the morning.

While Romano was demonstrating his remarkable powers, I was studying him in an attempt to learn the techniques he was using to make attunement with the minds of his observers. Gradually, I began to get similar impressions, which I did not voice but which occasionally corresponded to the impressions Romano was expressing concerning certain individuals. Romano, himself, when asked how he did it, would jovially respond, "Oh, those things will happen!" Actually, I learned much from this unusual man which I was to employ in my own development of these extra-sensory powers. . . .

Through Jacques Romano, Martha and I met Jacques' physician friend, Dr. Seymour S. (Cy) Wanderman, and his lovely, musically talented wife, Dorothy, who became and have remained among our dearest friends.

Cy Wanderman, ordinarily an "open-minded skeptic," had seen and tested Romano, as I had, and we were both impressed with his remarkable sensitivity. His mental feats had confounded Harry

Houdini,[2] who was reported to have stated: "Jacques Romano is the only man whose feats I could not duplicate."

[*How to Know What to Believe*, 1976]

By 1929, when the Shermans' younger daughter, Marcia Ann, was born, Harold was a successful writer and the family was living in a penthouse apartment on Riverside Drive in Manhattan.

In the early years of the Great Depression, two of Harold's plays were produced on Broadway. The first, Her Supporting Cast, *a farce comedy, opened at the Biltmore Theater on May 4, 1931, and ran for about a month. The other,* The Little Black Book, *was a domestic comedy that ran briefly after opening on December 26, 1932. Harold's unproduced plays included* Coo Coo Ism *and* Hocus Pocus, *two comedies debunking various "isms"—numerology, astrology, palmistry, etc.*

In 1932 Harold turned to social and political issues with his first adult novel, Dry Rot, *followed by* Let Freedom Ring!, *both illustrating the futility of the Prohibition law.*

In 1933 he spent four months in Hollywood writing continuity and dialogue for a sound picture, Are We Civilized? *Using newsreel clips and scenes from old historical feature pictures, Harold depicted man's inhumanity to man, from the days of primitive man on. The story illustrated that, as man has become more civilized, he has not become less savage—he has only improved his weapons of self-annihilation. The film depicted various nations conducting military maneuvers—testing new explosives, new and more destructive means of warfare—and asked the question: "Do nations prepare in this manner, who are preparing for peace?"*

When Are We Civilized? *opened at the Rivoli Theatre in New York, it drew favorable reviews.[3] Walter Winchell called it "the most stirring plea for peace ever produced." It was booked for distribution throughout the United States, and then the booking was mysteriously canceled. In* Your Miraculous Powers of ESP *(1969), Harold claimed that Adolf Hitler, through the German Embassy, had threatened to cancel all American-made showings of pictures in Germany if* Are We Civilized? *was released, as the story pictured the coming of World War II and "the shoe had fit too tightly."*

---

[2] Harry Houdini (1874-1926) was an internationally famous magician and escape artist.

[3] The film can be watched at www.archive.org. A book, *The Making of* Are We Civilized?, by Saskia Raevouri, is for sale at www.amazon.com.

While in Hollywood Harold became reacquainted with several New York friends, including the psychic Arthur Ford who introduced him to screenwriter William Hurlbut,[4] who in turn took him to meet veteran Hollywood director John Stahl.[5] All of these men were intrigued by Harold's ideas on how to meet personal problems by visualizing one's future, and they encouraged him to write a book on his philosophy of life. Harold was not sure that he had the background for it, but they said, "Well, you certainly have enough authority for us. What you have told us tonight is very helpful. Give some thought to it." And so, encouraged by his Hollywood friends, upon his return to New York Harold wrote Your Key to Happiness,[6] *which became a bestseller, going through many printings.*

In my first philosophically written book, *Your Key to Happiness,* I emphasized the value of meditative relaxation and gave the reader a simple technique for letting go of all body tensions, for making the conscious mind passive, for turning the attention of the conscious mind inward, and then in this relaxed state, freed of all physical stresses and strains, for placing a mental image in mind of what one wanted to do or be or have.

A year or so after this book on self-development was published, I received a phone call one night in my New York City apartment.

"Is this the Harold Sherman who is the author of *Your Key to Happiness?*" a man's voice asked.

"Yes," I answered.

"My name is H.C. Mattern," said the voice. "I've bought and given away over two thousand copies of your book—and I figured it was about time I was meeting you."

"Any person who has bought and given away that many copies of a book of mine, I want to meet!" I responded.

"Okay!" he laughed. "How about lunch at Stouffer's Restaurant on Forty-Second Street tomorrow noon?"

"It's a date!" I confirmed. "I'll be there!" You can imagine how piqued my curiosity was! What could cause any person to buy that many copies of a book?

When I arrived at the restaurant, I found a dark-haired, somewhat heavy-set man of about medium height waiting to greet me.

---

[4] William Hurlbut (1878-1957) wrote the screenplay for *Imitation of Life* (1934), *The Bride of Frankenstein* (1935) and other films.
[5] John Stahl (1886-1950) was best known for directing *Imitation of Life.*
[6] Harold M. Sherman, *Your Key to Happiness* (New York: G.P. Putnam's Sons, 1935).

His facial features were unusual; deep-set, penetrating blue eyes, and a determined square jaw. He could not shake hands with me immediately because he was carrying, in each hand, a strapped-together stack of my *Your Key to Happiness* books, all of them giving evidence of having been well read and well worn.

"Brought these along for you to autograph," he explained, as he set one stack down and gripped my hand with bone-bruising fervor. "When I told friends to whom I had given these copies that I was going to meet you today, they brought the books in for me to take to you. They said it would mean so much if you would put your 'John Henry' in them."

"Glad to do it," I said, as we took a table in a corner of the restaurant and he unstrapped the books. The first one he handed me gave me a shock. I saw that page after page had sentences and paragraphs which had been underlined with red, green, and blue pencils. He had also printed along the margins of pages which had been stapled together, instructions like these: *Do not open and read these pages until you are sure you understand and have mastered what you have studied thus far!*

I looked at Mattern questioningly. "How come all this?" I asked.

"That's to make sure they don't go through this little book too fast," he said. "Your book is not to be read lightly and tossed aside—it's to be studied and applied. I have made a text book out of it, as you see, and I make people to whom I give copies promise that they won't remove the staples until they're reasonably certain they have digested what they have read. This way, when they're through, they begin to get results."

Mattern went on to explain that he'd used the creative visualization techniques set out in Harold's book to invent a chemical solution to clean and preserve leather upholstery, which led to a successful business. Using the same techniques, he found his wife and partner, Mary.

By the time H.C. left this life he had bought and given away over ten thousand copies of *Your Key to Happiness*. Mary and H.C. became close friends of the Shermans[7] and we met many times as my lecture trips took me to the same same cities in which they were working.

[*How to Foresee and Control Your Future*, 1970]

---

[7] Harold later introduced the Matterns to Dr. Sadler and the Forum.

Harold on the radio in 1936
[University of Central Arkansas, Archives and Special Collections].

Your Key to Happiness was so popular that Columbia Broadcasting System signed Harold to a series of fifteen-minute radio spots in which he explained how to draw upon one's God-given powers within to attain one's goals. Within two months he was receiving so many letters a week that he took on several stenographers to help answer the mail. The show's success led to CBS giving Harold his own show, "All About You," which was on three times a week and lasted about six months, making Harold a known figure in the field of self-help.

In the middle 1930s, the idea came to me that I might dramatize, for radio, stage and screen, the life of America's great humorist, Mark Twain.[8] Inquiry revealed that the rights to do this would have to be secured through the Mark Twain Estate, which had been established following Twain's death for the purpose of handling the sale and other business relative to his many literary properties. I found that this Estate was managed by an attorney, Charles T. Lark, with offices on Fifth Avenue; that he was one of the trustees, and that he had been the lawyer who had drawn up Twain's will and acted as his executor. The Estate was being operated for Mark Twain's only surviving daughter, Clara,[9] at that time Mrs. Ossip Gabrilowitsch of Detroit.

I realized that my ambition to dramatize Mark Twain's life could not be achieved unless I was willing to invest my time and talent in preparation of a full and complete synopsis which might be presented to Mr. Lark in proof of my ability. It was evident that many writers of far greater reputation than mine had sought and were seeking the granting of these same valuable rights. I reasoned that these busy writers would perhaps not be willing nor have the time to prepare any material on speculation but would request these rights of the Estate based upon their established reputations. I therefore decided it was worth the gamble for me to devote all the spare time possible in a study of all writings on, about and by Mark Twain to saturate my consciousness with his life activities and character, and then to prepare a detailed dramatic outline to show the Estate just how I would propose to handle this subject for the stage. . . .

---

[8] Mark Twain (1835-1910) was the pen-name of Samuel Langhorne Clemens, author of such American classics as *The Adventures of Tom Sawyer* and *The Adventures of Huckleberry Finn.*

[9] Clara Clemens Gabrilowitsch (1873-1962) became friends with Harold and Martha Sherman after Harold was given exclusive dramatic rights to Twain's life, and after the three discovered a shared interest in spiritual matters.

When my outline was finally finished, I had it professionally typed and bound and, with that, I was now ready to make contact with Charles T. Lark for the first time. I phoned his office and made an appointment through his secretary. The night before keeping this appointment, in my period of meditation, I had what you might call an imaginary interview with Mr. Lark. I saw myself meeting and informing him of the purpose of my visit. . . .

During this meditation, a definite feeling came to me that Mr. Lark would agree to read the outline, and the instant I had this impression I relaxed and went to sleep in the faith that all would go well with my appointment.

Everything *did* turn out exactly as visualized. . . . In about ten days, Mr. Lark's secretary phoned and asked me to mail to the officer a copy of my bibliography. I knew from this that my outline was receiving serious consideration. Two weeks later, Mr. Lark himself called and invited me to lunch. He then reported that he had read the outline and had liked it so much he had mailed it on to the other trustees and [Twain's official biographer] Albert Bigelow Paine, and when he had received favorable replies from them, had sent the script to Mrs. Gabrilowitsch. She, too, had written, expressing her liking for the overall treatment. "And I suppose now," concluded Mr. Lark, "what you want is the go-ahead."

I told him it certainly was, that I desired to work in close association with the Estate in the dramatization and, after some discussion, the contract was agreed upon, granting me the exclusive rights in all dramatic forms. . . .

[*How to Make ESP Work for You,* 1964]

Almost immediately Harold sold Mark Twain *to Harry Moses, producer of the Broadway hit,* Grand Hotel. *While casting the* Twain *play, Moses fell ill and died several months later. Harold found it difficult to find a new producer. Financially, it was such a lean time for the Shermans that they gave up their apartment in July 1936. Martha and the girls moved back to Traverse City while Harold remained in New York at the City Club. They were rescued in January 1937 by City Club secretary Charles Whitmore, who had enough faith in Sherman's earning potential to underwrite the family for a period of five months in exchange for 7% of Harold's future net earnings from writings, for as long as Whit-*

more should live. This allowed the family to reunite and find new living quarters in New York.

In the fall of 1937, the Russians attempted to fly some planes nonstop over the North Pole and land them in the United States. Two of their ships made the historic flight, but the third was forced down some two hundred miles from the Pole and never heard from again. The Russians thought the fliers might still be alive in the Arctic wastes, so they arranged for the famed Arctic explorer, Sir Hubert Wilkins,[10] to outfit an expedition and fly north from New York City in search of them.

At that time, Sir Hubert and I were co-members of the City Club of New York. I did not know him well but often discussed his various polar adventures with him and with other club members. Shortly before he was to take off on his search flight, I met him in the club lounge and engaged him in conversation. I asked Wilkins what he would do, should his plane be forced down and the radio go out of commission as the Russians' had. Wilkins smiled and said, "It would be a long walk home." I then suggested, half-humorously, "Wouldn't it be great, should this happen, if all you would have to do would be to concentrate and send a telepathic message of your latitude and longitude to a trained human receiver who could then send a search party to that location to pick you up?"

"You're jesting," said Wilkins, "but I would not say that in perhaps fifty to a hundred years, the minds of some humans would not be developed to the point that this could be done."

This led me to confess to Wilkins that Martha and I had been experimenting privately for some years with sending and receiving thoughts and that I believed, under certain conditions, I had been able to score above chance results. Wilkins made a confession of his own—that he had had premonitions all his life of things that were going to happen, and many of them had come true. He then proposed that we might undertake an experiment in long-distance telepathy during the time he would be in the Far North searching for the lost Russian fliers. He suggested that I act as the receiver and that we set aside Monday, Tuesday, and Thursday nights, from eleven-thirty

[10] Sir George Hubert Wilkins (1888-1958) was an Australian polar explorer, aviator, photographer, cinematographer, naturalist, newspaper correspondent, soldier, military consultant, lecturer and author. Introduced to the Urantia manuscript by Harold Sherman in 1942, he became an avid student of the papers and read them on his frequent visits to Chicago.

to twelve midnight, Eastern Standard Time; and that he, as sender, would try to get off by himself, wherever he might be in the Far North, and transmit to me in mental imagery form, the outstanding things that had happened on his expedition that day. He would relive and review them in his mind's eye and put feeling behind them as he thought of me. It would be my assignment to make my mind receptive, while seated in my study in my New York apartment, and record in my own words what flashed across the screen of my mind in the form of mental pictures or deep feelings.

So that we would have witnesses to these experiments should they prove to be significant, friends arranged for us to meet Dr. Gardner Murphy, then head of the Psychology Department of Columbia University,[11] who requested that after recording impressions each night of thoughts I felt I was receiving from the mind of Wilkins, I make typewritten copies of them and put them in the mail that very night, addressing them to him at Columbia University. In this way, whatever I had received would be protected by government postmark, carrying automatic proof that long before I could get a check report from Wilkins' diary and log, I was on record as of those dates with Dr. Murphy. Other witnesses to these experiments were added,[12] whose affidavits appear with that of Dr. Murphy in the book written by Wilkins and myself, *Thoughts Through Space*.[13] After five and a half months, during which several hundred impressions were recorded by me, it was found that some seventy percent were remarkably accurate.

For example, one night at the appointed time when I was concentrating on Sir Hubert, I suddenly became conscious of a disturbing toothache. I actually felt this in my own jaw but I sensed, in this instance, that it was Wilkins' tooth that was aching, some three thousand miles away! I then recorded:

"Have feeling you have had bad toothache today. . . ."

Several weeks later, when Wilkins' check report from his diary and log was received in New York, his entry for the same date stated:

"Had severe toothache today. Flew to Edmonton to get tooth filled. . . ."

---

[11] Dr. Gardner Murphy (1895-1979) also served as president of both the American Psychological Society and the American Society for Psychical Research.
[12] Fellow City Club members Dr. A.E. Strath-Gordon, Samuel Emery, and Dr. Henry S.W. Hardwicke.
[13] Sir Hubert Wilkins and Harold M. Sherman, *Thoughts Through Space* (New York: Creative Age Press, 1942).

Sir Hubert Wilkins around the time of the experiments
[University of Central Arkansas, Archives and Special Collections].

On another occasion, with my mind attuned to that of Wilkins, I felt as though my head had been bumped a number of a times. I interpreted this feeling as follows:

"Sudden severe pain comes to me—right side of head—I seem to see or feel physical disturbance affecting another. . . ."

This impression was also confirmed some weeks later from Wilkins' diary and log, again synchronized with the approximate time of my recording:

"Am not sure that it happened this day, but each one of us could not seem to avoid bumping our heads on a sharp-edged stovepipe in the kitchen of our quarters. I bumped mine only twice but Dyne and Cheesman bumped often. Cheesman was laid out by the blow twice in one day. The pipe was at an awkward height. . . ."

In both of these cases it is evident that strong feeling was involved. These accurate impressions could not be attributed to guesswork since Wilkins had only one toothache in the five and a half months he was away, and I had picked up the impression of it on that very day. The head-bumping incident also occurred only once, close to the time I recorded the impression of it, when it was much on the minds of all concerned. It was interesting to me that I actually seemed to feel a momentary simulated toothache and these bumps on the head simultaneously with a mental sensing of such conditions.

I particularly recall my concern the night I had recorded my mental picture and strong feeling impression that Sir Hubert had been forced down on a flight due to bad weather, and had appeared at an Armistice Ball attired in an evening dress suit.

I remember saying to Martha, "I have a feeling I'm all wet tonight; that I've let my imagination run away with me. . . ."

Martha counseled me to wait until I might receive a check report from Wilkins' diary and log by air mail. She urged me to clear my mind of doubt, meanwhile, so it would be free and undisturbed to engage in the next experiment at the appointed time. This I did, but I had moments of uneasiness nevertheless. You can imagine the sense of relief that came over me when Wilkins' report finally arrived and I learned I had been right about that dress suit!

[*How to Make ESP Work for You*, 1964]

In December 1938 Harold was hired as editor of The Savings Bank Journal *but soon resigned as the full-time job left him no time for cre-*

ative writing. He then joined an advertising agency, Applied Merchandising, as Director of Radio.

The success of Your Key to Happiness *gave Harold the opportunity to give talks before groups such as Harriet McCollum's Applied Psychology class and autograph copies of his book, which by 1940 was in its fifth printing. In addition, the Wilkins experiments led to invitations to give presentations on ESP with Sir Hubert Wilkins and Charles Francis Potter,[14] at such venues as the Psychic Forum in New York. Harold and Sir Hubert were also busy co-writing the manuscript of what was to become* Thoughts Through Space, *the account of their long-distance telepathic experiment.*

Around this time Jesse L. Lasky,[15] one of Hollywood's top producers, asked the Mark Twain Estate for permission to produce a film about Mark Twain. The estate agreed, stipulating that Harold Sherman be involved in the writing of the film. Contracted to go to Hollywood as soon as Lasky could overcome certain creative and financial hurdles, Harold began preliminary work on a "master chronology" of Twain's life while still in New York.[16]

[14] Charles Francis Potter (1885-1962) was a Baptist preacher turned Unitarian turned humanist. In 1923-24 he became nationally known for participating in a series of radio debates with conservative Baptist Rev. John Roach Straton, which were published in four volumes: *The Battle Over the Bible, Evolution versus Creation, The Virgin Birth—Fact or Fiction?* and *Was Christ Both Man and God?* In 1925 he served as advisor for Clarence Darrow and the defense during the Scopes evolution trial. In 1929 he published his first book, *The Story of Religion,* followed by two books on humanism. In the late 1930s he developed an interest in ESP and telepathy, which led to a lasting friendship with Harold Sherman.

[15] Jesse L. Lasky (1880-1958) was a pioneer filmmaker. In 1914 he and his partner Cecil B. DeMille, with financial backing from Lasky's brother-in-law Sam Goldfish (later Goldwyn), produced the first Hollywood feature-length film, *The Squaw Man,* a big hit. Co-founder of Paramount Studios, he left the company in 1935 and became a successful independent producer of films, including *Sergeant York, The Adventures of Mark Twain,* and *Rhapsody in Blue.* During the writing phase of *Mark Twain,* the Laskys and the Shermans became friends.

[16] A book, *Behind the Screenplay: The Making of* The Adventures of Mark Twain, by Saskia Raevouri, is available at www.amazon.com.

PART II

HARRY LOOSE

1

A Flow
of Astounding Letters

The impact of that great personal adventure of meeting Harry Loose in 1921 had made as deep an impression on Martha as it had on me. It carried us through almost the next twenty years; our change of residence from Marion to New York City, as Harry had predicted; my struggles to gain a foothold in the writing profession, first as juvenile sports-story author, with its many ups and downs; while devoting much of my spare time to a study and practice of telepathy, as we sought greater and greater knowledge concerning the mysteries of the mind. During this time we tried on several occasions to make contact with Harry Loose, but letters addressed to the Chicago Police Department and the Redpath Chautauqua Circuit were returned, marked "no forwarding address" or "whereabouts unknown," seeming to confirm Harry's statement that he would not be available for a time, while on a "mission." . . .

With the finish of the Wilkins experiments and with time to study and evaluate them, it became clear to me that I had, in my way, been able to receive specific and detailed impressions of events from Wilkins' mind, comparable to the type of communication that Harry Loose and his wife had apparently demonstrated years before. I had never doubted the validity of what I had witnessed that night in the Marion Hotel, and my memory of it had given me the faith that if I persisted, I would hopefully, one day, acquire the ability to duplicate what the Looses had done.

Thinking of them so strongly renewed my desire to make contact with Harry again, and one day, as if in response to this desire, an amazing thing happened. The chances for this occurrence were literally ten thousand to one, for Wilkins and I received thousands of letters from people all over the world, following publication of a feature article in the March 1939 issue of *Cosmopolitan* magazine,[1] telling about the success of our long-distance telepathic adventure. We divided the mail between us and set out to try to reply to all the interested correspondents, a task which took some months.

As I was writing Walter M. Germain, head of the Crime Prevention Department, Saginaw Police Force, Saginaw, Michigan, I suddenly had the feeling that he might know the whereabouts of Harry J. Loose, so, acting on impulse, I added a postscript: "Would you happen to know the present address of Harry J. Loose, former Chicago policeman and detective in charge of Hull House? . . ."[2]

By return mail came Loose's address! He was retired and now living at 123 Elizabeth Street, Monterey Park, California. I wrote him at once, filling him in on our family background and a few highlights on what had happened since our first memorable meeting. . . .

[*How to Know What to Believe*, 1976]

> 380 Riverside Dr.,
> New York, N.Y.
> January 31, 1941

Dear Mr. Loose:

Do you remember meeting a young man, then a newspaper reporter on the *Marion Chronicle*, I believe it was the summer of 1922 or 3, in Marion, Indiana—who called on you at the old Marion Hotel and spent, for him, an unforgettable evening? You indicated to him then a knowledge of mental powers far beyond the comprehension of average humans—and wrote him a letter which Mrs. Sherman and this young man, now slightly older, still cherish as an inspiration!!

We have carried you in mind all these years, and as I have pursued my research in the higher powers of mind—it has al-

---

[1] See Appendix A.

[2] It was really after Sherman's and Wilkins' appearance on the "Strange As It Seems" radio show, on December 12, 1940, that Walter M. Germain sent in his letter. Both the *Cosmopolitan* article and the radio appearance drew large amounts of mail.

ways been with the thought and hope that our paths would cross again some day. At the time you told me I would go to New York City, and you felt you had a mission to perform which would take you the next ten years and that the next time we met it would be in the east. I went to New York City in the spring of 1924, to follow a writing career. Since that time I have written over sixty published sport and adventure books for boys and girls which have sold over 7,000,000 copies; I have had plays on Broadway, have been in Hollywood and written for pictures, and have written a bestselling book on the mind, *Your Key to Happiness*. This would perhaps interest you more than all else— together with the experiments in long-distance telepathy which were conducted with Sir Hubert Wilkins, under supervision of Dr. Gardner Murphy, head of the Parapsychology Department of Columbia University. You may find an account of this work in the *Cosmopolitan* magazine, March 1939, perhaps on file at any public library.

Your fine interest in me and what you told me that memorable night, while you were on your Redpath Chautauqua tour, meant much to me and spurred me on my way—and I have always been deeply grateful.

I have never had the urge to try to locate you until recently, for I felt that you might, one day, get in touch with me. But, of late, you have been particularly in mind. It is interesting to know that you are apparently west.

I may come west with my family—wife and two daughters, Mary, aged 19, and Marcia, 11. I hold the exclusive rights, from the Mark Twain Estate, for the dramatization of the life of Mark Twain for radio, stage and screen . . . and recently sold the picture rights, being busy now on the scenario. If production plans go forward on schedule it may bring me back to Hollywood within the next three months.

I sincerely hope that things have been well with you and that you have been enabled to accomplish much in service to the world. There is a great crisis looming ahead for this nation which is going to require inner wisdom to meet.

If you have not seen my book, *Your Key to Happiness*, I should like the pleasure of sending you a copy as soon as I have had acknowledgement of this communication.

With warmest regards and good wishes to you and yours!
Sincerely,
Harold M. Sherman

An immediate reply came from Harry, indicative in every way of the unusual nature and character of the man as I had remembered and been inspired by him:

> 123 N. Elizabeth Ave.,
> Monterey Park, Ca.
> February 4, 1941

Greetings:-[3]

Mary and Marcia. Both are Biblical. Marcia is a derivative of Martha. With a good wife and two beautiful and dutiful daughters, you are very fortunate. I congratulate you. I am pleased with your writing success also. You have been helped—as you helped yourself. I will be much pleased to receive your book, *Your Key to Happiness.*

Long-distance telepathy—or short-distance—is much in use and operates perfectly. It has been in operation for thousands of years amongst certain groupings in all periods. Its method is very simple when once understood. Time or space is nothing.

I live, on a very modest income, in an old brown house in a small and humble suburb of Los Angeles. Very different from 380 Riverside Drive. Seven miles from Los Angeles Plaza. I drive downtown in 12 minutes. My time is not occupied physically. My lot is large but I am a sad farmer.

May I thank you for your letter. It came early. I was not given to expect it until later in the month. There is a reason. You may be called to serve. I do not know. Many have been. Do not be afraid if called. I do believe you have been in the preparatory stage for a long time. If called it will probably be for some specialized working. Time alone will answer. I do not know. I am merely surmising.

Intelligences with whom I am in contact have accomplished much in service to this atom of a world. I serve in a very humble capacity. My mission has not been completed. I have progressed but had hoped for release and much greater progress before this. Much has been done in regard to the crisis looming for this nation, but the forces in opposition are of tremendous psychic power. An untaught, untrained mind could not comprehend.

There is nothing else real but "mind." "It is the Spirit that quickeneth, the flesh profiteth nothing."

---

[3] The letter as it appeared in *How to Know What to Believe* was heavily edited; we are reproducing the original letter here.

I do not know your present development. I have to be careful. I do not want to talk over your head and be misunderstood.

I was in New York City in May 1926 as I had anticipated. Owing to circumstances beyond my control, I did not see you there as expected.

Remember to watch for a tremendous book which will be published in about two years. It has been now 35 years in the building. It is not mine but I had something to do with it. You will recognize it when it appears. It will be world shocking. It will clarify so very much that is cloudy in our present-day Bible. It is a true spiritual revelation to this age written by intelligences that have never been earthbound and who have to do with the governing of this tiny earth in this very limited universe. Please believe every astonishing word. It is the TRUTH. I KNOW.

I talked with you on the night of July 21st, 1921, in my room in the old Marion Hotel at Marion, Indiana. Nearly 20 years ago. I knew so little myself then. You were one who was ready to receive. The seed did not fall on stony ground—though it often does—you would be surprised.

It is all an individual proposition—whether there will be growth or not. No one can grow for you. This applies hereafter just as much as here. You will not be satisfied to sit on a damp cloud and play on a 4-string harp forever. You would get very tired of it after the first few hundred years. You will find that you will be kept very busy instead of cloud-sitting.

Excuse my long letter. I will be looking for the book. Thanks a lot.

With every good thought to surround and support you and yours,

Sincerely, *Harry J. Loose*

This was the start of a flow of astounding letters, each one an individual revelation in itself, as Harry informed and instructed us, step by step, giving us an enlarged vista of life and the universe; a broadened concept of the Creator and creation; a beginning grasp of our purpose on this planet; and the suggestion that each human creature comes into this life with a potential mission to perform in service to humanity.

This idea of each person being born with a mission—a debt, so to speak, to society, which he or she was given the freewill opportunity to pay—was new to us. It was new and yet it appealed to our sense of logic and rightness. It helped give us a feeling of rhyme and reason behind all things—observing as we did the interrelatedness and interdependence of all forms of life, one upon the other.

[*How to Know What to Believe*, 1976]

HAROLD SHERMAN to HARRY LOOSE

New York, February 8, 1941

Friend Loose:

I knew your letter would reach me yesterday afternoon and hurried home from downtown to get at it.

Mrs. Sherman and I have developed through the years together—which has helped immeasurably. No doubt this has been true of Mrs. Loose and yourself. We have found, as you long since discovered, that the more that is revealed, the more remains to be revealed . . . and one becomes most humble in what little knowledge has been gained.

My apprenticeship has been long and trying—physically and mentally. It will be thrilling to meet and compare notes when the time is right.

To think of my being drawn to you that night, of your knowing of my coming, of the message and inspiration you were able to give me then—at a time when I needed just that demonstration—of the years that have intervened, now but a snap of the fingers covering this "illusion Time."

I have been helped greatly—as you know—and have striven to the best of my small ability to be worthy—to earn the right for advancement. There is much that we both could say to each other.

I was on the radio in a dramatization of the telepathic experiments with Sir Hubert Wilkins, the "Strange As It Seems" hour, December 12th, 1940—and was also interviewed at that time. Our broadcast broke all mail return records—over seven thousand letters, voluntarily written, expressive of interest and wanting to know more. This broadcast brought me a letter from Walter M. Germain, Supervisor, Crime Prevention Division, Police Department, Saginaw, Michigan—and I got the immediate impression he knew where you were. I wrote and asked him and got your address by return mail. He is enormously interested in higher powers of mind. I could write SO MUCH. May we meet in body soon!

My best to you and yours,

HARRY LOOSE to HAROLD SHERMAN

Monterey Park, February 12, 1941

My Friend:-

May I thank you for your letter, the book *Your Key to Happiness*, and the magazine. They arrived a day ahead of me. I was away on a long journey. I have not yet had time to read either the article or the book, and I have them before me as a treat. May I thank you for the inscription on the first page.[4] I appreciate it a great deal. I also want to report to you that the parcel had been opened by someone for inspection and re-closed and tied with a brown string and so delivered.

This is my second letter to you today. I had been given permission to write you and was very happy about it. I was of course to be much circumscribed as to amount, and to two subjects. They are subjects that should not be written about. There is no authentic written data on one of the subjects and there should be none. After I had finished it, I read it to Mrs. Loose who agreed with me that it was as clear and understandable as was possible under the circumstances. And then we decided that I had better not mail it. It lays here, stamped and addressed.

You see, you have been my responsibility for many years, and I am so afraid that you could not yet understand and it would give us both great grief if you had not progressed to be able to understand and would disbelieve what had been written—I know that you have grown but I do not know to what depth lays your yet-so-limited receptivity. Yet you must have information. I have not been able to find what Intelligence is to give it—nor whether earthbound or free. I was hopeful that I would be given the work.

When you called before, I was able to help. You did not know whom you were calling. Now you call me. I hear you calling—and I cannot answer you because you know my personality. It was easy to answer you before because I had only the receptive and open mind to satisfy, but now I have memory, mental eyesight—individuality—personality, etc., given to Mind to confuse it . . . You too will sometime have the same responsibility—it is the Law—and you too may have your problems when the time comes for advancement of your responsibility—when you too will be released.

---

[4] "To Harry J. Loose, who inspired me early in my quest for true knowledge of self, and who has remained in consciousness through the years, as a deeply esteemed guide along my pathway of life."

I know that you are chosen for advancement and that you will have some beginning in what mortality calls paranormal but which is really perfectly normal—merely operating on little known or understood normal laws. What would radio be called 100 short years ago? A child can tell you today that it is not supernormal.

I imagine that in *Your Key to Happiness* you are probably trying to tell the multitude some plain and normal mental laws. A hundred years ago these very same laws were in existence, but how many knew about them. They were none the less true then than they are now. They have been so since the beginning—but how many knew anything about them. So then, many things that are supernormal to the mass are perfectly normal to the few who understand the perfectly normal laws upon which they operate.

What would you say if I told you that the Astral is perfectly true? The nearest to me of my Order is a Catholic priest in one of the So. Americas. I told you in the beginning of this letter that I had been on a long journey. So I had. I had been to visit him. I spent some 20 hours away from here. I have an appointment with him to visit me here in April. We visit back and forth quite occasionally. These visits are made back and forth under perfectly normal laws. When you understand these laws you will be also able to so operate.

But one of the degrees upon which the Astral operates on this dimension requires the cooperating between the two. I cannot go where I am not desired and no astral can intrude upon my privacy—I have got to desire the visitor. In the next dimension you go where you desire without any cooperation required.

There is so very, very much. I must be careful—I am getting close to dangerous ground.

I made a mistake in my last letter to you for which I have been corrected. I remarked, "Many are called." This is not so. I meant, and should have written, "Many are considered but few are called."

I have tried to get through to you in the Astral. I cannot. The Law against intrusion operates against me. You do not yet understand advanced telepathy. I nearly make it, when you grow weaker and get away. You scatter your forces. You do not understand this conservation yet. When you get a year in advanced telepathy, you will see that your earlier efforts would be confusing.

So, the long letter—addressed, sealed, stamped—lays here on my desk. I do not yet know what to do with it. I will not destroy it until I first try to think my way into the clear. I may get a different viewpoint in your answer to this letter.

I would like to have you meet my friend the Catholic priest. Maybe when you are here, he will visit. We generally meet in our little local park where we can sit and watch the children. He can only stay 10 hours because of his church duties. He comes home to dinner with me at noon time but he cannot eat anything. Air and water are necessary to him, however. He will be perfectly visible to you. I know that you would enjoy talking to him. I would like to have you see him when he starts for his home particularly. No, I am not a Catholic.

Well, I must wait. There is nothing else that I can do. I may be instructed to mail my letter to you. I know so very little. It appears now that I will not make contact with you until you come west. Well, that is not such a long time. If I do finally lay some background by way of my letter, it would be perfectly all right—though I would like to be able to give—teach a little—just two or three months. And then again, I would be merely an old man, in the way, once you get started—and you have your family and your work to do. I would ask you to please answer this—it may help me with my problem. I have not been so perplexed in many years.

With all good thought over and under and around you all.

Harry J. Loose

[*Handwritten addition:*] I am old and tired and know that I must soon toss the torch to some younger and more virile mortal. I am so hopeful that it may be you. I do not know.

HAROLD SHERMAN to HARRY LOOSE

New York, February 17, 1941

Friend Loose:

There is so very, very much that I could say! And so very much that must be said when the time is at hand to say it.

I feel and have felt, since your first letter came, that I could open a door to you. I have sensed you close at hand, inwardly, and have spent a restless week as a result. I knew you were writing that letter and spoke of it several times to Martha, my wife. I did not respond to the urges that came, at times when you seemed near, because I did not feel settled enough in body and conscious mind.

Need I explain by saying that such little knowledge as I have gained has come to me in what might be termed "the hard way." I have had to seek this knowledge within myself through arduous trial and error, having found very little of it in books, years ago. I have had to intuitively perceive these mental laws and then endeavor to learn their operation through long years of experimentation—attracting to myself such knowledge and help as I might be able to *earn* from other intelligences, whether recognized by me on occasion or not.

The Wilkins experiments were undertaken under supervision of Dr. Gardner Murphy, head of the Parapsychology Department of Columbia University, and other scientifically interested persons here, giving me the first opportunity to test powers of which I had been aware, under controlled conditions, operating on regular schedule.

I undertook this work while under great economic strain, and was required to do from ten to twelve hours of creative writing a day in addition to this higher mental work three nights a week. The strain of mind and body was almost too much. I developed ulcers of the stomach and suffered severe hemorrhages which nearly took my life. When the five months of intensive mental work were completed, during which time I had become so sensitized that when I dropped off to sleep after an "appointment with Wilkins," I was projected automatically into the astral and made "unbidden" journeys to distant points, I decided I must place a conscious check upon my development for the time being until I could gain better command over my physical. I have kept a record of my most outstanding experiences in this "unsought field of phenomena" which I later hope to show you for analysis and evaluation—as well as interpretation. One of my comparatively recent experiences of still a different nature, I am asked by my wife to send you now. She recorded it for me—it being her interpretation that the "youth" referred to is my higher self. I will await your own interpretation. It is significant that the guide was a "monk."[5]

When you say that I "scatter my forces" too much, as yet, you are perfectly right. My creative activities have been terrifically varied.

Since you saw me in Marion, Indiana, at which time I was getting a newspaper background, I have successfully gained experience in advertising, publicity work, juvenile writing, radio, stage, screen, adult novels, philosophic writing, editing of trade magazines—ending up, just last year, as editor of *The Savings Bank Journal*, a well-known financial publication, because I was impressed that I *must* gain an in-

---

[5] This record has not been found.

side knowledge of the type of minds that control the financial affairs of this country. I was sent to Washington to do a job of interviewing summer before last, during which time I met most of the outstanding Senators and many government officials, which gave me an immense insight into forces and activities.

Early in life there came to me the clear vision that a tortuous apprenticeship lay ahead . . . that I was to develop in myself the creative facility to express myself successfully in every medium of expression—utilizing every important channel of communication—the press, magazine, book, radio, stage and screen fields. I sensed that my real opportunity for service would not be at hand until I had encompassed this job. It seemed to me that when this time had arrived, there would be given to me inspiration for the creation of stories and messages of vital import which I could then dramatize for mankind under the guise of entertainment—and thus reach mass consciousness with truths so direly needed in order to accomplish a degree of liberation and advancement for many.

I have not spared myself in devotion to what has seemed to me a first duty. I have deliberately resigned from writing activities which paid good money, and started all over again in a different writing field altogether because my inner self told me that I had completed my experience where I was—and it was time for me to move on. This has not been easy, when one is carrying the burden economically of one's family and others dependent on him.

I am deeply grateful for such development and understanding as *has* come to me under the circumstances.

I have the physical weight now that you said I needed years ago. I am close to 175 pounds stripped and about five feet ten in height. In fact, I am about ten pounds heavier than I should be, in my opinion, yet my doctor wishes me to carry a little extra weight as insurance against any possible flare-up from the stomach. I have my occasional stomach pains, indicating that I have not entirely eliminated that condition. My last, most serious attack, was a year ago in February— when I came close to passing over. I know this was a test and perhaps a warning to give more thought to balance on all planes.

Now, as is always the case when one is approaching a moment of great change, conditions are unsettled. I am awaiting word from the coast from Jesse L. Lasky, who has purchased the Mark Twain play. He is endeavoring to complete releasing arrangements through a major company, and the moment he is able to do this he will send for me—and I will store my furniture here and bring the family west with me.

I said to Martha, before I consciously knew that you were west, that I felt this Mark Twain work, as important as it might prove to me from the writing standpoint, was intended to bring me west for spiritual purposes . . . that I would at last discover what my real mission in life is to be.

I did not feel, in all the time since my one physical contact with you, that I had earned the right to try to reach you again until recently—and then forces placed at my disposal opened the channel easily and speedily. How much you have known of my actual physical and mental struggles during those years I, of course, cannot tell. I have felt you close to me many, many times, however.

This last week or ten days I have been busy clearing up writing odds and ends, and my conscious mind has been more aware of unsettled external conditions, which has not been conducive to receptivity. I have one assignment remaining before I would be ready to leave for the coast . . . and that is completion of the book Sir Hubert Wilkins and I are writing, telling the "inside story" of our telepathic experiments, under the title of *Thoughts Through Space*. I have put off writing this book until now . . . when my mind would be freed of other commercial obligations. You can appreciate the battle I have had to undergo for years—doing many things in the nature of development which would not have been first choice of the inner mind but which I knew had to be faced.

It has seemed to me that my job was to be a simplifying of these mental laws—a "practicalizing" of them for the benefit of mass humanity . . . a "down-to-earth" description of them so that people of all faiths could grasp basic truths and, according to their own understanding, make use of them. Obviously one can only tell so much in print, and even that in more or less rudimentary form. But there is a reaching out now—on the part of all humanity—for certain truths, for an understanding of Self, for some satisfying explanation as to "why" certain things are happening in the world . . . and this need is going to be overwhelming in the next few years to come—when external evidences of chaos will be spread over the face of the earth.

I am sending you a little poem which came to me, in a higher state of meditation, *already written*. I simply seized pencil and paper and wrote it right off as I heard it spoken in consciousness. It came as a result of my desire to be given the power to express my belief, concisely and in such an inspired manner that it might "ring a bell" in the lives of others seeking to express their own inner feelings ordinarily incapable of being put into words.

ETERNITY AND I
Deep down within the depths of me
   There stirs a mighty, timeless sea.
Its waves of memory touch the shore
   Of consciousness and, more and more,
As time unreels in worlds of space
   My self reveals its God-like face:
A God-force breathing through each form
   Of life I've lived. About me swarm
The eons past in which I've dwelled,
   Vague, fleeting glimpses now beheld.
One day, an inner voice persists,
   I'll reach beyond all that exists
And Time and Space no longer bind
   The new dimension of my mind.
Until then, plodding I must go,
   With patience, reaping as I sow,
From birth to death and birth again;
   Nor asking how nor why nor when
The "I am I" of me content
   To know that it is heaven-bent;
A heaven not as dreamed of yore—
   A blessed state—the open door
To realms above the sense desires
   Where burn the great creative fires
And, one with those who have attained,
   Freed now from all that had me chained,
Eternity and I embrace
   At last I meet God face to face.

I feel inwardly—tremendous thoughts waiting to be expressed. I feel a communion with higher spirits or intelligences which I have not yet tried to identify . . . because there has come with this sensing the impression that "the time is not yet." I have said to Martha, "I feel I will one day be used as the instrument for some form of expression that will electrify the world," but I must not let myself become impatient . . . *I must not try to pull this inspiration from my inner self now.* If I do, I will expose it before its time . . . and give premature birth to it, which would be fatal. I must be given unmistakable signs that the time is at hand . . . and conditions exactly right.

Economic freedom is one of the things that must occur to provide the period necessary for the illumination I sense may come through such guidance as yours. I have never striven for the sake of money . . . I have striven only to *prepare*—firm in the faith that, at the proper time, resources would be given me as a result of my having earned them . . . to grant the liberation needed for performance of higher duties.

I still have not the absolute physical assurance of conditions working out to bring me to the coast at any definite time . . . although my inner feeling tells me it will not be too long. Complete consummation of the *Mark Twain* contract would solve all economic problems at once and free me to commence on further preparation for the real work ahead.

It would be a great privilege to be able to enjoy association with you. It would also be a rare privilege to be able to commune with your friend, the Catholic priest. I hope I may be given the power to earn this right . . . and to be able to visit with you and see you in my own home. I do not think it would take too long for me to develop this ability for astral traveling . . . but I need to know how to control my physical reactions a bit better yet. You see, I have had to pay the price for such advancement as has come to me, discovering these different functions of body and mind as concentration has revealed them to me . . . but at the cost of certain ignorance which could only be banished by experience. And yet, the things I have absolutely needed to know, in critical moments, have been shown to me.

The close spiritual bond between my wife and myself has made what little I have been able to accomplish possible. She has traveled the road with me, maintaining at all times a soldier-like faith in me . . . and our common ideals, that has bolstered me when the trial seemed almost too much to bear.

I have written as I have been impulsed to write. Perhaps what I have said may disclose to you what you wish to know at this moment.

My deepest affection goes out to you and yours from all of us,

HAROLD'S NOTE   *New York, February 17, 1941*

After receipt of the second letter from Harry J. Loose, I made my first effort to assume a receptive state of mind and to invite impressions from or about him.

I stretched out on my cot, relaxed my body and turned my thoughts inward. I remained in this receptive state until about 11:45 a.m. EST, from about ten minutes after eleven.

As I opened my eyes, I saw, distinctly against the wall in front of me, next to the door, the outline of a pink rose, with green stem and leaves, as though it were a color picture or print.

To make certain it was not inner vision, I shut my eyes and the rose disappeared. I opened my eyes again and its image was still there, flat against the wall, larger than natural size, and next to the framed words of Fra Giovanni which have meant so much to me.

This is the first time, in my recollection, of ever having had such an experience. It caused me to wonder if this were an experiment that some mind or intelligence was trying—to determine if I were ready or could receive such impressions or images.

2

"CHOSEN FOR ADVANCEMENT"

HARRY LOOSE to HAROLD SHERMAN
Monterey Park, February 17, 1941

My Friend:

I am writing you a long but necessitous letter.[1] You will find herein some things you should know. I am leading you gently. I would prefer that you should read this after your evening meal. I would prefer it read aloud between you two, and all at one time. You will need your Bible. Please believe and have faith.

You have been chosen for advancement. I have been released from my responsibility and you stand alone on your own two feet figuratively. This is my swan song after nearly twenty years. Both Mrs. Loose and I are so glad that the long pull is over and all has turned out so well so far.

We have finally agreed that it is best not to send you the other letter that I wrote you about. Although I was given permission to write you briefly of some subjects, the decision was left to me. We have decided that it is not yet the time and that they are matters that should not be put into writing. Also, the information should rightfully come

---

[1] This letter was written before Loose had received Sherman's letter of February 17th.

to you from another source. So my long letter has been consigned to the little wood fire burning in the grate—with the stamp cut off economically and soaking in a cup of water so that it can be removed and used again.

I am not fast on the typewriter and I guess that I have a several hours' job ahead of me. Too long a letter to reread for any correction and so please excuse any minor errors that may appear herein.

Before I get into the body of this letter, I want to tell you that I have read your book, *Your Key to Happiness*, through once with pleasure. I am going to read it again. You have really and truly done a remarkable job in its creation. It is clear, concise and at once available to the varied mentalities of the multitude—to the gallon-sized mind just the same as to the pint-sized. The type is very acceptable—it makes easy and non-tiring reading. I read it, too, as your own personal philosophy and it is fine and constructive. I am proud of your accomplishment. I am extra proud of what you write on page one of my copy. I could not help but think of it all as so apropos of poor Job's sad remark, "That which I greatly feared has come upon me," and also another one, "As a man thinketh in his heart, so is he." It has already done a great deal of good in its help to confused minds and should surely run into additional editions. Your writing style is "different." Nothing stilted. It is very natural, friendly and conversational. The little story of Grandma Morrow[2] is so personal, friendly and neighborly, so intimately confidential. On the whole, a difficult job well done.

I have not yet been able to read fully and consecutively the article in the *Cosmopolitan*. I liked the picture of you. You are not much changed. Older, yes. I am glad that you shave smooth. I have often

---

[2] From *Your Key to Happiness* (pp. 90-91): "My grandmother, Mary A. Morrow, was a remarkable woman physically, mentally and spiritually. She lived to be eighty-three and was active all her years until but a few days before her passing. She said to me upon one occasion: 'You know, it's so hard to grow old gracefully.' And yet, Grandmother Morrow was setting a marvelous example of doing that very thing. She had a deep and abiding faith in God, in the universe, in the fundamental rightness of things. She bore such afflictions as came to her with a rare patience and fortitude which was expressed in a clipping that she had treasured and which I came across after she had gone. It said: 'Life is a battle. We all have work to do. We must not expect to sail to Heaven on flowery beds of ease; while others fought to win the prize and sailed through bloody seas.' Grandmother Morrow believed that happiness must be *earned,* both here and hereafter. Yet when her time came to go, with loved ones gathering about her bedside, clinging to her, she was able to face this supreme moment and to say: 'You who love me, do not hold me here. I want to go. There are many dear ones over there. It will be a happy release.'"

listened to the "Strange As It Seems" program and am sorry that I missed the one of December 12th, 1940.

Now as to criticism. There is one place in the book where you are wrong deliberately. I dislike very much to disagree with you, but I speak from direct knowledge—not from deduction or theories. You are to learn this difference very thoroughly and well in the not-far-distant future. The part to which I refer is on pages 43 and 44.[3] The truth is that once you leave this dimension you never return to it, nor do you ever at any future time have a second earth experience.[4] You never appear here or on any other earth again in the flesh—spiritualism and ghosts and such manifestations to the contrary. There are too many millions of inhabited worlds in this smallest Universe to ever need to return here, if a second earth experience was required, and there is far too much to do in the second dimension to require a second period of service on this or any other earth. Once you leave this dimension, you never return to it.

There are, however, certain entities, or Intelligences, from other dimensions whose presence here in this first dimension, in the flesh, for varying periods, is required for especial missions. Let me tell you a little story here; in its way, it will be illuminating:

Years ago, I was at a meeting of a group of men folks at the home of Dr. Weir S. Mitchell [sic], the famous Philadelphia neurologist.[5] His life work with the inner mechanism of the mind and nervous system should have tended, and doubtless did, to make him cynical as regards supernormal phenomena, but during the evening he told us men sitting there what was to him a strange story. I had heard that he had related it before, and I was interested to hear it from his own lips. He told us in a way that left us with a feeling that there was a question in his mind as to its significance. It was the sole mysterious incident of his long medical career.

---

[3] See Appendix B to read this part as well as the revised version as it appeared in the 1943 edition.

[4] *A mortal never returns to his native planet during the dispensation of his temporal existence* . . . (39:4.15). [*Ed. note:* This passage from the Urantia Book and others to follow are cited according to paper, section and paragraph (in this case, Paper 39, section 4, para. 14).]

[5] Loose copied this whole account from pp. 12-14 of George K. Cherrie's book, *Dark Trails: Adventures of a Naturalist* (New York: G.P. Putnam's Sons, 1930). Silas Weir Mitchell (1829-1914) was known for his writings on nerve injuries in the Civil War. Erythromyalgia is now known as Weir Mitchell's disease.

One evening, after an exhausting day with patients, he had got into his dressing gown and retired with a book to rest. After reading a few moments, he dozed. He was awakened by the violent ringing of his front doorbell. When the maid did not answer, he arose and went to the door himself. There he found a little girl, thinly clad, and plainly in distress. Without waiting to be accosted, she said, "It's my mother, sir. Won't you come please?" The night was cold with snow whirling and drifting before a bitter wind. Dr. Mitchell was very tired. He expostulated with the child and suggested that there were other doctors at a nearby hospital. Besides, the little girl was a perfect stranger to him. But the little messenger would not be put off—she argued—she wept—and there was something in the way she spoke— or her personality—or some other unknown impression, that caused Dr. Mitchell to relent. Bidding her to wait in the warm hall, he got into his clothing and overcoat and followed her.

He found the mother ill with a violent form of pneumonia. She turned out to be an old servant of years before. Anyway, Mitchell telephoned for proper medical aid and other medical assistance. Some days later, when the woman was past the crisis, and conscious, he sat at her bedside and complimented the sick woman on the intelligence and persistence of her small daughter. "But my child died three years ago. Her shoes, her dress and her little coat are in a box in that closet." Mitchell took the box from the shelf and saw the exact garments worn by the little girl. And Mitchell concluded with a gesture of spreading hands and said, "Not that I hold any brief for ghosts, but what was it that I saw? What was it that walked with me and talked with me?"

These things happen. There is a reason. By a singular coincidence, I now know the reason why that particular phenomena was produced. I have been cognizant of many similar events happening since. When I can talk to you, if I ever do on this dimension, I will tell you the reasons "why" of the "poltergeists" and other "ghosts" and materializations. They appear and there is a reason for their appearances. They are perfectly true and do happen. I am leading you along gently. I hope I have your full attention.

Before I go any further, and make another criticism, I want to get this little extraneous bit into the picture. Read it well. I am hopeful that you do not get too far afield in some of your perhaps lonely, and not-so-well-guided, meditations and explorations. I have seen disturbing conditions arising from a lone student getting so far afield that they were unable to return without help. Be sure of your groundwork, and until you have recognizable help, advance but step by step. Always be sure of your way back before you go out. Slowly—step by step—remember. You may receive a demonstration and/or information from some authentic source as you help yourself, however.

In my years of sending, it has always been of much concern to both Mrs. Loose and myself that it was not too much for assimilation—just little by little—but now that you will be on your own, I want to warn you seriously. I want to counsel you, however, to patience. These matters generally move very slowly. I speak from experience. It may be weeks—or months—before actualities occur. Count your blessings when you have a tendency to become impatient. You can perceive. Look backwards. You will then recognize actualities that have already occurred—always for a reason—and always making for this present crux.

Now to the second and last criticism. It is a technical one but it gives me opportunity to pass to you a bit of other information at the tail end which is true and accurate. We are not of the two-brained type.[6] We are the three-brained type. There are other planets that are inhabited by either a two-brain or a one-brain type of being. It depends upon the development. Anyway, we are the three-brained type. The cerebrum at the top, the cerebellum at the back and the medulla oblongata at the extreme rear.[7] The spinal cord begins at this third brain, which is about the size of a fifty-cent piece. It is entirely separate from the other two and its functions are to itself alone. Really, nothing is definitely known of what it has jurisdiction over. It is presumed by the medicos to have to do with the cardiac and respiratory systems.

Now follows the true interpretation. This is of the three combined. Brain, the fleshy content of the cranial cavity, they are all collectively the switchboard in the powerhouse over which the Ego—Cosmos—

---

[6] In *Your Key to Happiness,* Sherman never mentioned that humans are two-brained; he said that humans had two minds—the conscious and the subconscious.
[7] Contrast: *[T]here are three basic organizations of the brain mechanism: the one-, the two-, and the three-brained types. Urantians are of the two-brained type . . . From the two-hemisphere type of the Urantian cerebral cortex you can, by analogy, grasp something of the one-brained type. The third brain of the three-brained orders is best conceived as an evolvement of your lower or rudimentary form of brain, which is developed to the point where it functions chiefly in control of physical activities, leaving the two superior brains free for higher engagements . . .* (49:5.14).

I—Spirit—Soul—Intelligence—whichever you wish to call it—operates, and through which it has jurisdiction over its subject, the body.

In addition to the duties of the subconscious that you write about, it is the storehouse of memory and it also has jurisdiction over all of the involuntary movements of the body, within and without, from birth to death, and it is the *last* of the human body to die. While the conscious mind sleeps, the subconscious never sleeps—from the cradle to the grave—and neither does the mysterious medulla oblongata. Some people say, "My memory is becoming poor," when as a matter of fact the memory never fails. What fails is the ability of the conscious mind to *re*-collect from the subconscious.

Yes, I know that it would have been much more difficult to develop without Mrs. Sherman's help and co-operation. I also know, as a truth, that you could not have reached the degree where you now are as a single man. He is not whole until he is joined with a woman (womb-man), the Life carrier, in this dimension. A single man or a single womb-man develops psychically to a lesser degree—never fully.

I could go on but now is not the time. During the probably long forthcoming period, please keep a quiet, well-ordered and receptive mind, week after week. Talk together fully—exchange opinions—give your imaginations full and free rein—discuss freely all the angles of your coming advancement as they present themselves to you—the more thought and conversation the better. Avoid discord of any kind. Positively do not let it appear in your home. Be helpful, cheerful, happy, thoughtful of each other. Do not indulge the flesh in any excesses—anything and everything in moderation is all right. Guard your emotions. Beware of anger, hate, jealousy, or worry, and avoid discord of any kind. Anticipate good. Look expectantly for good. Fill yourselves with LOVE. Beware of constipation. Drink much water. Things will normally happen in their own time. Take things easy. You have naught to fear and nothing to worry about. Do not be anxious. Be casual and relaxed.

Do not talk to or in the hearing of the children of these things. These are matters of direct import to you, and that single word does not mean either of you singly. You are only YOU when it means both—you were made one and you are one—physically—mentally and in spiritual thought. Let the matter be one that is exclusive to just YOU and carefully exclude the children. There will come a time when it must be given to the children—a little at a time—but not now. You will be given to know when and how much.

You must treat this letter, and all and any following evidences, most seriously and sacredly. It is not to be transmitted to any persons beyond YOU. It must be strictly private to you. It must in no way be written about—nor commercialized—no part may be in any stories, plays or motion pictures. Any digression from this would be instantly known and you would lose a great deal—in progress I mean. I also warn you that it is better to accept, you will be given your free choice, without any mental reservation—and with full knowledge and intent to give service. You have an extremely rare opportunity. There is no punishment, either here or in the next dimension, for failure. But I assure you that it would mean loss to you—and no profit to you.

So relax—read—write—have no differences—be "of one mind" and continue so—both—and "be not weary of well doing"—continue any religious contacts that you may have—pray—earnestly—and in your own most secret place—that is, pray within you, inaudibly—you do not have to kneel—you do not even need to close your eyes to commune with your Father—he IS your Father—you are a cosmic citizen, with all the rights of all cosmic citizens, and a part, though a very infinitesimal part, of the Great Intelligence—and remember, "God is Spirit and must be worshipped in Spirit and in Truth." Become friendly with him—read your Bible. Don't forget Proverbs and Psalms. Both are good—especially Proverbs.

You have been chosen for further development. But what the development is to be—in what direction—and there are several—I do not know. I do know that, whatever the course, it will be several years before you will be far enough along to begin to be of service. Do not expect anything of a sudden nature—although things not evidential to your understanding will be happening all the while.

I know that you have been in preparation for responsibility for years. In conversation I could, permissibly, tell you much in answer to questions that I know are very present with you. Things about this whole matter. Things that are to you of great import.

In regard to one thought on which you wish confirmation—that is, whether there is a continuity of individual LIFE—I can answer you most positively YES. It will not be long now, I am sure, when you will have other and more positive assurances than what my mere statements represent. I am trying to lead you gently—little by little—as always.

Now I want you to get out your Bible and read the references I will give you below. You cannot read further of this letter understandingly without the background of the Bible references. Read the following consecutively: Genesis 14:18; Psalms 110:4; Hebrews 5:6-10; Hebrews 6:1-20; Hebrews 7.[8]

Please know, O my friend, that this Order is in existence in direct and unbroken descent, and the written matter pertaining to the Order and other matters of interest, from those times up to the present, is in existence.

To this order belonged one who signed himself in Americ [sic], not Hebrew—Joshua ben Joseph—which means "Joshua son of Joseph"[9]—the word Jesus being the Greek for Joshua. Christ is also a Greek word meaning "Messiah" and was in no way attached to the name of Jesus until 400 years after his death.[10] I have seen that signature. It and the mass of writings are safe in a "Shangri-La" sort of a place. You will visit there some day too. From the written records there, which I have seen—with translations attached—how different is the truth, how much more fully informative than our own present Bible—so full of inaccuracies and errors of translation.

For instance, I have read the translation from the original statement there and it tells the story of much of His life written at the time, and the last is the account of his death—to be accurate, within three months of his death. A description of the cross on which he died. A much different cross than that which is generally pictured. With what was called a "Roman saddle," a round stick of wood in a hole and on which the person on the cross sat with legs crossed and which partially suspended the weight. The bottom of the cross, where the feet were placed, was a measured three feet from the ground.[11]

---

[8] See Appendix C.

[9] The name Joshua ben Joseph is Hebrew, not Aramaic. "Ben" is Hebrew for "son of"; "bar" is the Aramaic form of "ben."

[10] The Urantia Book indicates that Jesus was proclaimed as the Christ immediately after Pentecost: *What has happened to these men whom Jesus had ordained to go forth preaching the gospel of the kingdom, the fatherhood of God and the brotherhood of man? They have a new gospel ... Their message has suddenly shifted to the proclamation of the risen Christ* ... (194:4.4).

[11] Compare: *The soldiers first bound the Master's arms with cords to the crossbeam, and then they nailed his hands to the wood. When they had hoisted this crossbeam up on the post, and after they had nailed it securely to the upright timber of the cross, they bound and nailed his feet to the wood, using one long nail to penetrate both feet. The upright timber had a large peg, inserted at the proper height, which served as a sort of saddle for supporting the body weight. The cross was not high, the Master's feet being only about three feet from the ground* (187:2.1).

It tells me that Joshua learned the trade of carpenter in the shop of his father, Joseph, which shop adjoined the home in Nazareth.[12] It tells of Joseph advancing from carpenter to the business of contracting.[13] He was quite successful and had the contracts and did the erecting of several large public buildings. He was finally killed in the fall of a derrick at Carthage where he had the contract for the erection of a large, new public building.[14] I have not seen the contract but I was informed that it was there amongst the records.

At the time of the death of Joseph, Joshua was not living at home. He was in partnership with the Zebedee brothers, James and John, at Galilee where they built boats exclusively—for use on the Sea of Galilee.[15] Jesus began working with the Zebedees several years later. On the death of Joseph, Joshua immediately returned to his home in Nazareth where He, the oldest child and son, took over as provider and head of the household. His mother, Mary, was pregnant with child. This child was born six months after the death of Joseph and was named Ruth. Ruth grew to womanhood and married Jacob, son of the stonemason who lived next door to the family in Nazareth.[16] Out of the seven brothers and sisters of Joshua, this sister, Ruth, and the brother, James (who became head of the new Church in Jerusalem, instituted after the death of Joshua), were the only ones in the family outside Mary, the mother, who believed Joshua was what and who he represented himself to be.

At any rate, Joshua opened the old carpenter shop and did carpenter work there—but not enough to support the large family—and so he added tent making—rope making—and working in leather— to bring in more revenue. Later in his life, when his disciples asked him, "Lord, how shall we pray?", He gave them what has since been called "The Lord's Prayer," which he wrote originally with charcoal on

---

[12] *[The boy Jesus] began doing regular work in the home carpenter shop . . .* (124:4.1).
[13] *Joseph himself was a carpenter and later a contractor* (122:1.1).
[14] According to the Urantia Book, Joseph's fatal accident occurred in Sepphoris: *[A] runner from Sepphoris brought to this Nazareth home the tragic news that Joseph had been severely injured by the falling of a derrick while at work on the governor's residence* (126:2.1).
[15] The Urantia Book states that Jesus was working at Joseph's caravan repair shop at the time of Joseph's death: *The messenger from Sepphoris had stopped at the shop on the way to Joseph's home, informing Jesus of his father's accident, and they went together to the house to break the sad news to Mary* (126:2.1).
[16] According to the Urantia Book, Jacob, the stonemason's son, married Jesus' sister Miriam (128:5.8), not Ruth. Ruth married David Zebedee (190:1.10).

a smooth board and affixed to the wall in the carpenter shop, where he taught the younger children, His brothers and sisters, to read. While Joshua worked at his carpenter's bench or at his tentmaking, he taught the younger children to read by the use of that prayer written with charcoal on a smooth board on the wall of the carpenter shop— and it was this prayer that they all used in the home life.[17] Pardon the repetition but it is so worth repeating. This is the true and accurate way in which we acquired "The Lord's Prayer."

In the same line of thought, I will tell you that the now generally accepted pictures and personality expressed therein of Joshua are wrong, badly. He was a man of medium height, judged by present-day standards, but full-fleshed, virile and powerful. With titian shoulder-long hair that curled and a reddish short beard and small mustache— large brown eyes that were very expressive and full of Life. There was nothing weak nor effeminate about him. He was all man.[18] Please know that this Intelligence, Joshua ben Joseph, was only one of many of an Order whose sole office was, and is, the introduction of Man to the Great Intelligence.

At a certain period in the growth and development of Life on these new worlds, whose making continually goes on, comes a time when Man searches for God and the "why" and mystery of Life. After a long period of Man's groping in the darkness for the answer, and at the proper time, comes one of the fully spiritual Order to which

---

[17] Compare: *During this year [A.D. 9] Jesus first formulated the prayer which he subsequently taught to his apostles, and which to many has become known as "The Lord's Prayer". . . . [O]ne evening in October he sat down by the little squat lamp on the low stone table, and, on a piece of smooth cedar board about eighteen inches square, with a piece of charcoal he wrote out the prayer which became from that time on the standard family petition (126:3.4). Later that year, . . . Jesus climbed the Nazareth hill with James and, when they returned home, wrote out the Ten Commandments in Greek on two smooth boards in charcoal. Subsequently Martha colored and decorated these boards, and for long they hung on the wall over James's small workbench (126:4.9).*

[18] Loose may be alluding here to an apocryphal description of Jesus, purportedly written by a Publius Lentulus to Tiberius Caesar, Emperor of Rome: "He is a man of medium size. . . ; he has a venerable aspect, and his beholders can both fear and love him. His hair is of the colour of the ripe hazel-nut, straight down to the ears, but below the ears wavy and curled, with a bluish and bright reflection, flowing over his shoulders. . . . His beard is abundant, of the colour of his hair, not long, but divided at the chin. His aspect is simple and mature, his eyes are changeable and bright. He is terrible in his reprimands, sweet and amiable in his admonitions, cheerful without loss of gravity. . . . His stature is straight, his hands and arms beautiful to behold. . . ."

Joshua belonged. On each young world, the procedure is the same. No individual Intelligence, a member of this Order, could answer the need. There are a great number. It is one of the works proceeding from growth.

The appearance of Joshua ben Joseph here was his 7th and last presentation in this step of progress and growth. He was the "Son of God" truly. You, too, are a Son of God. Read your Bible.

Nazareth was the crossroads of several busy caravan routes.[19] Joshua became a caravan conductor, after some years back in the old carpenter shop, He had the responsibility for the safety of the caravan, the many employees and animals and their loads of freight and the "mail"—written messages to be delivered in the towns through which the caravan passed—he was also responsible for the passengers that for safety accompanied it, and the paid guard, etc.[20]

On one of these routes he met a very rich Persian who traveled as a passenger. This man had a son of 16 years who accompanied him. For some years Joshua traveled with this man as tutor to the son. He visited Rome and much of the then-known world in the company of this man and his son.[21]

I could write on and on. I could tell you of Abner. He was a disciple of John [the Baptist] before the coming of "the Christ." But after the Christ came, Abner became His disciple. He was one of the seventy-two disciples that were sent out to carry the message to far places and establish Churches. (See your Bible.) And Abner did establish and build a Church in Philadelphia in Perea—across the Galilean Sea—and this Church remained there for 800 years after the passing of Joshua. It was finally destroyed—burned—and leveled to the ground by the Arabs. Abner did not agree with James, the brother of Joshua, who became head of the new Church in Jerusalem, or with Paul, who became head of the new Church in Antioch, because of

[19] *Nazareth was a caravan way station and crossroads of travel and largely gentile in population . . .* (123:5.7).
[20] The Urantia Book reports that during his year as a caravan conductor, *Jesus functioned . . . in an executive capacity, being responsible for the material intrusted to his charge and for the safe conduct of the travelers making up the caravan party. And he most faithfully, efficiently, and wisely discharged his multiple duties* (134:2.4).
[21] According to the Urantia Book, Jesus visited Rome before working as a caravan conductor. His companions on the Roman trip were Gonod, a wealthy businessman from India (not Persia), and his teenage son Ganid. (See Papers 129 to 133.)

their concessions to the religious cults of the day to help gain converts, and because they tried to make a religion of Joshua and his life and miracles instead of what Joshua taught. However, Abner left his own writings of his experiences, and they were not destroyed.[22] It was to Abner's Church in the little town of Philadelphia that Lazarus fled in fear of the Pharisees after being raised from the dead by Joshua, and who labored there with Abner.[23]

O I could go on and on and on. But I must get on with my letter. I am still leading you gently. I would like to take just these few lines though to become a bit personal and remark that you will be tremendously intrigued when you are introduced to real advanced telepathy. You will use it frivolously somewhat at first—just as I did. We are all the same.

I would like to see you in the flesh—right here on this dimension—and talk with you, but I am in doubt as to whether it will ever occur. It would be better not. I have an idea, too, that it would be a bit disappointing to you to see me—merely a tired old man, in wrinkled clothes, like many of those that you see on the park benches when you pass. Except that I could, perhaps, permissibly talk to you of matters of interest to us both. I am old. Older than you think. I have been in service for a long time and am tired. I know that my virility is leaving me slowly though I have been well preserved. In the very natural course of human events I will be released in the not-far-distant future. It does not seem in accord that I should go on to the next dimension without leaving some younger, stronger, more virile mortal that which has been given me of these things in all these years.

---

[22] Compare: *The seventy were ordained by Jesus on Sabbath afternoon, November 19, at the Magadan Camp, and Abner was placed at the head of these gospel preachers and teachers. This corps of seventy consisted of Abner and ten of the former apostles of John, fifty-one of the earlier evangelists, and eight other disciples who had distinguished themselves in the service of the kingdom* (163:1.1). *Abner became the head of the Philadelphia church, continuing as such until his death. . . . It was the apparent misfortune of Abner to be at variance with all of the leaders of the early Christian church. He fell out with Peter and James (Jesus' brother) over questions of administration and the jurisdiction of the Jerusalem church; he parted company with Paul over differences of philosophy and theology* (166:5.4). *[F]rom Philadelphia the missionaries of the Abnerian version of the kingdom of heaven spread throughout Mesopotamia and Arabia until the later times when these uncompromising emissaries of the teachings of Jesus were overwhelmed by the sudden rise of Islam* (171:1.6).
[23] *And so Lazarus took hasty leave of his sisters at Bethany, . . . never permitting himself to rest long until he had reached Philadelphia. Lazarus knew Abner well, and here he felt safe from the murderous intrigues of the wicked Sanhedrin* (168:5.2).

Someone on this dimension has to take over my particular duties. I have been hopeful that it might be you—and yet it is a hard and exacting service—there are other services. I do not know. I know so little. I do know that it would take several years before anyone could be sufficiently developed to carry on. I cannot think but that I must soon throw the torch to some younger mortal than I. The size of this Order has always been limited to a certain number. Never more and never less. The follower is always chosen by the individual active member and he is developed through the years by ways which, I hope, you will one day know. You too will have the right to choose your follower, or successor, and develop him until he is advanced. When your time for advancement to the next dimension comes, your successor will fill your place and take your number in the great old Order. You will be as nearly overcome as was I when the number is given you and you realize the years of service behind that number. I do not know if you are to receive from me, or elsewhere, certain definite and most important information, a little of which was in my letter to you inferentially and not as direct information. Nor do I know when you are to receive this—and other information.

I do not ask you to believe any of the statements that have gone before or any that are to follow. I would rather that you honestly did not believe until you have had further and more visible corroboration. I do not mean vision with the physical eye—that will come later on—but I mean vision with the mind. I know that I would not believe the statements myself under exactly the same circumstances were our positions reversed. Because of my now long association, I sometimes fail to remember that there was a preparatory time when I, too, had to be introduced over a period of several years and little by little until the picture was before me believably. To try to deliver any but a small, a very small, portion would not be possible because of the inability of the receiver to conceive. An ant could not conceive operating a bicycle. It would not be possible to give a child calculus—it would have to have a background of years in thought to bring it to that level of understanding.

The subject matter to follow is tremendous. The totality staggers the mortal imagination. I can tell you only that which is the truth, however. This earth does not operate itself any more than any piece of intricate machinery operates itself. It takes a trained mortal intelligence to operate and control intricate machinery in this dimension. Your automobile does not operate itself. It also takes an Intelligence—or many Intelligences, rather—to operate the great forces and intricacies involved in the operation of this planet. This does not apply alone to this small world in this smallest and newest Universe. It also applies to the other millions of other inhabited worlds in this newest, and smallest, and last Universe—the 7th, by the way. It applies also to the dark islands of space that are other worlds in formation and to which there has been given neither light nor Life.[24] It takes in all those things which mankind calls "natural" or "nature." All animal life, the winds that blow, all growing things—the rivers—the rivers that flow into the oceans—the flowers—their very odors and colors—the grass— the grains—all the many things that have to do with LIFE. Everything except mortal intelligences as we know it on this planet. Everything, ad infinitum onto ad infinitum, is under the jurisdiction of these Intelligences of the next dimension. They govern and oversee them all.

We are surrounded by forces and powers that very few mortals have any conception of, and these very few who do know are cognizant of only a very small number. Most mortals know of but one—the law of gravity—and there are many who do not even know that lone one. The very few, however, who know and recognize *some* of these forces and powers also recognize that there are others, many of them because of certain effects that must originate from a cause—and then there are still others, a very few, who have added information from certain sources—I refer to the members of this ancient Order.

These Intelligences that have to do with the operation of this world have full or partial charge of most of these powers.[25] All does not go well at all times in these vast operations. There are accidents, mistakes, troubles of different kinds, etc. Much the same as on this dimension. When these things occur, the result is felt here in the usual so-called "great calamities" of NATURE.

Some of these Intelligences have had earth experiences—never on this particular planet—many have never had an experience on this

---

[24] Compare: *The Dark Islands of Space. These are the dead suns and other large aggregations of matter devoid of light and heat* (15:6.11).

[25] *[The control and manipulation of power] is carried on by the versatile directors, centers, and controllers of physical energy in the grand universe . . . These Universe Power Directors assume the more or less complete control of twenty-one of the thirty phases of energy constituting the present energy system of the seven superuniverses* (42:2.14).

dimension—that is, an experience in the flesh. There are many more without an earth experience than those with one. Many without an earth experience would very much like to have one.

Please know that all is not perfection in the next dimension. FAR from it. Remember, there is still trouble, still disorder, still the undesirable, still many imperfections, still limited mentalities, just the same as here.

You are still you in the next dimension. You do not become somebody else. You do not become anything or anybody else or different than when you left here. You do not become any different mentally. The growth that you made here is the very same growth that you arrive there with.[26] You know the differing mentalities here—well, simply going to the next dimension does not advance them. No more than the movement of a schoolchild from Los Angeles to New York gives it more intelligence from just the movement. No—it will arrive in New York with just the same intelligence as it had when it left Los Angeles. And so, as it must all be learned eventually, why not learn as much here and now as is possible.

You will find on the next dimension that those Intelligences of fuller development are in the more advanced operations with the greater responsibility, while those of the lesser development have to be used in operations where there is less responsibility and where it can be overseen by the higher Intelligences. Much the same as the "boss and employee" system—modified much—with the foreman and plant superintendents, etc., as we use on this dimension.

For very definite reasons which you will understand fully later, the use of earthbound mortal Intelligences still in the flesh is necessary to the contacting here of these higher Intelligences from the next dimension—and dimensions beyond—higher and still higher Intelligences who have jurisdiction in other, much further advanced Universes—with Intelligences who have jurisdiction over and on this world of ours—known celestially as Urantia. The still-earthbound Intelligences used in these most frequent, I could very nearly say continual, contacts are always taken from the membership of this aged Order. I cannot go into details at this present stage. It is forbidden.

---

[26] *On mansion world number one (or another in case of advanced status) you will resume your intellectual training and spiritual development at the exact level whereon they were interrupted by death. . . . You begin over there right where you left off down here* (47:3.7).

Messengers from other Universes make this a stopping place at times, with messages and orders, and for other reasons that you will know later. In fact, many of them *must* stop even if they have no orders or messages, for messengers are most frequently taken from the second dimension—and you are still earthbound, though not in the flesh, in the second dimension. You still need air and water at intervals and there is also a certain force drawn from the earth contact that you still must have at intervals—so earth contact still must be made by those in the second dimension—you are not yet wholly free from the earth. There are still strict limitations in the next dimension. They still know death. This same first dimension is applicable to all the planets of the grade of this earth—Urantia. By the very same experience by which they gained the second dimension, they progress to the next dimension—by way of death.

You are an individual Intelligence when you arrive here and you remain an individual Intelligence until you pass to the next dimension—you continue to remain an individual Intelligence for all eternity. You are an Intelligence whether you are burdened with the flesh or whether you are free from it. The same that applies to you applies to every Intelligence in the flesh. Whether you are in the flesh or have been freed from it, you are a certain degree of Intelligence. You don't suddenly become different in the degree on attaining the next dimension. You are still you. Your growth depends on yourself. No one else can grow for you. It is all an individual proposition—not alone from the cradle to the grave—but for all time.

"It is the Spirit that quickeneth," etc. The world's population is not ready, will not be ready for thousands of years, en masse, to be able to receive. Imagine the gleeful suicides—the madness—that would follow the broadcasting of definite assurances of a continuity of Life.

Do not waste the emotions. Do not indulge the flesh. Everything and anything in moderation is perfectly all right. Get plenty of sleep and rest. No worry. No fear. Just *let go*. Drink plenty of water. Don't allow constipation. You will sense and feel when actual positives are happening or are about to happen or have happened. You will not see them with the physical eye for a long time. Teaching some very necessary things will probably eventuate from some other than I—though I have been hopeful. There will follow some contacts. Do not be afraid.

In about three years you should be capable of continuing your growth with but little help. Do not lose faith. Even though there may seemingly be nothing evidential to you happening. There will be. You will know later. Remember Mrs. Sherman's credit due. Be especially tender with her. You will need her help much as you continue.

"Seek and ye shall find. Knock and it shall be opened unto you" is the very truth. Please keep and read and reread this. All is in perfect accord with Biblical teaching. There is no conflict—only corroboration and substantiation. I go to no particular Church. I have no choice. They are all based on what is true. They merely travel different highways having the same destination in the end.

I am still sure that I did correctly in destroying my last letter.

I see that I have been writing this for nearly 4 hours right now. I hope that I have not made any errors for which I may again be corrected. I have written this hurriedly as usual and will not reread before enclosing. Excuse my bad spelling. *Do not destroy this.* Read and reread. You will know later when to destroy.

You may question yourself and remark something I want to forestall—your question would be, "How would he dare—how could he run the risk of writing these things on paper to us whom he has never seen. How does he know that we will not talk and betray to others what has been written here?" Well, that has all been cared for. To illustrate one of the forces of which I wrote, one of these very forces protects this letter. You cannot pass this letter on nor can you even repeat that which has been given you herein. Just stop reading for the moment and question whether this is so or not. I have no fear for your answer. No, my friend, you could not betray this letter.

I wish you to be as fortunate with your student as I have been, and I wish you the best of fortune in advancement and understanding. I feel that you will grow rapidly once the usually long-drawn-out preliminaries are over.

I want to thank you for the courage and industry and intelligent cooperation of the past twenty years in this difficult and most intricate operation. You have always been very responsive and helpful. You even called me some weeks before expected. That call to me was my information that you were through as my student. I had been given to expect it nearer to March. I pray you serve your novitiate seriously and successfully. May I ask you to please acknowledge receipt of this letter. Thanking you again for all. With all good thought over and under and around you all,

I am finished,

HAROLD SHERMAN to HARRY LOOSE

New York, February 21, 1941

Friend Loose:

Your letter came late this afternoon when I was downtown. I opened it just before dinner, having asked Mrs. Sherman to come into my study with me, feeling that she was to be present at the reading. When I read the first few lines, we put the letter away, as requested, until we should have dinner and could give it our undivided attention. We waited until both our daughters were in bed, then retired ourselves, and sat up, reading and referring to the Bible, as instructed. You can well know that it was a most sacred and privileged occasion.

I had sensed that reference was going to be made to *Your Key to Happiness* and had brought a copy of it into the bedroom before our reading began. Thank you for your criticisms. I marvel that I have not made more mistakes in this little volume . . . but practically everything else in that book I had been able to demonstrate in my very own life . . . and I had not waited for the same knowledge to come, through experience, with respect to the subject matter covered on pages 43 and 44. This is a good and severe lesson. You see, my progress has been made thus far, with my having been compelled to *prove* every step of the way—and I have stepped out of bounds in this particular.

I have endeavored to keep my mind open and to develop final conclusions on nothing . . . being ready to expand as deeper understanding has come.

Do you know that we had kept the one and only letter you had ever written us all these years, in our family Bible (written on Whiting Hotel stationery, Traverse City, Michigan) . . . and the contents of this letter had served as a guide and an inspiration . . . and the other day, when your second letter arrived, Martha went to the Bible to get this first letter—only to find it had vanished! Of course it is possible it became dislodged and was inadvertently thrown out—but with all the loving care and protection we gave it all this time—it seems surprisingly strange that it should be "lost" now . . . when we wished to keep it with these other spiritual treasures of yours—for ourselves alone.[27]

We enjoyed your sense of humor with respect to my autographing of your *Key to Happiness* book and your comment, "the thing you

---

[27] The Shermans later found the letter. It is reproduced on pp. 41-42 of this volume.

feared most, coming upon you"! To have had me for a responsibility for twenty years has been no easy assignment, I can imagine. Having a vivid recollection of what I have had to undergo in the nature of an apprenticeship—with the consciousness of having fallen far short many times . . . but always with the will and faith to keep trying again, which I can honestly say I have done . . . I was able to relax and laugh at the thought of your watchful attention and concern . . . with possible shakings of the head, as much as to say, "I wonder, sometimes, whether this fellow Sherman is ever going to make it!"

Dear friend, to have earned . . . and to deserve what you have said about us, up to this point, is to have found all we have had to experience, the trials and discouragements and hardships—immensely worthwhile.

You have answered many questions we have raised in our own souls through this letter. I am sure you have made Martha supremely happy as you have me—in the knowledge that true development is meant to take place between man and wife—that progress from dimension to dimension, while a solitary pathway as it concerns each individual intelligence, is still fundamentally bi-une.

Of course I have a consuming desire to clasp your hand and to look into your eyes while you are still here in the flesh. I have stilled this desire in my heart all these years—the while I have felt an unexplainable closeness to you—for I sensed that I had much to accomplish before I might ever be in touch with you again. But now that contact has once more been permitted—it is my prayer that the intelligences who possess the power and the word, may let circumstances bring us together. I am sure I would profit immeasurably thereby. I have long since gone beyond being influenced by any physical appearances . . . and I only wish that I had the development which could enable me to greet you—perhaps a "tired old man in wrinkled clothes, seated on a bench on Riverside Drive" . . .

I will try to prepare myself to be ready, physically and mentally, for the new experiences which are to come to me. I know, despite one's knowledge, that certain kinds of visitations must be awesome when first experienced, however well prepared one may be. I would welcome such demonstrations when I have earned the right to have them happen.

You are right—we have both needed the information you have been allowed to give us. We need *more*. We are hungry for more—and our prayer is to be fitted to serve . . . to have revealed to us the capabilities in which we can best serve others.

I have been impressed recently to accept invitations to talk on the mind, along the lines of the subject matter in the book, *Your Key to Happiness,* which has seemed to be of such great help to some thousands of people. I find that I have the power to hold audiences spellbound in such talks—and the gift has been given me to answer all manner of personal questions at the conclusion. Certainly there are many thousands ready to take a step up in their own advancement once a little of the way is shown them. I, of course, cannot reveal any further than I have walked myself—and I am not referring to the advanced knowledge you are covering in your letters to us . . . but the practical application of mental laws for successful everyday living. As you know, when humans start out on this basis, they open doors within themselves for higher development.

I have never sought money for money's sake . . . nor have I sought personal glory. I have never wished anything to happen for the sake of giving me a life of ease at the expense of my own development. Martha has stood by me, through all our ups and downs, with the same vision and aspirations. We have been interested only in developing together.

I was on the coast only once, from December 1933 to March 1934, during which time I was in Hollywood and wrote the original story, continuity and dialogue for a feature picture entitled, *Are We Civilized?,* which dramatically prophesied the coming second world war. It was a fiction story based upon fact and my own intuitive knowledge of what was coming. It aroused the opposition of Germany, and a boycott of all major distributing companies was threatened if this picture was shown in chain theatres . . . although Germany's name was not mentioned . . . and the story pertained to all so-called dictator countries. I wish sometime you could see a private showing of this picture . . . I have grown much even since that time . . . gained in knowledge of world forces.

Now, for the first time, even before contacting you, I have felt the pull westward again . . . and oh, there is so much apparent reason for our going west now . . . but we have become used to sacrifice . . . and if there is work to be done here . . . or elsewhere . . . we will respond, as we have in the past, when the way has been clearly shown.

It is futile, of course, to attempt to express appreciation for your labor of love in our behalf. We can only promise to continue to try to fulfill, in every way, the faith you have in us. Martha joins me in sending love to you and yours—love that will reach you both in whatever dimension you may be, now or henceforth.

We trust and pray you will be permitted to write us again and to reveal more of what you will be given to feel we should know.

Until then, we humbly and obediently await whatever is to come.

HARRY LOOSE to HAROLD SHERMAN

Monterey Park, February 22, 1941

My Friend:-

Thanks a lot for your letter [of February 17]. It was a beautiful thing. The very writing of it was good for you. It also told me that which I wished verification about.

I want to also thank you for the poem. It is momentous. Terrific in its import. One of the finest and most powerful that I remember to have read. There isn't a wasted word. It, however, cannot be read with understanding materially. It must be read with spiritual understanding to perceive. It is too heavy—too deep—and far too spiritual for any magazine of my acquaintance. I surely would keep it carefully and sometime in the future have a hand-painted script of it made and then framed for hanging in some esteemed place in your own home. Its translation and effect would be understandable to some visitors— but far from all. Analysis is to each individual a different picture. (But see my disagreement with the philosophy in my last letter.)

Receival of my last letter and the fact that you have made this long waited contact, should do much to clarify the dream. It is very apparent to me. I could write a translation, which would perhaps tally much with your own—but it would make this present letter too long to indite it here—and now. However, to go further, the impression on me is the receipt of this dream as long ago as the date given, makes it strong evidence of fore-vision. Remember many sensitives are extremely clairvoyant—fore-vision is an advance of general clairvoyancy.

Your load has been heavy all these years. You seemingly have abused and neglected the physical in favor of Mind. *This will truly not do.* I know very little of physical conditions although I have had, and still have, my share. Will you please ask your doctor, on the next contact, to check for possible Myocarditis—or a heart enlargement—and to tell you the truth of his findings.

Your primal physical condition was "nerves," evidenced probably in "nervous indigestion" first and the stomach ulcers came after. Extreme "nerves" are usually indicative of a mental exhaustion. They are sometimes dangerous symptoms. Re-education of the human Will with mental rest—and freedom from worry—lots of sleep—good food—together with *desired*, congenial, mental companionship, are all helps too. I am afraid of any chronic, debilitating thing attaching itself that would affect your advancement. I know that it surely would. So please bend every effort at accomplishing as near to perfection, for your age, in the physical as possible. I know that you never could assume any service until and unless you were in good physical and nervous condition. I want to very seriously ask you to follow fully and completely the advice of your physician and please help him mentally yourself. Relax your abdomen physically—let it protrude, if it will—stop tensing and restricting it—just "let go." You are so near, and yet so far to realization as long as the physical and nervous condition remains.

Well, you are in the best of company as far as "nerves" are concerned. The world's work is done by "nervous" people. The best executives, the best lawyers, the best actors and actresses, the best writers, and so on ad infinitum, are ALL "nervous" people. All really great people are nervous, although not all nervous people are great. There are the drinkers, the habit-forming drug users, etc., who are generally quite nervous—but there is a difference. It harks back to the old saying, "All great people have great noses, but not all people with great noses are great." However, *nothing* really great is ever done by the plodding, *never nervous*, vegetable or animal type of mind. *All* great people really pay with "nerves" as the penalty of being great.

You are in good control physically. Outwardly little, if any, evidence of nervousness—the same as all great ones. Mrs. Sherman is the only one, probably, who sees the evidence of nervousness.

I will give all that I can to reconstruct. You will feel me. If you will but cooperate and call me when you go to bed. You will sleep soundly and restfully but you must strongly cooperate and have "faith." Remember in the Bible before the healing when Joshua asked, "Believest thou that I can do this?"—and how he criticized others by saying, "O ye of little faith." And again, "If ye had the faith of a grain of mustard seed," etc. I can help and I am very desirous to, but I cannot help unless you will call, cooperate and most of all have faith.

I must be more careful. I have again been corrected. In my last letter to you, I said that James and Ruth were the only ones in the family that had belief in Joshua and his works and message. I left one more brother out—his name was Jude. I make so many errors—and never reread for correction—I really should.

I also must tell you that I have been forbidden to write you more of things psychical. I must keep my instructions. However, I did tell you a little bit in my last letter. Keep it and reread it. You will be given when to destroy.

When you so desire, write down any questions that you care to—no matter how serious or how foolish they may sound—so that when I see you—which I sometime hope to do—I may, permissibly, answer them.

I, too, have little. These people seldom have. Remember the Bible where Joshua said, "Take no thought of what ye shall eat and what ye should put on," etc. See Matthew 6:25, and Luke 12:15. "A man's life consisteth not in the abundance of things which he possesseth." I, too, have been fed and supplied when the need was. It, also, came somehow or other.

My Mother was released, at a great age, last January 23rd and went on. I had supported her for the last 18 years. And as Joshua, the "wayshower," was raised up in three days, so was she. And I know that she is busy and much happier than being confined and restricted in the aged flesh. SHE was aged—but remember the Bible again, what Joshua said in reference to death, "No man knoweth, not even the Son but the Father."

You have by now digested, somewhat, my registered letter. I was the "well" from which you drew—with much self-help and travail. I knew nothing of the physical or mental struggles. Those are forbidden matters in developments of this kind. The whole process has been entirely free from generally-thought "contacts." It has been on a higher plane and a continued plane than the lower and irregular other operation. Also, my mental activities can have naught to do with a physical condition occasioned largely, if not entirely, by the action of your own Mind. I should say Will and Mind. The Mind before the Will, unless it is in answer to your own desire. To do any other than such would mean taking possession of your Mind and this is absolutely prohibited.

It is ALL an individual proposition, not from the cradle to the grave but for ALL TIME. As long as there is LIFE—in this dimension—or the next dimension or the next. The only ones who can supersede rightfully, even to the withdrawal of LIFE, are the Ancients of Days.***[28]

I must be careful again. I can help you if you call me and then only in a manner not to interfere with the operation of your own Mind and Will arising. If you call me and ask for help, I can give help—but I can not permissably overcome your own Will—*and* you must have Faith in my ability so to do.

I do not want to forget to tell you that I most certainly appreciate the great courage and tenacity you have displayed in carrying on. However, please remember, ALL come up the "hard way." No one can do your thinking for you. You can plant a rose, and water it, and give it care and sunshine, *but* it has to do its own growing.

For your safety and for the sake of the possibilities that lie ahead, you must make every sacrifice to regain physical and nervous health. You must *again* consciously control any psychic activities. My advice is to completely stop them—any meditations or explorations—until the physical and nervous health is at par again. You now have a big and important job ahead of you to accomplish this. The Great Intelligence be with you—I pray for all good.

Such writing, as your letter suggests, of these things for educational purposes is a little beyond any thought I had given. Such possible writing for the public in the way that you have outlined may be the very service which you may be called upon to do. I have no knowledge of what your service may be. Personally, I do not see how such involved matters could be put understandably to these many minds of such mixed mentalities. So to what purpose. You may, however, have instant answer when the time comes. To me, it seems that they, too, would also have to come up the hard way—even as you and I—and the rest of those from this Order that are in service. "Seek and ye shall find. Knock and it shall be opened unto you." However, I have seen things, as much involved, worked out satisfactorily, much to my astonishment, and so I have ceased to wonder when such things do mature. I know so little.

---

[28] *[O]nly the Ancients of Days may sit in executive judgment on the issues of eternal life and death* (15:12.2).

I bounce back to a subject already remarked but much present with me. I believe that with your many and varied activities, you have been much overdoing. You must slack up and get rid of both things that interfere with so much. The hysteric gets rid of his nervousness by the very fact of his hysteria—he gets a fit of it and hollers and yells and rants around but in the end it is over and he has rid himself of the repressed emotion and is relieved. But your type, the non-hysteric, holds on to all that repressed emotion—with no outlet—and in the end it "burns him up" or "blows him up," and nerves, nervous indigestion, stomach ulcers and worse, follow.

If you only had a real friend there now to whom you could go— any day—every day—at your disposal at any time—with whom you could converse with implicit confidence—you could get rid of many mental pins that you are sitting on that are a constant irritation. However, you are the same as the rest of the "different people," these strange "sensitives," these people that are "set apart" (see your Bible), they are not the same as the ordinary run of folks. With ALL of your acquaintances, you can number your *real friends* on the fingers of one hand. And amongst these very few, there probably is not even one that really and truly understands you. I would wager, if I was one who gambled, that the only one in New York who really knows you—who really understands you—is Mrs. Sherman. Unless you take care of yourself and maintain your best physical and nervous health, you are not acting square with Mrs. Sherman. You are what she has to rely on and you must not fail her.

Another thing. Years ago Mrs. Loose insisted that for the time when I ceased to be productive, or if anything happened to me before that time, we should have a "back log" in the shape of a modest home that we owned, clear of any encumbrance. Mrs. Loose is the better "manager" than I and so the matter ended by us having this old place clear of any encumbrance. Now, in protection of yourself and Mrs. Sherman and for a time when you, too, will not be producing, and as a protection for her should anything unforeseen happen to you, don't you think it would be a wise move so to do yourselves? . . . Counsel with Mrs. Sherman about this. Both of you would feel safer so to do and you really would be safer—it would be a grand "fall back" for Mrs. Sherman if anything happened to you.

I just heard the news broadcast and they said that so far this year, 1941, some 200 and over had been killed since Jan. 1st in Los Angeles.

I'll bet most of these people did not expect it. I do hope that I get this across to you understandably.

Well, slack up as much as you can. Get through with the commercials as soon as you can and "let go." Remember, please, that concentrated mental activities, particularly psychic, when the physical and nervous health is not good, especially the nervous health, are very debilitating—and NOT good. When you have to force yourself to do mental work when you are in a nervously exhausted condition, it is really mental masturbation and you must restrict such mental output if it is a possible thing and consciously control emotion and any other mental practice that would tend to deplete the nerve force.

When you write again, I would be very glad to hear that you have been open to suggestion and recommendation and are going to follow through with the program toward health that I have herein so repeatedly suggested.

I never have quite so missed the possession of money as right at this particular time. If I had it, I could think of no more profitable way to employ it than to be able to finance a complete release for you from all mental activities for a few months. But as I do not have it, it is just another one of those impossibles.

That [*Cosmopolitan*] article said that you sat with eyes open and concentrated to receive from Wilkins. I hope that she wrote wrong. Never attempt concentration for reception with open eyes. This also goes for sending. There is a positive and distinct loss of force in the open-eye process. Much of your present condition might be traced to loss of nerve force to this very wrong posture. I would not be explaining this to you if I did not expect you to call me.

Remember—relaxed—not too warm—abdomen with no internal tensing—eyes shut—laying position if possible—or if sitting then perfectly limp and with head in a hanging position forward—mild concentration—not blank—and FAITH. I must write no more.

With the very best from both Ma Loose and I to you all—and with protecting and uplifting thought,

HAROLD SHERMAN to HARRY LOOSE

New York, February 26, 1941

Friend Loose:

I am so glad you liked the poem. While it came through me, it does something uplifting and exhilarating every time I reread it. My oldest daughter, Mary, who is interested in art and designing, had already begun to letter this poem in hand-painted script, ready for framing. When she has completed it, I shall send you a copy.

Thank you for your comments with regard to my physical body and suggestions, which will be followed. I am possessed of almost boundless high nervous energy and no doubt waste quite a deal of it. I seldom feel debilitated. Even when I have been plagued with the stomach ulcers, the severe pain which has kept me awake night after night, I have still been able to call forth the energy to continue as before, each day. Obviously this has, nevertheless, been a strain. I am much better now than I was this time a year ago, when I was just getting over the hemorrhages, which have not re-occurred . . . although they did come in January and February of 1939 and 1940. In 1935 and 1936 I fought off a fungus growth which developed on my throat and tongue—a mycosis belonging to the family leptothrix, which ordinarily proves fatal in a few months' time. I was on the radio then, giving talks on the mind—telling other people how to overcome their fears and worries—and it seemed as though this affliction came upon me to determine whether I could "take my own medicine." The fungus growth was cauliflower-like in form and as tenuous as a hard rubber tire. It grew to a height of half an inch or so over the back part of my tongue and down into my throat within half an inch of the windpipe.

It took me a year and some months to eliminate this, with the aid of Dr. Seymour S. Wanderman, an absolute genius whom I wish you could meet. (He is now curing cases of leukemia and streptococcus viridans in the last stages, but is not yet ready to announce his treatments to the world. Also curing hitherto incurable cases of arthritis within a few weeks' time—and is an amazing heart specialist. He is one of my dearest and closest friends, with a great understanding of life, and next to Mrs. Sherman is the one I could discuss many of these mysteries of life with . . . although some subjects are barred . . . and Mrs. Sherman is the *only* one with whom I can "go the limit.")

I hope, when the financial situation clears and resources are given me above those needed for current expenses, to purchase a home at the place we are supposed to locate as a family—so that Mrs. Sherman and the girls may enjoy this feeling of security.

I have refrained from attempting any sustained mental phenomena since the Wilkins experiments, as I told you. Let me say, as you have surmised, that Inez Haynes Irwin [writer of the *Cosmopolitan* article] was wrong in her statement that I "concentrated with my eyes open." I did it with the lights off, sitting in darkness in my study . . . and used a flashlight which I switched on and off as impressions came, so that I could see to write them down. I learned early in my experience that operating with the eyes open proved inhibiting and nerve exhausting, since what the physical eyes saw were thrown upon the "screen of the inner mind," competing with the impressions being projected by the "subconscious" from the mind of the sender, and making it extremely difficult to maintain clear reception.

I will put myself in a receptive mood each night as I retire, which is usually between 12 and 1 o'clock our time—and perhaps we may meet in the higher plane of consciousness.

I know, with so many years lived, you must feel the urge to go on—but I selfishly am glad you are still on earth since I have drawn courage and inspiration from you. I am sure now that we have come a long way together—as time is counted far beyond the span of our years here.

How Mrs. Sherman and I would like to be with you and Mrs. Loose physically—and, with proper visualization and things working out on the coast to bring us there—this can happen! It will be one of life's greatest thrills on this earth plane.

Again—our love to you and our best and highest thoughts.

3

ACCIDENTS, MISTAKES, AND HYBRIDS

HARRY LOOSE to HAROLD and MARTHA SHERMAN
Monterey Park, March 8, 1941

My Friend:-

Thanks a lot for your last letter. I will be glad to get the hand-painted script of the poem when Mary gets it ready. It is a very fine thing. I am also glad that you have such a fine doctor, and much further relieved in knowing that you have such confidence in his knowledge and ability. If he says that there is no great nervous depletion, we should be satisfied. I still would like to be assured by him that there is no Myocarditis or heart enlargement. That was surely a strange fungus growth—it must be a rare condition—I have never heard of it before. I am also glad that you have your Doctor to talk to confidentially.

I do so hope that in my so sketchily writing you, you have in no way confused these matters with "ghosts" or other forms of supernormal phenomena.

Just as an illustration, away back in the beginning of things on this particular planet, a grievous mistake and partly an accident so happened together that its aftereffects affected a great number of minor Intelligences on this present First or "beginning" dimension, which left them earthbound here—unable to advance. They are a sort of a "hybrid"—that is the only word in this language to give the near-

104

est expression understandable of their status. They are not fully in the next dimension, nor fully in this, and because of the mistake and accident, they cannot make full progress to the next dimension.

For these many earth years, theirs has been a rather sad lot. They must have air and water as regularly as a fleshed Intelligence. Those *fully* in the next dimension also need air and water but not nearly in the amount or as regularly as do these poor "hybrids." The "gravity pull" still operates against their free and full movement—and they are still subject to "gravity Law"—which is still different. You would be tremendously interested.

These "hybrids" are fully organized—much the same as any earth Order, and they have done and are doing much good here. Some seven earth years ago they petitioned for a hearing of their grievances before the group of Intelligences having to do with the adjudication of matters in that particular scale, and of [other Intelligences] in the same scale having to do with the administrating of the LAW in this dimension on ALL planets in this particular Universe. Because they are still earthbound and unable to leave this planet without especial permission and especial care, a messenger of the Second dimension was assigned, at the request of these "hybrids," by the group of Intelligences having jurisdiction over this particular planet, to carry a petition to the planet whereon the Superior Intelligences serve, a much more highly developed planet than this one of Urantia. We, here, know that particular planet as Bogaluse. It is so large that it could contain, if hollow, our planet and its sun, and both could make their regular orbits therein.[1] An order came through from the Superior Intelligences at Bogaluse allowing a committee of these "hybrids," numbering Seven, a passage through to Bogaluse by especial transport. The Seven were made temporarily full Second Dimension

---

[1] Loose's description of "Bogaluse" is similar to the Urantia Book's description of an unnamed star in Orvonton, which in turn is similar to Arthur S. Eddington's account of the star Betelgeuse given in his book *Stars and Atoms* (1926). From the Urantia Book: *Another of the Orvonton giants now has a surface temperature a trifle under three thousand degrees. Its diameter is over three hundred million miles—ample room to accommodate your sun and the present orbit of the earth. And yet, for all this enormous size, over forty million times that of your sun, its mass is only about thirty times greater* (41:4.7). Eddington states: "By spectroscopic analysis we know that Betelgeuse has a surface temperature about 3,000°. The diameter is about 300 million miles. Betelgeuse is large enough to contain the whole orbit of the earth inside it . . . Its volume is about fifty million times the volume of the sun. . . . We can . . . deduce [that its mass is] equal to 35 x sun" (p. 82). Bogaluse is a town in Louisiana.

Intelligences. Because of the still partially earthbound members of the second dimension, there had to be stops usual to such travelers along the way.

One of the Seven leaving stations in this jurisdiction is some 200 miles from where we live, in a National Reserve, a very beautiful place.[2] Humanly it is a very strange place also—with mysteries not solved by earth scientists who ponder "why," even on the stillest of days, in a relatively small area a cold wind always blows, the temperature is always ten degrees lower, and a compass whirls ceaselessly. There are great powers there. It is a very busy place always, with the transport of all those who the world here says have just "died" taking off—thousands upon thousands of them. You will see it all, too, sometime.

The Committee of Seven left from that Station in custody of full Second Dimension Intelligences caretakers. The time to Bogaluse by transport is nineteen of our days in summer—a little longer in winter—the gravitational "pull" is heavier in winter—all Intelligences in the second dimension are still subject to the gravitational "pull"—and the gravitational "pull" goes through all orbits of all planets—the Sun planet in each local Universe has a much greater gravitational "pull" than a Life planet—and the dark islands of space to which has not yet been given Light nor life, have the greatest "pull" of all. The Committee returned here a year of our earth time later.

Matters have been satisfactorily adjusted, and this present year is to see a migration of these "hybrids" in their proper and full elevation to the Second Dimension. All of them assigned away from this particular planet as is the usual proceeding. Those left here will be full Second Dimension Intelligences also, but they are engaged here in important work and missions that cannot be left to the care and custody of untrained Intelligences. So they will continue here until such newcomers in the Second Dimension, from some other planet, can be taught to take their individual places. Do not fail, too, to remember that Intelligences from both the Second and Third dimensions are here *now* on special missions in the flesh for that particular time—and also please know that through all earth time such Intelligences have been present here in the flesh on missions of one kind or

---

[2] Loose is referring to a particular area in Sequoia National Park, near the Grizzly Bear Tree, discussed in more detail in future correspondence.

another. Joshua ben Joseph (Jesus) is just a mortally very well-known example. There were many thousands before Him and there have been many thousands since. Melchizedek was another. I could name you another hundred or so.

This earth that we ride upon is celestially known as Urantia, and it is also known locally to this Universe, the 7th and last, as "the dark world" because of its lack of progress in the Spiritual.[3] It would also interest you to know that the little world that we know here as the Moon is a "prison world," or, perhaps more accurately, as a detaining world for the detention of some Intelligences that have violated restrictions or the Law. They are kept there until they have had a hearing and their new assignments are made or other judgments rendered.

Regarding writing you, I have been forbidden much. I am eager to give and so I must be double careful and sure not to overwrite myself. You see, so far you are, or have been, just learning your "numbers." You still have addition, multiplication, division, etc., etc., yet to go. And because of your yet-so-limited receptivity, it makes it hard writing to your present understanding.

Regarding that man that said to you, "If I could only find a reason for life or my being here," etc.[4] That is exactly the same question that a child in school asks. Ask a child in the lower grades "why" he has to go to school, and see what answer you get. He does not understand the reason. As they reach the higher grades, they begin to get a better perspective of the reasons for school. This "first Life" on this planet corresponds to the school life of the child. This Life is but the beginning of the *individual* Life experience. As there is progress or growth in understanding here and elevation to the next dimension from this planet Urantia, so the child goes in school from grade to grade through the grammar on into the High School.

Please remember that this Urantia is a "first Life" planet—and a very backward one at that—known, as I have remarked before, as

---

[3] Compare: *Your world, Urantia, is one of many similar inhabited planets which comprise the local universe of Nebadon. This universe, together with similar creations, makes up the superuniverse of Orvonton, from whose capital, Uversa, our commission hails. Orvonton is one of the seven evolutionary superuniverses of time and space which circle the never-beginning, never-ending creation of divine perfection—the central universe of Havona (0:0.5). It is a fact that Urantia has become known among other neighboring inhabited planets as the "World of the Cross"* (188:4.1).

[4] Loose is apparently vaguely referring to something in *Your Key to Happiness*.

Urantia the "dark world." Please remember that this is one of the far from fully developed worlds spiritually—it is a very backward world—there is very little spiritual wisdom yet. There has been so little spiritual development here that this world, Urantia, is known in this smallest, and last, Universe, the 7th, as the "dark world" because of its backwardness in learning and its great lack of spiritual growth. Some Church denominations, with other factors, have been much to blame. By far the most of these planets, in the same class as Urantia, and on which there is Light and Life, are far ahead of this one in their spiritual growth.

There are *many* different orders of planets in this great scheme of things. Some, for instance, are "home" to Intelligences of the higher, and much higher, dimensions that have never had an earth experience in the flesh. There is not the same development here as on most other planets in the same class as Urantia. Many do not kill their "Christs," as was done here after only three years of teaching.[5] How much more our "Christ" could have taught had he been allowed to live for ten years here and been cooperated with. Some of these planets have kept their "Wayshowers" with them for MANY earth years—some until they have been called for continued services elsewhere. You can readily understand how much more was learned by people of these planets than this dark world which kept its "Wayshower" only three short turbulent years and that ended as they did in his torturous death.

If you can imagine a vast business institution in this present dimension right here, with a Superintendent who has charge entirely of the whole institution at the head, and who is responsible for its activities and progress, and then follow your imagination through the whole organization of the personnel of the vast business institution, with its many different divisional heads—and then the foremen and below them the other workers, you will have a very fairly correct picture of the highly specialized operation of this planet. And this method of operation is the same as that of every planet, no matter how advanced spiritually.

---

[5] Compare: *[Y]ou should not entertain the idea that [bestowal Sons] always meet with the tragic end encountered by the Creator Son who sojourned on your world nineteen hundred years ago. . . . It is not necessary that such inhuman treatment be accorded a Son of God, and the vast majority of planets have afforded them a more considerate reception, allowing them to finish their mortal careers, terminate the age, adjudicate the sleeping survivors, and inaugurate a new dispensation, without imposing a violent death* (20:6.6).

On some of the planets on which there is a much higher developed spiritual learning, there are advantages given far in excess to what are given on this planet for advancement because of their greater growth and understanding—which then gives an added ability to further absorb.

I am responsible here to a higher member of the Order. He is responsible to the Superior. The Superior is responsible to a yet Higher Intelligence.

There are honest and sometimes serious mistakes in the operations of this great and ancient Order. There are honest and sometimes serious mistakes in the operations of intricate matters under jurisdiction of the Second dimension, and there are sometimes, rarely, deliberately planned, wrongful, oppositional happenings there. Remember, Mind, Soul—Ego—Cosmos—etc., does not suddenly change and become immediately different on its passage from this dimension. Dillinger is still Dillinger. Capone is still Capone. It is not all *perfection* in the Second Dimension. NOR IS ALL PERFECTION IN THE THIRD DIMENSION EITHER. None here on this First Dimension are perfect and without mistakes, and these mistakes and accidents happen in other dimensions just the same as they do here. The Second Dimension is but a much further advanced dimension spiritually than here now on this earth and in this First Dimension. And it is only by growth and understanding and work and study that you advance there—just the same as here.

There are 173 references in your Bible about "understanding." It is a long, long way of "SERVICE" before you are given the "Embrace of the Father," the Great Intelligence. Lucifer, one of the great ones of this particular planet, a Prince, with jurisdiction over this planet, had never seen the Father nor had he ever had the Embrace of the Father. Yet Lucifer was spiritually conceived—without the experience in the flesh, yet he denied the Father and led a rebellion against Him in which he was joined by many higher Intelligences who also denied. This is only to illustrate to you how all is not perfection and order yet even in advanced dimensions. See Isaiah starting at Chapter 14:12.[6] Isaiah, by the way, is written in our Bible as the writings of ONE man when it is really the writings of TWO men, one much earlier than

---

[6] How art thou fallen from heaven, O Lucifer, son of the morning! how art thou cut down to the ground, which didst weaken the nations!

the other—and it should be so divided in our Bible. Also, by the way, this same Lucifer is one who is still held, with many others, on the detention world, our Moon, which I have written about above, and on whom no judgment has yet been passed.

Harold, are you following me a little and learning a little in these small introductory writings?? I would like to have you answer me when you write.

Dear Martha:-

I would like to express to you my appreciation for what you have done for Harold in all these years. I have lately however been much concerned about the stomach ulcers, their cause, etc., but I have been assured by Harold's last letter that he has not been debilitated and that his nervous condition is good. I also am concerned as to his heart condition and have asked him to have it checked by the doctor. I would like to be assured. He is so near—and yet so far—to the realization of what we have all been working toward these many years.

As you have so helped him in the past, I know that you will continue to so do. He has before him a strenuous time in which he should be fortified with all the physical strength and nervous force he can muster. I am so hopeful that nothing intervenes to halt or delay so much that he has in prospect—and he will need you still more as he goes onward. So please watch your physical health just as you watch his. He needs you.

I wrote in a recent letter that a sensitive of either sex who was single could not advance here in this dimension as far as a sensitive of either sex who was married. I either wrote wrongly to Harold or he misunderstood what I wrote, for when his return letter came he wrote of that part of my letter as meaning there was bi-une progress in the next dimension. I am sorry. It is all an individual proposition in the next dimension and there is no married or other bi-une state existing there. Singleness is the natural state of existence in the next dimension just the same as a bi-une existence is the normal for this planet. Sex is a condition that exists in the flesh only—there is no flesh in the next dimension—hence there is no sex.

You will have company from the very instant of your arrival—the THIRD DAY after your passage from here by way of "death"—the same "three days" that intervened between the death of the "Wayshower" and his resurrection—and when you wake you will have been transported away from this planet, and your first sight will be of a Morontia Intelligence, who will be with you from then until your experience on the Second Dimension is through and you leave for the Third Dimension.[7] There is always a deep affection gendered between the Morontia Intelligence and their charge, and when the time for separation comes there is much real grief. There is much better understanding of progress and continuation when the time for the second "death" arrives, and it is not regarded so seriously as it is regarded in this dimension.

I write away on the old typewriter and send without rereading or correction and so I am subject to minor errors such as misspelled words and maybe repetition—so please excuse. I am much restricted in writing, Martha, and yet I am trying to get as much information to Harold as is allowed me. I have written some long letters with this idea before me—and I am desirous to know if it makes too much for him to read and absorb or if it is tiring to him.

This ending of nearly twenty years of responsibility is a big thing for Mrs. Loose and myself, and we find the final breaking off quite something to accomplish. You see, I am an old man now, a very old man, so old that you would think it but the vaporizing of an unsound mind if I attempted to tell you. I do not expect to be detained on this dimension a great while longer. I sometimes feel the urge to see Harold in the flesh before I go this time and then again I am a little afraid that it would not be for the best, and so very probably we will never see each other here. I am so glad to be assured about his nervous health and I would so like to be assured about the heart.

I have had in mind maybe to tell Harold of some of his people away back, just for his interest, in some of these letters that I am given permission to write. They were Iberians who lived in Kant, which many years later was called Egypt. Maybe it would be quite entertaining besides being educational to him. I must close now,

With much LOVE to you ALL and with the best thought over and under and around you all,

Sincerely,

---

[7] *One of [the Morontia Companions] will certainly be on hand to welcome you when you awaken on the initial mansion world . . . And from the time you are thus formally welcomed on awakening to that day when you leave the local universe as a first-stage spirit, these Morontia Companions are ever with you* (48:3.8).

HAROLD SHERMAN to HARRY LOOSE

New York, March 8, 1941

Friend Loose:

I have just finished an intensive ten days of creative writing, during which time there has been no further written word from you—but the *very definite sensing* of your presence on many occasions. Particularly has this been true at night, for I have slept much more soundly and without disturbance during the night, when formerly I have had little sieges with my stomach.

I am endeavoring to follow all your suggestions relative to taking things more casually, drinking more water, etc., and am noting results.

The book on my telepathic experiments with Sir Hubert Wilkins is done, and if you would be interested in checking a copy of the manuscript when it has been typed off, I would be happy to send it to you, before publication. I am calling the book, *Thoughts Through Space— An Adventure in the Realm of Mind*, by Sir Hubert Wilkins and Harold M. Sherman. (Do you think the subtitle should be "realm" or "realms" of mind? I originally had designated it "realms," feeling this was more descriptive of the actual state of things, and was criticized for it by a literary friend.)

As much as it would mean to me for production to start on the Mark Twain picture, I have hoped that I would not be called west until the Wilkins book was completed . . . for I know that this work on the mind would be indefinitely postponed once I had to give my full attention to *Twain*. Apparently my prayer has been answered, for the coast delays have enabled me to do this job and I have such a "released" feeling in consciousness now . . . READY FOR THE CHANGE, with all the important work in the east now done.

I have heard nothing from Lasky for two weeks—but know him to be busy producing *Sergeant York* with Gary Cooper for Warner Bros. Perhaps the good word that everything is ready will be forthcoming soon and the Shermans can then "pull stakes" here.

Martha and I have read and reread your letters, getting more illumination from them each time. You write sublimely of these great truths with an unconscious majesty. This is especially true of your writing on the lower half of page 6, in the registered letter [of Feb. 17th], wherein you describe the millions of other inhabited worlds, the dark islands of space, etc. I wonder that you have not been permitted to put *some* of these truths, which the world *could* know, into such form as to be published, for they would carry great inspiration.

I am constantly having to check myself from going off into avenues which would consume pages . . . things I'd like to discuss with you!

We are being led to interesting people here—one last week, a Dr. Alfred J. Fox, M.D., who has specialized in suggestion and hypnotism as a means of treating disease. He told at a lecture his results attained, and said to me afterward that he positively *knew* astral traveling was a fact . . . that he could send certain entities out of the body, under hypnotic control . . . that he had reason to believe we could ultimately visit different planets . . . that he was sure that we did after death occurred . . . and that he had discovered, beginning as an atheist and agnostic, that God dwells within . . . that our purpose here is to be awakened to the existence of that Great Intelligence within us.

Sunday, Martha and I have been invited to visit the estate of Pierre A. Bernard[8] in Nyack, up the Hudson. He has been referred to as "the Omnipotent Oom," a white man who has absorbed the wisdom of the Indian philosophies and who founded what is known as the Clarkstown Country Club, financed by wealthy people, containing everything the heart could desire in recreational, cultural and artistic surroundings. "It shall be easier for a camel to go through the eye of a needle, than for a rich man", etc.!! But, following a policy long established, I have welcomed the opportunity to meet such persons and study them.

I met last week a Mr. James B. Schafer, who founded the Church of the Radiant Life here and received nationwide publicity when he stated that he had an advanced class in visualization—six students whom he was going to teach how to make a million dollars apiece, in

---

[8] Pierre Bernard (1875-1955) and his wife Blanche De Vries (1891-1984) helped popularize yoga in America. In 1905, after a sojourn in India, Bernard began teaching his system of Tantric and Hatha yoga, first in San Francisco and later in New York. In 1910 he made headlines when two young female students sued him for abduction and for running a "love cult" at his Temple of Mystery school. The case was dismissed when the women refused to testify at the trial, but not before he had become known to the press and public as "Oom the Omnipotent." In 1911 he founded the New York Sanskrit College, which taught yoga exercises, Sanskrit, health and religion. In 1920 he opened the Clarkstown Country Club, which flourished for over thirty years.

a year's time; and who also announced that he was raising "an immortal baby" in his "Shangri-La" . . . by protecting the child from worldly vibrations, etc. He is learning now, to his sorrow, that you cannot commercialize these higher truths . . . and is going through hell trying to attract enough money, through freewill offerings, to keep a theatre he is running open as a center for "classes in truth."

On every hand one witnesses such abuse of powers of mind and the principles behind them. I have written a farce comedy [*Hocus Pocus*], debunking these isms and revealing the gullibilities of humanity which lead them into neuroticisms, hallucinations, etc., which should be done some day as a means of educating as well as entertaining.

I am hoping some day that I may be permitted to give Dr. Wanderman some comprehension of these truths, for I consider him to be an advanced soul—receptive to this type of thought. He believes there is a great intelligence at work in the universe, and is already living a life of service in medicine, unselfishly doing all he can in his power for humanity. If I am to go to the coast reasonably soon, I would like Dr. Wanderman to visit me . . . and for you to meet him. He is a rare human being. He must have been given to me to help preserve me in the physical trials I have gone through . . . because I definitely owe my life to him on at least two occasions.

I mentioned to him some years ago that I had met a highly developed soul, in you, and that you had been an inspiration to me through life, although I had never been in touch with you since . . . and Dr. Wanderman was deeply interested. He said he was certain that everything that happened to us in life had a purpose . . . and that there were higher intelligences at work. I believe, at the right time, if he could know some of the truths that he might be entitled to know, it would give him the illumination and fortitude to persevere in certain research which now requires such economic sacrifice to accomplish. He is a Jew—but, with all we hear about the Jewish race today, if all Gentiles were of his calibre, this would be a wonderful human race. Thank God I am free of prejudices against races, creeds and colors!

How much can I tell Dr. Wanderman—being mindful of your saying that if I had some friend with whom I could discuss many things on my mind it would be helpful to me? Having trusted him with my life, I feel that I could certainly trust him with any information it was right for him to know.

I shall await further instruction from you, and am enclosing another dream impression that Martha felt you should have, and interpret for us.[9]

Our best to you and "Ma Loose," always—

HARRY LOOSE to HAROLD SHERMAN

Monterey Park, March 10, 1941

My Friend:-

I am writing you hurriedly in answer to your letter which arrived an hour ago. You should get a long letter from me this Wednesday the 12th. I mailed it Saturday last.

Yes, I have been with you at times. You are some harder to help though, now that these things have become known to you. I am so grateful that you have been sleeping better. I am so hopeful that you will continue calling me. Yes, please follow my suggestions faithfully regarding taking things more casually, drinking more water, etc., and please get all the sleep and rest that you can. "LET GO."

Glad that you are through with the Wilkins book and that it is out of the way. Do NOT send me the manuscript to read before publication. The subtitle should be REALM. One Mind, one Realm. Two Minds, two Realms.

So glad that things are working out so satisfactorily with the Lasky people about the Twain matter. Maybe you will be coming out here sooner than expected.

Am so glad that you and Martha are rereading the letters and that you keep them. As they are, their reading must be confined to you and Martha. Keep them closely to yourselves or they will dematerialize as did the one from the Whiting Hotel. If your time is delayed much later in coming here than you expect, I would put them in a safety deposit box if you feel that they are not safe from other eyes, or fire, where you now have them.

Dr. Fox has been convinced of some very real facts. I will make inquiry of and about him and at the same time will inquire if it is advisable to tell him some small truths.

To go back to my letters again, I am told specifically that they must be "safely kept." I am hopeful that, as you suggest, some use may be made of them for the benefit of such humanity as could un-

---

[9] This dream impression has not been identified.

derstand, by you putting them in some way into book form. I do not know. I do know, however, that the whole world is due very shortly for a great spiritual revival and attempt at understanding, and I do know that the great book, "The Book of Urantia," should be out in the next year-and-a-half to two years. And please remember when reading it and I am not here anymore, that although I had nothing to do with the writing of it, I have had other things to do with it for now over thirty-five years.

Anyway, I am so very restricted in my writing, not alone by direct orders, but I have to hold myself so much back because of your yet so limited understanding. You cannot yet understand calculus when you are just getting acquainted with your numbers. I know very well, too, that if any writings appeared of my letters and information, which would of necessity have to be so very restricted, I could in no way appear by inference or otherwise. My identity would have to remain absolutely unknown even though gone on for some time.

I think here would be a very good place to just drop the information to you, as permission was today given me, that you were some hundreds of earth years ago chosen for a special mission at this particular period. This has been done many times before in history, as you have already perceived without my remarking it at all. You were made to make contact with me when and as you did, but you were in the formative stage, or period, for years before that particular contact. You have been guided and helped much since then and you have been my especial responsibility for nearly twenty years. I am nearing the complete end of that responsibility. You are to go ahead. What mortal Intelligence could you tell that to?? In time you, too, will have your responsibility to raise—and I wish you just as much success as I have had.

Go to visit Bernard in Nyack. He is a rank impostor. You will recognize it. "Many shall appear in my name." The same applies to James B. Schafer.

You have done all so wonderfully well, and I am very proud, *except* for the physical body. I am so very hopeful that you will do all possible to right the condition. A quiet undisturbed Mind—"Let Go"—plenty of water—rest—sleep—follow your doctor's instructions—no worry—no overwork mentally—do not do any more intensive explorations—there is MUCH efficacy in prayer (in some of my later writings I will explain to you the Intelligence that really hears and adjudicates your supplications) and in your prayers thank the Great Intelligence for Martha and again thank him for Martha. Be at Peace.

Yes—there is so much to talk about and letters are such unsatisfactory mediums except that it forces me to give you a very little at a time and I must NOT force feed you—and I am so restricted besides. The balance of the human mind is a very delicate thing. You could not accept nor absorb great things delivered unto you without some sort of preparation. We would defeat our own purposes. Remember that I am trying to give you an outline of thousands of years here—and in other dimensions—in the short time that I am to be here. I grieve also that I am so earth old, so very old, and not so strong physically, and I do have to conserve my physical strength. And yet, I too "am constantly having to check myself from going off into avenues that would consume pages," just the same as you remark in your letter.

Because of your physical, you do not receive fully the dreams as sent. Make haste to correct the physical and nervous, and please remember—quiet—and peace—think of that little bit in our present faulty Bible that says, "Be still and know that I am God." He meant to be mentally quiet and at peace, restful and still, AND NOT TRY BY WORRY AND MUCH THOUGHT to do HIS work. And read Isaiah 26:3, "Thou wilt keep him in perfect PEACE, whose MIND is STAYED on THEE, because he trusteth in THEE."

I would appreciate it if you would please acknowledge receipt of my long letter which you should receive Wednesday.

With much love from Ma Loose and myself to you ALL,

As also with every good thought over and under and around you ALL,

I am,

4

QUESTIONS
IN THE WAITING PERIOD

HAROLD SHERMAN to HARRY LOOSE

New York, March 12, 1941

Friend Loose:

Yes, I am following you with profound interest, absorbing everything you write and crying out, like the baby that I still am, hungrily—for *more!*

If this twenty years has been a great responsibility for you and Mrs. Loose—it has been an exciting, inspiring and punishing twenty years for me . . . and it will seem an extreme penalty to be denied seeing you and having a heart-to-heart visit in the flesh.

Just think—two precious hours in Marion, Indiana—and twenty years of physical silence!

I have known, since a boy, intuitively, that I was going to be required to serve a terrific apprenticeship which could fit me to perform some unusual service—and I have gone forward, facing every obstacle and apparent setback, to the best of my ability, in that faith. *You* know it hasn't been easy—but I have found that one can endure anything—if the goal is worth the price . . . and I have always felt that it was.

Of course I have made mistakes . . . many of which I am now conscious . . . others of which I am not, as yet. But I have tried to correct them, when discovered . . . and to improve on my actions of the past.

Can you answer me these questions?

Have we existed in some form before we became conscious of life on this earth?

Have we worked together, in other planes of consciousness, before this?

What relation do I have to my people back in Egyptian days? (I am enclosing a vision of mine about Egypt which will demonstrate to you that I was conscious of my connection with this period in some way. I was compelled, for lack of knowledge, to interpret it as a possible incarnation in that time.)

Gradually, you are touching upon elements in me which have risen to the surface of consciousness from deep down within . . . giving me visions and impressions which I have copied in my "little black book.[1] How I wish I could go over it all with you!

Your description of the activities of Intelligence on all planes makes sense and begins to answer many questions.

I have always rejected the spiritualists' concept of heaven—and the spirit's return to tell Friend Wifie how to invest the money left her and where to find the lost will, etc., etc.!! You should read my play debunking the isms, which will do much, some day, to clear the atmosphere on all this fraudulent, misguided business.

You say in your [March 8th] letter, "before I go *this time.*" Have you been on earth to render some service in the flesh before? And isn't so-called reincarnation a fact in some instances, even though not the rule?

Since my youth, something has told me that we visit other spheres and worlds after we "die" . . . that our destiny lies far beyond this puny earth. I believe my father was a highly advanced soul. He planted the first seeds in me and bequeathed me a mind freed of any churchified concepts. My brother, Edward, too, who died from a fall from a tree in our front yard in Traverse City, at the age of eleven, I am sure, was developed "beyond this world." His death had a profound influence upon me. I was sixteen at the time and, from that moment, I was a man, overnight. Father died in 1921, operated on for a brain tumor in Battle Creek Sanitarium. . . .

---

[1] Harold's visions, dream impressions, the later Ara and other inspirational messages and poems were typed up and neatly assembled by the Shermans in a small, black three-ring binder. They are published separately as *The Ara Messages* (Square Circles Publishing, 2015).

And, in a sense, you took over my guardianship after Dad went on . . . I seem to feel this now . . . for Dad died March 1, 1921 . . . and you came into my life a few months later.

How much there is to understand . . . and to put together . . . like a weaver of patterns! And how, step by step, all the amazing things that have happened to me begin to fit into the mosaic!

Why I have been helped along the way, in my poor strivings, is beyond my comprehension. I must possess a background . . . a tie-up with what we consider the past, of which I have not yet been made conscious. How you could have known that I possessed potentialities to be worth all the time and attention you have given to me through the years . . . and all the loving thought you are pouring out to Martha and me now . . . is still beyond ordinary senses to conceive. We are both humbly grateful.

Apparently Martha and I have gone on several marvelous astral journeys to other planes or spheres . . . for I have recorded a number of dream-like experiences which I will one day want to show you. We have considered them too sacred to be shown to others.

This letter may sound a bit rambling but many thoughts are coursing through my consciousness. Let me ask you this: If we should not be permitted to see each other in the flesh—will we meet again in some future moment of so-called "Time" . . . and recognize each other . . . and do we retain the same names as are given us in earth . . . or have we already been "named" and come to recognize this identity later?

Your account of the "hybrids" was fascinating . . . also the manner in which we depart this earth plane.

And now about the physical—I still have flurries with this sensitized solar plexus of mine and in the stomach area. I weigh around 185 with clothes on . . . 15 pounds over what I should weigh . . . but Dr. Wanderman says, because of the ulcer condition, he does not want me dieting. He would prefer I take pounds off when tennis season resumes again. Tennis, while a strenuous sport, has been a lifesaver.

Due to the economic battle through the years . . . to accomplish what I have required of myself in the creative field, in development and preparation, and still earn a living—the strain has been great. Without some such big deal as the *Mark Twain* situation (which, if it is confirmed or consummated by April 25th by payment of sizable amount, will bring instant economic relief), living in the writing field is "up and down."

I am going through a temporary lean period now—another waiting period, when I have done everything that can be done—and must wait upon the judgment and action of others. Such periods are always difficult and, with current expenses to be met, exact a strain, however developed one may be.

I have been willing to keep pressing onward, confident in the faith that when economic liberation is my due . . . it will come. It has been a gruelling test of patience . . . for there seem to be so many thoughts of real moment and worth ready to pour through my consciousness onto paper . . . which are not economically feasible to invite now. It would require a quiet period for meditation to do justice to them . . . the type of solitude that cannot be broken in upon by landlords, grocers, butchers and—you name the rest!

Despite hell, high water and everything else—I have finished the Wilkins book, which is now being copied, as I reported. And another book manuscript, entitled "A New Philosophy of Selling," adapting my psychology in *Your Key to Happiness* to this field, is done, and under consideration.

I have interest now in several of my plays for Broadway, written strictly for light entertainment. I have visualized success in this field as a means of furnishing me with all money necessary to subsidize the real work I have come here to do—when this work is revealed to me. Just think—I have around 30 full-length plays written—awaiting the day when the big break comes . . . in addition to all the books I have written . . . all this creative effort tending to polish my style of expression and get me ready for the big job.

I am sure I will not shirk the real task when it appears . . . and can laugh at most physical and mental obstacles that might cross my path . . . thanks to the apprenticeship that has been given me. I do feel, though, that I should be able to earn a little release from these *plaguings of the flesh* . . . for a few years, at least. My energy is almost boundless despite the physical things I have had to go through . . . as I think Martha will tell you . . . but this doesn't mean I've entirely licked the stomach kick-backs, etc. . . . due largely to economic pressure which has existed, off and on, through the years. . .

I'm not complaining. I can see very clearly that if my first Broadway play had been a big success, it would have meant Hollywood at a big writing salary and the possible pigeonholing of other higher development that has meant so very much—in fact, life itself, to me.

But I somehow feel now that I've reached a turning point when success will not be denied me on the monetary side . . . in order that other gifts may be released.

You have received, since you wrote your last letter, another communication from me, telling you more of Dr. Wanderman, who says my heart is okay. He *did* state that an inexperienced examiner might have said, some years ago, that I had a mild myocarditis condition, but he said it is just a "characteristic" and not a condition . . . and I have played tennis strenuously for years with no ill effects. As I stated to you before, Dr. Wanderman is absolutely the only friend I know . . . the only person outside of Martha, with whom I feel I could talk of these things of which you write. I yearn to broach some of these subjects to Dr. Wanderman but, of course, would not and could not do so without permission and direction from you.

As you have repeatedly said, you "know so little" . . . and if you know so little . . . how much less must *I* know! How does one reach the point where he could recognize the ability of anyone else to carry on in his behalf, when he shall leave the earth plane?

I can sense your presence almost every night when I retire. Today, around eleven o'clock, I said to Martha, "I feel there is a letter from Harry Loose in our mailbox downstairs." This second delivery is never brought to our door. I phoned downstairs and the letter was sent up.

I would like to be able to see you and converse with you in the astral . . . but this is probably beyond me, as yet. I no doubt have journeyed in the astral without my knowledge quite often . . . and you may have communed with me many times without my being aware. I have a sensing that you have.

I KNOW that whether the Mark Twain deal materializes at present or not, IF we are to meet in this life—nothing will stop the means being placed at our disposal to cross the country to one another! When one is required to go it alone so long . . . should he be denied stopping at an oasis, such as your presence, for a short drink of spiritual truth . . . before another lone trek in the wilderness? Martha and I would count ourselves privileged beyond words to be able to spend a quiet time with Mrs. Loose and yourself. May the fates decree that this can happen!

Our love to you always!

VISION IMPRESSION   *New York, February 12, 1939*

Last night, between twelve and one o'clock, as I was about to drop off to sleep, I had a vivid vision in my mind's eye. I was conscious, keenly aware of what I was seeing, in an entirely relaxed state. As nearly as I can describe it, I seemed to see a motion picture of a past civilization taking place in consciousness ... only more real than a motion picture and three dimensional!

I found myself active in the construction of the Great Pyramid in Egypt. In a few flashing seconds of time, I saw myself superintending the loading of great stones upon specially constructed barges at a distance of five hundred miles or more from the site of the pyramid.

These stones were then transported down the river Nile and through a specially built canal by thousands of slaves or workers who had hold of thousands of ropes, attached to these barges. These workers ran along specially built runways on both banks of the canal, pulling the barges at incredible speed considering human manpower. They were relieved by thousands of fellow workers at different points along the route, the original workers then returning to their starting point to bring down the next loaded barge.

At the site of the pyramid, I now watched the great stones being put into place, high above the desert sands. I saw huge platforms on wheels, pushed and pulled by hundreds of humans—brought along on special tracks.

These platforms were rolled out onto *mammoth elevator lifts,* the shafts sunk into the ground *for as deep a distance as the pyramid was to be high!* Yes, even deeper.

And through certain powerful lifting devices, these elevator tubes would rise higher and higher into the air, beside the pyramid structure, until they reached the level desired, when these huge stones were rolled off on their platforms, onto scaffolding runways and taken to the exact spot designated for them.

My impression is that there were four elevator shafts, one on each side of the pyramid, sunk great distances into the ground. The elevators were lowered to the earth level when empty, awaiting the next lifting operation.

The area around the Great Pyramid, for some miles, seemed to swarm with ant-like humans, feverishly busy, under armies of foremen, cursing and sweating—but all knowing precisely the part they were playing in the building of this enormous structure which was to stand the test of time.

It seemed to me that certain knowledge and control of gravitational forces was a help in this construction—but manpower
was a tremendous factor.

I do not recall ever having heard or read a supposition that
these huge stones were transported to the pyramid site through
a specially constructed canal. I should be interested if scientists
could determine the possible existence of these great elevator
shafts, some traces of which might still be found, far beneath
the earth's surface.

I have done no reading or thinking in recent years that even
suggested the pyramids.

NOTE TO FRIEND LOOSE: I should be most interested to know
whether this vision ties in with "my people" . . . and what my connection with them has been. Apparently inner faculties of my mind have
begun to open up, revealing glimpses. I am eager for more unfoldment . . . as is Martha!

HARRY LOOSE to HAROLD SHERMAN
Monterey Park, March 15, 1941

My Friend:-

In my last letter to you, in my desire to get other matters introduced into your consciousness, I failed to mention some things which
one of your letters remarked upon.

For instance, you wrote of being unable to find my first letter to
you, written from the Whiting Hotel at Traverse City, Michigan, and
you wondered where it had gone and when. That letter had served its
original purpose and was dematerialized in a perfectly normal and
natural manner. I, personally, had nothing to do with the matter, but
you may be sure that it was done for a good and sufficient reason. I
have seen such dematerializations, and of much greater things than
a letter, many times. For your information also, such things do not
happen theatrically at all. They are almost always done very quietly—
but seldom secretly. It is such a simple thing to do, if it is but a small
matter. All that is required is the suggestion to a human who comes
in contact with the article to be disposed of, and the article is gone by
their assistance. Afterwards they generally wonder to themselves why
they did it. You have heard someone occasionally say, "I just don't
know *why* I did" this or that.

This does not apply to all such manifestations, however. Sometimes direct full dematerializations do have to occur, very often in-

stantly. They are not mysterious or shocking to see. The inanimate object is there, and while you look it is gone—like a moving picture—that is all that there is to it. Dematerialization, in a way, is practiced by all living things daily. And because it is so generally practiced, it receives no attention. I mean, the eating of food, which is simple dematerialization of solids and semi-solids. But, make no mistake, there are Intelligences that can, and do, dematerialize inanimate objects instantaneously—and at any distance—there is no distance to thought. Just the same as all unfleshed Intelligences travel almost instantaneously. Just the same as you, in the flesh, can travel instantly to any destination mentally, just the same as you can really travel in what are called "local" distances when you have been released from the flesh.

There are no wings used in such transportation such as pictures of "Angels" would try to make mortals believe. There are no such things as "Angels" *in the generally accepted understanding* of the word. The idea of wings was the only explanation that early man could give for the sudden appearance, and as sudden disappearance, of seemingly solid personalities with whom he sometimes came in contact, whose bodies were suspended in the air, like a bird, without any contact with the earth. His only explanation was that they must have wings to so support them—hence came his strong belief in these beings having wings.[2] There is an Order of service that is known as Angels, that is correct, and this Order of service is graduated into and out of, and they have a specific purpose to perform—as do all these many Orders—on this dimension as well as those upon the next. So Angels are not winged by any manner of means. Wings are associated with flesh. There is no flesh in advancing dimensions. Any such accouterment as wings would be very much in the way and perfectly needless.

Also, you wrote of and about your strange dream. Normal human dreams are occasioned when, on the verge of the very thin line of demarcation between the conscious and the subconscious, where the mixed rambling of the then-ungoverned subconscious goes on

---

[2] Compare: *The erroneous idea that angels possess wings is not wholly due to olden notions that they must have wings to fly through the air. Human beings have sometimes been permitted to observe seraphim that were being prepared for transport service, and the traditions of these experiences have largely determined the Urantian concept of angels. In observing a transport seraphim being made ready to receive a passenger for interplanetary transit, there may be seen what are apparently double sets of wings extending from the head to the foot of the angel. In reality these wings are energy insulators—friction shields* (39:5.12).

ceaselessly, the conscious reasoning mind sees for the fraction of a second the mind pictures of the subconscious. It then instantly puts the mental house in order and the "dream" fades away. That is the way of a normal dream. However, your "unbidden Astral visits" may be what are termed the beginning of "true" or "full" unfleshed Astral explorations, which is something different again—very much a different substance than dreams. I would have to know their nature intimately before I could be sure.

Anyone dreams naturally, but dreams are often "sent" for some direct and enlightening purpose. Your Bible has many and many illustrations of this. You have been sent dreams on occasions—both memorandums of the dreams that you have sent me were sent dreams. But you do not get the correct impressions because of faulty physical interference—meaning your body difficulties. In each of the dream memorandums that you have sent me, there are present two dreams—not one. There should have been just the one, and its purpose you would have very shortly reasoned out. As it is, neither one is clear.

Unless a stronger sending is arranged in the future, you may have difficulty in one of our very much used methods of contact and communication. You see, while the conscious mind is sleeping, the sender has no interference in reaching the subconscious with the message to the conscious mind that you want delivered on wakening. You order the subconscious so to do, and so at once on wakening you get the full and complete message. This method is much used when there is the necessity of sending many orders and reports. It is much preferable so to do than to send such routine matters to the awake, conscious mind that has sometimes much about to interfere with proper full and immediate reception. I do hope that I have got this across to you. Look up the night visions and dreams—all with meaning—all messages—in your present Bible. You will find a great number.

I do not believe that in my other letters to you I have told you that December 25th, Christmas Day (Christ Mass, from the Catholic Church), is not the birthday of Christ as it is so widely celebrated. His real birthday was on a day that now falls on the present world's almanac as August 21st.[3] This little bit was to break away from the heavier matter above.

---

[3] . . . Jesus was born August 21 at noon, 7 B.C. (122:8.7).

All that the human eye can see is but the outward expression of thought. Thought is the expression of Mind, whether that which is looked upon is man-made or something expressed in nature. There is first the thought before it can be externalized, whether it be in the human or above-human expressions—ALL is thought first. The flesh of the brain can no more think by itself than can the flesh of the arm or leg. The brain is merely the instrument over which the Spirit, or Soul, operates. It is the UNFLESHED you that does the thinking.

And do not mix the animal instincts and the desires of the animal body with "thought." Their instincts, not thought, have to do with their animal desires necessary to the upkeep of the body—they are not emanations of the subconscious at all either. Food—water—a dog to bark—a chicken to crow—these are instincts—not mental requirements. Animals have no associative memories. Their instincts lay always in ahead of them. They cannot "think backwards." A cow is frightened and runs down the field—by the time it has got to the end of the field, it cannot remember why it ran. I do hope I get this rather involved thought across to you.

No one in the flesh has ever seen the real YOU. They have merely seen the house, or as Jesus called it, the "Temple" that the real YOU resides in—and resides there alone. You live with yourself *alone* more than four-fifths of your earth life—and so does everybody else confined in the flesh. If, in your own meditations, you will but forget your man-made name, and think of yourself first as an Intelligence and second a *degree* of Intelligence, it will not lose your identity to you at all, you will still be you, and after a time will be very helpful in much. However, you will find this quite a task to fully accomplish.

In my last long letter to you—and in the shorter one that followed, I have given you a great deal to be thoroughly digested, hence this lighter letter this time.

Please do not lose sight of the thought, which is the truth, that you are a "sensitive"—that you are not quite like others in the flesh—that you are a highly developed sensitive with a body that is imperfect. Please remember that now, so far as I am given to know, nothing will retard your development except the physical. I pray that you use every means that I have suggested and the advice of your doctor to gain as near as perfect in the physical and nervous as possible.

As much as I would like to see you in the body—and then become afraid to—I believe that I would like to see Martha. I do so want to be assured that she is taking every care of you. I believe surely that she is—and she has been so reported to me on my asking such affirmation—but it would be a satisfaction to be able to look at her once—then I would know and be absolutely *sure*. Please do not be in any haste or hurry—if you do these things and worry, you will tear down faster than you can build up—so much depends on this. I feel so very much like here saying, "Mind Martha," and yet, I hope, that is not necessary.

Please remember that, at best, it will be three years at least before you will be advanced far enough to see and do—and walk alone. You will then have things to see and Intelligences to talk to and travels to make. . . . In all these approximate three years, things will be happening to you that you cannot see and mostly you will not be much recognizant of—all toward your building and benefit. You will have enlightening experiences. There is so very much.

Please remember that I do not hold out in prospect to you any riches or wealth or material profit of any kind. You may be as poor as the proverbial "Job's turkey" as far as this world's wealth is concerned. But remember too, as has happened before, you will be surely cared for. You will really not "want." There will always be something come along just at the proper time, as has happened before. Wealth means nothing. "What worth is it that a man gains the whole world and in so doing lose his own Soul." With avenues that I have had open to me, I could have acquired much material wealth here. I know too much. I prefer to be as I am and as I have always lived.

Your letter [of March 8th] spoke of it being "as easy as a camel to go through the eye of a needle," etc. That is the way that our Bible expresses it. Just another small inaccuracy. That passage was written originally in the real Americ [Aramaic] and it was translated wrong. The word "rope" was wrongly translated as "camel." The passage read correctly should go: "It is as easy for a rope to pass through the eye of a needle," etc.[4]

Another passage that I just happen to think of as I write—where just a wrong or left-out word or two changes the whole concept, is the one that goes: "He who looketh on a woman," etc. Well, that passage

---

[4] The substitution of "rope" for "camel" was made by George M. Lamsa in his *The New Testament According to the Eastern Text: Translated from the Aramaic Sources,* published in 1940.

in our Bible is also a word or two out of correctness and which words make a big change in its understanding. It should read, "He who looketh on a woman WITH INTENT," etc. You see how different? There are so many inaccuracies—one denying and confounding the other—and many through the years and inaccuracies seeming to give the lie or being totally not understandable, even when trying spiritually to discern.

Regarding my trying to convey to you that you will be kept very busy in the next dimension and the dimension to follow, please read St. John 5:17, which says, "But Jesus answered them, 'My Father worketh hitherto and I work.'" Does that not open anything to your understanding in reference to your continuity of working in the next dimension?? I tell you that there is work there to be done and you will be kept very busy.

In my long letter to you which you have already received, I asked Martha if she thought it would be interesting to you if I told you some about your people. They were Iberian, in the old land of Kempt, sometimes also called Kant, meaning the land that many earth years later became Egypt. I thought, too, of telling you the strange beginning of those peoples that we now call Esquimaux, but all this mainly as a kind of a "let down" from heavier reading. I do not now feel that I will have much time for this, and it would be better to take what time I have left to give you as much as I am permitted before you receive a real teacher. You should be ready to receive in about three years.

The Doctor was right when he said, "The Kingdom of God is within you." When Jesus said that, He spoke the actual truth. But He did not mean the physical heart or brain or liver or lungs. He meant that tiny, infinitesimal bit of the Great Intelligence which we all have given to us, every one, as the Soul or Spirit—the REAL non-flesh YOU that lives alone in its house of flesh and bone and which operates over the switchboard in the powerhouse of the fleshy content of the cranial cavity—the fleshy brain.

Your letter remarks of my writing of millions of inhabited worlds in this Universe. Harold, this is the 7th and last Universe and it is the smallest of them all. And ALL of the 6 other Universes are much more populous with inhabited worlds. There are uncounted BILLIONS of them, if you can conceive the majestic number.

I have never been away from this small Universe. The Order of the Finality[5] has been closing the barriers at the outermost edges of the collective Universes for a time that I cannot tell you—I dare not.

Tell me, Harold, how could I convey to your esteemed Doctor friend things that I have already given you believably. He has not had the background—not alone in this life—nor the earth preparatory that you have had. It would be impossible for him to conceive. He would be entertained only—and make your life unhappy later by trying to keep up with you confidentially when he *could not.* It is of you that I am thinking. The "after a while" for you. I could not get permission so to do for you. He also very correctly would promptly consider me the usual "crackpot" and want to move me into safe quarters reserved for those with unsound minds.

Now, Martha, be sure to be very careful of your boy. His food— no roughage of any kind—oils—milk—boiled greens—everything "bland." He needs you so very much now. Talk with him—he has implicit confidence—be "Mother" in addition to wife. Be careful of him. So much depends on YOU.

Well, the postman has just been to the door and given me your letter [of March 12th]. I will read it and see if there is anything to be answered.

I am reading your letter and answering as I go along.

You ask me questions that, if answered directly, you could not understand. I am placed in a hard position by the fact that although you are now what is called "an awakened Soul," you are unafraid—as many times when newly awakened, they are, and you ask questions that, though perfectly legitimate, cannot be answered to your present, yet very partial development.

You were chosen some hundreds of earth years ago for birth and development at this particular period and for a very definite purpose. This is a "First Life" planet. This is not a First Life planet for you.

You ask questions that are too advanced for answering in your yet understanding. Yes, you have been a terrific responsibility for the past twenty years. I have given much force and strength to you in

---

[5] *The present known destiny of surviving mortals is the Paradise Corps of the Finality . . . At present the Paradise finaliters are working throughout the grand universe in many undertakings, but we all conjecture that they will have other and even more supernal tasks to perform in the distant future after the seven superuniverses have become settled in light and life, and when the finite God has finally emerged from the mystery which now surrounds this Supreme Deity* (112:7.15).

these years to aid you to carry on. You have been alternately easy and then hard to handle and teach and help and push upward and onward—because you are a full Intelligence unto yourself and have felt inherently a sense of another existence. There have been times when my only contact has been through Martha. Now I have great difficulty to make direct contact, and even then I can only give you the sensing or impression of my presence. Because of your imperfect physical, I have great trouble in even sending you word pictures and messages by way of dreams—or visions. You even have your individual dreams to double up and confuse with what I send you and so confuse the message or picture. You now know too much for me to have the usual easy access that I had before.

There is so much that you want to know, and your desire for progress is perfectly legitimate, but there is so much that you cannot understand yet.

My work is closing. It will be in the neighborhood of three years before you will be having contact with higher Intelligences. I tell you this because it is the usual in such developing.

This is a "First Life" planet of the three-brain type of development. This is not a "First Life" planet for you. I cannot tell you more than that without permission, which I do not have.

Your people were Iberians who lived in the land which later became Egypt. You are VERY close to the one, the particular one I had in mind to write you about. If I could tell you the story of this Iberian understandably, you would see the connection between your present self, the Iberian of so long ago, and my humble self.

I ask you here and NOW to read again the story of the "hybrids." Yes, I have been present here in the flesh before. This is not a "First Life" planet for YOU. There is no reincarnation back from the Second Dimension to the First Dimension. THIS SOUNDS CONTRADICTORY TO WHAT I HAVE GIVEN YOU BEFORE BUT THESE SENTENCES IN NO WAY CONFLICT. Think it over—and look things over—that I have written you.

Yes, you do visit other planets after your first passage from this earth—but you do not visit other Universes for many celestial "years," so called, after leaving here. A celestial day is the length of three of our earth months.[6] This will give you the period of what would be

---

[6] Compare: *The standard day of the superuniverse of Orvonton is equal to almost thirty days of Urantia time . . .* (15:7.2).

called a celestial year—but there is no such reckoning of time after you leave this dimension. . . .

I am so often mistaken, I do not like to make a definite prophecy, but I do not expect to ever see you in the flesh. If we are forbidden to meet here, we will make contact again later on. I very well know that. In fact, I already have some orders relative to that particular time already—in something near 160 earth years away.

You have done everything so very exceptionally well, it seems such a pity to have the physical condition present. You have a Myocarditis and you have a slightly enlarged heart in addition to the ulcers. The heart enlargement is on the right side. We knew of the condition, but the only way that you would accept it was through the doctor. Bland foods—milk—eggs—oils—very little condiments if any—plenty of water and liquid foods—and *nothing iced.*

Do you wonder that I press you, as soon as economically convenient, to protect Martha with a modest, owned home. Things would be much easier economically all around if you had that house now for a permanent home for Martha and the girls. As a safety move for you both, you surely must start on this—before the time comes when you can produce less. I do hope that I can impress this on you.

No, you will not take over my particular duties when I have finished my little time here and am released. I do not know this but am resigned to it now. You have a much more specific assignment, I am now sure of. I do also believe that your especial assignment will have to do with writing. Still I do not know.

I believe that you have already made some "unbidden Astral journeys"—which is unusual for one in such a yet early development. No, not now, will we ever meet in the Astral. I used to visit you quite regularly for a long time. But not anymore. That time has gone by for me.

I can see by your letter that you have missed some important information in my last letter. Study it a bit more. Possibly my letters are too long—in my eagerness to help as much as I can, I may be overdoing.

This particular door giving access to you is slowly closing in my face. I am holding to the contact through force of 20 years of necessity so to do. But my responsibility is over. Your further development and the ways in which it will be brought forth are not within my province anymore. I feel that I must try again to impress on you the absolute necessity of bettering your physical condition. I must again tell you that if it is not much corrected, there will be much interference with your advancement.

I also want to tell you that I may at any time now be instructed to bid you farewell and to cease contact with you—that I may be interfering in some way with the program that another Intelligence may be at present operating. You will know our sadness when this should occur. I do so hope that you study these letters. I hope that our contact may continue for a time—but I am fearful. I would like to get a few more letters to you if possible. But do not grieve—I will see you again—in something like 160 earth years from my passing and release.

The Iberian was a "hybrid"—you are also one, and so am I. That should tell you a great deal.

With much love to you ALL from Ma Loose and myself,

And with every good thought over and under and around you all, I am,

[*Handwritten addition:*] I have been rereading your today's letter. Please reread my small outline regarding the hybrids. You were in Kempt (Egypt) long before it was called Egypt. It is very probable that you were engaged in the work you describe. I was not there at that time. I had met the Iberian there much earlier than the time of the building of the Pyramids. You see, the hybrid has never been *completely* in the next dimension nor fully free from this earth. You have a service yet to perform—and so have I for a little time.

Yes, we have worked together in this partially freed *non-flesh state*—not fully in the next dimension. You will know all about it—the whole and full story at the proper time.

Please relax—all that I have here written should be helpful. Mind Martha.

HAROLD SHERMAN to HARRY LOOSE

New York, March 19, 1941

Friend Loose:

No, your letters aren't too long—and what you are telling us is soaking deep into consciousness. We are reading and rereading and will continue to do so. We need the presence of these letters for some time in order to entirely absorb their contents. Each rereading brings a new illumination . . . and many things that have happened to us are now being made understandable.

I will set myself to the task of eliminating these physical difficulties. I have fought off, with help, the serious threats against my life on other occasions . . . and do you not believe it possible that I can clear up this ulcer condition and myocarditis? I presume, in some degrees, physical conditions come as a test. I know it has been helpful to other persons who have bemoaned their physical state as being a handicap to achievement . . . who have said to me, "If I hadn't been sick, etc." . . . "*You* haven't had to go through anything like I have. If you had, *you* couldn't have gotten anywhere either." And, for me to be able to reveal that I have faced seemingly insurmountable physical conditions, at various times, has given these people new confidence that they could get hold of themselves and accomplish something after all. One has profound respect for others who have *experienced*, as against those who simply theorize!

I have been thanking the Higher Intelligence for Martha ever since she was given to me as my life companion. Our experience and growth together has been wonderful beyond words. How I wish you *could* meet her. She has taken such splendid care of me . . . and has gone forward with me uncomplainingly, making willing sacrifices always, when I felt I must gain certain experience, whatever the economic or other costs.

I would like to know more of the Iberian and my relationship with you in that period of so-called Time. I felt that you were telling me the story of the "hybrids" preparatory to my realization that we *belonged*. Martha feels that I should now send you another dream impression which goes back to a most primitive state[7] and which was profoundly moving to me at the time. I am sorry that my imperfect physical state has inhibited the proper receiving of impressions or messages sent me. I shall give my best endeavor toward correcting it.

There are so many, many questions that my inner self desires answered. Why the mystery of the different languages, the different colored races, the widely varying grades of consciousness on this little ball of earth? The "English language" is apparently unknown on billions of other inhabited worlds. What is the universal language of communication. Does it lie beyond words—beyond language?

Why, also, our inability to know our past experience in the incomprehensible period of time which has gone before we became

---

[7] Dream impression of January 17, 1939, follows this letter.

conscious of this present existence? I have always been confident that I would, one day, *know*. But is this part of the penalty of our "hybrid existence," and does full knowledge come with the release or the "evolvement." (Words are so futile to convey absolutely true meanings.)

Apparently we are to be liberated from this "hybrid" cycle when this present earth experience is over and our service has been rendered. Apparently, too, we have been "locked" in this first dimension through past *mistakes* and *accidents*, existing in flesh and semi-fleshly bodies as we strove to rise above conditions into which we had plunged ourselves. And, to this degree, reincarnation, for want of a better term, has functioned for us—causing breaks in our continuity of understanding . . . and because we are related to all hybrids . . . none of us can gain escape into the full Second Dimension until we have aided all others toward this same level.

I have never asked to SEE what my service was to be. I have accepted a profound inner feeling with complete faith and have striven always toward a never-doubted end. The way has been hard and the trials, mentally and physically, have been grueling . . . but I have known, as I know now, and as you confirm, that—for some as yet undivined reason—some great Intelligence had chosen me to render some outstanding service to Humanity. I have felt that when this time should arrive, my one task was to be prepared . . . that the greatest "sin" I could commit would be the "sin" of unpreparedness. There has been gradually welling up in me the conviction that I am almost prepared to face anything. That, if great responsibility were placed in my hands, I would find myself possessed with the inner wisdom to accept and execute it . . . that I would be inspired to do and say what would be expected of me to do and say.

I have been prevented from joining any church group or any organization, for some Intelligence within has said: "When the time comes, you will be mercilessly examined by all manner of people who will be looking for the 'ax you have to grind' and they must find no evidence of any ax whatsoever. They will not be able to place a label upon you, giving them an excuse to misinterpret what you will say or reveal . . . they will be unable to pervert your message . . . and will have to concede that it comes from higher sources, uninfluenced by earth organization or worldly desire."

I have increasingly felt that Time, as we conceive it here, is one of the great illusions. This was more impressed upon me in the telepathic experiments with Wilkins. I was enabled to receive pre-visions of the only two accidents which befell his plane, some days before the accidents occurred.

This raised the question in mind—were they *destined* to happen? Could anything have prevented them? And how much free choice do we have in this dimension . . .

There is also the miracle of birth. If I was *destined* to be born at this time, as I *know* I was and have known, without being able to explain it, since a boy . . . could I have come into this world through any other set of parents than the ones who gave my soul this physical envelope?

Science, which sees only the physical side of life, would say that one spermatozoon, uniting with one ovum, results in the human embryo. Yet there are supposed to be millions—yes, possibly two billion of these spermatozoa in each ejection! Only ONE of them, however, makes union with the ovum.

Question: Does the spirit or soul enter in at the time of conception? What determines *which one* of the millions of spermatozoa is to make union with the ovum . . . and would the consciousness and identity of the inhabiting EGO be the same, in any case?

I have long believed that Sex and its expression is one of the great mysteries . . . and that we could come as close to an understanding of the great creative forces in this universe if we could gain a true understanding of the function of sex. Certainly some of the most indescribably beautiful experiences in life come through this union on physical, mental and spiritual planes of being . . .

I have never been told this . . . but am I right in sensing that: No father and mother experience the same physical reaction or mental or spiritual in any two sex acts. We have the mystery of the highest type of man and woman in a community marrying. They have three children—two of whom are truly representative of them . . . the other a "black sheep" . . . a "no good." And people in the community shake their heads and say: "How can such a child ever have been born to such fine parents, in such a fine environment?" etc.

Now, if my understanding is correct—isn't it possible that this man and woman had sex expression on the highest possible plane in the two instances when they attracted to themselves a high type of soul . . . and that, in the third instance, the sex act was repulsive to husband or wife for reasons of physical weariness, temperamental or emotional maladjustment . . . and this *so lowered* the rate and character of the "magnetized" or "vibrating" spermatozoa and ovum that it permitted the attunement or attraction of a low-vibrating entity seeking physical experience?

I perhaps haven't used the right words in describing this thought . . . but I think you will get the sense of my question. Isn't it necessary for the spirit seeking experience on this earth plane, to attune itself to a "conceiving body" containing the same rate and character of vibration as has been developed by the soul or intelligence?

Which leads to another question: IF anything had caused my own father or mother not to have been born, or any break had occurred in the mysterious line that stretches back, ancestrally—WOULD I STILL HAVE COME INTO BEING, WITH THE SAME AWARENESS OF SELF, THAT I POSSESS TODAY? Or COULD any break have occurred, with all the births and deaths and apparent choice of life mates which have gone on for some hundreds of years, prior to my ARRIVAL at this point!???

I am getting a sensing of a tremendous pattern and a oneness of the whole . . . and you must realize that my thoughts are going far beyond these little questions here as I reach out for even more fundamental knowledge in my desire to get a foundation under me . . . and the proper perspective to face what is to come.

I am a bit appalled at the thought of being separated from you, after having been restored to you again, on this plane. I feel no inner fear of what may be required of me . . . but I do feel the need for guidance and the support of such Intelligences as yourself. I suppose it will be given to me to recognize, beyond any doubt, the *real* teacher, when he comes?

Martha is interested to know, when it is right for her to know, what a woman's place is in the scheme of things. An awareness has begun to come to her. She knows that her destiny, at present, is to care for me, and I, in turn, am doing my best to care for her.

Martha has been left her parents' home in Traverse City, Michigan—empowered to make use of it whenever she wishes. . . . I have not been back to my home town in ten years and, while it was a grand place as a boy, I have not felt we could ever go back there to live.

We have never had the desire to get "settled" in the east . . . and I have thought, increasingly, that any home we would ever buy . . . might be west. Martha has felt a strong pull west for years . . . but has never been west of Chicago. If I am to render my service through some form of writing, I should be either near New York or Hollywood, the way the world is organized today.

Should the Mark Twain deal be consummated, it would bring me the money to secure a modest home. We have never and *would* never—want luxury. But I can clearly see that I must attract a sufficient amount of money soon to give me complete physical and mental freedom. I would not be in the physical condition I find myself, temporarily, today—were it not for my terrific efforts to achieve development, against the economic struggle of making enough to support my dear family at the same time.

I definitely feel that this is coming . . . and, with it, my liberation, to begin the work I came here to do!

In that connection, if you are "released," can Martha and I have the privilege of doing what we can for Ma Loose, for so long as she may be destined to remain here? Martha would so much like to know more of her . . . and to know her . . . as would I.

Martha wishes me to ask you, in connection with this First Life Planet, if there are places for souls "coming into this life," as there are places for their taking off? She is not yet aware of the previous portion of this letter and does not realize that I have been aiming at such a question with my own questions on "sex expression," etc.

She would also like you to explain, if you are permitted, the term "First Life planet" . . . and what *our* First Life planet may have been . . . and how *our* spark of Intelligence became individualized! (A small order, I am sure—but one which has caused me no end of meditation.)

What a great debt of love and appreciation we owe to you . . . for your care of us and your guidance through the years. . .

I particularly appreciate your patience and your tolerant consideration of my shortcomings. I shall try to measure up to your estimate of me . . . of the capacity and promise that is mine . . . I will try to justify your guardianship through what I may be able to perform, through such help as you have given. I know you want and ask no credit . . . but my being able to fulfill what you have seen for me is the only possible way I can begin to make up to you for what has been done for me . . . the only way, at least, that I can see at present. Is there anything at all—WE CAN DO FOR YOU?

Yes, what you say of Dr. Wanderman is undoubtedly true . . . and a good analysis. When so many humans, like the doctor, are rendering such a fine service to humanity, it is a bit hard to understand why enlightenment cannot come to them. What would a man like Dr. Wanderman have to do to qualify for higher understanding and development. Is there any way suggestions could be given him, without revealing anything, which would open his mind to receive and be prepared?

Sir Hubert Wilkins is another highly developed soul with whom I could go a long way in matters of this kind . . . he has said to me that he feels the universe is filled with Intelligence of infinitely high and low grade, in a state of unfoldment.

Again there crowds in on me all the pent-up questions with which I have wrestled for years . . . and a great eagerness to "know," or have revealed to me again what I perhaps already know, pervades my consciousness!

I hope you will be permitted contact with me for a little longer time . . . as I feel the need so much!! But I do not wish to trespass upon you in any way . . . or to selfishly keep you here. And I can look forward now to our reunion—160 years from this moment—as the taking of one deep, inspired breath in the eternality of "time." It will seem no more than that—a mere snapping of the fingers covering this span—when the moment has arrived! Perhaps then I can look you in the eyes with the consciousness of having performed the task assigned me . . . prepared, as a result, to undertake a much greater work with you!

Martha and I now join in sending our deepest love to Ma Loose and yourself, looking forward to the next communication from you with reverent appreciation.

DREAM   *January 17, 1939*

Last night I had another vivid dream that seems to have been related to some "incarnative" experiences. I was so moved by it that I awakened sobbing, the pillow wet with tears.

It seems that I was living again some moments that were mine in quite a primitive age, when humans traveled in tribes and fought one another with clubs for domination. Men had an animal-like regard for one another; respect was created only by fear of brute force; even supposed tribal friends or flesh-and-blood brothers were suspicious of one another, jealous and greedy. Constant physical combats ensued for possessions or command of followers in the tribe. Individuals were bludgeoned, severely beaten, or killed.

I was able to recognize the five Morrow boys, sons of my Uncle Arthur Morrow, my mother's brother, who were born and brought up in my mother's home town of Marion, Indiana. Lowell, Kenneth, Lawrence, Owen and Gus—all were tribal members; and my own brother Edward (now deceased) and my other brother, Arthur (I being the oldest in this life), all were in these primitive scenes.

Edward was least combative of all and avoided all conflicts where he could. He was beset often, without cause, because of his keeping aloof. I was repelled by the constant battling but had to fight in self-defense—and no doubt did my share of battering and killing.

The occasion which moved me greatly was a terrific tribal battle in which many were injured—and killed.

Understanding seemed to have come to me in that experience. I saw clearly the futility of such a struggle to gain human ends, the need for the expression of real brotherhood and love for one another. I made impassioned pleas to the assembled tribes, with many of their members—those I knew and could recognize amongst them—for them to give up their warlike pursuits.

I can see them yet, staring at me with their strange-shaped heads, which did not admit of too much intelligence, such as monkeys or gorillas stare at humans, as though trying to make them out, to comprehend. In some faces was a dawning light of understanding; in others a dull, sullen expression. But all were moved in strange ways by my plea because I was one of them, and had apparently felt some deep urge within me that they hadn't felt or couldn't yet feel, because their bitter experiences—the law of the primeval in them, the struggle for survival of the fittest—had smothered a consciousness of any higher laws.

As I was awakening from this experience, vaguely conscious that I was crying in my sleep, and with this scene receding from me, there came a flash of another scene and a totally different type of advanced civilization, where I was making this self-same plea for brotherhood and understanding between the peoples of the world on a much broader scale, and these two scenes seemed to fuse, as though being part of the same keynote!

Then came the flashing consciousness that both these "incarnations" were impinging on my present moment, that I had come back into this life in an effort to bring greater understanding of themselves and their fellow men to the humans alive today, who were alive in other ages in which I had lived; and this was the reason that I, in my poor way, had been so profoundly interested in studying the hidden powers of mind and trying to discover the laws behind the operation of the human consciousness.

I was impressed, too, that I had a "karmic" relationship to these two experiences, and that—but for my having progressed further than many of my associates in the primitive experience—I should have been born back into this life, in the Morrow family, as one of Arthur Morrow's sons, my identity being distinct. Even so, the law of attraction was such that I was born into this world through Arthur Morrow's sister, my mother, Mrs. Alcinda E. Sherman.

I have never felt closely drawn to any of the Morrow boys. They are more on the physical than the mental side, every one of them, and their development has been on the physical— the plodding, unimaginative, mechanical path of life, working largely with the hands.

As I was unable to save my brother, Edward, in this life from meeting with a fatal experience, so was I unable to save him then, from being beaten and killed by his primitive brothers . . .

It is worthy of reflection, this feeling that has come to me, through this unexplainable dream experience, that what the soul has gone through, in all of what we consider to be the past, could be brought to the surface *if* we but knew how to strike the keynote!—for instance, my deeply rooted desire, born of past experience, to cause mankind to realize the futility of physical struggle against itself. I attempted to put this message across in my picture, *Are We Civilized?*, dramatizing man's inhumanity to man throughout the ages. I have been devoting all my time and thought that I could spare, to a study of mankind and the effect of wrong and right mental attitudes upon individuals as well as the masses. In this study I have been seeking the fundamental answer to the world's ills, and this dream makes me see more clearly my purposes in life—why I have had this *driving urge* since childhood.

We are driven into higher and higher development through our bitter experiences being the result of our own greed and ignorance. Could we but strike the right keynote, it would bring up harmonics along the entire life line of our soul's experience. When a keynote is struck, vibration extends from the present moment of our conscious entity back into the so-called past and simultaneously into the so-called future. Events truly cast their shadows before, and the shadows are as real, potentially, as the events!

HARRY LOOSE to HAROLD and MARTHA SHERMAN
Monterey Park, March 22, 1941

My Friend:-

I am so glad to have been able to give to you your first light in some of the confused darkness in which you have been feeling your way. I have tried to gently lead you.

Now you know that you are, too, one of the hybrids who rightfully should have been fully in the next dimension, or beyond, but through accident and mistake away back in the beginning of things on this planet, have been tied here earthbound all this period when we should have been making full progress onward and upward. As you make progress here in your mission and meet teacher Intelligences, the long and intricate story of the accident and mistake will be broken to your consciousness little by little. I may, myself, yet get opportunity partially so to do before I am instructed to conclude my letters to you. I have also wanted to be able to write to you the full story of the crucifixion if I could get the time so to do. It has really never been written and the Biblical story is so meager and incomplete.

Telling the story of the hybrids and the cause and reason for their condition, in detail, would require explanations and descriptions and introductions—and each one a book in itself. It would be a most tremendous production to try to effect at this period when there is so little time left for me, and which little I would prefer to use for your immediate benefit in getting as much information to you as is possible, with permission.

I so cautiously gave you the Iberian lead to see if it would, this early, arouse recollections of former earth appearances. I get instant and astonishing response with your letter, with its fully written delineation and the Egyptian dream in addition. Can you not see now, your slow awakening to consciousness of some of the sights and scenes of prior existences. And so you grope in the flesh appearance until contact is established with your responsibility, or your responsibility with you.

We never operate singly in fleshed earth experiences—always by twos. You see, YOU WERE THE IBERIAN—does this clarify it a bit further than my last letter in which I closed by saying, "the Iberian was a hybrid—you are one—and so am I."

Now we can go ahead a little further and get it down to where it rightfully belongs. YOU were the Iberian. You were on a fleshed mission at the time and so was I. You were a much older earthly man than I in that same appearance. Now you must know further, that you are already a member of the great Order of whose existence I wrote you in the earlier letters. So are ALL hybrids. You will know all that you desire to know of the Order when teaching begins.

I so pray you to do all possible to help the physical.

Do you begin to see how impossible now it would have been to merely announce to you, in my first letter, that which I have had to give you little by little up to the present period. . . . If I had bluntly told you then, without any preliminary information, what I have been able to convey to you in these several letters, you could not have accepted and would merely have ended the correspondence at once. Now, however, with a very small introduction established and your Soul wakening you will be able to further digest—and in larger mindfuls.

To illustrate how hard it is to teach and illustrate what is otherwise beyond the comprehension of certain lower degrees of mentalities, and they are numerically far the greater, Christ had to use what were then called "Parables," and that word merely means "story," and it was only through the story that he could get his hearers to visualize what He was trying to convey. Every one of his Parables was used for a purpose—read from your Bible. There were no newspapers in those days, no telephone, no telegraph, or radio. There was great illiteracy.

You cannot conceive the correct answer to a problem unless you are introduced, step by step, to the limit of your intelligence, in the process involved making toward the complete ending crux or sum total. To hurry such mental processes, the teacher uses the blackboard and chalk, the pupil his pad and pencil—and, earlier in his life, the slate and slate-pencil. But supposing this all occurred when there were no blackboards and chalk—no pencils and paper—no slate and no slate-pencil—no education—and no ability to write, how could you faster, better and more believably teach a simple and restricted mentality—why, just as the present-day kindergarten children are taught—by song—by story—by word pictures to illustrate. . . .

Just to use one of many illustrations as to how early dissemination of the life of Jesus and His death on this earth occurred, there is even today existing a portion of a small playlet that the preacher had to use to place the picture to his audience of limited mentalities to their understanding. There is only a small bit left—the rest has gone into oblivion, but this little bit is still with us after nearly two thousand years of earth time. It is the old "Punch and Judy" show. The characters are Punch, his wife Hariot, Judy, another man, and a baby. In the original, the humpbacked, huge-nosed, caricatured "Punch" was Pontius Pilate, who finally sentenced Christ to the cross. Hariot, Punch's wife in the playlet, was Herod, the governor of Galilee, the friend of Pontius Pilate, who gave the order to slay all babies under two years of age in his Galilean jurisdiction (Herod's slaughter of the innocents). The original Judy was Judas, the disciple who betrayed the Christ. If you have seen a Punch and Judy show, you will remember that its presumed humor built about a crying child, which in the finale is supposed to be beaten to death with a club by Punch, ably assisted by Judy, over the vocal objections of Hariot. In the course of the years, the origin of this playlet was lost and it is now not known.[8] I am here giving it to you in this earth period merely to try further to illustrate the point desired to your consciousness.

Dear Martha:-

May I thank you for your letter.[9] I had wanted to see an untouched snapshot of you, or even to see you once, but this illuminative letter has very well taken the place of the snapshot or really seeing you. I have so, too, wanted to see Harold, but I realize that it would not be to his present benefit as it would personalize me to him too much. I had looked forward to you folks coming to California later in the year, at which time I could see him and you fully in the flesh and reminisce with him over things that occurred in the long past, and perhaps bring more strongly before him some of the pages and pictures so

---

[8] According to *The Dictionary of Phrase and Fable*, "The most popular derivation of Punch and Judy is Pontius cum Judæis (Matt. xxvii. 19), an old mystery play of Pontius Pilate and the Jews . . ."

[9] None of Martha's letters to Harry Loose were preserved.

very long agone. But it is wisest and best, under the conditions, that we pass this by. He will probably not be far enough advanced yet to remember or visualize in full, and the very last thing I want to do is to try to force anything into his consciousness. It must all come slowly, by his own free *will* and desire to advance.

I am grateful that you reread my letters. Each time that you read them, with concentration, something new will open itself up to you. You see, you have a man that is really and truly "not the same as other folks." You have probably come to this conclusion yourself a long time ago. He is different. There is so very much to tell and so little time for me, individually, to tell it. And there is so much, too, that I cannot tell permissibly, and there is so little that you can yet understand—even if told!

So the greatest speed that we can make is to "make haste slowly." It takes quite a few years of intensive study to make a lawyer, a doctor, a writer, an artist, a farmer or a bricklayer. None of these highly trained people can give you the information, and experience, necessary in any one of these occupations through the exchange of a few letters on the subject, or an interview or two, or even by a month's association. What they have, they had to get by individual endeavor—no one could have simply given to them against their will—even if they had really desired it. They themselves would have to make their own individual effort—meaning work—application—and the desire so to do in addition. On paper, I am doing all that I can to convey to you and Harold as much as I permissibly can, and to your understanding, that which goes a great deal further back than the earth time necessary to make a lawyer or a doctor. I can only, perhaps, just arouse your legitimate questioning interest.

Really, my work is done. It was concluded when Harold, of his own will, made the original contact by letter. However, just the same as you will grieve to lose your contact with your Morontia Intelligence on leaving the next dimension, just the same I grieve at losing my contact of nearly twenty years with Harold. Although his route was planned many years before this present earth experience, and we were closely associated then, and though I know that the earth years will pass, still I have dreaded the direct separation.

The book, *A Dweller on Two Planets*, must have a leaning to or a bearing on Theosophy. I believe it is their general concept that all souls continue to make return visits here until they reach perfection. There is no such thing as perfection on this planet. Jesus once said, "Why call ye Me good? There is NONE good except my Father which is in heaven." And by the way, that name, heaven, is just another small Bible inaccuracy. The correct way of spelling it is HAVONA. Very like the Cuban city of Havana.

Harold has been here before, many times, but this appearance is his last here. This is his First Life planet—as it is also mine. This is my last appearance here also. All this because of the decision affecting the hybrids, about all of which I have already written.

You may be comfortingly assured that there is a continuance of individual Life. You, with your but-human intelligence, would not uselessly and needlessly create and give LIFE to your child for no other reason than just to merely destroy it, and you may rest assured that the Great Intelligence is just as kind to His creation as you. What would be the use of creating all—just to destroy—to no purpose. Your own reasoning tells you differently.

Yes, there IS much to learn on this planet. Not, however, of the material or physical—that means nothing in the continuation. But there is so much to learn in the Spiritual. And, to quote a widely used ad for flour, Pillsbury's I think: "Eventually. Why not now?" The more you know of the Spiritual here—the further along you are in the very next dimension.

Harold's quasi-spiritual background has been of much help to you, though you, too, have been under watchful care and guidance. I cannot go into detail.

Your attention to the material has been of inestimable value to Harold. I grieve because of the stomach condition. He can and will be helped but he also must help himself and continue in the WILL so to do. If the Doctor says to play tennis, then he should do so. So very much depends on his physical and nervous health, particularly for the coming three years, and too, so VERY much depends on you for this period particularly. Continue to ever remind him to concentrate on me at night. If he will so help himself, I can help him. I can do nothing without his desire and co-operation.

At the time Harold's weight went to 123 pounds, Dr. Wanderman was led normally and naturally onto the scene.

Please remember that my contact with Harold was not just a "happening." It was arranged beforetime—even to my being on that particular circuit for Redpath on Chautauqua.

Your living expenses in New York *have* been too high at times and so have other expenses. I want to call your attention to the fact that you can remember that, somehow or other, something always seemed to happen at the right time to adjust matters in some way, and there was really no "want."

Your description of the periods at which time these stomach troubles are accentuated furthers my before information that "nerves" have much to do with the condition. The condition is perhaps only mild but is aggravated at these particular periods. And that means that some of it is mental—or "nerves."

I wish that I could explain or even hint at what occurs to him, or to any of us, in sleep—but I cannot permissibly.

About Mrs. Loose—she is a woman of German extraction, a former resident of Brooklyn, New York. She is five feet high and quite well-fleshed. Glasses—is a distinct homebody. The full domestic and "mother" type. Without her, I would be completely lost. She is highly developed spiritually. She has been a member of the Christian Science Church for many years. I am not a member of the Christian Science Church and have not attended their services in some time. I may just add this thought here—of all the present-day religions, Christian Science comes closest to the real teachings of Christ.

Mrs. Loose is, of course, very well acquainted with my spiritual background but is just as non-talkative about it as I know that you now are and will be as the future unrolls itself. Mrs. Loose's spiritual knowledge far supersedes that which is taught by the Christian Science Church.

From my deductions, I believe Harold's especial mission at this time on this, his last earth visitation, will be one of assistance to the great coming spiritual revival by writing a book based on information conveyed in these letters that I am permitted to write, by information from other Intelligences, and his own "light" or individual illumination which will be given him. I am not sure of this, but indications all point that way. I am in no way an author or writer.[10] I have written more to Harold since he has discovered himself than I have written collectively for many years together.

Do you honestly think that this world, or the Universe, or the other planets and other Universes, run themselves without jurisdiction??

---

[10] In 1920 Loose published a novel, *The Shamus* (Boston: The Christopher Publishing House), based on his days as a Chicago policeman.

Does it not take great forces and powers so to do? Do these great forces and powers operate themselves without jurisdiction of Intelligences? Jesus once said, "My Father worketh hitherto, and I work." Do you honestly think that only the Father and Jesus, or those of his Order, work in this and other dimensions and Universes while uncounted billions of Intelligences sit around and play on harps?? Does it not seem, even to human reason, that these uncounted billions of Intelligences are busily employed? Would you be happy for eternity sitting on a damp cloud and playing on a four-string harp??

A Morontia Intelligence is a degree of service in the second dimension. When the period of learning and service in the second dimension is finished and the passage through the "second death" has been accomplished, amongst many advancing services of choice is this one called the Order of the Morontia. Amongst the duties of the MANY Morontia services is this one of first contact, guidance and guardianship of the newly released and arrived Soul. You yourself may choose the Morontia way of progress on leaving this second dimension.

You are not correct, Martha, in saying, "Why has man always been chosen to present the great spiritual truths to the world as we know it?" Mrs. Mary Baker Eddy[11] alone introduced her philosophy and concepts by way of her book, *Science and Health*, and I have above told you that it is the nearest religion today to the teaching of Jesus Christ. Yet I have told you that I hold no other bias than this for it. I am not a member of this Church. I went to their services last some three years ago. Mrs. Loose is a member of a local church and a regular attendant and Sunday School teacher—but her spiritual knowledge far exceeds the teachings of this worthy Church. Its members number among the millions with thousands of churches in every land and it is the fastest growing Church of any denomination—not even excluding the Roman Catholic Church.

If you and Harold get any mental help or consolation from Theosophical thought or teaching, by all manner of means please do con-

---

[11] Mary Baker Eddy (1821-1910) was the founder of Christian Science. Claiming insight into Jesus' healing techniques, she established herself as a healer and began to teach others how to heal. Her book, *Science and Health with Key to the Scriptures* (1875), has remained the textbook of Christian Science. In 1879, she founded the Church of Christ, Scientist and later the popular daily newspaper, the *Christian Science Monitor*. Before she died, the religion she established had spread around much of the world.

tinue. As I suggested in one of my letters, "Continue any Church contacts that you may have," etc. I am not at all interested in any particular form of creed or worship. I am trying to get to Harold all the helpful information possible to make his progress easier when he stands alone in the not far distant future. I am not interested in proselyting for any Church, creed or denomination.

The mailman has arrived with a letter from Harold. I will read it and answer right along with this letter.

Yes, you can greatly help and ameliorate all of the physical conditions by mental attitudes toward them. Forget them as far as possible but remember to observe all the doctor's orders. If he says that you can play tennis, then play it. But don't overdo it to the point of exhaustion or breathlessness. "No man knoweth, not even the Son, but the Father." You can actually bring on real physical conditions by too much mental attention to small physical evidences. A part of health build-up is *laughing*. In laughter we must have forgotten that which perplexed or worried us before. Cultivate laughter. You have not had enough of it in your present earth life. Laugh—if you will practice making a job of it to see that you get one "belly laugh" a day—and be sure to connive or scheme in some way to give Martha a good laugh once a day—a funny story—a ludicrous sight or happening— anything to give her a laugh. Remember that humor is one of the few things that we take with us when we leave this planet.[12]

Remember Martha's dependence on you—and also your dependence on Martha. Hers has also been a way of responsibility and hardship. Thank her courage and trust and confidence in you. Supposing that you had married another instead of Martha—someone without her many attributes. Your answer is, of course, "Unthinkable"—that is correct also. You and Martha together was arranged long aforetime. In your mission to accomplish here, everything was long provided for.

As your physical state improves with the months of your WILL, your attention to your doctor's orders, your cooperation and the help that has always been given you, all these should improve much your ability to *receive* and to *perceive*. I have before written directly and have otherwise indicated that the human mind is a very delicate bal-

---

[12] *[Y]ou will enjoy the celestial equivalents of your earthly humor all the way up through your long morontia, and then increasingly spiritual, careers* (48:4.2).

ance—and its reception is really very limited—and more especially so when unprepared.

I must keep myself to leading you slowly and gently to these small learnings because of the inability to conceive at once the many and so much greater things you will be gradually inducted into consciousness of. It would be humanly possible to do irreparable injury by allowing myself to overburden you.

The "why" of the different languages, the different colored races, the widely varying grades of consciousness on this planet, is a very reasonable question. It cannot be answered in a sentence or two—or a page or two—but would require a great deal of writing right at this particular instant when time is of the very essence in getting to you much more essential information. I will, however, just give you an oddity that will be interesting. You know, of course, that we have the red man, the black man, the yellow man, the brown man, and the white man. Well, away back in the beginning of things here, there was a blue man. It would have been much better if the black man, with his generally lowered capacity mentally, had disappeared and the blue man had remained, for the blue man had a much better brain development and possibilities.[13] However, the blue man disappeared and the black man is still with us.

There is a universal language which begins in the second dimension. It is a present which is given you on arrival. You know it without effort when you awake.[14] It is a combination of pleasing sounds much more elastic than any earth language, with many more gradations of conveyance. Understandings are possible with its usage, and the ability to express is magnified many times over that of any earth

---

[13] Compare: *On those worlds having all six evolutionary races the superior peoples are the first, third, and fifth races—the red, the yellow, and the blue. The evolutionary races thus alternate in capacity for intellectual growth and spiritual development, the second, fourth, and sixth being somewhat less endowed. . . . It is a misfortune on Urantia that you so largely lost your superior blue men, except as they persist in your amalgamated "white race." The loss of your orange and green stocks is not of such serious concern* (51:4.3).

[14] Compare: *You will not acquire new languages automatically; you will learn a language over there much as you do down here, and these brilliant beings will be your language teachers. The first study on the mansion worlds will be the tongue of Satania and then the language of Nebadon. And while you are mastering these new tongues, the Morontia Companions will be your efficient interpreters and patient translators. You will never encounter a visitor on any of these worlds but that some one of the Morontia Companions will be able to officiate as interpreter* (48:3.13).

language. It is the same with music—there has never yet been born on this planet a real musician—there will be one some day.[15] The music is as different in the second dimension as is language.

You and I are recognizant of other flesh appearances because of the condition we have been in since the beginning of things here, *but because of the limitations of the fleshly human mind with which we are here burdened in these fleshly appearances,* we could not conceivably carry and retain full memories of such great magnitude—and such, if possible, would totally unfit us for the mission we were sent here to do—to have to also carry us, *in detail,* all these unusable memories. As you grow and progress, more and more will be given you by Intelligences, who you will eventually recognize as such—and also by information that will "come" to you mentally—which really is also delivered for your particular advancement.

This present year sees the liberation of all but a few hybrids from this planet, as I have explained in my last letter. I happen to be one of the few whose mission is not complete. When my mission is ended I too will go, my work here is then done. When your mission is complete you too will receive your release—and not until then. We have been locked in this hybrid existence since the beginning of things not because of what either you or I did, or did not do, but because of a great mistake and partly an accident that happened through those Intelligences who had jurisdiction over this planet at that time. There was no readjustment made because of the many intricacies involved, until by their own WILL and organization, [the hybrids] put the petition through in the way that all such jurisdictional matters are brought to the attention of the Superior Intelligences, and then there was action. This all happened as described in my prior letter.

Do you remember me calling your attention in former letters that all is not perfect in the next dimension. That simply passage to the next dimension does not mean "perfection"? To further try to convey this fact that all is not perfect in the next dimension, I call attention to the best human evidence available. I mean our present Bible. See Mark 9:5, Rev. 18:2, Isa 19:14, Mark 5:13, Luke 7:21, Luke 8:12, Acts 19:12-16, and there are many, many more. I am above quoting from memory, as always, and hope that I have not misquoted.

---

[15] *[S]ome day a real musician may appear on Urantia, and whole peoples will be enthralled by the magnificent strains of his melodies. One such human being could forever change the course of a whole nation, even the entire civilized world* (44:1.15).

Yes, it is probably best that you have not joined any particular church group—though I hope that you have gone to some place of worship on occasion—and with Martha. Please do not forget to give her every attention and be very gentle with her—and be sure that the girls get some religious instruction.

There is no such thing as Time. It is entirely a man-made innovation. Time has always been, and always will be.

Yes, you did have fore-vision with the incidents you mention in the Wilkins matter. True fore-vision is a very advanced operation. Far beyond true clairvoyance or true clairaudience. For fore-vision to occur once in a life-cycle is remarked upon, but for such to occur as often as you report is something else again. I must make enquiry about its evidentials. These fore-vision incidents were to be, you could not stop them or do anything about them.

You were born at this particular and definite period by manipulations that I do not understand. Yet these are happenings that are within the scope of operations of the second dimension. I am acquainted with much of operable nature in the second dimension but my acquaintance is not full. Just exactly the same as although you and I are at present in this first dimension, and we know much of the operables here—yet our knowledge is FAR from ALL. There are far higher operations than that which we discuss—which are far beyond my understanding—but I cannot refuse them simply because I do not understand, for I see them in operation and then the full and completed culmination. All that I can explain in such is that when certain Intelligences designate a happening to be in this first dimension, that thing happens, it simply IS.

There is a restriction to my quasi-human understanding, too. I know many things happen, but the methods by which such occurs I am not conversant with. Nor do I know the "why." You and I observe the huge mountain. It is there, we recognize its presence, we know the physics of its happening, but the "why" of its occurrence is beyond our understanding. Yet there IS a purpose and a "why" or it would not be there. I am often told that such and such WILL BE and IT SO OCCURS. Do you now see WHY I so often repeat to you that "I know so little." Handicapped by still being but a hybrid, and really not fully in the second dimension, my understanding and vision is limited.

There are 7 dimensions[16]—each of greater knowledge and freedom of action than the preceding dimension. How can the second dimension know in comparison with the third dimension. How can the third dimension know as much as the fourth dimension, and so on and so on?? It is all a matter of slow and deserved progress.

In reference to sex, which your letter discusses. Sex exists only on First Life planets. Sex is the only way to produce and continue the purely flesh animal that we in the flesh all are. There are many First Life, or flesh, planets in this Universe. There are also many planets in this Universe that have never seen flesh—that are inhabited either by advancing Intelligences from the flesh worlds, or First Life planets, or by Intelligences that are entirely spiritually conceived and who have never had an experience in the flesh.

You see, in the next dimension, you still need air and water.[17] You are not without restrictions. If you did not have air and water in the next dimension, you would perish just the same as you would perish on this dimension without them. So, on those planets that are fields of operation for the first and second dimensions, there must be both air and water. On the third dimension, the need for water is gone but you still need air. Beyond this dimension, I do not know the requirements. Because of the necessity for both air and water in the second dimension and the need for air in the third dimension, Intelligences of these dimensions are restricted to such planets in their Universes which are supplied with such essentials. They are also under other restrictions that have no place here in repeating.

Some years ago we were informed that because of assistance needed in the emergency that was present, a convoy of earthbound Intelligences (humans in full flesh) from a planet that was to be destroyed, were to be dipped through this earth envelope while they were being taken on their convoyed way to their destination, a new First Life planet that was already prepared with Light, air, and water and ready for its First Life beginners. Because they were of the First Life grade,

---

[16] Compare: *The nearer consciousness approaches the awareness of seven cosmic dimensions, the more does the concept of potential space approach ultimacy* (130:7.6).

[17] *Though you have morontia bodies, you continue, through all seven of these [mansion] worlds, to eat, drink, and rest. You partake of the morontia order of food, a kingdom of living energy unknown on the material worlds. Both food and water are fully utilized in the morontia body; there is no residual waste* (47:4.6).

their continuance of Life depended on their being brought through the earth envelope of attraction at certain periods of the journey. Always these passages through earth envelopes cause brilliant and unexplained lightings in the sky. They are always remarked upon by observant citizens, newspapers and scientists as unexplainable celestial happenings. You have quite probably read of just such things in the newspaper. I am only quoting this First Life transference because it seemed a good place to begin that which I may be able to finish sometime later, a story of why we came here and how.

Remember that we human animals here are arrived at by progression upwards until we reach a certain period in our development when we begin our search for God. At this time, there is then introduced into the human race the blending with more advanced and higher Intelligences brought here from older and more developed First Life planets by such transportation as I have above tried to describe.[18] Now, Harold, you will find your answer to the "why" and "how" of the colors of men here—and for the background of later-developing different languages. I am glad to be able to get this short and concise partial explanation in here instead of having to leave it obscure—see the preceding page.

All that I have written so far in this letter is in answer to your questions. I am still continuing.

I will ask your very close attention here for I am about to introduce to you a so-far-unmentioned entity, which will explain so VERY much to your consciousness. There is no individual Life to the spermatozoa, unless it at once contacts the ovum. There is no individual Life to the ovum; unless it at once contacts the spermatozoon, it is extinct. They are merely two halves of a whole. One cannot exist without the other. Once the spermatozoon meets the ovum and the ovum encircles the spermatozoon there is no Life—there is merely a *dormant* but completely fertilized egg. The womb, by a sucking process and slow movement, induces entrance of the fertilized ovum. And yet there is no individual Life. There follows a period of gestation wherein the fetus forms. At least the fetus is partially complete—and is identifiable. There is still no individual Life. It is still nothing but a growing portion of the woman's body—just as if it were a permanent attachment—it has no other life than hers.

---

[18] Compare: *[The] six evolutionary races are destined to be blended and exalted by amalgamation with the progeny of the Adamic uplifters* (51:4.8).

At or about the 4th month of gestation, through mediums entirely free from the woman's volition, the Intelligence whose work it is so to do inculcates the first great gift of the Great Intelligence—LIFE—to that which has before been nothing but a part of the woman's body. It is now a separate and distinct Life from that of the mother. And within two weeks after this time of presentation, the woman reports the individual movements of the child and says that she "feels Life." We now have a living thing yet unborn. Still, it is merely something of animal flesh and without a Soul. So it lives until its appearance at birth—freed from its mother—and we have a distinct individual.

Now—at the very instant of its first breath showing continued Life in the Individual, from those much higher Intelligences having charge as their particular work comes the second present from the Great Intelligence—it is that tiny bit of Him—the human Soul so-called, that makes the new Life entirely different from all animal Life. And that tiny bit of the Father makes that new animal Life something that belongs to HIM. And so we now have a new Life and a new Soul.

And so the baby grows, subject *entirely* to the rule of the mind of the mother—not knowing good from evil. All this until the fifth (5) year of the life of the child when another wonderful thing happens. Comes NOW the higher Intelligences whose work it is to so deliver, bringing what is known celestially as the "Thought Adjuster,"[19] or what we humans have called "Conscience."[20] Just as the Morontia Intelligence meets the new arrival of the human Soul just released from the flesh to the next dimension, so does the "Thought Adjuster," or what we call Conscience, meet the now new Life and the new Soul on its entrance to the first dimension on the First Life planet as a distinct Individual.

So, you see, you are only the flesh parents, born of human physical lust, just as the Bible tells you, of these new Souls. The real parent of these new Spiritual creations is really the Great Intelligence, the real Father of us ALL. The "Thought Adjuster" or Conscience then

---

[19] *Adjusters reach their human subjects on Urantia, on the average, just prior to the sixth birthday. In the present generation it is running five years, ten months, and four days; that is, on the 2,134th day of terrestrial life* (108:2.1).

[20] Compare: *Do not confuse and confound the mission and influence of the Adjuster with what is commonly called conscience; they are not directly related. . . . Conscience, rightly, admonishes you to do right; but the Adjuster, in addition, endeavors to tell you what truly is right; that is, when and as you are able to perceive the Monitor's leading* (110:5.1).

remains with the Individual for the period of earth residence of the Soul. You may, right now or at any time, anywhere, listen and hear, in your consciousness, the soft inner voice of the "Thought Adjuster." It is with you ALWAYS, in every waking moment, consciously, and unconsciously, in your sleep.

Regarding the question about the two good children and the "black sheep" in the same family. All voluntary acts of the individual, after Life, Soul, and the Thought Adjuster have been given, are the sole responsibility of the Individual. Whether he is the good child or the "black sheep" is dependent entirely on the Individual—that is his responsibility. And unless there are extenuating instrument-box, or fleshy brain, circumstances which prevent proper functioning, the Individual is held strictly to account for its deportment.

To answer another question. Your particular advent into the flesh was not following the usual pattern. If your father, or mother, had not been born, you would have arrived on schedule by some other route. You would also have had the very same awareness you have always had.

Do not be afraid to lose me. You will be cared for—if you follow your own WILL and desire—but remember, you are not freed from earth's responsibilities any more than I have been—I have had to eat—to breathe—to clothe myself—and have had my earthly cares just the same as you have had—and will continue to have. I have done my best for you—the rest is up to YOU individually. Keep on as you have been doing and I do not fear the rest—the only thing that can slow down the process—and can also COMPLETELY DEFEAT IT, is your own physical and nervous health. If you are "weighed in the balance and found wanting" as you progress, that will be a fatal occurrence as far as a continuance in advancement in this particular operation is concerned. I know no further than this. So take great care to observe everything of benefit to correct the prevailing conditions. . . . Don't look for a teacher for three years—don't try to rush or force things—you cannot and will retard your own growth. Don't try to do the work of higher Intelligences. You cannot.

In regards to Martha's question—woman, as a whole, is usually further advanced spiritually than is man on this planet and on ALL First Life planets. They are inherently so, unknowingly, for they are the lone carriers of the sacred LIFE of the new Souls to be. And to further the command "Be fruitful and multiply" to provide for the appearance of these new Souls. Woman is a more necessary creation than is man in many ways—and her place in succeeding non-flesh dimensions is in exactly the same ratio as man's.

I am so glad that Martha has the old home in Traverse City as a place of safety for herself and the girls in any unlooked-for necessity. I have no suggestion where it would be best for you to settle. You folks would have to decide where would be best. However, living expenses here in California are about 60% of what they are in the east and there are no severe winters. I only suggested the stabilization and security of an owned home because of Martha and the girls.

Regarding Martha's next question, it is pretty well answered in the forepart of this letter. The new Soul is a part of the Great Intelligence and resides with HIM until the time for its earth presentation.

In reference to a "First Life" planet. There are different Orders of planets because of the different stages of the development of Spiritual Life existing thereon. This Urantia is one of the First Life Order. It is Martha's First Life planet—and yours—and mine. Martha will go onward from here. You and I, hybrids, have been here since the beginning of things and have made many flesh appearances—yet it is our First Life planet.

To your next question. No—if your mission is what I feel sure that it is—that is, to write the story, I want no connection with such story in any way public. It must remain between Martha and yourself, and the higher Intelligences.

Just to give you a small illustration of the powers which are interested in this whole matter, just to prove it to your human thought. This information to you, as has been given, is now so protected that Martha cannot convey it understandably to anyone—unless she should have with her this whole series of communications in her hands and read them as she tried to convey. And she could not do this, for the papers would dematerialize as she tried to read. Ask her right now if she honestly thinks that she could so explain—without the papers. She may think for the moment before answering—but in the end her answer will be "No." This very same protection now also applies to yourself—and will so apply until such time as you receive instructions to incorporate the information into book form—and this may come from your own "light," by dream instructions, by way of your own "Thought Adjuster," or by way of separate higher Intelligences. How it will come, I DO NOT KNOW.

When this book is published, see that Dr. Wanderman receives a copy. When he has finished reading it, you may confide in him the whole story—withholding my name of course. You see, when this book is published you should be a very much sought-for man, you should be literally stormed by people seeking further information—you will be asked to give talks, etc.—use your own thought here.

Be sure that you properly protect Martha with some of the gains. Get her a Life Annuity with some large Life Insurance Company so as to assure her that she will not "want" no matter what happens. I personally want nothing—if I am here. And be sure to know that I have no knowledge when I am to be released.

No, there is nothing that you can do for me—and if I go and Ma is left, there is nothing that you can do for her. She is already taken care of for her time here. Just the same as with Martha, so it is with Ma Loose—she cannot talk of these things—it is the LAW. If you were to question her, she would refer you to me: "I cannot talk of these things, you will have to talk with Harry." Just the words which Martha would use under any such circumstances. The subject, and knowledge, is too sacred and too filled with POWER for any minds except those that are CHOSEN. Even should you be released before Martha, she then could not talk of these things either.

I have looked over your letter and find that I have just about answered every question that you ask. I will get along to the conclusion of this communication.

I may in all probability be still here, gardening in the yard, or going for the groceries, or on some mission, when you do come west, but even so, for the sake of your future, it would be best that we did not meet in the flesh. You would then personalize me too much—you would inherently "lean" on my understanding instead of doing your own individual constructive work. You would tend to release to me some of the responsibilities that are truly yours by your own WILL and desire and endeavor. Of course, I have a very distinct longing to see you in the flesh but I would much rather sacrifice my personal desires to your own betterment.

I would very much like you to read a few verses every night aloud to Martha from the Bible before you go to bed. I would like you to begin with Proverbs, and then when there is a finish, then go to Psalms. Only a few verses. Then when you go to bed, CALL me quietly after complete relaxation.

About your dream [of January 17, 1939]. You are getting things plainer. How well you write—how descriptatory. You now are receiving some verifications of your existence away back in the beginning of things. The presence of the boys known in your youth was an infringement from the subconscious. You sure do draw a fine word-picture. Yes, that is your beginning. Your Soul has gone through—as have other hybrids—all these things that are now being pictured to you. You see, you and I are what are also called celestially "Old Souls."

Martha, will you tell me, please, if I am giving Harold too much at a time. I do not want in any way to interfere with any of his activities—either physical or mental—and I do not want to tire him.

Thanks again for your letter, Martha. I am going to reread this long letter and see if I can correct the many mistakes. I don't usually do this when I write to you all.

I will be very much obliged if you would acknowledge receipt of this letter. I have been working away on it for several hours.

With much LOVE to you ALL, and with the very best thought over and under and about you ALL,

HAROLD SHERMAN to HARRY LOOSE
New York, March 26, 1941
Friend Loose:

Your letters are the spiritual tonic I have been reaching out for—for years! I can't seem to get enough of the *very much* I need to know . . . and each letter throws more light on experiences of the past . . . making it seemingly necessary for me to reveal more dream and other impressions to you—for analysis or evaluation as you may desire. I will include more with this letter.[21]

You say so much each time . . . and I do not wish to over-burden you with questions and comments, but I am eager to progress as fast as you can comfortably help me.

I sensed that you meant I was the Iberian . . . but it seemed egoistic for me to assume this since, apparently, the Iberian was a highly developed soul . . . an *old soul* . . . and I feel so humble and have always

---

[21] Dream impression of January 1938 follows this letter.

so felt. I have recognized the worldly necessity of establishing one's identity with the public—so that one's name can command attention . . . but I am sure Martha would tell you that whatever I have been able to accomplish has not aroused the ego within me. I have been interested only in how effective an instrument I might make of myself in expressing the thoughts and ideas given me.

I have said to Martha many times that I felt things within me . . . deep down in consciousness . . . that I *did not dare* permit to come to the surface as yet . . . for I sensed that I did not possess the maturity to give full expression to them . . . and that if I exposed them before their time, I would impair their quality and usefulness. Now I can begin to understand why I have not been permitted to try to express these profound truths existent within me until I should be "awakened."

I can understand your feeling that my meeting you in the flesh might retard rather than help. I am willing to abide by whatever the Intelligences decree . . . but I think I am beyond being affected by sight of physical form, which does not represent the real you or me. (I should like to know what the REAL FORM does look like, however . . . the REAL INDIVIDUALITY.) And I will not, as yet, abandon the hope that I may be found worthy of meeting you and Ma Loose before the great change comes . . . which very natural desire Martha shares with me. . .

It is thrilling beyond words to describe—in whatever small ability has come to me for expression—the JOY of this REUNION with you. I can look back over these marvelous but gruelling twenty years . . . and feel how worthwhile they all were . . . to have led me back to you. If your service has been to enlighten and prepare me for my mission here . . . what must I have at one time done for you to have deserved such guidance now?

What service did I, as the Iberian, perform with you? Did we both, of our own choice, enter fleshly bodies in order to serve those who were residing here in this, a First Life Planet for them? And were we imprisoned here, beyond the "time" ordinarily counted on—by this mistake or accident?

When and on what First Life planet did we originate as individualities or souls, if this can be answered? And when you speak of being so *old*—is it because you now have come into a consciousness of your earth years on this planet . . . has your recollection of the past enabled you to feel the weight of those years of service . . . as you now prepare to drop life's overcoat on this earth plane . . . and enter the dimension long denied? Your mother, herself, must have been an advanced soul.

Has it been our destiny to work together? Is this what you mean by service being rendered by TWOS? And how did we come together in the first place—if the answer is knowable? I shall never forget how drawn to you I was, from hearing you speak in Marion . . . it wasn't from anything you said . . . for you obviously weren't talking on these subjects . . . but something in me said, "I must meet this man Loose personally" . . . and I told Martha, on our way home, that I must try to locate you at the hotel that night after dinner . . . and *then* to *learn* that you were in the hotel room, actually waiting for me to visit you . . . ! How thrilling and worthwhile everything is in this indescribable universe when understanding begins to come! And now I shall look forward to our meeting 160 years hence! We must have looked forward, in times far distant past, to meetings in what then *seemed* the future!

I feel that I have come close to licking every other obstacle but the one of economic pressure. My regard for my family and its care has weighed in heavily upon me. I haven't mentioned my brother, Arthur, whom you met in Traverse City and who has never ceased to talk about you and ask if I have heard from you, being so impressed just by merely shaking your hand! But Arthur has had a strange "karma." His [hoped-for] marriage to a girl who was of Catholic faith in Marion, where Mother and Arthur went to live after Dad's death, was opposed by my well-meaning Methodist mother and the girl's mother . . . so Arthur, to get away from it all, took a job in a bank in Detroit . . . and his emotions were so dammed up within him that he had a mental lapse . . . and disappeared from Detroit and came to his senses four days later on a train a hundred miles from Denver, Colorado, with no knowledge of what had happened to him. This was the "escape mechanism" operating and gave him the excuse to break his engagement . . .

I then brought him on to New York and took him, in bad nervous condition, to Johns Hopkins in Baltimore, where the fluid was drawn from the brain due to intercranial pressure. Arthur, seemingly recovered, went to sea for two years for his health, was hurt on shipboard, hospitalized, met a girl . . . and married without advising me. I accepted it with good grace even though Arthur had no job . . . and he has had work only spasmodically since . . . being my own special care and responsibility in addition to my dear mother, who spends part of every year with us and the other part with her widowed sister in Marion . . . or visiting friends and relatives in the home town of Traverse. Arthur has had three children in his impoverished state . . . and has had to go on relief at different times when things hit rock bottom with me on certain occasions. . . .

Arthur has high ideals, is quite religious, quotes the Bible . . . responds to suggestion . . . but instinctively knows he can lean on me . . . that no matter how tough the struggle is for me, he can always depend on my getting the money somewhere to see him and his little family through. His faith in me is like a man's in God. He lives in one of the new WPA developments in QUEENS . . . a big housing project . . . where thousands of families live on relief . . . fraternize . . . and decided that this is a good enough existence for them. I give you this much of a personal picture so that you can appreciate the burdens I have gladly sought to carry, in addition to my own not-inconsiderable problems . . . while I have been seeking at the same time to carry on my own work and to gain this priceless knowledge which is now coming to me through you.

Long years of up and down economic struggle, despite the ample evidence of help at critical times, has gone to my solar plexus region . . . and despite my knowledge of mental laws and how to throw off fears and worries . . . it cuts like a knife at times. For myself I fear nothing . . . my only concern is my dear ones. Also—it has not seemed right that dear friends, on occasion, and, in some instances, strangers, should have to advance me monies, as they have . . . to see me through.

I have always had an independent nature . . . a *tremendous energy drive* . . . as Martha will tell you . . . there just is no quit in me . . . I have always been conscious of having been born with this quality . . . it's a power I possess, stimulated by the deep knowledge that I have come here for a purpose and am willing to undergo any hardship and sacrifice in order to work unquestioningly toward the fulfillment of that purpose.

I shall try more and more to relax and invite your help. I *do* seem to need *this much* of a boost. I relaxed yesterday afternoon, lying on my cot in the study next the bedroom—*adjoining*, I should say. There came to me two vivid impressions: "Great good news is coming" . . . and the phrase, "Be still and know that I am God!" (Incidentally, some days ago, while relaxing, I felt you in your little home, on the left side of the house, downstairs, a back room overlooking a garden of some sort . . . a place you seem to use for doing your concentrating. I seemed to see you sitting in a chair before a little table, thinking of me. (By left side, I mean left side facing the house from the street.)

I know that what you say is true—I have staged a real comeback from my serious ulcer condition of a year ago . . . and nerves tie up the stomach muscles . . . causing cramps, gas pains, etc. . . . when the economic pressure is strong in consciousness, with current bills due . . . and nothing that I can momentarily do to bring money in except WAIT for the TIDE to come in, on work already accomplished! I MUST overcome this—despite everything—and I WILL! It is the severest form of test I know . . . at least, for me. But I so want the RESOURCES I need to be attracted to me, through my own efforts, and not through the help of friends, as has happened in other critical moments of past years, on occasion. However, if I had stopped to think of money ahead of everything else . . . on many projects and many past courses of action, I would have missed DEVELOPMENT . . . and I always chose this road, with Martha's consent . . . her entire confidence . . . and faith. I *do* thank the Higher Intelligences for her, time and again.

Martha would like to know, is this a First Life Planet for her? Has she been here as many times as we . . . and associated with me before . . . and does our destiny lie together in future points of "time"? We feel so indescribably CLOSE in every way, as though we have always belonged to each other . . . almost as though we were one and the same identity!

TIME OUT: Charles H. Forbell and wife arrived for dinner and to spend the evening. I am picking up this letter to you this morning, March 27th. You will remember Forbell's work when I tell you that he is a cartoonist and that for years, in the old *Life* humorous magazine, he had a full-page cartoon showing "Ye Ancient Knights in Armor." He did a lot of funny stone-age stuff and take-offs on ancient civilizations, sometimes crossing their activities with the modern-day methods. Charlie also did a series entitled "Club Life in America" which ran in the *Judge* magazine, showing pot-bellied old men in spats, asleep on sofas in the Harvard Club, with cobwebs over their feet, etc., indicative of those intellectuals making no real use of all their "culture" and "higher education."[22]

The Forbells are two of our dearest friends, possessing a deep knowledge of these subjects. Mrs. Forbell has been a profound student for years and has worked out a system of prognostication based upon so-called astrology, numerology and the Kabbala which is astounding. She drew a chart for me last night which took her three hours, and then said: "Harold, you have had a terrific struggle all your life. You have come up through all manner of obstacles . . . and you are about to emerge into a new cycle which is going to see you gain world fame. You have had to go it alone . . . and your success will be self-made—but *you've got to watch your health!* You could have died about a year ago . . . in fact, I congratulate you for being here. . . . Martha—you take charge of Harold and see that he does it. Martha is the finest person in the universe for you . . . and her destiny is wrapped up in yours. She will gain world fame with you . . . and your charts and those of your two girls show travel . . .. you are going to change your location . . . MONEY is going to come to you . . . LOTS OF IT . . . but through your work in the MYSTICAL. The theatre is going to open up as well, giving you opportunity to do something inspiring in it . . . But—WATCH YOUR HEALTH . . ."

Martha and I feel that the Forbells were sent to us last night to reinforce what you already have told us . . . to *make certain* I am properly impressed to PUT MYSELF IN SHAPE. They are such sincere, trustworthy people. Charlie said, "Harold, I am sure you are being helped by Higher Intelligences and that you are living almost as much in the next dimension as you are in this." There is no doubt in my mind, and there never has been since we first met—but that you have come here to render a great service . . . and despite all the hell you have had to go through, you are going to accomplish it. The tide will turn one of these days soon . . . and all the worthwhile things you have worked on so long will come to pass at once!"

Martha and I made no comments but listened and checked with one another . . . as the Forbells poured out their spiritual assurances in the loving, vitally interested manner so characteristic of them. Some day, it would seem that people like the Forbells should be permitted

[22] Charles Forbell (1884-1946) also designed "Mr. Peanut" for the Planters Peanut Co., as well as the two elves, Hap-Pea and Pea-Wee, that symbolize Andersen's Split Pea Soup.

to know a few things . . . but probably this is all taken care of as they reach certain development.

It would be a great privilege to be entrusted to write such a book as you suggest—based on what has been revealed to me through you and other Intelligences . . . and the illumination which may come to me later. Certainly, after this war, world consciousness will need some SHOCKING SPIRITUAL REVELATIONS to lift spirits high and give millions the opportunity of working toward their own liberation. I have sensed that my work was to be with the masses . . . that what I might one day say and write would have a profound impression on them.

Another of our friends—a man who has had a profound influence on our lives—is Jacques Romano. I have learned much of mental operation from him, since he possesses the ability to "tune in" on the subconscious minds of people and tell them what has happened to them, giving names, dates and places on occasion . . . the highlights of their life experiences. He has been a world traveler, was born in Spain, formerly spoke quite a few languages, spent some time in India, was all over Europe, in South America and Mexico . . . as well as China and Japan. Jacques is now 77 years of age, the youngest and most vital appearing man for that age I know. He has a deep knowledge of the occult . . . but is a terrific exhibitionist! His ego is enormous. He loves to demonstrate his powers and *must* be the shining light in every gathering. He blankets the field, regardless of other important personages present whom you might like to hear from.

But, despite this great weakness, Jacques has accomplished great good in awakening hundreds of skeptical people in all walks of life to the actual existence of such powers of mind. No one is precisely the same, in mental attitude or outlook, after seeing him perform. He is a most lovable personality with it all, and loves to serve others, going out of his way time and again to administer to people in sickness or do them a favor. He is a chemist by profession and has developed several iodine preparations which are dispensed by the well-known drug firm of Eimer & Amend. He is not well-to-do and is not interested in money, as such. I have often thought, but for his weaknesses, Jacques could be one of the highest developed individuals I know. He tells stories of his visit to monasteries and the fact that he is going back to visit one in 1953, etc. . . . but I am sure there is a curious blend of fact and fancy in all such stories as he tells . . . since he appropriates, vividly, what is told him by other seekers of occult truths . . .

In Jacques' quieter moments, when he has had me alone, he has looked at me significantly and said: "Harold, you don't know who I am . . . but one day you will. I was meant to get in touch with you and put you in touch with Dr. Wanderman . . . and to help see you through. My role is to play the fool in public . . . the entertainer . . . and to mix in these mental feats to awaken an interest in people . . . I am not interested in what others think of me . . . I have nothing to sell . . . if they believe my mental feats are trickery, if they are not advanced enough to perceive . . . that is all right . . . they are not ready."

You can see from these remarks that he has the elements of the mystic . . . but it has been hard for me, devoted to him as I am, to balance his great and his weak qualities in my mind. He makes a terrific impression on people the first time they see him—for his feats are unparalleled. I have no exhibitionist complex in me . . . and would not demonstrate my "psychic qualities" in public, if I could. Many times I get impressions of people while Jacques is demonstrating, and later he tunes in and gives out the same impressions, to the amazement of the subjects. I have been willing to put such powers as I possess under scientific observation . . . and have avoided being labeled with any ismic belief or spiritualistic brush.

Jacques has often stated: "I'm now going to give you a demonstration of spiritualism or what I could call spiritualism . . . although I don't believe in it." Then he tells the individual to think of some dear one who has passed on. Jacques rolls up a piece of cigarette paper into a ball and gives it to the individual to hold, having them press the point of a pencil against it. He proceeds to tell them the first name of the deceased . . . and then goes on to give a full and convincing description of the outstanding events in their former life. At the finish, he has the individual open the cigarette paper and the first name of the deceased is written thereon! It's a startling combination of trickery and actual sensing of conditions which pertained to the life of the "departed."

Jacques always frankly states when what he does is a trick and when it is a genuine phenomenon . . . he does not try to take credit for feats that are simply sleight-of-hand on the basis of supernormal faculties. He does amazing things with cards . . . adding actual suggestion and "mind-reading" to the tricks to make them absolutely unexplainable to the ordinary person. In his way, Jacques has rendered a tremendous service.

I am wondering, though, if he has not forfeited much, in his own development, by letting his ego run away with him . . . and by appropriating spiritual experiences of others . . . and recounting them as having happened to himself! What a pity if this is so . . . for I would say he could have expressed on a high plane. Perhaps you will have some information pertaining to him . . . and perhaps this outward manifestation of Romano's has point and purpose not ordinarily discernible. Certainly he has compelled Martha and me to expand our mental horizons by his absolutely original viewpoints on life, entirely uninhibited by education, religion or any of the other elements which so often narrow and warp an individual.

I have meant to mention my interest in the Book of Urantia which you say is to be published. I should like to know more about it. Will the true story of what is behind this universe begin to be revealed to humanity during my lifetime . . . are humans to be permitted to know the real truth, with regard to some vital matters, soon? It would seem necessary, to balance other destructive factors now running rampant.

Your explanation of creation on the physical plane was of great interest and helped clarify certain wonderments.

How very much there is to discuss with you—it would take several weeks to even get up to date on the things I would like to check that have happened to me in these twenty years, did we get together for a physical talk.

Tell me, as I am asked pointed questions following public talks on the mind—must I withhold the revealed knowledge that is being given me and give answers which I know now are what might be termed partial truths? I am remembering your statement about the pages in my book, 43 and 44, and while many such points are surmises in the minds of many so-called authorities . . . I do not wish to assume the responsibility of giving out wrong information even as a theory or supposition. Actually, I am discovering that many things I sensed and did not completely interpret, actually do exist, but not in quite the way I have explained them. I presume mankind grows in this way, from partial truths to whole truths . . . and perhaps we could not stand the unadulterated truth at first. But as true wisdom is being added to me . . . for my own advancement . . . how long must all of it be withheld and will I be shown later just how it is to be used. . .

It is perfectly plain that this knowledge is not available in books—at least, not as yet . . . and is not widely disseminated. I have been impressed that I must be able to demonstrate certain mental laws in my own life before I could write about them or pass on information about them to others. In my "primer for average men and women"—*Your Key to Happiness*—I wrote with the conviction that came through actual experience.

When my book with Wilkins reaches the public—it may open many doors for much more advanced presentations. Wilkins is a world-renowned character and will attract the comment of radio commentators such as Lowell Thomas[23] . . . the columnists . . . feature writers . . . magazine and newspaper people . . . *Thoughts Through Space* should awaken millions to possibilities within themselves . . . it may be the beginning of my real work. I should be interested to know your own view on this.

Well, I could write more and more and more . . . and I am closing with many questions unanswered, eager to learn more about my past as it relates to the present and future. I am sending out the call every night . . . a little too tense yet, I know . . . but I'll make progress.

Our love to Ma Loose and yourself . . . and our profound appreciation for all you have done and are doing for us!

DREAM   *New York, January 1938*

Since I have been carrying on these telepathic experiments with Wilkins, I seem to have awakened channels in consciousness which have brought me unusual dreams of different civilizations or planes. Here is one of the most vivid of these experiences.

I found myself, with Martha, attired in a form of luxurious evening dress. I do not recall just what I was wearing, except the feeling that I was well-appointed, but Martha was radiantly beautiful in a rich, purple gown which trailed as she walked. A bejeweled star shone at her throat, and this, with her dark eyes and hair, made a stunning picture.

We were apparently paying a visit to some important personages and were just arriving at their residence. But the build-

---

[23] Lowell Thomas (1892-1981) went on to be a best-selling author and motion picture and television producer. He wrote 52 books, among them *Lawrence of Arabia, Beyond the Khyber Pass, A Life of Kipling*, and in 1961 *Sir Hubert Wilkins: His World of Adventure*.

ings of this very advanced civilization were much different from those of today. They were built in great circular, tubular tiers, like mammoth automobile tires piled one upon another with a common entrance on one side—the tires being joined and compacted at this side but separating at various angles on the opposite sides so that each circular tier of dwelling places stood out into space alone and distinct.

This building was of tremendous height. Entering at a point or level midway between the top and bottom by our modernized car or conveyance, which I remember only indistinctly, carrying us right inside, we got out and the car was immediately discharged, apparently by some magnetic force, to its parking place. I was conscious of a myriad of great passageways, some sloping up and circling around and around onto the different circular tubing levels. Martha and I passed through a great reception room, high-ceilinged, something like the Radio City Music Hall, but much grander in size and architecture. We crossed this apparent lobby, passing many impressive men and women, all handsomely dressed and all apparently knowing exactly where they were going.

We stepped into some kind of an elevator and I felt ourselves being transported upward, easily and silently, a great distance. We got out upon a certain tier. I recall now simply having spoken the number of this tier while in the elevator and this had started the mechanism.

Walking out along the corridor at this level was somewhat like being in the salon of a Zeppelin for we could see for miles, as we followed around the circular tube, every time we came to a great, circular window. In one direction, I remember a great expanse of ocean in the distance. In another, hundreds of other great dwellings like the one we were in.

The scene now appeared to be night, with all the circular, porthole-like windows gleaming or glowing with an inner light, making the whole outer world look like dazzling bands of luminosity as far as the eye could see.

I had the impression that everything one could wish for in this life was contained in each one of these great buildings, and yet Martha and I accepted what we saw, for the most part, as though we were accustomed to it.

Only once did I feel wonderment and make an inquiry and that was when we came into a great music room and Martha went over to a mammoth organ unlike anything I have ever seen, seated herself, and commenced playing music of indescribable beauty. (Martha plays no musical instrument in this life.) I listened, spellbound, overwhelmed in admiration. It seemed that the beauty of her soul was being transmuted to music—or that I was hearing, for the first time, *the music of her soul!*

I suddenly felt a presence and turned to find a kindly-appearing, mature-aged gentleman regarding me, smiling.

"To whom are we indebted for this?" I heard myself ask him. And he, giving me an unforgettable knowing look, said quietly, "You may refer to me as the *Governor*."

When Martha had finished at the organ, which was played by pushing a myriad of buttons rather than keys, she dismounted from the sumptuous seat and took my arm, and we continued on toward our destination on this same circular level.

I was conscious that magnificent dwellings were enclosed in these great circular tiers opening off these corridors. We stopped at a certain door and spoke, I believe, the name "Byron," when the door opened by unseen hand, and we stepped inside to be greeted by a charming man and wife who stood side by side as they took our hands in greeting.

The scene dissolved as though we were not supposed to remember what transpired there.

The next thing of which I was conscious was awakening to find myself on the outer side of a huge bed, with Martha, at an elevation above a corridor, or overlooking a passageway. I had been awakened by the voices of a couple passing below who were unconscious of our presence even though they were extremely near us.

The impression was most vivid and I seemed to understand what they were saying as I lay there and watched them going by. But something at this moment actually awakened me and as I came to my outer consciousness, in my own bed, I carried over the impression of my dream momentarily into this dimension, for the couple now stood, for a second, beside my bed talking.

I looked up and saw them, conscious they were talking a language now foreign to my ears. I had no sense of fear—only of great interest—and, as I became wider awake, they faded from external sight and hearing, even as I looked.

My lasting impression, with this dream over, was one of great inner happiness, as though Martha and I had been on some mission in space together, and were developed with powers beyond our conscious awareness, being much more closely united than we have any imagining.

[This dream] was recorded January, 1938, before any of the knowledge you have now given us. In the light of this, I now wonder if Martha and I weren't fully on the Second dimension and speaking in the language you say is given to us there, a language which seemed natural to me then, and which seemed foreign to me when I "came to" on this earth plane? Perhaps this vision or dream or actual experience will mean something to you. . . .

5

"Your Class of *One*"

HAROLD SHERMAN to HARRY LOOSE

New York, March 31, 1941

Friend Loose:

Your class of *one* (Martha and I) is now coming at you with a barrage of questions! We read and reread your letters each night, usually between the hours of 12 to 1:30 a.m. our time, discussing them and giving free rein to "imagination" and inspiration. Then, at the conclusion, I always relax and send out the call to you.

One apparent contradiction has appeared: On page 4 of your letter sent under postmark of March 15th, you say pointedly three times: "This is a First Life Planet. This is NOT a First Life Planet for YOU." Now, in your most recent letter, mailed under date of March 22nd, you say on page 3: "Harold has been here before, many times, but this appearance is his last here. This is *his* First Life Planet, as it is also mine."

You apparently do not connect Martha with the same background that has been common with us. Has she come from another First Life Planet to be of aid to me and to join forces at this time? Is this her first appearance here and also her last?

Are the "hybrids" comparatively few in number? And were they *all*, at the time of the "mistake and accident," imprisoned here, though highly developed souls or intelligences even then? And are the majority of humans really First Life entities, reaching this state of consciousness for the first time? (There is still some little confusion about these points.)

If *most* of the hybrids are to go over this year, then it would seem that many millions of humans are not hybrids. And are we correct in interpreting that those *few* hybrids who are left here will become full second dimension intelligences *while yet in the flesh* in order to raise their capacity for service in the critical time to come? Is this an experience that might come to you and to me before we leave this first dimension? Do the hybrids belong to the order of Melchisedek?

Martha is interested to know: If I did not follow the usual pattern in coming into this life, how did my coming differ?

We would appreciate more light on the two- and three-brained type of development and its significance.

Martha wishes further to know if your friend the Catholic priest is a member of the Order, and if *none* of the hybrids, through all the centuries, have been released until this year?

She is also interested to know: To what service are criminals and murderers and such types put when they leave this dimension if they are permitted only one life on this planet?

Have none but the hybrids had reincarnative experience on this earth? And is *she* a hybrid, or has she come through another influence entirely?

These other questions may seem unrelated and are not being asked in order:

What became of the "blue man" and why was he blue? We can get a sensing of the why of the origin of different colors and languages, and feel that fuller illumination will soon come.

What causes gravity?

Is the "thought adjustor" a separate entity? Does it have anything to do with creation on the earth plane?

Are poltergeists actual intelligences? You mentioned that you would explain the so-called ghost phenomenon. We have never believed that we contacted, in any ordinary séances, however purportedly genuine, the actual intelligence of the departed. And yet strange, unexplainable things have often happened. (Apparently there is a reflective intelligence closely connected with the fleshly body which has some kind of a shadow existence of itself for a time, under certain conditions. It is hard to put this thought into words.)

Martha feels that I should now send you the report of an impression I received on February 17th, after receipt of your second letter.[1] There seems to be so much to report to you, we simply await the inspiration to send different material.

A letter this morning from Jesse Lasky has this to say: "I am happy to advise you that negotiations have been resumed on the Mark Twain picture and I hope to have good news for you within the next two weeks." I had also been inspired to send a copy of my book, *Your Key to Happiness,* to Mrs. Lasky, who I had been told is much interested in these subjects. About this, Mr. Lasky writes: "By the way, Mrs. Lasky received the copy of your book and I had a chance to read the first two or three chapters. In the meantime, Mrs. Lasky read it and enjoyed it so much, she is urging me to finish it which I certainly will do." I have a feeling that, with the proper spiritual appreciation being developed, the Laskys may enable me to express on a high plane through the medium of pictures!

There has been no report, as yet, from Whittlesey House, currently considering the Wilkins book. I made the change from "realms" to "realm." Thank you for your correction. The editors at Whittlesey House stated that it was possible Wilkins and I had a book which would interest the *Reader's Digest* and the Book-of-the-Month Club. If this should be the destiny of such a book, it would open the door wide for this later book to which you refer, and I could easily see how its reception and interest would be worldwide.

God speed the day when my real service can begin! I have felt this urge in me from my earliest moments of recollection, and I can feel my body health improving! It MUST and it WILL!

I have done such an enormous amount of writing . . . much of which should prove commercially productive once things begin to move. Certainly I desire to have my financial problems cleared up once and for all, as a result of my own efforts—putting me beyond all necessity for such aid coming from outside sources.

It will be difficult not to be able to confide many things in you which cannot be put in letter form, things that I feel we must have exchanged in the long, long ago . . . or feelings or thoughts or experiences that have come to us in some other plane of association.

---

[1] This report is on p. 75, above.

I have long sensed the great mystery of SLEEP . . . and *know* I must have been in the presence of great intelligences many times, in this state. Here is where we must have met on numerous occasions . . . and I am eager for this veil to be lifted a bit.

I awaken now with such a satisfied sense . . . as though I have been with you . . . although I cannot yet recall anything specific.

Well—another letter from you is on the way . . . and I already hunger for it. This is the food and drink I have been seeking.

With all our deeper love to Ma Loose and yourself, now and for-ever, I am,

In eternal gratitude,

HARRY LOOSE to HAROLD SHERMAN

Monterey Park, March 31, 1941

My Friend:-

Your letters received.[2] Thank you both. I was glad for the questions and will answer them and any you may send in the future which I permissibly can.

You have *not* been doing right by Arthur to accept any of his impositions re money advances or other responsibility. You are taking away from him his right to growth and progress. He is utterly wrong to ask or expect such. The kindest thing you can do for him is to refuse from this day to carry any more financial or other responsibility for him. It is all right to help anyone "over the hill" but it is wrong to allow imposition. I do hope you get this. You have enough legitimate adjustments and expense of your own. You have much to do to read-just much of your thinking—to open new avenues of thought—to get yourself physically and nervously well—to prepare yourself for the future. You are of too great value to this and succeeding generations to allow yourself to do harm to yourself by a wrong program. I am only making suggestions to you. I cannot dictate your WILL.

Your description of and the location of my room and its pur-pose—even to the window and its location—are *exactly* correct. I congratulate you. You surely are making definite progress.

My old body is ill. I cannot use the typewriter. In a few days I should be up and will write you on it.

Love from Ma and myself to you all.

---

[2] Martha's letter has not survived.

P.S. Please don't put so many stamps on your letters unless it is really a necessary thing.

HAROLD SHERMAN to HARRY LOOSE

New York, April 4, 1941

Friend Loose:

I have had an uneasy feeling concerning you the past few days. I was certain I would get some word from you today and was sorry to have this feeling confirmed by the written knowledge that your body had been ill.

I hope that I have not been, in any way, the cause—that I have been too much a drain on you in the physical effort you have put forth to supply me with what I have so needed to know. I doubt if you can tire me, physically or mentally, with however much you might write . . . but I would not want to overtax you.

You speak of your body almost as though it were another intelligence apart . . . with kindness and appreciation of its service to you . . . and sympathy for its illness. I have wondered, sometimes, if the body *were* not a form of entity itself which we, as the higher intelligence inhabiting it, abide with and direct for a time—unless we let its lower elements rule us—in which case we are the worse for our earth experience. If we *lift* the elements in our body to a higher plane through mastering them—then this body entity advances along its scale of "evolution" too, and is the better for our having inhabited it. Does any of this make sense? It is so difficult to express in words. (And, if I am even partially on the right track—does this explain why this body entity "takes on" a reflection of our REAL INTELLIGENCE which manifests after so-called death . . . and which is NOT the real US at all? And does this "reflection" exist in the earth atmosphere until all the elements have been dissipated or transmuted into other forms?) Is this often what so-called mediums communicate with instead of the "real spirits." Is this close to an explanation of poltergeist (uncontrolled physical force), etc.?

I will not burden you with more questions now but will await further word. The time draws nearer when we will leave, as a family, for Hollywood. Wires are being exchanged relative to terms in the final contract and it would not surprise me if we were west in about six weeks, maybe sooner.

I am so glad I was able to demonstrate my sense of nearness to you by "visiting your study mentally" and retaining accurate impressions of it.

OUR LOVE to Ma Loose and yourself—and our prayers for new physical strength to sustain you.

HARRY LOOSE to HAROLD SHERMAN

Monterey Park, April 3, 1941

My Friend:-

I am glad to again acknowledge receipt of both your letters [Harold's letter of March 25th; Martha's letter has not survived]. I am glad for the questions that you both ask and will answer every one that I permissibly can.

Because of the present and very probable greater future circumstances, I would like to head this letter with a suggestion in justice to yourself and those of your immediate family. You are not helping Arthur nor yourself in continuing to allow yourself to be responsible for him, financially or otherwise. In justice to him and his family, try to rectify the absolute wrong you have been doing him by allowing him to impose on you. . . .

I am going to read your letters as I sit here and answer all the questions that I permissibly can. I will begin with Martha's letter.

Question—What is the reason for miscarriage?[3] Answer—The reasons for miscarriage have to do with the human animal and the flesh almost entirely. The Spiritual has nothing of any kind to do with miscarriage. The deliberate, knowing and willful production of miscarriage (abortion) after the present of "Life" has been given to the unborn child is as much what is termed murder as would be the taking of Life from a child or adult fully in this First Dimension.

Question—What place has the premature Soul in the scheme of things? Answer—There is a place in the Second Dimension where all such juvenile Souls are kept and normally developed, in reproduction of the earth experience, until what would be the earth age of 14 years. Residents attaining this age are removed from such temporary surroundings and given their choice of many different paths of service,

---

[3] Martha had suffered a miscarriage early in their marriage and sought reassurance of the baby's survival potential.

each path leading to full service in an established Order of which the Ascendant Soul is but a part.[4]

Question—Are miscarried beings Souls which need more than just a passing through the earth's atmosphere for air and water but not a full life experience? Answer—No, that is not their status. Most miscarriages are deliberately produced, or induced, by physical or medical means. These are deliberate abortions, and an abortion of an unborn to whom Life has been given is the "taking of a life" as truly as though by some other physical means you should take the life of a full-born. I have not made inquiry regarding the responsibility for the use of a contraceptive.

Human Souls of the first dimension asleep in the flesh in convoy transport from one First Life planet to another in this same Order, for implanting purposes, require earth contact for air and water and also because they need to be revivified by certain earth electrical forces that all flesh are *attuned* to receiving—and which all receive during the actual flesh existence. These electrical forces are received in full and visible form at the *positive,* or reception point, of this earth, at what humans call the North Pole, in what has been named the Aurora Borealis. After their passage through the earth, [these forces] are finally discharged at the *negative* point, which is termed the South Pole. The same procedure occurs in all planets of this order.

I mentioned the Eskimo because of the strange story that lies behind these peoples. Not because they have a bearing on present-day humans or that they were progenitors of either of you folks. It is a long and strange story and one which I hope to some day be able to write you of in full. However, there are so many more introductory matters that are of more immediate and direct import that I feel that the present time should be used to get as much of these other things to you as possible. I will only mention this bit as an indication. They are, or were before general contact with the white man, the direct and perfect lineal descendants of a pair of twins, brother and sister, who,

---

[4] *The infant-receiving schools of Satania are situated on the finaliter world, the first of the Jerusem transition-culture spheres. These infant-receiving schools are enterprises devoted to the nurture and training of the children of time, including those who have died on the evolutionary worlds of space before the acquirement of individual status on the universe records. . . . Any time after sixteen, if final choice has been made, [these children] translate to the first mansion world and begin their Paradise ascent. Some make a choice before this age and go on to the ascension spheres, but very few children under sixteen years of age, as reckoned by Urantia standards, will be found on the mansion worlds* (47:2.1,5).

of their own volition, separated themselves voluntarily from the family clan and went northward from a point where Indo-China is now located [*sic*]. This twin brother and sister were the forebears of these peoples now termed Eskimo (Esquimaux). In their natural state, they have made so little advance that they are little more ahead than they were these ages agone. They still have the "short" language filled with the same gutturals. They have the same color, only little added height, the same eyes and features and many of the age-old habits. They are the very last peoples of this earth to retain so very much of the appearance, stature, etc., of their long-ago beginnings.[5] Some tribes of these peoples who have had very little or no contact with the whites, bear even much more of the beginning resemblances to these long-ago peoples from whom they sprang. It is all a very strange and very interesting story that I hope to write to you some day. Just as I hope to be able to write you the *real* story of the crucifixion. That should really be done before the Eskimo story. . . .

I forgot to mention in one of my letters where I told a little of the life story of Jesus and His family, that Joseph, the husband of Mary, had been married before, and that he had five sons by his first wife. His wife died—the five sons were of mature age—Mary was much younger than Joseph. Joshua ben Joseph was the first child to be born of Mary. The next child was James. Then followed Jude, and three months after the death of Joseph little Ruth was born.[6]

---

[5] Compare: *Asia is the homeland of the human race. It was on a southern peninsula of this continent that Andon and Fonta were born* . . . (79:0.1). *Very early [Andon and Fonta] learned to engage in verbal communication; by the age of ten they had worked out an improved sign and word language of almost half a hundred ideas and had greatly improved and expanded the crude communicative technique of their ancestors* (62:5.7). *[B]y reason of their own intelligent choice, the twins* . . . *migrated northward to a secluded region where they escaped the possibility of biologic degradation through admixture with their inferior relatives of the Primates tribes* (62:5.9). *And the sole survivors of these Urantia aborigines, the Eskimos, even now prefer to dwell in frigid northern climes* (61:6.3). *Primitive man—the Andonites—had black eyes and a swarthy complexion, something of a cross between yellow and red. . . . In general appearance and skin color these early Andonites more nearly resembled the present-day Eskimo than any other type of living human beings* (63:4.1).

[6] The Urantia Book says that the brothers of Jesus mentioned in the New Testament (Matt. 13:55; Mk. 3.6) were the children of Mary and Joseph. According to *Hastings' Dictionary of the Bible*: "The tradition that [Joseph] was a widower and had children by his former wife probably arose in the interest of the dogma of Mary's perpetual virginity." Joseph and Mary had eight children in addition to Jesus, their first-born: James, Miriam, Joseph, Simon, Martha, Jude, Amos, and Ruth, who was born six months after the death of Joseph.

The Iberian was an "old Soul" then, and many earth years have passed since that period. The same Soul that resided with that Iberian now resides within the fleshy content of the cranial cavity of Harold M. Sherman—in company with the very same "Thought Adjuster" or Conscience.

You are "built in the (physical) image and likeness of the Father," as the Bible tells you. The physical is merely a fleshy reproduction of a much more beautiful spiritual counterpart.

You will meet Intelligences later who are in this Spiritual form. You will talk to them—be advised by them—they are no different in appearance than you and I. There does, however, emanate from them a feeling of great power that will be very evident. You will make no mistake regarding these entities. Remember, too, that there are always many full Spiritual entities from the Second Dimension here on this dimension on special missions. There are probably always some from the Third Dimension also. I know little of their activities from my own knowledge.

Please remember, Martha, that you have a most responsible place in this particular development. Without your great help it is very probable that Harold might not be able to reach the height that he is enfleshed for. You, the balance for a sensitive, are in a very needful position. Keep him to his schedule—remind him when he is remiss. Counsel patience—the building of the physical—the nervous—make him laugh—laugh easily yourself—lighten and make less any burdens—remind him to "Let Go"—to relax physically and mentally whenever time or opportunity presents—"fix" his hair—smooth his forehead—"mother" him—your physical touch means so very much to him.

Please remember that my little informative letters must in no way be construed as "teaching." What he will receive from "teacher" Intelligences later (in three years) will *really be something*. You will know, too, Martha, very, very much. But you must keep your share of the load to carry during all this time.

Harold, because of what you have been given to know—so very far beyond so very many—you must now educate yourself away from the human "death fear." Do not allow thoughts to enter your consciousness that make for such fear or fear of any kind. Disregard all minor forms of physical manifestations that would otherwise tend to unquiet you.' Cultivate the legitimate poise you will positively have to have as development continues. Would a nervous, unstrung, shaky, unpoised and unposed man be the best one to talk before large audiences on the book that will eventually be written of those things??

The "Thought Adjuster" is but one of the paths of service and progress of an Order operating out of the *Third* Dimension. This path of further progress and service is one of a great many offered in the Third Dimension and is subject to the choice of the individual advancing Soul. You yourself may choose this particular pathway of further learning and progress upwards when this time comes.[7]

The Iberian and I performed a service in the ancient land of Kempt, which much later became Egypt. It was a fleshed appearance, in which the Iberian was an older earth-man than I. The experiment and service was for a period covering a normal life range of the time and had to do with the introduction, propagation, and transplanting of trees and other vegetation in the land which at that time surrounded a great sea which is now the Sahara Desert.

PLEASE remember that all tree life and other vegetation had to be brought to this planet in the beginning of things. No tree or plant evolved itself here. ALL was brought here. All has even been helped in development since arriving here—and all as services by different Orders of Intelligences. NOTHING has happened here all by itself. There has been an Intelligence working behind EVERYTHING. Please remember, in addition, that every other expression of LIFE was brought here. It DID NOT evolve itself. It has been developed here—but it did not ORIGINATE here.[8]

Please also remember, Harold, that there is NO "great change" to suddenly come to you. You will reach a place of growth and understanding very far above those in this dimension. You came here, of

---

[7] Compare: *On the mansion worlds the seraphic evangels will help you to choose wisely among the optional routes to Edentia, Salvington, Uversa, and Havona. If there are a number of equally advisable routes, these will be put before you, and you will be permitted to select the one that most appeals to you. . . . You are not given unrestricted choice as to your future course; but you may choose within the limits of that which the transition ministers and their superiors wisely determine to be most suitable for your future spirit attainment* (48:6.5-6).

[8] Contrast: *That we are called Life Carriers should not confuse you. We can and do carry life to the planets, but we brought no life to Urantia. Urantia life is unique, original with the planet. This sphere is a life-modification world; all life appearing hereon was formulated by us right here on the planet; and there is no other world in all Satania, even in all Nebadon, that has a life existence just like that of Urantia* (58:4.1).

your own volition, to perform a great service. You have made very excellent progress—you STILL have much to do—you are not fearful—you welcome the work that means progression. Just as you have EARNED your progress to date, just so you will still work and earn your further progress. You will be much helped, as always, but none can do your GROWING. Just go ahead now as you have in the past—and in addition do all possible to right the body conditions. Remember, as the Bible says, "We see now as through a glass but darkly." "Make haste slowly," have much patience. Do not try to do the work of higher Intelligences. All will come out right at the proper time—with your continued effort—and with Martha's help and cooperation.

We both, of our own choice, entered these fleshy bodies to perform a service to those who are residing normally and humanly in the First Dimension on the First Life planet. It is also your First Life planet as it is mine and also Martha's. The difference is only that at the time that you and I should have passed normally to the Second Dimension, there was a mistake and accident happened that neither you nor I were in any way responsible for, which left us both and many other thousands in a position and condition that I have tried best to illustrate by giving the word "hybrid." Neither of us, or the other many thousands, are fully in this present dimension nor are we fully in the Second Dimension.

At the conclusion of other earth experiences, at the conclusion of other missions, we remained on this earth occupied in such services as we were capable of. We were not released fully from this earth and promoted fully into the Second Dimension. This condition has now been rectified and this year there will be the migration of these "hybrids" to their really proper dimension. Many thousands have already gone. Many are concluding missions here, fleshed and unfleshed, that must be concluded before they CAN leave. It just so happens that you and I are amongst those so situated.

Right here, before I again forget to remark it, I want to be sure to tell you of a much out of the ordinary method of transportation that was used in those far-off days away back in the beginning of things. Some day, some earth scientist will come in contact with some of the bones, maybe, and other evidences of a huge prehistoric bird, as large as, or larger than, the much later mastodon. These birds were alive, in full flesh and feather, away back in the beginning. They too had their purpose—in the eating of foods with indigestible seeds which were passed out with other excrementa, and in this way those seeds, and fertilizer, were transferred to distant places with the flight of these huge birds. They were an extremely unintelligent form of life and very cowardly and inoffensive.[9] These huge birds were much used by early man for transportation purposes—ten to twelve could ride very comfortably on their backs at one time. In the wise planning of the Great Intelligence and other Superior Intelligences, this method of transportation also accounted for some of the implanting of MAN to faraway places on this continent.

I could go into many pages of description of this bird—its appearance, its purpose here, and the reasons for its final and total extinction—but now is not the time nor is this the place for it. However, this great bird had something to do with the implanting of early man on the great continent that has been called Atlantis, which finally disappeared long ago in a great calamity that was also caused by a VERY bad mistake occasioned by those Intelligences having jurisdiction over this planet at the time. Atlantis was the name given this lost continent by the great Greek philosopher and poet, Homer, in his great poem, "The Iliad," and was really NOT the name of this lost continent. As a matter of fact, it had no name to VERY early man. The name came MUCH later when the continent had many, many inhabitants.

Harold, you are very worthy of meeting Ma and I, and the very same applies to Martha. We would dearly love to see you both. But for the sake of your continued individual progress—your mind and thought—it is very probable that we will never meet here. I have asked which would be so and I have not been answered. I would not dare to do so unless given direct instructions so to do, and must resign myself to accept what greater Intelligences indicate is for the best.

I am not quite sure that you yet realize the great responsibility of this operation and how much depends on you AND ON MARTHA.

---

[9] Compare: *The early races also make extensive use of the larger flying animals. These enormous birds [called "fandors"] are able to carry one or two average-sized men for a nonstop flight of over five hundred miles. On some planets these birds are of great service since they possess a high order of intelligence, often being able to speak many words of the languages of the realm. These birds are most intelligent, very obedient, and unbelievably affectionate. Such passenger birds have been long extinct on Urantia, but your early ancestors enjoyed their services* (52:1.5).

I don't know why, but I have so much the feeling to always remark in these letters to "mind Martha"—perhaps I am very wrong in this feeling, but it is there. I know that you are a very highly developed sensitive. I know SOME of your mental and physical struggle—and I know the "balance" that Martha has been to you through it all. And I know your dependence on her—and I know how wonderful she has been—and how very helpless you would be without her—and I know how much she means to your future development—and so I am going to risk offence by really saying "mind Martha." I plead with you both to "be of one mind"—your progress has been very wonderful—you deserve all that is in the future—don't let the physical or the nervous defeat or much delay you now. Do not "be weighed in the balance and found wanting."

You are in close touch and contact with great forces and powers that have work for you to do. I believe that work to be a book on these matters—with all the additional publicity of stage, screen, radio, and platform work. I have not been directly so informed but all evidences point to that particular thing.

This is my First Life planet, as it is yours. You have never left this planet nor have I. You have made many appearances here in the flesh BUT YOU HAVE NEVER LEFT THIS PLANET—your First Life planet. This is why you are a hybrid. You are neither FULL in the flesh nor are you FULL in the spiritual.

I do not think of the flesh as "old," but when you further progress and come slowly to know and recognize your beginnings and know the full history of your "hybrid" existence, from far greater authority than I—when you know all this and much more, you will come to the realization that you are really what you are called in the full second dimension, "an Old Soul." Please remember that I have had to go through just what you are now going through—and had to learn just as you are now—and will so continue. Your very "visions" (they are *not* true dreams) tell you a little. You too, the same as I, are an "Old Soul."

There is a Superior Intelligence who is in charge of this particular operation. I and you, both, are operating under his jurisdiction. No operation of a hybrid is of his own individual choice. The hybrid can refuse or accept voluntarily to proceed upon such mission under the jurisdiction of such Superior Intelligence. You may liken us to two soldiers operating under the jurisdiction of a superior officer. So it is with all operations of hybrids enfleshed for missions. They always operate in twos for their own protection in the operation.

All operations do not progress as far as we have gone successfully. Mistakes and accidents, unlooked for, occur. Either you or I might have something occur to the human before the "graduation" and "awakening." We might have a serious accident—we might become alcoholics or drug addicts before such time and be "weighed in the balance and found wanting." We might so neglect the body that we would develop some physical thing that would disqualify us for furtherance in the mission.

I can give you an illustration of one that failed whom you may know of. There was a hybrid in New York City that was sent here on a mission of importance. His name was O'Fallon [sic].[10] He was a lawyer in New York who was called "The Great Mouthpiece." He failed utterly and completely through his uncontrolled desire for alcohol. I just happen to know that the mission he was sent here on is still not completed because of his failure. There are many failures of missions by hybrids on this dimension. Our operation, by much struggle and pain and travail, has been successful SO FAR, but although my personal work is done, you are not yet through—you are not even yet qualified to continue—until the physical and nervous conditions are met or much improved.

My mother was NOT an advanced Soul. Your mother is not an advanced Soul. Both your mother and my mother were merely the necessary means of the flesh production of the temporal residence of two "old Souls" with a mission.

You may be absolutely positive of the continuance of individual existence. You may be as sure of advancement as a reward for your own individual effort in the next dimension—exactly the same as in the present dimension. No one has ever advanced *in anything* except by individual effort—and that same rule applies in every dimension up to and including the 7th. The whole history of individual LIFE is individual effort. "My Father worketh hitherto and I work." Everything is "work and order" and routine—observe the same regular routine and order of this earth—and of the stars that you see in the heavens at night. Would you be satisfied right now to sit and do nothing for years. YOU are exactly the same YOU in the next dimension.

---

[10] For more details, see Gene Fowler, *The Great Mouthpiece: A Life Story of William J. Fallon* (New York: Blue Ribbon Books, 1931).

Don't scatter your forces anymore by observation of any strange cults or "isms" or sleight of hand tricks. Don't allow yourself to be confused or distracted or lose any of your forces by attention to these things that you now know to be untrue and false. Use your own thought to help unfold and enlarge the prospectus given you in these letters. Open your mind to them. Can you now see what great difficulty Jesus had to get the great truths that he taught to the understanding and acceptance of so many? "Think on these things" . . .

I have asked information on the economic matter mentioned in your letters and the question has been brushed aside—so, from past experiences, I believe that the matter will eventually be adjusted in some manner. If you have done your best about it, then don't worry about it—you will so injure yourself to no benefit.

The Book of Urantia is a revelation to this age which will take the place of our present-day Bible. It is definite and authentic in full, and completely descriptatory. Wherein our present-day Bible is obscure and contradictory. It is a very wonderful thing and you will read it. When you do, please remember my long contact with its building. It is FULLY by Intelligences from the succeeding two dimensions. My work with it was distinctly apart from the mission that I and you came here to do.

The morning's mail has just come. I have just read your letter of March 31st. I will reread and answer the questions when I finish with my answers to your questions in the letter that came before.

The difficulty in presenting answers to audience questions is the authority back of such answers. However, the human mind is such a little-understood organ of operation that all answers to such questions have a very liberal range—it being a matter of the individual opinion. Your answers would come in a perfectly proper range under the circumstances. Your answers, being entirely new thought, would arouse considerable argument probably. My reaction is that I think it would be very proper, in such talks as you indicate, to tell your audience questioners the mint truth—what [the mind] is—what operates over the fleshy brain, etc.—but do not connect me in any way with the matter.

Remember, the truth is that the fleshy Mind is but the instrument-box over which the real Soul—the real YOU—the real Intelligence—operates in its jurisdiction over its subject—the body. Remember too to include in such description that such jurisdiction is often in combat with the human WILL and all other instincts and desires of the animal Life of flesh in which the Soul or real YOU resides. It is too early, probably, to tell them of the "Thought Adjuster" or Conscience, which resides there too with the Soul. I am afraid you would begin to get into deep water there, until your book about it all first comes out—with the explanations all in print. You will find that you will raise a storm of controversy once that the information just about the mind and its resident is really circulated.

ALL of your earth work has been tending toward the eventual presentation of the fuller and greater work—that is my full belief. *Your Key to Happiness*, your *Thoughts Through Space* are all indicative.

I have read your very beautiful vision (dream). It is beyond me to unroll it to my understanding. I am sufficiently interested in it to ask of a higher Intelligence to give me some light on its interpretation. I may not be able to make such connection for some days, however.

I am now taking up your letter of March 31st.

There is no contradiction on page 4 of my letter sent under postmark of March 15th. *THIS IS YOUR FIRST LIFE PLANET.* At the time when you should have left here normally and progressed through the second dimension, a mistake and accident occurred through no fault of yours or mine—but occasioned by those having jurisdiction over this planet at that time. Because of this mistake and accident, thousands and thousands of Souls, which should normally have gone forward—advanced—were kept here. Since that time, we have not been fully in this dimension nor fully in the second dimension. We have continued on here—in the flesh on missions—or in the second dimension PARTLY. So, although this is TRULY your First Life planet, you have made many appearances here. Your ascending Soul and mine, amongst the many thousands, were caught here by that accident and mistake, and the best way that I know of to describe the conditions is that we are "half and half" or "hybrids."

This is Martha's First Life planet, the same as yours and mine. BUT this is her first appearance in the flesh—and she will make the normal exit and progression. As far as I know, she would not normally make a return visit. To my knowledge, Martha's background has not been the same as either yours or mine. *At the peril of seeming to reverse myself,* I might remark this extenuating sentence or two: I presume Martha's presence here to be a normal residence—although the procedure in similar operations is that the woman that the man marries is usually prepared long aforetime. For all that I definitely know, Martha's presence here may have a part in all this planning—beyond just that of "wife." IF this is so, I know nothing of it—though it could be perfectly possible without my having any recognition of it. So again I say, to be definitely truthful, I do not know of my own knowledge anything else but that Martha is perfectly normal as to entrance to this Life and perfectly normal as to exit. And again I say it could all be different—I do not know.

The hybrids are of a great number. Their entire efforts, fleshed or unfleshed, are spent in some useful and helpful endeavor on this, their First Life planet. These hybrids were not highly developed Souls at the time the accident and mistake occurred which held them here. They were perfectly normal released Souls at that time. It has been their experiences since that time which have advanced them beyond the normal. You are not the normal human. Neither am I. You know it—and so do I.

ALL of the humans existing here are on their First Life planet. However, remember that there are always fleshed entities here from other dimensions on missions of one kind or another—always for the betterment of mankind. I have no knowledge of their number. There are also always a number of hybrids so operating. I have no knowledge of their number.

ALL hybrids are members of the Order of Melchisedek. They are the only members. This of course also applies in answer to the question regarding the Catholic Priest. He is a hybrid and a member of the great Order.

You will pass from this dimension directly and in full to the second dimension and no further until you have earned the right to ascend to the third dimension by way of the second so-called "death." There will be, of course, some recompense for the service as a hybrid. I have no knowledge of what it would be.

You will not become IN FULL a member of the second dimension until you pass to it by way of the "first death," so-called, from the first dimension. As a hybrid enfleshed, you will so advance from here when your mission is concluded. NONE of the hybrids have been released until this present year.

As I have before written, the simple passage from this dimension does in no way change the real YOU. Neither Capone or Dillinger, or any other murderer, will be changed to any other identity. It is ALL an individual proposition—ALL THE WAY THROUGH. Capone and Dillinger, and all other murderers or other criminal types, will be exactly the same in passage to the next dimension and will so continue until they make their own ascendant progress. After a certain period, if there is no progress, and on the proper and orderly presentation of such facts before the ANCIENTS OF DAYS sitting in judgment over such and other great matters, on a finding by them, "LIFE" is withdrawn from such ascendant Souls, and they are no more.

I do not know the procedure in the matter of additional enfleshed experiences for entities above the second dimension, but I do know that enfleshed entities from such higher dimensions do appear on earth missions. The appearance of hybrids enfleshed in this dimension for the purpose of accomplishing missions is probably more frequent in occurrence—but I do not know for certain.

To my own knowledge, Martha is not a hybrid. She MAY be—it is perfectly possible—but if so, I do not know it of my own knowledge.

The "blue man" disappeared. I do not know the reason why. There is nothing strange in the color—we still have the other colored men—white—black—yellow—brown.

Poltergeists have an Intelligence as a background. As do other phenomena of the same order—simply called "ghosts." They are exactly the same. Make no mistake about the validity of both. It is probably too large a subject to be cleared in a few sentences, or a page, of writing. I have often remarked that the same individual YOU continues to exist after passage from this dimension by way of death. This YOU does not remain on this planet. If so, they too would be hybrids—at least as far as their activity is concerned. But they have no such jurisdiction. They simply are transported from this planet.

However, there is no such thing as Time or Distance. How quickly can you "think" of California—or Marion?? Instantly, of course. Just so, no matter to what planet these ascending Souls are adjudicated, they can instantly remove themselves by "thought" or "concentration" to the planet of their leaving. They do not personally appear BUT it is perfectly possible, under certain psychological conditions, for certain Intelligences to make their identity known through the surroundings of their former earth life OR through individuals in the flesh who have, above others, certain sensibilities that are not very much understood or even recognized by physicists and scientists. In fact, most of the public and all the physicists and most scientific men ridicule and "pooh pooh" the idea of such claims. However, there are such—physicists and scientists to the contrary—who allow the projection of a specter of themselves and incidents of their past existence to appear, through these certain "sensitives," to the visual attunement of the usual human optic. This very same phenomenon also pertains to the organs of hearing.

You will observe this development from another angle when you see the artist, musician, author, mathematician, and others whose equipment is developed at birth far above the normal. Just so, there are some people who, under certain conditions, can use their particular overdevelopment to assist, with the cooperation with the entity, the production of these TRUE Astral visibilities to the human eye. The former physical surroundings of certain entities of those in the second dimension also, on occasion, do operate. However, these appearances to humans are not countenanced by jurisdictional Intelligences of the second dimension, and are accomplished only with loss to the entity that allows such manifestations to occur with their collaboration.

Make no mistake however in believing that there are uncounted numbers of these *unseen* entities present at all times in this dimension. All occupied on tasks of one kind or another, in Orders of different kinds. Take notice, too, I beg of you, that most of the so-called phenomena of the kind under discussion is charlatanry, produced for money by human trickery, and is entirely false so far as having any true spiritual background.

I am so glad to receive the information from Lasky regarding the Mark Twain picture. I do hope that it all goes through—and soon.

Thanks so much for your continuing effort to build the physical. You can do it if you so WILL.

I am thankful that you are beginning to appreciate Sleep. Someday when the stress for these other things has passed, I do so hope to be able to tell you more about Sleep—the "little sister of death."

Gravity is a celestial Law under the direct supervision of the Great Intelligence, and none but Him knows its makeup or method of operation.

Remember, this is your First Life planet. You have made other flesh appearances here than the one you are now representing. It remains true that although you have presented yourself in the flesh here more than once, you have never left this planet, and it remains your FIRST LIFE PLANET.

I have written another LONG letter. Surely enough for this time. My old body has a heart condition of long standing. It lays me down suddenly on occasions. It will very probably be the manner and means by which I will be released from here.

With all good thought over and under and around you ALL and with much love from Ma Loose and myself, I am,

HAROLD SHERMAN to HARRY LOOSE

New York, April 8, 1941

Friend Loose:

Your most welcome long letter at hand which Martha and I have carefully read and reread and will go over many times in the future until the full import of all you have said sinks in . . . or calls forth the knowledge from us as a reawakening.

I can see the wisdom of your putting what we should know on paper . . . and I would wish to continue such procedure when we arrive in California, since this gives us a chance to review the thoughts time and again . . . instead of depending upon human memory from having such facts "told to us by word of mouth." For true development I can readily comprehend that a written exchange of thoughts can have a more profound and lasting value.

Let me ask—is much of the knowledge you are revealing to me known to my inner identity as the IBERIAN? Have we both had intervals when we have been aware of all that has happened to us thus far . . . and made our conscious, voluntary choice of services we have desired to render in what earth regards as "future time"?

I presume, with our operating in twos, that your mission is not completed until mine is accomplished . . . essentially. In other words, I have borne as great a responsibility in my way toward you as you have borne to me. It has been as necessary for me to fulfill my tests and complete my development . . . as it has been for you to lead me and to help give me strength and wisdom?

Obviously, much that we must know in our very souls is withheld. I have little or no conscious knowledge or recollection now of "tree planting," etc. I have not had time to "get back to nature" with this drive that is in me to gain the experience I sense I must have. But I have dreamed of a day when I might be able to meditate and to crystallize, away from the pressure of big city living, the thoughts I feel deep down within my being.

"MARK TWAIN" will be a great spiritual picture. You will THRILL when you may know of my great cosmic beginning and ending . . . and the other inspirational touches I am weaving naturally into the story. I hope "MARK TWAIN" will open up the opportunities for me to do things in PICTURES, on the RADIO and STAGE never heretofore presented . . . leaving a lasting impress on human consciousness!!

I possess now, through years of preparation, a knowledge of the technique of expression in all these mediums, as I have stated before . . . and I have sensed, for years, that I must make every sacrifice to gain this knowledge . . . that *great ideas* would be given me to be put in the *guise of entertainment* for humanity's enlightenment. I have striven through the years, never losing sight of this objective, secure in the faith that when the proper time came, the IDEAS would be revealed to me and I would find myself in position to carry them out!

Martha and I spent an interesting, revealing day at Bernard's in Nyack. He, together with Schafer, is a rank impostor as you say. He has sold a bill of goods to many idle rich who want to "play" at spiritual things in a recreational background for body and mind with emphasis upon sex. We talked for two hours with the "Omnipotent Oom" in his private library and I asked him testing, fundamental questions. He expounded expansively, smoking big black cigars the while and spitting in the general direction of the big fireplace. Whenever he used words a little too big for him, he couldn't spit over his chin. But his was the voice of authority; he is interested in no opinions but his own; he is the Oracle of Delphi and all other oracles thrown in, and there must be no other intellectual or other gods before him! We have seen enough of such man-made monstrosities . . . and will withdraw, as you suggest, from such observations in the future.

I had known of O'Fallon [*sic*], of course, and recall his tragic crackup. . . .

I am interested in what you say about the economic. There is increasing evidence that the MARK TWAIN deal is moving toward early culmination . . . meanwhile the last vestiges of economic struggle are hanging on to the very end of this difficult cycle . . . but I can sense that this whole condition is going to change soon . . . and I will be liberated to enter a field of intense service activity when I will not be weighed down by such matters.

My health condition is improving. I do not know what your impression was of the picture we sent you . . . but I have sensed a vast improvement in poise and outward and inner calm during the past year. Martha has always been my balance wheel . . . she has done and is doing the very things you suggest. Words can never convey my appreciation of her great, untiring and unfailing service to me. I do SO wish you could meet her in the flesh.

Will I have to wait until the Book of Urantia is published before I can have access to it or those in this dimension responsible for its execution?

I await eagerly your ability to tell me the true story of the crucifixion. Was I on earth at this time, the time of Jesus' mission here?

I also, at the proper time, would like to know more of the mystery of sleep—"the little sister of death."

Your comments on the Eskimo were of interest. What controls SIZE of any creation in life? Is it significant that some races are short and stunted . . . and that some people are midgets, etc.? Of course, there must be a reason why many souls are born into this FIRST LIFE PLANET, for a first life experience, CRIPPLED? How is this explained when they apparently do not have an equal opportunity for advancement, unfoldment and activity on this dimension? What explains the varying grades of consciousness and awareness among peoples IF this is their FIRST LIFE EXPERIENCE? What prevents them from starting on a seemingly equal basis of understanding, etc.?

Is there a condition BEFORE a first life experience which has determined the state of consciousness of the first life human?

Have we come up through so-called lower earth forms to the HUMAN level? I once had a vivid impression, awakening from a sleep state, that I existed in the form of an enormous lobster with conical shaped head, dark brown or black in color, with long extended feelers . . . and that my hands were great claws. I actually got this sensation that I was alive in this body and, momentarily and vividly, I seemed to exist in this form, while lying in bed. The impression died away from me slowly . . . and I was amazed at the sensation that my consciousness was *just the same* . . . and that I felt perfectly naturally in this body encasement which would ordinarily have seemed repulsive to me, as I would have viewed a lobster's form while aware that I existed in a human body. Awake and with my eyes open, this impression of this body form lingered an appreciable moment and I held up one arm to look at it, seeing it in the form of a great claw! It was uncanny the instant it lasted and has given me much thought. Can you explain it?

Do we reach a state BEYOND the so-called LIFE STATE as we progress through the seven dimensions? Who are the Ancients of Days and do they relate to the Order of the Finality? And why are these "borders" between universes being closed?

Oh, there is SO MUCH that I yearn to know . . . and it will be an indescribable privilege to be able to see and converse with Intelligences from the higher dimensions! My one desire is to be found WORTHY and entirely capable of fully assuming ALL RESPONSIBILITIES that may ultimately be assigned me.

I believe I am not so far from conquering the "death fear." I have been close a number of times . . . almost as though these periods were a testing to see how I would react. I have an absolutely TERRIFIC determination to SURMOUNT all obstacles and conditions which might lead to my demise BEFORE my mission is accomplished. This URGE is deeply ingrained in me. But I can sense, too, that when my inner self will know, beyond all doubt, that my mission has been performed . . . I will be GLAD to go!

What a glorious release it will be for us BOTH, with our missions here satisfactorily executed! The realization which must come of the long path we have trod toward this moment! I will be unrelenting in my pursuit of the steps I must take from this time on . . . and with such help as yours, I have no concern for the future!

Martha and I wish to express our gratitude again for all that you and Ma Loose have done for us.

Our LOVE and our BEST THOUGHTS go out to you.

P.S. Martha feels that I should now send a description of *this* experience to you![11]

HARRY LOOSE to HAROLD SHERMAN

Monterey Park, April 11, 1941

My Friend:-

I am glad that you recognize the reason I have been writing you of these matters in preference to their being a voice proposition. At

---

[11] The record of this experience has not been identified.

this stage, it is better that such preparatory information as I am allowed to give you is by way of writing. As you say, you may refresh your memory at any time by rereading instead of trusting to memory. Also, this written information will be helpful in the writing of your book of these matters.

Remember, in these letters I am not even "scratching the surface."

I am writing so extensively for *many reasons*. It is not regularly done in similar developments. My writing, as fully as I have been permitted, is to try to prepare your perception for greater matters to follow. I am trying to arouse in you what you have already evidenced fully—ability you have—interest you have—your mind is opening—you have receptivity and capacity to understand—your mental development is good—you are a perfect sensitive—you have feared much—and most of the things you have feared have not happened—in Martha you have a perfect balance—your physical and nervous must have care and attention—you do not relax and "let go" readily yet—you worry and magnify trifles sometimes—your WILL is fine—you can correct all the adverse, with Martha's willing cooperation.

I am now answering your questions.

Your beginning goes much further back than the Iberian. I only identify the Iberian to your consciousness because he was together with me on an operation in the flesh at that time. I try by mention of the Iberian to arouse a possible latent memory in the subconsciousness. With this possible memory would come such and other associated memories that would help to build back other fleshed and unfleshed recognition. You already have a starting point in your "dream-visions." I read the one enclosed in your last—the misty curtain that hangs between waved a bit for you—you were just visualizing a tiny bit at the edge of the second dimension. I am waiting to turn the several dreams over to another entity for verification of my several analyses.

I know my telling you of the great bird in my last letter might be hard for you to visualize but nevertheless it is very accurate and true. As you continue, you will learn many other very strange things to your developing consciousness.

Yes. You have borne just as great a responsibility, or greater, as I have borne. No. My part of this mission is completed. My work is done. Yours is about to begin *knowingly*.

Your time for meditation will come and so will gradually arrive your remembrance of the long past—as you develop and are developed.

I am glad for your expressions regarding Bernard and Schafer. I knew that you could not be fooled. You have a more *real* knowledge right now than these two men together have. *And* you are in a position to know a great deal more. You will get many quiet laughs at past part-beliefs as you go onward. I would here suggest again that you do not confuse yourself anymore with similar charlatans. "Come out and be ye separate"—Christ.

The economic will be adjusted to your satisfaction.

The picture [you sent] of Martha was a little indefinite but her letters were positive enough. She is all that I expected. Her care, cooperation and mental companionship, plus your really good body, blood, and mental vigor—all these have sustained you. Yes, your health condition should be greatly improving—with your now knowledge—with Martha's knowledge—and with what I have been sending you.

You will have to await the publishing of the Book of Urantia before having access to it. You will probably meet some of those in the second dimension who had to do with it before meeting those in this dimension who aided in its building.

I am writing against time. I do not know when I will be told to cease. But if I get the time, I would like to write you more of the Eskimo and more of the mystery of sleep. There are literally thousands and thousands of things that I would like to write to you of to aid in the development. I know that I will never be allowed the time so to do. You will advance by other means than mine.

NO. We never came up through lower earth forms to the human level. We came here as animals, that is true, but there was a difference. Man began the long struggle upwards—groping—and by torturous, painful and tedious ways. When, at the proper time in his searching and seeking, came the Great Intelligence, who mixed the then human-animal with the implantation of higher developments brought here by convoy transportation from older and further advanced First Life planets. And also, by the introduction of Adam and Eve and Lilith[12]—who all really lived—and who were really enfleshed

---

[12] A female demon of Jewish folklore, somewhat equivalent to a vampire. In the Rabbinical literature Lilith becomes the first wife of Adam, but flies away from him and becomes a demon. Lilith is not mentioned in the Urantia teachings.

spirituals. From then on, the ascent of man was much accelerated.[13] The different colors of man comes from the implantations from other First Life but further advanced planets, away back in the beginning of things.[14] Adam DID disobey his instructions from the Great Intelligence and so did Eve. Lilith did not. The punishment of Adam and Eve was much similar to the way that the Bible states. And it was at this time, in the confusion of things, that the great accident and mistake occurred that resulted in the "hybrid."

No. There is no condition before the First Life experience. Before that time, that bit of the Great Intelligence that is now YOU rested as a part of HIM.

The question that you ask about the cripple is answered by Jesus in the New Testament. He was asked, "Did this man or his parents sin, that he be born blind?" And Jesus answered, "Neither did this man nor his parents sin, but that the works of God might be made manifest in him." It is not clear to me, but this is his answer. This answer can also apply to the question regarding the different grades of mentality. However, the same soul—the same bit of the Great Intelligence—resides in each the same.

Now to tell you of a peculiar happening. I had asked for the story of the crucifixion and sat at my old typewriter waiting. You saying that you would like it in your last letter had started me. I knew that it would be a long story, as I had received it before several times. I started to type as the voice came through, and at once recognized that it was not the story of the crucifixion but something else. It seems to be copies of letters sent between Pontius Pilate and the Roman emperors of the time—and Herod—and then an account of Pilate's trial and death evidently from some records of the time.[15] It was the first time that I had heard it and it was quite interesting to me. Anyway, I

---

[13] *The result of the gift of the Adamic life plasm to the mortal races is an immediate upstepping of intellectual capacity and an acceleration of spiritual progress. There is usually some physical improvement also* (52:3.6).

[14] Compare: *On an average evolutionary planet the six evolutionary races of color appear one by one; the red man is the first to evolve, and for ages he roams the world before the succeeding colored races make their appearance. The simultaneous emergence of all six races on Urantia, and in one family, was most unusual* (64:6.1).

[15] Loose copied these from "Letters of Herod and Pilate: Connecting Roman History with the Death of Christ at Jerusalem," in *The Apocryphal Books of the New Testament* (Philadelphia: David McKay, publisher, 1890, 1901).

am sending it along in this letter hoping it will be enlightening and of interest.[16]

Now that was the first peculiar thing. The second one was the arrival of the information on the partly typed sheet at the front of this letter.[17] It is from an entirely different entity. It has nothing to do with the Pontius Pilate reports, etc.[18] The voice stopped just at the end of the sentence and there was no more. I waited nearly an hour for a continuance but nothing came. I do not understand it at all. It has absolutely nothing to do with the Pilate information. Anyway, I am sending it along. I may receive more to go with it. Will make inquiry anyway.

There are no "borders" between the different Universes. The Order of the Finality has to do with the final closing of the borders around ALL the Universes. As a fence around a whole apple—not around a dimension of the apple.

The Ancients of Days are mentioned in your Bible. Look them up. They have existed for aeons of time before this planet ever was. They are very high spiritual entities who have to do with the very important adjudication regarding ALL Universes. This includes the withdrawal of Life from a non-advancing Soul.

You will meet higher Intelligences as you advance and KEEP THE FAITH and the physical and nervous conditions are righted— you will begin to meet them knowingly in about 3 years. That is the usual pace of development.

I am subject to accidents—mistakes—honest errors in judg-ment—just the same as any other human. Nowhere is there perfec-tion. Nowhere is there infallibility. I am some corrected and told to make such correction to you. I am told to tell you that there is a posi-tive intelligence behind a legitimate "ghost." It is a true astral projec-tion from its original by operations that are not fully understood by me, and even that which I do understand is not yet explainable to you. To accomplish such astral production, or reproduction, requires the presence of a borderline sensitive in the flesh who is capable of retaining more of the average force of elemental so-called "electric"

[16] See Appendix D.
[17] See Appendix E.
[18] Some of the message's information seems to have come from the article, "Agrippina (elder)," in *Encyclopaedia Britannica*.

earth forces derived from the usual and regular accepted sources of such forces by way of what is here designated the "Aurora Borealis." Such forces are depleted in the human sensitive in such operation and such sensitives are early exhausted by the drain and loss of real power. The real borderline sensitive will tell you later in the progress of such production, "I feel the power leaving me"—"I am getting weaker. The power is going"—"The reception is failing me," etc.

Now as to the poltergeist. I am further instructed to tell you that *most* such demonstrations are occasioned by Intelligences that occupy the same celestial position that you occupy—the "hybrid"—who is then not operative on a flesh mission. Remember, humor is one of the things that you take with you when you go to the next dimension. And the activities of the hybrids in the phenomena they exhibit in poltergeist activities bears witness of this humor continuance. Remember, the unfleshed hybrid sees you and your reactions to such phenomena—and is entertained and amused by it. Remember, too, that ALL so-called "poltergeist" demonstrations are not caused by the unfleshed hybrid. The balance of other so-called "poltergeist" phenomena is at present unexplainable.

You see, in your present state of fleshed hybrid for mission purposes, you are still a hybrid until your present mission is concluded. You then proceed fully into the second dimension because of the ruling I have before written you about. In your other many flesh appearances, on the conclusion of such flesh appearance by way of death of the flesh, you would return to your continued hybrid state of *an earthbound spirit*—unable to leave here and fully enter the second dimension. In this hybrid spirit state, you would continue here on this planet in this invisible spirit form occupied with many duties until you would again volunteer, or be chosen, for another earth-mission in the flesh. All this because of this intricate mistake and accident happening away back in the beginning of things on this planet, as I have before explained. On leaving here this time, you will proceed fully to the second dimension and not be held here, earth bound, as you would have continued to be if the ruling affecting all hybrids had not happened, as I have before explained.

You have not been in any way responsible for the body's illness. It is the heart of the body that has weakened—and then it is real physical age.

Well, you again have a great deal to read in all that I am sending you today. I am hoping you are rereading and keeping abreast of things as I write. I do not believe that I will be permitted to write much longer.

With LOVE from both Ma and myself to you ALL and with the best thought over and under and around you all, I am,

HAROLD SHERMAN to HARRY LOOSE

New York, April 15, 1941

Friend Loose:

If you are not even "scratching the surface" you are going to have something TERRIFIC for me to release to the world by the time I am developed enough to receive it all and to confirm it by my own experience and knowledge!!!

I recognize the TRUTH of your statements but feel that I must experience contact with Higher Intelligences *myself* to give me the force of conviction I will need to face the world with such a book and with the various presentations which may be required of me through radio, stage and screen—and other means of reaching human consciousness en masse.

With regard to your assurance re the economic, I seem to be going through the last trying stages betwixt and between highly promising developments—consideration of the book *Thoughts Through Space* and final consummation of the Mark Twain picture deal . . . among others.

I am trying to hold myself free from other writing entanglements which could only be potboilers and not contribute to the big objectives toward which I have been striving. By yielding to economic pressure and taking on work which gets me nowhere, I close out the real opportunities when they are ready to happen. Developing the faith and "guts" to stand by during such periods has taken a bit of "doing" in times past. I'm sure you understand. But as you say, we have always been helped—seemingly at the last moment, in many instances.

It is an indescribable spiritual thrill to Martha and me each time one of your letters arrives in our house. We go off by ourselves, in my study, and read it aloud, absorbing and discussing as we go. Then we often reread many of your letters upon retiring . . . and I then relax and send out the call for contact with you . . . and drop off to sleep. I have been sleeping the nights through and awakening refreshed . . .

and my general condition is much improved. I played tennis four times this past week and am in the process of reducing—I hope! Still weigh 180 stripped . . . can you imagine that, from the thin-faced, slender young fellow you once saw?

While it probably was difficult to study the features, I thought that was a particularly good picture of Martha. She is the one on the LEFT as you look at the picture . . . NOT in the center, as I think she wrote you. Do you know—I had kept a picture of you, cut from a Redpath window card, for years . . . and Martha, in meditation after your first letter arrived, was impressed to destroy it. She did this without consulting me, a most unusual procedure, since we have considered all things of this nature as possessions in common. She said she felt as though you would not want us to look at your face as it was then . . . or to personalize you in this way. I, humanly, would have liked a really good photograph of you. Perhaps you can add some light to this!

The messages you received—apparently, as you say, *copies of letters sent between Pontius Pilate and the Roman emperors* of the time— were most interesting. I have had a feeling that *I* may have existed in *that day* also . . . and it is significant that the *other* message from the entirely different entity, intended for *me*, described a human or fleshed experience in the *same* period! I do not yet comprehend the full reason why this information should have been given me.

Strangely enough, I have wondered much WHY I should have had to be born and held prisoner on this little ball of earth . . . where so much hatred abounds and where a race of people called JEWS have crucified a CHRIST. And it has come to me that I might, as a Gentile, later bring forth some information which would do much to bring a BALANCE between all races . . . and do away with present HATREDS! Dr. Wanderman is of Jewish blood—and if all Jews were possessed of his high quality of character and integrity and humanity—they would be a credit to any and every race! Thank heaven I have kept free of all such hates and prejudices!

Let me ask—when this bit of the Great Intelligence which is NOW ME once departs from the FATHER on the long journey of INDIVIDUALIZATION . . . does it remain FOREVER cognizant of its IDENTITY in and with the FATHER, once this realization has come?

I still fail to see the justice in some humans being born, for the first time, crippled, blind, etc. while others are born with much great-

DETECTIVE
HARRY J. LOOSE
of the
CHICAGO POLICE DEPARTMENT

The photo of Harry Loose on the Redpath window card
[SPECIAL COLLECTIONS DEPARTMENT, UNIVERSITY OF IOWA LIBRARIES].

er advantages, UNLESS it is a matter of KARMA and they have carried these conditions over from some past life experiences in which they have failed to live up to certain universal laws and are now paying the penalty for their own acts . . . and are being given again an opportunity to fulfill the law and make God's work manifest in them!

I have thought many times—HOW DO I KNOW but what the SAME INTELLIGENCE which says "I AM I" in me—is not also saying "I AM I" in you . . . and but for a different individualized experience, we are ACTUALLY ONE AND THE SAME . . . in GOD or UNIVERSAL MIND?!

MY—the things I want to discuss with you—and the limitations of words and paper and time!!

Thanks for your clearer delineation of ghosts and poltergeists.

I am MOST EAGER to gain a knowledge of what happens DURING SLEEP! (The little sister of death, as you put it.)

The great bird description was thrilling and the import not missed by me. Sometimes I neglect to comment on an item such as this which has much impressed me.

With ways to PROVE the existence of these things . . . can you picture how WORLD SHOCKING a book—then a motion picture, of such conditions COULD BE . . . how it would tend to revolutionize thought and actions?

It seems to me that modern inventions are demonstrating to mass mind the POWER and REALITY of the INVISIBLE. There should come a time, with this world cataclysm reaching its zenith . . . and all material things taken away, when mankind will reach out for REAL KNOWLEDGE. At that time I hope I am fully ready to perform my service. I have known, since a boy, that I was going to live through one of the greatest upheavals ever to occur on this planet! Am I right? I can *feel* it coming! TREMENDOUS FORCES are gathering in anticipation of the event . . . a time when all humanity will tremble in the balance and real spiritual leadership must come forth to SAVE IT!

I received an astonishing confirmation of a dream or vision impression which came to me the night of JUNE 10, 1940, in last Sunday's *New York Times,* which news story was headlined: "BRAIN TRUST" WINS GERMAN VICTORIES . . . etc. the account going on to state how all German military plans were devised and executed by a staff of men trained in army, navy and air warfare—experts of all kinds forming a "brain trust board," laying out campaigns months and years before their actual operation.

Laurie Bowen, the man I mention in my "dream impression" was a boyhood friend—one of the highest and finest of young men I have ever known. He had a transcendent personality—actually seemed like a soul from another world . . . was a marvelous athlete, a true sportsman and a perfect gentleman . . . I would like your evaluation of this *experience* I went through with "him."[19] All hybrids are, of course, not highly developed. Were we more highly developed than most— and *caught* in the flesh—on a mission of service . . . at the time of the great accident and mistake? It is a privilege beyond words to be a member of this ancient order. You speak of the NUMBER being limited . . . and then again of us hybrids all being members of the order of Melchisedek. Can you clarify this? (I mean—all hybrids.)

Can you get any grasp of or throw any light on the ULTIMATE PURPOSE of the GREAT INTELLIGENCE in HIS universes? Or is this ULTIMATE PURPOSE in itself INFINITE and ETERNAL? How much are we CREATURES of FREE WILL and FREE CHOICE?

I would also like to gain a greater understanding of the great illusion TIME . . . and also SPACE . . . as regards our finite comprehension . . . I know THOUGHT transcends both easily.

I was most interested in your description of the vital forces that flow into this earth from the north to the south poles and the electrical display which occurs when souls are borne through the earth plane en route to other planets, etc. I would think, in great world catastrophes, when thousands upon thousands of humans are killed, that there would be electrical disturbances, etc., also . . . as souls "take off" for other planets, under guidance of higher intelligences?

Here is another question: WHY is a rock a ROCK and NOT a flower . . . or a HUMAN? And to what can a ROCK *aspire*? Does it have a rate and character and type of development consistent with its nature . . . or is it all a PART of INFINITE INTELLIGENCE and thus, really a PART of US . . . and we of IT? (This is pretty profound . . . but I've sometimes felt a strange and awesome kinship with all that exists!!)

I think this is a good letter to include also an amazing impression I received several years ago . . . Whenever in a certain sensitized

---

[19] See Appendix F.

mood I have asked myself a profound question . . . I have, on occasion, felt an overpowering URGE within me to pick up a pencil . . . that the answer was *welling* up in me, from some mysterious source . . . and I have written at great speed, with no CONSCIOUS thought, the ANSWER! Here is one of the cases in point.[20] What do you make of this, under date of February 22, 1939 . . . "Can there be any up and down in the universe?"

I do hope and pray that the other intelligences having supervision over your work will grant you permission to continue your work with me for a time . . . since I am gaining so very much from it, as is Martha! Until other intelligences put in their appearance—I know I shall miss you almost irreparably! . . . WILL IT BE POSSIBLE, DO YOU THINK, FOR YOU TO CONTACT ME FROM THE SECOND DIMENSION, WHEN YOU REACH IT . . . AND WILL YOU BE ABLE KNOWINGLY TO MANIFEST TO ME ON OCCASION . . . (*KNOWINGLY*, FROM MY STANDPOINT)?

I am sure when things are better organized . . . with the Mark Twain matter settled and my own plans laid . . . and I can give more time to meditation . . . perhaps under the inspiration of living west . . . I can begin to receive direct impressions and knowledge, much after the fashion you have developed. I would welcome demonstrations from other intelligences who have a work for me to do . . . and are interested in aiding me.

I have given thanks to the Higher Intelligences for your great service to me . . . and have prayed that I might NOT BE FOUND WANTING . . . when the TIME COMES for me to assume my full share of responsibility. With MARTHA at my side, I KNOW I can do the mission assigned me . . . and with such help and guidance as you are giving . . . I'll work night and day to be worthy!

OUR LOVE to Ma Loose and yourself in an unending stream!

IMPRESSION   *New York, February 22, 1939*
At 5:30 o'clock this morning, having spent a wakeful, painful night, due to the stomach disturbance that has been plaguing me, off and on, for months, I suddenly started to doze off and had the sensation of being in *limitless space.* Above and beneath me was an awesome void. There was no sensation of falling but a vital wonderment forced its way into my consciousness:

---

[20] Impression of February 22, 1939, follows this letter.

"Can there be any up or down in the universe?"

With this wonderment came an inner feeling that the answer existed coincidental with the question—that it was even then trying to express itself through my mind.

I was so physically weary that I tried to throw these impressions off but they persisted and I finally got up, being on the cot in my study, picked up pencil and paper, and wrote the following at *high speed*:

There is no up and down. The Universe extends in all directions from an endless succession of equa-centers. These centers are superimposed upon one another and synchronized with the center of every being in the cosmos so that each thing—animate and inanimate—is equi-distant from the equa-center or core which is forever expanding in an eternality of space-time!

The illusion is that the Universe has one center at some fixed point in space is due to man's finite concept. Actually we are all at that center through our at-one-ness with the creative elements manifesting in us.

There is naught in the universe but a center; there could only have been one focal point, not as Mankind thinks of focal points, but when it is said that "God is not in any one place but everywhere," and when Christ said: "Where my Father is, there I am also," it is meant that the most infinitesimal expression of our inadequate concept of God is centered in His Being—the bosom of the Universe.

The *forms* of this expression are as infinite as the radiations from this center and the movements of this center are always circular.

Our bodies are whirling in their own molecular space, following the vibratory pattern set up at the moment of conception when the new energies were individualized, permitting the union of our identities which *themselves* are revolving around a spiral center, taking on higher speeds of vibratory revolution and demanding, as they do so, more and more refined cellular houses for our habitat, made necessary through our increasing awareness and comprehension of the God force in action!

We cannot die out of the Universe any more than we can be born out of it. We could not have helped our being, since all that IS has always existed and no-one can conceive anything that is not. Nothing can ever be less than it is, though it can constantly alter its form.

Up and down in the universe—heaven as an imagined state *above;* and hell as an imagined state *below*—all these are false and childish concepts.

The entire universe is *inside ourselves,* and this is the mystery of BEING. We are searching through telescopes and microscopes for the center of things in some remote place from whence all energies flow.

God said, as the Bible symbolically reports: "Let there be light," and there *was* light. But where and from what place came the voice of God?

The union of centers or concentric relationship of all things establishes a center of balance that accounts for what is termed "gravitation." It is the force that gives to all matter a pulsation.

The voice of God is then the infinitely varying wave-lengths of this pulsation expressing forever-now in the infinite forms of worlds and stars and suns and all things and creatures thereon.

Up and down? How can there be an up and down to a center? Heaven and hell, as fixed localities, are non-existent—but AT-ONE-NESS with GOD—the Universe—is the GREAT REALITY!

6

ARA,
THE THOUGHT ADJUSTER

HARRY LOOSE to HAROLD SHERMAN

Monterey Park, April 20, 1941

My Friend:-

May I thank you for your two fine letters.[1] I am sitting here at the old typewriter again and it feels good. The old body creaks and groans and lays me down suddenly sometimes. However, it has been very kind and good to me for so many earth years. You have both asked questions and I want to answer all that I can permissibly.

Yes, it is a fact that the very little that I have written you is not even "scratching the surface" of the VERY LITTLE that I know. And the very tiny bit that I know is again VERY FAR from "scratching the surface" of what is known in the full second dimension. Please read the above over and over again.

It is far from possible to explain understandably to the mental capacity of an African aborigine the mechanical workings of the radio—the telephone—the airship, etc., ad infinitum. It is all far beyond his mental capacity to comprehend. It is just as impossible for me to explain to undeveloped human understanding very much of the mechanics, and the reasons therefor, of the operation of what is humanly termed the celestial. *Even the much-developed human mind is very*

---
[1] Martha's letter has not been preserved.

circumscribed and limited in its ability to comprehend. "Thus far shalt thou go and no further." You should now recognize quite fully the "why" of my oft-repeated statement, "I know so very little." There is so *very* much that I would so like to be informed about—exactly the same as you—but, from long trial, I find that with my present limited human mental capacity, I can go no further. . . .

Remember, PLEASE, that you have only known what you really are for a few months and have had only little embryonic bits given you in these letters, whereas I have known and have been taught for fifty years. And yet I have never been a teacher—though I would so liked to have been given the permission to teach you. Will not Marcia know more and be able to comprehend more 10 years from now—and again in 10 more years from that time? However, do not place yourself in the same position as either the aborigine or of Marcia. I am only using an illustration to convey—you are not in the same position because, you see, you have a background of preparation and spiritual and quasi-spiritual help in these understandings. If, for instance, I were to try to tell you some of the things NOW that you are to learn later little by little, you would neither believe nor be able to understand. It would be very harmful to you to be given that which is yet far beyond you—and, so, would very much retard the continuing development. . . .

My work is now done. Yours is but beginning—unless, in the last analysis, you are finally "weighed in the balance and found wanting." I have brought you up to your awakening with much satisfaction. You are a very fine development up to now—except for the physical and nervous condition—and I have two reports from your Thought Adjuster telling me of your real physical improvements—though not so great in the nervous or worry state that you still periodically indulge in. He also reports that the Myocarditic matter is stationary. Though these reports came from your Thought Adjuster direct, they did not come to me direct from him, but from him to another Intelligence, and from that Intelligence to me. I do so hope that I continue to occasionally receive such reports—of your progress. It is not a regular thing to receive such reports in operations of this kind—it just so happened that such came to me in an irregular way.

Sometime, when you have a quiet few moments, I am so very hopeful that you can sit very still and get a start on getting acquainted with your Thought Adjuster. Ask him questions and listen for his answer. He knows you better than you know yourself. You may, or may not, be able to converse with him the first few trials. You may be very successful the very first time, I do not know. Please know that this very Thought Adjuster is a very real and true and living identity from the full second dimension that resides with you and is absolutely separate and distinct from your Soul—or your material intelligence or instinct. You will find him always with you awake or asleep—he does not sleep. "If you take him one mile, he will take you two more miles." He will counsel and advise you, always to your benefit, but you will have your own individual choice of your WILL and following actions. You will soon find, however, that his advice is always for your best interests—and that he knows much more than your human intelligence.

It will take a little time and concentration, but to get acquainted and friendly with him will be much to your benefit. Remember, he is of the second dimension and knows much more and better. After a time—with much practice perhaps—you will find that you can talk with him at any time and he will talk back to you and reason with you as a distinct and separate identity. Please remember that in much of your future advancement, you will receive help from him. And, this is very important, a part of your continued learning depends on your closeness with him.

Read the following carefully. ***** The Sages, the mystics, the "wise men" of India, ad infinitum, are those who have been taught, or those who have learned by themselves through meditation, HOW to commune with their Thought Adjusters. They spend much time with them and through this cultivated friendship, they learn much—and they do things with the body that seem not possible. Please do as advised. Help me to help you. If you do not succeed at first—try and try again—you will be successful in the end. It is a part of "understanding." Sometimes I am a bit fearful as I very well know the old maxim, "Many are called and few are chosen"—I have seen it happen.

Enclosed please find a very good snapshot taken a week ago. Remember in the future that a side-face picture is always SAFE and a full face picture NEVER is.

I just happened to think of something of quite some interest to you. Through the Intelligence from whom I received the good report from your Thought Adjuster, I also learned quite something about

The snapshot Harry Loose sent to the Shermans, taken mid-April 1941
[Sherman Family Private Collection].

him. His First Life planet—his earth name at that time—and what his occupation was. I would like to get the [*Ed. note:* Sentence ended here.]

I must leave this letter unfinished and send as it is. I have just received instructions to cease my writing—and to report. I do not know if this means a complete and permanent quittal or not. I presume that it is although I will continue to hope for a release of the order. I hope that you have not been doing anything that you should not. Have you violated confidence in any way?? Remember—I warned you. If you have not, there is nothing to fear. There is so very much that I would so liked to have been able to permissibly give you.

With much love to you ALL and with the great and good thought under and over and around you ALL.

HAROLD SHERMAN to HARRY LOOSE

New York, April 24, 1941

Friend Loose:

It is strange that last Sunday night I was inspired, on retiring, to pick up the Bible and open it at random, with the feeling there would be a specific message there for me. I opened to the Fourteenth Chapter of St. John and read it through, being particularly impressed from the Twenty-sixth verse on . . . that the Comforter was my Thought Adjuster.[2]

And last night I was a bit restless, and went to my study, which adjoins the bedroom, to sleep on my cot. There, for the first time, I sought to commune with my Thought Adjuster and felt a Presence. It has seemed to me that the vibrations in my study are particularly protective and healthful . . . as though my meditation there has done something to the very atmosphere . . . it is "my retreat" from the world. I will certainly endeavor, with all my soul, to follow instructions and to accept whatever is to come. I have no sense of having done anything that I should not . . . or violating any confidence.

In anticipation of a call from Hollywood I have been quietly preparing the Mark Twain story outline for the motion picture, even be-

---

[2] John 14:26 But the Comforter, which is the Holy Ghost, whom the Father will send in my name, he shall teach you all things, and bring all things to your remembrance, whatsoever I have said unto you. 27 Peace I leave with you, my peace I give unto you: not as the world giveth, give I unto you. Let not your heart be troubled, neither let it be afraid.

fore contracted to do this end of the job—so I will be that far ahead when the time comes . . . and will be FREE to give more time and thought to these higher and finer things.

I have always been conscious of how VERY LITTLE I knew . . . so willing to pay the price for a little more knowledge in whatever understandable way might be required. I have no evidence at the moment that the knowledge you have started to give me may be available from another . . . but I accept on faith that it will be made possible to me—either through direct communication or from some higher intelligences who may come as teachers. I, too, am sorry and will regret it deeply if you are not permitted to teach me a little . . . or to go further with me . . . but you may be sure I will be carrying on, in a more aware state now than I have carried on before, through all the years that you have watched over me.

I hope to be given the wisdom to write the book of which you speak . . . and had hoped you could put much more in writing concerning the subject matter to be contained in it.

I have been working on my physical body—playing tennis three and four times a week—building up physical strength and tone . . . and can sense an improvement. Final developments from the coast have been extended on option to May 15th, but things can be consummated any time before that.

The snapshot of you is much appreciated. I am sorry that we have no such side photographs at the moment. We have had few pictures taken in our family. You do not look the age that you must be, and present a face of strong character and power. Time will pass—and if we are not to be permitted to meet on this old earth, I will look forward to our reunion 160 years from now. I hope I can have earned the right to have you say then, "Well done." If I have not, I do not see how I can face you at all.

I am so grateful for all your loving, protective, guiding thought which I have felt through the years . . . keeping you always in mind . . . though I was and am so meagre in understanding. But the DESIRE for KNOWLEDGE is burning within me. I do want to KNOW and PROGRESS and to be able to accept ANY RESPONSIBILITY which may be required of me.

I will continue doing the best I know how—in the faith that I will be shown the WAY.

I hope you will be permitted to answer some of the questions asked in our last letters at least. I had hoped I might have been permitted to spend the better part of several months with you in the west . . . not that I want to LEAN on you . . . but that I might ABSORB and AWAKEN and put myself in position to EXECUTE such knowledge and wisdom in the service of humanity as my abilities and past experiences will permit.

I have been learning a severe lesson in patience for years . . . it is one of the hardest, most gruelling lessons there is . . . especially with the economic factors tied up in it. But I can look back, seeing the wisdom of ventures which fell through . . . which, if they had succeeded, might have brought wealth to me before other needed development . . . experiences I would otherwise have missed.

Of profound interest to me would be more knowledge of my Thought Adjuster, which you had started to give me. I will endeavor to get better acquainted with him in daily meditation.

World conditions, which I have not permitted to affect me personally, are whirling toward a great crisis. I feel that whatever work is going to be required of me will be coming along in these next ten crucial years.

Martha has turned over some questions to me which she said she would appreciate your answering, as would I, if permissible. They are:

Are all souls permitted to choose their paths of service before entering this life? Or is this directed for them?

What is meant by borderline sensitives?

Can a poltergeist hybrid make his presence felt to all people? Under what conditions?

What is the state of hybrids between incarnations? What are their duties? Why permitted to make nuisances of themselves? (some of them)

Will the hybrids in the unfleshed dimension advance from there now—or will they have to have a final enfleshment before they are free to go on to the full second dimension?

Why should Intelligences who have never had a flesh experience particularly desire one?

How were the letters concerning the Christ crucifixion dictated, and did they come through a voice or a personality? Do you see the entity or just hear the voice or both?

Why the *two* letters so very similar from Augustus to Pilate?

There are a number of other questions I would like to ask you but will withhold them for the time being until I know what future developments are to be.

You have not said that I could not write you . . . and I hope that this door will be left open . . . even though I may not hear from you . . . if this should be the decree.

Mary has about finished her work on the poem, "Eternity and I," and it will be mailed to you, framed, later this week. This came to me from higher sources in a moment of great inspiration! How I wish such inspiration might be a part of my daily life!

I hope you can be the medium through which other Intelligences are brought to me for my advancement if your work is done. I will do all I can to attract them directly and work with my Thought Adjuster. I hope, too, that when you have gone on to the Second Dimension, I may reach a development whereby I may contact you on occasion.

I will await some sign or word from you—sending out a constant stream of love and gratitude—which flows from Martha and myself . . . and which will continue to flow for so long as we carry on in the earth experience here . . . and are released at last for service beyond this dimension.

New York, April 26, 1941

Friend Loose:

We thought this news item from this morning's *New York Times*[3] would interest you and are wondering if you consider it authentic.

Note the comment in the purported letter to Jesus relative to: ". . . For I have also heard that the Jews are muttering against you and want to do you evil. . ."

In the very long ago, was this mistake and accident connected in any way with the Jews as a race, on this first life planet? It would seem that this race is involved today in much of the mutterings of the times. Are the Jews associated away back with the Satanic hosts who sought to "overthrow God" and to deny Him. There are some mysteries here which have a bearing on the present world situation rising to a terrific climax involving all of humanity, I am sure.

Certain things are stirring in my consciousness. I believe, when my economic picture clears with complete consummation of the Mark Twain deal, I can accomplish much through meditation and concentration. I am feeling stronger each day, physically.

---

[3] See Appendix G.

I am going to NEED TO KNOW many things from some AU-
THENTIC SOURCE soon, if not yourself. I hope this source is made
possible to me, for I can feel strange powers welling up inside me.

Doesn't the ability to ask specific questions that the average person would not think of asking, indicate ordinarily the right to know
the answer? Doesn't the very fact that such questions are raised, imply
that I know the answer in my inner consciousness and have not yet
developed the faculty of pulling it through?

Our love to you—and may you sustain the vitality of your body
for as long as you wish it to serve you here.

HARRY LOOSE to HAROLD SHERMAN

Monterey Park, April 26, 1941

My Friend:-

I have not yet received word from you whether you have rec'd
my last letter. I am writing hurriedly and against time. I was needed
in an extreme and immediate emergency and because of this I was
instructed, in the first page or two of my last letter to you, to at once
cease writing and hold myself in instant readiness for movement. I
have been away for several days. While engaged in this particular
matter, I ascertained that it was not intended that I permanently cease
writing you at this period.

There is much confusion—"War, war, and rumors of war."

I will be engaged actively and busily for some days—I do not
know definitely how long. Until this period of activity is concluded, I
will not be able to write you. Possibly for a week to ten days. However,
"be of good cheer" and carry on.

Now ATTENTION PLEASE. Your first assignment follows. I am
requested to ask you for an acknowledgment of the safe receipt of
these instructions—and your desire to abide by them.

First—read John 14:16—and John 14:26—and John 15:26 and
John 16:7.[4] Now I may go a little further with you. I have given you

---

[4] John 14:16 And I will pray the Father, and he shall give you another Comforter,
that he may abide with you for ever. John 14:26 But the Comforter, which is the
Holy Ghost, whom the Father will send in my name, he shall teach you all things,
and bring all things to your remembrance, whatsoever I have said unto you. John
15:26 But when the Comforter is come, whom I will send unto you from the
Father, even the Spirit of truth, which proceedeth from the Father, he shall testify
of me: John 16:7 Nevertheless I tell you the truth; it is expedient for you that I go
away: for if I go not away, the Comforter will not come unto you; but if I depart,
I will send him unto you.

the name Thought Adjuster which resides with you as advisor and constant helper in thought to your Soul. The words "Thought Adjuster" are my own poor way of expressing to you that which you will find mentioned in these verses under the Biblical name of "the Comforter."⁵ I have so tried to convey to you some of the real telepathic—and the beginning of Spiritual, reception. I have so mentally urged you to find the Thought Adjuster your own self in your own Bible as the Comforter that Jesus promised to send, but I have not been successful. Before His time, there was none with humans. It was entirely His gift.

I may now venture a little bit further and open up a bit more to your understanding. It is through this very Thought Adjuster, or Comforter, that *very* much is accomplished with the real YOU in development furtherance as you advance. This Thought Adjuster has a part in what follows.

Now, with this little bit added to your general information— please follow through with the following. Earth contact is to be made on the night of Wednesday, May 7th. The visit is one of much importance, with jurisdictional superiors of Urantia concerned with matters of governmental domain meeting together with jurisdictional superiors assigned to Urantia. At this meeting there will also be the usual Urantia reports of the eastern jurisdiction. With jurisdictional superiors assigned to Urantia, no earthbound contact is needed in their work here, they are already so attuned. But with the still higher Superiors from distant planets, certain earth forces centered in this planet in earth humans are required for their transitory unfleshed appearance here. You have these necessary forces. Because of your advancing stage and known background, I suppose, you are required for this service on the night of May 7th.

On this day particularly do not allow any nervousness or unquiet. On this night refuse any entertainment or visitors. Be alone with

⁵ Compare: *I [a Solitary Messenger] doubt that I am able to explain to you just what the Adjusters do in your minds and for your souls. . . . It is all somewhat of a mystery to us, not as to the plan and purpose but as to the actual mode of accomplishment. And this is just why we are confronted with such difficulty in finding an appropriate name for these supernal gifts to mortal men* (108:5.7). According to the Urantia Book, "the Comforter" is another name for the Spirit of Truth: " . . . 6. *The subsequent bestowal of the spirit of the bestowal Sons, on Urantia called the Comforter or the Spirit of Truth*" (16:4.14).

Martha. Martha is the balance to your power and control. If there is any feeling of unquiet or nervousness at any time, hold her hand or have some sort of physical contact—holding her handkerchief or her dress will also help if needed. If you do not have a feeling of nervousness or unquiet, this will not be necessary—but under all circumstances have her present with you. Be relaxed—read some Proverbs or of Psalms—talk together thoughtfully and soberly—discuss this very occurrence—commune with your Thought Adjuster—these superior entities will be in the very room with you. Your Comforter may evidence himself in the presence of these identities—I do not know. I mean evidence himself to your awareness that higher Intelligences are present—that is all. I have told you purposely who the Thought Adjuster, or Comforter, is, so that you may have no human fear of any evidences he *may* exhibit.

The visit will be in the study of your apartment between 10:30 and 11:30 *at night*. The Intelligences will be gone by 11:30 at the very latest.

I should also add that should your Comforter so attune himself—if you are that close and friendly to him—he may *translate* to you *some* of the conversation going on in your presence—only understandable bits, if any, to you humanly—and according to your understanding. Please listen for him closely—just in hopes—I would so like to have you hear something from this little Urantia—beyond the little that I have so miserably sketched to you in these writings. I am so hopeful that you will succeed. I KNOW THAT YOU WILL FEEL THE PRESENCES AND SO WILL MARTHA, even if the Comforter does not translate for you. Do not be afraid—or nervous—be glad instead—and proud—and happy—that you are this early asked for service—it is just the very beginning, you know.

Be sure to notify me at once of the safe receipt of this communication and your acceptance or refusal of the service. It is all up to your WILL and desire.

I am so hopeful that you soon may become so well-acquainted with your Thought Adjuster that *most* of this writing between us may be begun to be done away with.

Remember to lean *heavily* on Martha if necessary. Be close together, where you can touch her at any time.

Do not eat heavily that day. Drink lots of water. Be sure to have a very good bowel evacuation.

In a week or ten days, I hope, I will be able to write fully and answer all the questions of your two letters of last week.

I have written longer than I thought. I have written some in haste. Please forgive any errors in writing—misspelled words, etc.

Much love and good thought,

HAROLD SHERMAN to HARRY LOOSE

New York, April 28, 1941

Friend Loose:

Our letters apparently crossed in the mail, mine bearing evidence that I *had* received your message and had already turned to the Bible references you now give me. So you see, you have been successful, after all.

I gladly accept the assignment of service and will prepare myself for this day and hour—as will Martha. In the interim, I will try to become better acquainted with my Thought Adjuster.

I take it that we are to sit quietly in the *light*, and can read and discuss this matter, as directed, *during* the time. I presume from what you have said heretofore, that any demonstrations which may come through higher intelligences, or through one's Comforter, are performed as easily in the light to those who have become aware. If I am wrong, and absence of light in some instances is an aid, I should like to be advised.

I desire to gain the utmost from this first experience and to avoid any possible mistake or unwitting lack of cooperation which might in any way prevent the finest result.

I *knew* that you were to be permitted to keep contact with me these last few days and was awaiting your letter this morning. I turned on inspiration to the *same* passages in the Bible last night, and had reread them with the feeling that they were all-important to me at this time.

It is wonderful beyond expression to be experiencing this unfoldment and I am sure you feel my gratitude. It is all so *right*, so *logical* and so *ringing* with *truth!*

Sometime I would like to know the significance of the higher intelligences being actually present in my room—whether their conferences must take place on this planet in areas where they have channels through which they can draw forces, enabling them to commune. Whether like meetings are taking place at the same time in other parts of this world . . . and whether all higher intelligences, from whatever earth or human forces they are drawing—are in simultaneous communication with each other even though making contact with this planet at different points!

This question seems a bit involved but I think you can sense what I mean.

I do hope we may be made aware of much that transpires that night. We are looking forward to it as one of our most sacred moments.

I do not fear. To my knowledge I have never feared for myself alone . . . I have only had concern for my loved ones—the economic condition in which they might be left had anything happened to me . . . but this concern is also vanishing as I gain greater faith and understanding.

We will be looking forward to further word from you, when it is possible to write. Meanwhile, our love to you and Ma Loose and an abundance of physical vitality!

HARRY LOOSE to HAROLD SHERMAN

Monterey Park, April 30, 1941

My Friend:-

My additional work is concluded beforetime. I had not expected to be finished for some additional days but it has been taken over by another—I am glad, for I am tired.

I wrote you a letter and sent it air mail. I hope that you have received it safely. The meeting that was to have occurred at your apartment on the night of May 7th is not to be held there. It is to be at some other location and at an earlier date.

I now have your last letters [April 15th, 24th and 26th] before me. One came yesterday afternoon containing the news clip. I have them here and I will read them one by one and answer your questions as I read along.

I believe that you are to write a book. I do not know this of my own knowledge, but from indications I would judge so. I have no such instructions to give. You will be told by someone else other than I, if this is to be. When the proper time comes you will be instructed just what your duties are to be. I do not definitely know them.

The economic will be adjusted to your satisfaction.

[*Evaluating a picture of Martha and Harold:*] Martha told me in her letter that she was the one in white. That the lady in black was an old friend. You are dominant in the picture. Martha is indefinite. Her letter answered the picture quest. There is no personality to Martha's *picture*—there is plenty personality to the letter she wrote.

[*Evaluating a picture of Harold:*] There is personality, individuality, courage, tenderness, pity, love of music, spirituality, confusion, fear. Particularly love of your own—of those that belong to you; the love of music is not of the jazz variety—there is love of the music of quartettes of the male voices—love of beauty in nature and surroundings, love of good and beautiful minds. Not a good "material" manager or money handler—no banking instinct—no saver of money as money—deeply religious feeling—a worrier over trifles or imaginary conditions—you can and do make yourself physically ill by thought—a seeker for truth—an investigator—has possibilities not at all recognized—very possibly has several espatulate fingers—absolutely *needs* the evidence of physical affections exhibited—domestic quiet must rule—a quasi-executive eye that could be operative under necessity—it tells me the most vulnerable weakness and the greatest strength—it tells me a whole book full—AND SO DO ALL OTHER OR ANY FULL FACED PHOTOS—and they tell the same exactly to those who know and understand what is written here. THE PROFILE OR SIDE FACE TELLS ABSOLUTELY NOTHING in a photo.

If the picture that Martha destroyed was full face, she did right. There is no harm in side-face pictures.

As long as you "call" me, I can help you much. When you cease to "call" I have no way of entering in. It all must come by way of your own desire and WILL.

I believe the other entity who introduced herself in the message was about to start on the true crucifixion story, which I had made request for you. She got just that far when something intervened. I, of course, do not know the reason for the stoppage and I have not asked. I do not always get what I ask for at all times. I get many silences; I do not know why—except that I very possibly ask for things that are beyond my comprehension—or because what I ask for is judged as curiosity. I remember one time asking for the number belonging to the Order whose assigned duties are the introduction of man to the Great Intelligence—the Order to which Jesus Christ belonged—and I was not answered—and I afterwards recognized that it was a question of mere curiosity—and not necessary—and beyond me.

Yes, once the realization has come that you are a bit of the Great Intelligence on its way to Individualization, it forever is cognizant of its identity with and in the Father. However, you continue to remain a distinct individual of FREE WILL, and the simple recognition and knowledge of the relation you bear to the Great Intelligence does not "make" you do anything against your own WILL and desire. It is all up to YOU—what you will do—what part you will take. Your "Thought Adjuster" is given you to take counsel with—to help you—to guide you—yet do you always counsel with him or take his advice. If you take him one mile with you, he will immediately take you two more miles with him.

You are absolutely correct in the thought that "we are actually one and the same in God—or Universal Mind." You are getting around the edges of something very deep here as you will learn later on.

Regarding the ghosts and poltergeists—I cannot explain much—it would take a large book to go into detail. I should have remarked also that not all people can see ghosts or poltergeists. I know quite some about these two species—but there are others that are not seen by anyone—many more than those that ARE visualized—and there are so many different varieties. Sounds different than what you may have thought before—but very true. Some are true spirit astrals—some are human astrals—some are seized human astrals by secondary non-fleshed forces—I cannot describe them differently. It is a large, intricate section. I have been in contact with several varieties. But to be accurate, I have never particularly interested myself in them. They are not a very interesting lot and nothing can be learned from them. There was one that was a regular nuisance to us for a year or so where we once lived. He used to wake us at unreasonable hours at night and give foolish exhibitions. I threw a shoe at him several times. He finally went away.

I would like to very much write you something fully in regard to sleep and will if given time. Only sketchily as it is a tremendously long and deep subject in its entirety.

There is no time nor space. Thought easily transcends them both. Yet it cannot be explained on paper—even in a book—unless the one you are trying to explain to has reached a degree of development and understanding. To illustrate—a celestial day is three of our earth months long[6]—it takes 19 of our earth days to reach a distant planet in convoy transport by spirit—yet there is neither time nor space. This does not make sense to finite understanding—yet it is true. I do not fully comprehend it myself but I know sufficient to be able to understand that such can be so. I hope to be able sometime to give you the little understanding that I do have. The lower part of this paragraph does not conflict with the beginning—although I have perhaps written somewhat ambiguously.

NO—I cannot grasp anything of the ultimate purpose or plan of the Great Intelligence in His universes.

Hybrids were once in the flesh as humans. There were differences in their intelligences at that time. Since passing into the hybrid state so long ago, these differences in capacities have largely been adjusted to one level. There are still some differences—but rarely very great.

The Order of Melchisedek is limited. It is an Order existent only among hybrids and therefore limited to their numbers. The records of this Order existent on this planet are in a Shangri-La sort of a place that you will some day see—together with the mass of records—many thousands of them.

It is said in the Bible that when this earth is finally and completely destroyed the next time it will be by way of fire. When this happens, ALL WILL BE RETURNED AGAIN TO THE GASES FROM WHICH IT WAS ORIGINALLY FORMED. FIRE IS THE REAL AND COMPLETE END OF ALL PLANETS IN THE EVENTUAL. So will go the earth and all upon it. ALL under sufficient heat returns to the gases from which in the beginning they were originally formed.

A rock does not "aspire," neither does a fish or a cow or a tree. Man with the tiny bit of the Great Intelligence in him is the only earthly thing that "aspires"—or that continues.

You are very correct, there is neither "up nor down" in all the combined Universes. If you will lay your watch on a table and look at it from above, you will see how the great collective Universes are laid out. Divide the watch into seven sections and you have the seven Universes. The lower right-hand division is the Universe in which this planet Urantia resides.[7] It is the last and least populated with planets.

---

[6] See footnote on p. 131.

[7] ... Orvonton, the seventh superuniverse, ... swings on between superuniverses one and six, having not long since (as we reckon time) turned the southeastern bend of the superuniverse space level (15:1.5).

The position of your watch on the table is exactly the way the entire Universes are collectively in the sky. There is breadth but not the same depth by far. Just the same as with your watch, there is no up nor down; the movement is from the outside rim to the center inside and from the center inside to the other rim. This from any side of the watch. And so with the collective Universes. There is no up nor down. Only IN and OUT.

The information that you now have—without the slightest addition—would make a world shocking book—make no mistake about this statement—and you very well know it. This although you could not PROVE a single statement that you might make. Some minds are such that if you took them right into their so-called Heaven, they would not believe that they were there.[8] When Christ performed miracles, the people were entertained and most of them came to Him in crowds to see the miracles—NOT to listen to his talks to them and profit thereby. He said to them on one occasion, "O ye of little faith. Unless ye see signs and wonders, ye will not believe." You could not prove a single thing to your book audience in *Your Key to Happiness*. Those who profited had to follow through with the advice therein contained and by their own individual effort prove it to themselves—no one else could do their work for them.

Your book on the information that you now have would raise world-wide controversy. Few would believe. Very, very few of the non compos mentis type at all if any. Just a few of the thinkers. And you would be called a liar—and sneered and laughed at—and cursed and abused—by press and pulpit. You sure would be called a lot of names—and your life would be made a misery if you allowed your mind to be so distressed by the turmoil. What you wrote of the subject would not begin to be understood for a generation. The really intelligent—without axes to grind—and without mental quirks—would grasp the whole picture immediately and besiege you for more—and give you great veneration. But when even Jesus could

---

[8] Compare: *Were it possible for the lower orders of intelligence to be transported instantly into the presence of the Father himself, they would not know they were there. They would there be just as oblivious of the presence of the Universal Father as where they now are* (5:1.5). *If a Urantia mortal could be transported to Havona, he would there be deaf, blind, and utterly lacking in all other sense reactions; he could only function as a limited self-conscious being deprived of all environmental stimuli and all reactions thereto* (14:2.4).

not get the masses to understand or believe, what chance would you have.

Remember your own self just a few months ago. And you are a brilliant mind. Could you then have believed your own self?? So please believe me now—that there is no way of "proving" anything to the masses now by book, motion pictures nor personal appearances. No more than there was of "proving" anything to the masses in Jesus' time. You would raise a terrific clamor in the world—in press and pulpit and lecture platform—and you would start the intelligent who could see the thing as it was—but you could PROVE nothing to nobody. IT STILL REVERTS BACK TO WHAT I HAVE SO OFTEN TOLD YOU***THAT IT IS ALL AN INDIVIDUAL PROPOSITION. Each must "get it" BY HIMSELF. I do hope that this is clear to you.

Yes. You are right. You are right now—and have been for some years—living through the very greatest upheaval ever to take place upon this planet. Human thought is much limited—as you know—and there is the unthinking inability to so recognize the limited spectrum—so the most of them recognize no upheaval, either now or in the past or to come in the future. There should be a great religious awakening to follow this period—and there must be new religious thought to accompany it—some advancement—some further directional opening to help them to advance. That is what I have pictured to myself was your mission in the book that I have HOPED it would be your duty to write. But I do not KNOW of a surety that this is to be your mission. You may be sure that you would be in an enviable, and a not enviable, position once such book was printed—and both at the very same time.

Yes, I too hope and pray that higher Intelligences having supervision over my work here will grant me permission to continue my work with you for a longer time. It is possible but not probable. I do not know this future.

YES—it will be possible for me to contact you from the second dimension. I will be very able to contact you KNOWINGLY from your standpoint. I expect you to be so advanced by that time that I will visit you knowingly and visually as much as if I were to walk into your study right now in the flesh. You may be SURE of this. And with no equivocation. I expect to keep very close watch over and contact with you. You and I will be bound together for probably the complete tour of the second dimension.

By three years from now, I fully expect you to be able to receive sight direct. You will be receiving demonstrations and impressions from other Intelligences knowingly. However, you cannot hasten things other than by growth and understanding—by your own application and endeavor—and by getting close to your Thought Adjuster—the Comforter—and by being able to contact and advise with him. No one can do this for you. All is an individual experience by way of your own WILL so to do. Have patience—do not try to otherwise hasten things—except by your own application as above outlined.

A Soul does not become such until the first individual breath of individual LIFE after birth. Up to 4½ months [in the womb], it has life but not individual LIFE. It is still a living part of the mother. With the coming of "life" at 4½ months, it is then a degree higher in the "life step." With full individual life with the first individual living breath comes the individual Soul. Until this second, the individual Soul did not exist. No new Soul is permitted, or able, to choose its path of service before birth. There was no new Soul until birth. Neither is such service directed for them. There are notable exceptions—the birth of Christ is one—and there are similar others—hybrids for example, with a mission to perform. However, this present year closes any further appearances of hybrids ever coming again in such manner.

I was born Sept. 13th, 1869.[9] I will be 71 [sic] years old this coming Sept. 13th. I have not thought so much of my body being old or of great earth age but of the age of the hybrid existence. An "old Soul." You are one also. You are as old as I.

A "borderline" sensitive is one so attuned that he far transcends the ordinary sensitive. The borderline sensitive is one who, though fully in the flesh, is at the very border of the spirit much of the time. Unless helped to find himself, he is usually a pretty unhappy person— continually seeking—seeking—seeking. Trying this—trying that— seeking and not finding—until, mayhap, he discovers by himself—or he is recognized by an advanced Soul and is taught who and what he is—then comes satisfaction and relief.

Neither a ghost nor or a poltergeist can make their presence known to all people or at any time they choose. The person who is the

---

[9] Loose's obituary, in the November 22, 1943 issue of the *Chicago Daily News,* states that he died at the age of 63. His gravestone in El Monte, Calif. gives his birth year as 1880.

perceiver must be one so nervously and physically constituted that such ghost or poltergeist can draw from such person, asleep or awake, certain forces which will allow them sufficient strength to perform. Some houses or locations are permeated with such as to allow such force withdrawals and to permit such appearances thereby.

Between flesh incarnations upon especial missions, hybrids are occupied in the full duties of second dimension spirit entities on this earth alone. Up to this year, they have been so restricted because of the bad mistake and accident that I have before written you of.

On conclusion of their present flesh or quasi-spiritual missions here, the hybrid ascends fully to the second dimension and leaves the precincts of this particular planet for good—except under very extraordinary circumstances which may bring him back in the Spirit for the rounding out of some special mission.

You have never had an experience, knowingly, in the second dimension—so you would like to experience such. The Intelligences who have been entirely spiritually conceived have never had an earth experience. So, many of them would like to have the experience of an earth existence. Not all, by far, such Intelligences so conceived so desire. Just exactly the same as many who are now going through this earth experience do not especially desire to leave here for an experience in the second dimension. It is all an individual desire—one way—or the other.

I would very much like to see you. I have not been definitely forbidden so to do—I may be. I do not know. I now do not think that you would try to "lean" on me. See Proverbs 3:5-7—and do them.[10]

I fear your disillusionment in seeing me. You have built up a picture of me and you will be disappointed upon its non-realization. I am but an old man—a kind of a shabby old fellow—just about the same that you will see on any park bench. I have no long beard nor patriarchal appearance. I don't appear even of average intelligence. You would ask me questions that I would very probably have to ask permission to answer before I replied. I am pretty sure that I would come far from measuring up to your expectations—and you would

---

[10] Proverbs 3:5 Trust in the LORD with all thine heart; and lean not unto thine own understanding. 6 In all thy ways acknowledge him, and he shall direct thy paths. 7 Be not wise in thine own eyes: fear the LORD, and depart from evil.

be greatly disappointed. Because of this, I fear harm would come to you in your interest and endeavor for advancement.

The Christ letters were dictated in full hearing voice to the Comforter in the old language and translated by the Comforter to me. Sometimes the dictator would get ahead of my typing and the Comforter would request slower. They had a little by-conversation occasionally. I was not given the name of the sender. RIGHT NOW WHILE THUS WRITING, I am being requested to ask you NOT at any time to divulge those letters. I had full-voice English reception of the other communication—the one that was directed to you and that stopped so suddenly.

All spiritual struggle is being made to keep the western hemisphere out of the continuance of war. There is a possibility of not war being declared by the United States but of war being declared on the United States. This is not to be discussed openly. The next few weeks will decide.

I have so often told you that we are surrounded by forces that we do not know or understand. I note the following in today's paper. "Scientists at Columbia University, New York, have for the first time isolated in a pure state the element known as U-235, which is a close relative of Uranium. Only minute quantities have, as yet, been produced, but it is estimated that one pound of U-235 has as much energy as five million pounds of coal or three million pounds of gasoline." Does this help you to realize how very little we ALL know.

I now ask you to meditate with your Comforter. Get understandably close to him. Counsel with him. Much of your future advancement absolutely depends on this. Much of your beginning perceptions will be through his cooperation and HELP. If you are earnest and intent, you will make progress in this—soon I hope. You may be able to contact him so far that much of this writing may be done away with—at least some of it I hope.

I, and others, have tried to make your study your spiritual retreat. I, and others, are so very happy to have your recognition and acknowledgment of your discovery.

You must not lean on me. You must lean on your own understanding. The only one from whom you can borrow strength legitimately—your reservoir—is Martha. If, when you go out on something nervously or mentally strenuous, you would carry something intimate of hers—a used handkerchief, a stocking, something that you can conveniently carry and reach with your hand—you will be at once relieved of any nervousness by so grasping and holding it for a bit. Try it and see.

I have tried to learn something of Martha's background but it is all a closed book so far. I will continue to try. There is a great deal that is not plain nor clear to me.

The reason for the two letters of Pilate to Tiberius was because of the dangers to the messengers who carried them. To insure the safe delivery of at least one such report, it was the custom at this early time to always dispatch two messengers with similar reports some days apart.

I surely will be very glad to receive "Eternity and I," with great thanks to Mary for her work thereon.

The clipping from the paper that you enclosed is correct and bona fide. It is not new, however. I have known of and read about it some years ago.

The Jews were really and truly a chosen race. They were not attached in any way to the Satanic hosts. They have been greatly punished for their sin of the crucifixion. Christ told them that their city of Jerusalem would be "taken" and despoiled and not a stone of their holy building, "the Temple," would be left standing one upon another, and that they would be driven over the face of the earth—a nation without a country. And so it was—and is. Because of His crucifixion by the Jews, Pilate was beheaded and his body eventually carried to Vienne—now in Austria—and thrown into the River Rhone (Rhine),[11] and Tiberius, the Roman Emperor, tore down the Temple and scattered the Jews. Since that time, they themselves have referred much to themselves as the "accursed race."

I am tremendously glad and proud that you, at last, are aroused and that "certain things are stirring in your consciousness." I am so glad and so is Ma. You CAN accomplish much through meditation and concentration. You are "on your way"—I am so very glad.

---

[11] Loose lifted this from "The Death of Pilate, Who Condemned Jesus," in *The Apocryphal Books of the New Testament* (Philadelphia: David McKay, publisher, 1890, 1901).

One of your finest evidences—I feel like cheering—is that last paragraph. It is FINE. Do you remember it?? I will repeat it here: "Doesn't the ability to ask specific questions that the average person would not think of asking, indicate ordinarily the right to know the answer. Doesn't the very fact that such questions are raised imply that I know the answer in my inner consciousness and have not yet developed the faculty of pulling it through." That is magnificent. I have been trying so very hard to bring this very word-for-word paragraph from you—as well as to give it to you.

Now, having worked this out—and now having this understanding—you have started to go toward the window to open it. *Now* knowing the Thought Adjuster, the Comforter, and having your reasoning MIND to reject the chaff and to winnow out the grain, and with Martha to draw strength from and to balance—with that good mind to adjudicate—you are at last beginning. I am so cheered.

I have written so long—and I am quite physically tired—I must be careful not to overtax for this little time.

Martha, I have not written directly to you in this. Forgive me. There was so much that I was eager to get to Harold—and I fear I have so little time left. I will try to do better soon. Write when you can. Be very tender of her, Harold—be very careful and tender—make her smile—make her laugh—you are TOO sober—laugh a lot—you should. Martha is very needful to you—more needful now than you know.

The way for me has been hard and long. The burden is slipping slowly from my shoulders. I am glad. The boy is aware—he now knows—there will be no more seeking—no more questing—no more foolishness with charlatans and "isms"—he is on the right highway now.

With much love to you ALL and with the very best thought over and under and around you ALL,

HAROLD SHERMAN to HARRY LOOSE

New York, May 3, 1941

Friend Loose:

Still no word from the Hollywood sector relative to closing of arrangements. What patience and faith one is required to develop and maintain! It seems so many real achievements have been deferred and deferred in my life. I have been so close to many fine accomplishments, only to have them disappear for no fault of mine, due to circumstances beyond control. Of course, I have accepted these happenings as for my best at all times—as hard as they have been to "take" economically and otherwise. Martha's faith and understanding through it all has been my "rock of Gibraltar" and then some.

I am, as you can realize, eager to make the change from east to west now—as are all members of my little family. I am preparing the physical by playing tennis almost every day and the weather for April has been fair throughout, not even April showers . . . good for *me* but bad for crops! I weigh 177 pounds now and have had no more stomach "back talk" for weeks, with an endurance that enables me to play five to six sets of hard tennis a day and no fatigue or depletion. Not bad for a young man going on 43 years.

I'll be 43 on July *13th!* Did I tell you I was born July *13th,* 1898? I was amazed and thrilled to find you were born on September 13th, 1869. My mother's birthday is also on September *13th*—1874! 13's run in our family. My next brother, Edward, was born February 13th, 1903, and died October *13th,* 1914. (Result of the accident I mentioned in a previous letter . . . fall from tree in our front yard in Traverse.) Dad was born January 31 (13 turned around), 1867, and died March 1, 1921. Martha was born December 5, 1898. My brother Arthur's birthday was July 17, 1905. If you will note—the name Harold Sherman (without the middle initial "M") has thirteen letters in it. I used this name in my book, *Your Key to Happiness,* and the "M" with my juvenile work. Somehow I have the pull to go back to "M". What do you think?

Interesting—your analysis of the picture and the qualities you give as mine. Very accurate. The picture Martha destroyed of yours was side view and I was sorry to lose it . . . but am *so glad* to have this new and recent one which is now in a little frame, standing upon the cabinet which contains my row of books.

I have not been calling you the past nights because I did not wish to place a greater burden on you—knowing the special work you had to do. I regret, in a way, that the plans had to be countermanded relative to May 7th, as Martha and I were looking forward, eager to be of service . . . and hope we can deserve to be of help on some other occasion in the near future.

Martha wonders if individuals who come into this life to render service have certain talents in different directions, which they have developed heretofore, "subdued or restrained within," in order that they may concentrate on the specific talents required for the mission . . . rather than diverging into other fields which active use of other talents would permit? Her wonderment is occasioned by the fact that she observes other women in the limelight because of their musical or other talents, when she seems to have little faculty in these directions and her urge has been to make a home for me.

Your account of ghosts and poltergeists was interesting to us—particularly your own personal experience. Martha and I had one strange occurrence when we were living uptown at 134 Haven Avenue, overlooking the Hudson River, almost opposite the great George Washington Bridge, the construction of which we watched, as from a grandstand seat, from the laying of the first cable.

Martha was carrying Marcia at the time and it was close to the end of her time . . . I think in the month of July. On hot nights she did not sleep well . . . and so I would get up and go down the hall, making a turn to the right, and into my study, where I would sleep the rest of the night on my cot.

On this night, I was awakened by the startling sound of someone whispering directly into my ear. I can feel goose pimples now as I relate this experience. I sat up, thinking that something had happened and Martha had come into the room to awaken me . . . but there was no one there. Then I thought Martha must have whispered to me from the hall and, getting no response, had gone back to bed . . . so I jumped up and went out in the hall and around to our bedroom, some distance away, separated by walls . . . and asked Martha, finding she was awake, if she had been out of bed.

"No," said Martha, "*but did you whisper to me* a few moments ago?"

"No," said I, "that's what I was coming to ask you . . . did you whisper to *me*?"

"No," she said, "but this whisper wakened me . . . it was right next to my ear."

We then confessed to each other having had the most uncanny feeling . . . almost as though an evil presence had been in the apartment. No one had lived in the apartment before as the building was new when we moved in.

I have always wondered how Martha and I could have heard the same whisper at the same time. From what source had it come?

I have had a great many so-called psychic experiences, a number of which will have to wait until we are privileged to meet, which I deeply hope we will do.

If the burden is not too great upon you, I would want to continue our correspondence even though we might not be so far apart, after we get to California . . . because I agree that this method permits a retention of much you have said which might be lost if given verbally.

Of course, when I develop so that I can practically take dictation from you . . . or we can communicate from mind to mind . . . and I am also able to commune knowingly with my Thought Adjustor . . . then it will be quite different.

Just now, what you are are so good as to put down on paper is milk and meat to me.

Oh—I must tell you of some interesting things that are beginning to happen. On two different mornings, as I have been awakening, I have been shown a white paper on which an account of some sort has been printed. For an instant, I have known the entire contents . . . and then it has been withdrawn from me and I, reaching a waking consciousness, have only been able to retain fragments . . . but the recollection of the reading matter having been most vivid has remained.

For instance, April 29th, at 7:15 in the morning, I came to after such a vision, recalling distinctly these two strange lines:

Knowing my reach and hold
I lay in store by the sea.

Then I recalled having heard a voice say to me, at the time I was looking at this printed page:

"The story of thy life shall be
released by God."

I have no explanation to offer but felt I should report the above happening.

This morning I seemed to be reading the ancient report of a peasant whose master had been away, fighting in some war, and who was reporting his return home, in spirit, the master having been killed. How he knew of it was because hay had been thrown down for the cattle in the barn and the cattle sensed the master's presence and made sounds such as they made when he had physically been around them. I vaguely recall the language of telling as having been old style . . . but it escapes me now.

Such thoughts and impressions as these have no association with my normal waking life, as you can see.

I was also impressed, after meditation, to turn to the third chapter of Ephesians which seemed to contain a personal message for me at this time.

Your promise to write me about some of the mystery of sleep is appreciated. This should open up new comprehensions within me as I long have been aware that strange and amazing things happen during the sleep state.

Referring to the poem, "Eternity and I," which you have received by this time, I had some photostatic copies made of Mary's work and when I called for the prints, I heard a woman's voice say, "Oh, is that Mr. Sherman out there? Please let me take the job out to him." I am not well known in this photographic place . . . but this middle-aged woman came out from an inner room, bringing the job with her, and gave me an odd look. I have never seen her before.

"Did you write this, Mr. Sherman?" she asked.

"It came to me," I answered.

"It's the most beautiful poem I ever read," she said. "And something tells me every word of it is true. It's a beautiful thing . . . beautiful!"

I told her I was glad it meant so much to her . . . and she stood looking after me as I went out.

I was reminded then of Marcia's reaction at the time I made a typewritten copy, a few days after having received the poem inspirationally. I had said nothing to the girls about it and took this copy of the poem to the living room to show to Martha. I laid it on the radio table and Marcia, then nine years of age, came in and picked it up. I was amazed to have her show any interest in any creative material of mine, which she had never heretofore done, and when she started reading the poem, I was further surprised for I had considered it too profound for her comprehension.

Martha made an immediate record of Marcia's reaction to the poem which I will now copy . . . after first telling you that we had been having trouble with her, at that time, following an operation for the removal of her tonsils. She apparently had had a terrifying experience under ether . . . and was afraid to go to sleep at night . . . or be

⚞ Eternity and I ⚟

eep down within the depths of me
There stirs a mighty timeless sea.
Its waves of memory touch the shore
Of consciousness and, more and more,
As Time unreels in world of Space
My Self reveals its God-like face;
A God-force breathing through each form
Of life I've lived. About me swarm
The aeons past in which I've dwelled,
Vague fleeting glimpses now beheld.
One day, an inner voice persists,
I'll reach beyond all that exists
And Time and Space no longer bind
The new dimension of my mind.
Until then, plodding I must go,
With patience, reaping as I sow,
From birth to death and birth again;
Nor asking how nor why nor when—
The "I am I" of me content
To know that it is heaven-bent;
A heaven not as dreamed of yore—
A blessed state – the open door
To realms above the sense desires
Where burn the great Creative Fires
And, one with those who have attained,
Freed now from all that had me chained,
Eternity and I embrace.
At last I meet God face to face.

Harold Sherman 1939

"Eternity and I" in Mary's calligraphy
[SHERMAN FAMILY PRIVATE COLLECTION].

in the dark. She would awaken with frightful nightmares, the feeling that evil presences were in the room, under the bed, pursuing her. At other times, she would feel that she was growing smaller and smaller and would hysterically cry out that she was dwindling into nothing . . . that she was *dying*.

But now, after reading the poem, here is her reaction as recorded by Martha:

When she finished, Harold asked her if she liked it. Her face aglow, she replied, "Oh, Daddy, I think it is wonderful. I feel it is *true*. It makes me feel so at ease, so comfortable. I feel as though I were old and that I would live on and on . . . and I am not afraid to die. I know it will be all right. I feel so peaceful and rested inside . . . The words are so beautiful. It is the most beautiful poem I ever read. Some poems are just silly but this one is all true. It will make you very famous."

I turned to her and said, "Marcia, Daddy felt when he wrote that poem that someone helped him write it."

"Yes, I believe God did," she replied. "God or Jesus or some of his helpers . . . but I believe it was God. I shall never be afraid any more . . . I just can't tell you in words how wonderful it is."

And she couldn't drop the subject, for an hour later when she went to bed, she was still speaking of it and placed the copy of the poem under her pillow. But before she went to sleep she told Harold she saw just how he had written it. That he lay down on his cot and suddenly reached for a piece of paper upon which something was already written, folded it over on the inside and commenced to write. He was amazed himself at what came and showed it to Mother right away and she thought it was very fine, too.

This was exact in every detail . . . and then Marcia went on to give Harold advice about writing more poems. Never must he think them out but sometime when he was *tired* (relaxed) just to lie down with a paper and pencil and see what would come. The next poem, she said, would be a further carrying out of the thought embodied in the first . . . and before she fell asleep she said again, "This is going to make Daddy famous."

This ends the record . . . but isn't it remarkable what *thought* can do to a supposedly "young mind"? If this poem can bring such a reaction—what can the RIGHT BOOK, supported by some kind of authoritative evidence if only in the RIGHT APPEAL to men's souls—do for humanity? I grant you it will take courage to write such a book . . . and to weather the storms of materialism . . . but the havoc in the world on the *destructive* side and the great advance of science and invention on the *constructive* side are doing much to sweep away the age-old foundations of materialism and pave the way for the religious revival you foresee.

People are hungry for true knowledge . . . and witness how all the cults and isms are being exposed and blown up by human perversion of thought and body . . . the latest being the Rosicrucian mess. Bernard here is in trouble again[12] . . . and [his nephew] Theos Bernard, a young man who claims to be the only White Lama, is being sued[13] . . . the "I Ams" of Los Angeles[14] . . . and all these profaners of true spiritual knowledge are being exposed . . . leaving a trail of emotionally unbalanced and insane followers behind them. This all by way of making room for the coming into this world of TRUE KNOWLEDGE, clean and pure and free from the perversion of either malicious or well-meaning SECTS.

I am most interested in world conditions. Poor Lindbergh. He has needed, during all his public career, a good public relations counsel.[15] A man must be sure that he has not left himself open to

---

[12] Before the U.S. entered World War II, Pierre Bernard temporarily closed down his Nyack country club to house refugees from the Nazis. His secretary managed the program and was shot, though not fatally, by a Nazi sympathizer in January 1941.

[13] Theos Bernard, purportedly the first white person admitted to the Tibetan Buddhist priesthood, became a yoga instructor and published numerous books on the subject. In 1941 he was involved in a sex scandal with a student whose husband sued him for $25,000.

[14] THE I AMERS. An occult group that was formed in the early 1930s by Kansas-born Guy W. Ballard, his wife Edna and their son Donald. In 1931 the Ballards established the Saint Germain Foundation, under whose auspices Guy, using the pen-name Godfre Ray King, published his accounts of his purported experiences with Saint Germain, a 700-year-old mystic and "Ascended Master." The Ballards held classes in Chicago and other U.S. cities, selecting students as "appointed messengers" to tour the country. Shortly before his death in 1939, Ballard was accused by a former student, Gerald Bryan, author of *Psychic Dictatorship in America* (1940), of plagiarizing much of the religion from old occult books. Lawsuits against the Foundation were initiated, leading to a criminal indictment of Edna and Donald Ballard in 1942 for mail fraud. The conviction was overturned in 1946.

[15] Charles Lindbergh (1902-1974). U.S. aviator known for his historic non-stop flight from New York to Paris in 1927. In 1941 he and his family returned to the United States after spending several years in Europe, and he became a leading spokesman for the America First Committee, an organization that opposed voluntary American entry into World War II. After President Roosevelt publicly denounced him he resigned his commission in the Army Air Corps and moved into the private sector.

VULNERABLE POINTS of attack, when he enters public life. Lindbergh, regardless of his personal feelings, to convince ALL elements of the American public of his lack of bias or prejudice, should have decried Germany's war machine and returned his medal [which he had been given by Germany in 1938]. In all his speeches, while stating sincerely his interest in defending America . . . he has never once said anything disparaging against Germany. In decrying all war and taking a neutral point of view, for the EFFECT his messages could have had upon the American public, in my opinion he should have bemoaned the attitude of both sides in the conflict abroad. Surely no nation, big or small, is entirely guiltless. And today, men are considered PRO in public life the moment they become CON. There is no middle ground remaining, it seems.

I can sense a tremendous SPIRITUAL STRUGGLE teeming under the surface . . . and I feel that my real work will BEGIN in the chaotic period following the conflict which is rapidly approaching a terrific climax, involving this country. The urge to get out of New York is coming stronger and stronger. There is so much for me to say to you . . . which I can only hint at because of time and other factors. Of course we see beneath the surface and the real causes and necessity for this coming cataclysm. It leaves me inwardly undisturbed and free of malice toward any country or peoples.

I am overjoyed that I am showing evidences of development to you . . . and Martha and I are counselling much together . . . I will arrange to spend more and more time with my Comforter. It was reassuring to know that you will be close, even when you have reached the Second Dimension . . . and I am sure that I have gone beyond physical appearances in my development and understanding, not to be retarded at all by a personal meeting with you in the flesh.

Your reference to the window [*Ed. note:* See p. 215.] refers back to one of the dreams I related to you. I catch the significance. A man made a strange remark to me whom I met on the street the other day. He is a Mr. Kane whom I have known at the City Club, a great student of mind, whom I helped through a nervous breakdown several years ago. He said, "Sherman, you have a rare type of mind . . . few have what you have . . . your mind has a skylight in it, which you're going to open more and more and take inspiration direct from higher intelligences. I envy you and yet I would not want the responsibility you are going to have to assume before very long for the world!" He did not amplify this statement and I gave no sign that it made a deep impression on me . . . but said he wished to see me again soon and have a further talk. He also observed: "When I saw you last you had just finished the Wilkins experiments and were run down in health . . . but you give every indication now of having reached a mental and physical balance . . . you've controlled these powers of mind in your body . . . which got out of control with me. You deserve great credit. Few people are capable of doing it . . . I wasn't."

Now this is wisdom coming from strange places! It is difficult, sometimes, not to give voice to some things one has come to know and to feel . . . but I have observed absolute control, despite the indication, at times, that some people I have met possess a glimmering knowledge and may be uttering things which I NEED to hear, beyond their own comprehension!

Our love once more to Ma Loose and yourself . . . our gratitude for all you are doing for us . . . and our constant prayer going out each day and night that we may be made increasingly worthy to receive more.

May the Hollywood matter be closed SOON and the trip westward become a reality!

New York, May 6, 1941

Friend Loose:

I have set aside a time roughly between eight and nine o'clock each morning for a session with my Comforter.

This morning the attached material seemed to come through.[16] It is based upon some truths you revealed to me and I am a bit self-conscious and over-sensitized about it. You see, I am so desirous of not permitting any "coloring" nor letting my imagination enter in . . . and gaining knowledge direct from a higher source, unpolluted. I will need, eventually, the proof of sight and actual sensing of higher intelligences as confirmation. Not that I doubt—but I am thinking in terms of the world and my ability to testify that these things are so . . . I know they are so, because I have experienced them. This has been my procedure in my stumbling way through this life.

I must have possessed this WISDOM in other earth experiences . . . but apparently it has to be brought through the flesh existence, in a little different form, each enfleshment. Perhaps I, as the Iberian, possessed a greater earth wisdom at that time than you did . . . and

---

[16] This material follows the letter.

it may have been my province to help you in your advancement then ... just as you now are helping me. Much of this is still so mysterious.

I would like your estimate of this material and your frank statement if you find any of it to be coloring. I have not asked you what the *accident* and mistake WAS ... feeling that you would tell me when the right time comes. You can state if this impression conforms to the TRUTH and perhaps you can give a fuller explanation to me if you find I have tapped something in line with the real happening.

I have seen so much drivel that has come through well-meaning but misguided souls under the guise of "automatic writing" ... I want to be SO SURE my own development carries me above subconscious meanderings. For this reason, I would like to be able to sense KNOW-INGLY the existence of my Comforter and hear his voice. I can feel a Presence but cannot isolate it as yet for a sufficiently long period to feel an entity apart. I'm sure you understand what I mean.

I will await, with interest, your report on this material. I am sure there is a tremendous lot more waiting to come through, once I can get properly attuned.

Our LOVE to you and Ma Loose as ever!

Tuesday Morning, May 6, 1941

Before the Iberian was I am.

Back in the early beginning of things my spirit moved in the gaseous vapors of earth. Dispatched as I was from the bosom of the Great Intelligence, with a host of other developed souls, to bring Light to the dark corner of this, His Seventh and Last universe.

We brought with us the vibratory essence of all that was needed to create a new First Life Planet and this area in Space-Time became a new magnetic center for the play and inter-play of universal forces in furtherance of the incomprehensible scheme of the Great Intelligence.

I moved behind the crystallizing and solidifying of these forces—the Higher Self of me—then responsive to the direct orders of Him who was giving expression of Himself through me.

And all would have been well had not certain parts of Him, given dominion over the creation of this world, become intoxicated with the power given into their hands. Through exercise of their Will and not *His* Will, lower forces were given power and control in the birth of this planet and the Great Intelligence, holding all responsible for this great mistake and error, issued the command that those who were here in the beginning should remain unto the end of such time as the great mistake might be rectified through all forms of life and manifestations which He had destined to occur.

Thus, I am as old as the planet Urantia in Him and grieve in my Higher Self for the cosmic severance of those long ago Intelligences from the following of His plan.

But now my Spirit rejoices, for the illumination has come that I am near the parting of the ways when I will be divided from all that has gone before and taken unto another dimension once I have fulfilled this, my last mission upon earth, where all that has long been denied will be added unto me, yea—all that He had intended should be mine from the beginning.

And the mystery of my Being shall be made known as will the mystery of Martha, that other half of me, contained also in Him—both of us a gift to each other that His work might be made manifest through us.

This little glimmer of knowledge given to me more as a test from my Comforter who signs himself "ARA" if my poor receptacle of thought has interpreted the word-sound correctly.

FOOTNOTE:

An elucidation of this meditation came to me following the sitting:

That the army of Intelligences sent to create this world had changed the plans of the Great Architect and had erected a structure containing fundamental flaws which caused these same flaws to be passed down through the ages, necessitating a rebuilding job under direction of Higher Forces in conflict with lower forces wrongfully given power over elements they should not have controlled.

Once the planet Urantia had been given material form it was impossible to correct these flaws except as they were worked out and expiated by those responsible for the great mistake involving all life and happenings on the earth.

God, the Great Intelligence, in His compassion, has permitted those who brought about this great mistake the opportunity for redemption and has left the door open for all humanity to find its way back to Him.

It is our purpose to help open this door and reveal this Light to humanity which was plunged into darkness by the great mistake so long ago.

HARRY LOOSE to MARTHA SHERMAN

Monterey Park, May 11, 1941

Dear Martha:-

Please excuse the paper that I am writing on. It just happens to be the only bit at hand at the present. May I thank you for your very fine letter. I am glad for the details therein describing your background in lieu of a better picture. Your handwriting told me much which your letter further clarifies. It also told me a great deal which your letter does not remark.

I want to here acknowledge receipt of Harold's letters and I want to answer some of his questions contained therein. One of the big reasons I want you to be sure to read the Book of Urantia is that it goes into much detail as to the great mistake and accident away back in the beginning of things that occasioned the hybrid. There are many pages of this description. Before concluding this letter I want to add a short clarifying bit which is in no way so descriptatory as what you will find in the Book of Urantia.

Darkness does not add to nor take away from any of the ability to contact your Comforter or higher Intelligences. Neither does noise, nor location, nor quiet nor the presence of other humans. NOTHING can halt such contacts AFTER the ability to make such contacts is established. It DOES take quiet meditation in either darkness or light, in the beginning, to learn of your Comforter and to become acquainted with him—to hear his still, quiet voice in answer to your questioning—and remember, you are his responsibility and he always answers you to your benefit.

There are certain powers that you inherently possess as a fleshed entity. Some humans possess such powers in excess of other humans. These powers are not possessed by unfleshed entities not directly associated with earth work or assigned on earth-missions. This particular arrangement is presumably for the purpose of excluding unfleshed entities who have no proper reason for a return to, or a visit to, a planet to which they are not assigned. This accounts for the non-return of legitimate spirits to the planet they left in earth-death EXCEPT on direct missions or with permission so to do for some personal good performance or for some other good cause. These, too, can only appear through an earth individual, or house, or grounds, which person or house or grounds possesses in excess such powers. This accounts for the fact that many people can neither see nor attract ghosts. I am not making expression here for other than legitimate spirits, the poltergeists or other classes of illegitimate appearances.

The best word that I can find to express such legitimate appearances is the double word "spirit-astral." These appearances can be made by these "spirit astrals" better in such locations where there is a normal wetness or moist atmosphere, which seems to be more conductive to such earth forces and powers as spoken of above. In line with this, remember that electricity is active in moist temperatures. Your car runs better in moist temperature, etc.

The above does not by any means describe the whole coterie of phenomena which we call "ghosts"—for want of a better term. I do not understand much of or about the subject. The above is mostly given in partial explanation of the significance of the presence of higher Intelligences in your room. I do not know, nor understand, much of their channels of operation except to really know that there is ALWAYS much movement and that this planet, and all other planets in full Life, or in the making, are under the strictest surveillance and observation—even more so than any huge and important business institution in operation in any one of our great business centers.

Conferences such as were to have taken place in your apartment are in progress all the time in many sections of the world everyday. NOT, however, with the attendance of superior Intelligences from other and higher executive worlds. Such conferences are only occasional as far as my limited understanding goes. I know so very little. If you were able to live ten thousand earth lives of one thousand earthyears each, you would be able to learn only a very minute amount of what there is to know.

One of the local papers yesterday had quite a long article about Bernard at Nyack, whom you and Martha visited, and about another Bernard. A suit by a husband over the loss of his wife by way of her becoming demented through the study of Bernard's philosophy. Your letter states that you have read of it in N.Y.C. papers. The article went into some detail about some of the tenets and studies of the cult—gave some of the naked postures of its pupils pursuing their studies by sitting in peculiar positions nude and with heads downcast, intensely observing their nude abdomens. By the very furthest stretch of the imagination, of what interest would it be to the Great Intelligence, or to ANY Spirit Intelligence, what posture any poor human twisted his fleshly form into. How can people who have even a below-par intelligence believe such utter twaddle as this Bernard teaches—and his believing clientele is presumed to be that of humans with super-minds and super-wealth, with none below par intelligence. How CAN people be such utter fools.

Our eyes are attuned to the perception of a limited few colors. Many humans are really even color-blind. There are many different colors that are earth-present but which our human eyes are not attuned to see. Scientific tests have established that most animals and birds see other colors than those limited to the human vision. Because we cannot conceive other colors than those which we can recognize by sight, it is very natural for us to deny the existence of that which we cannot perceive. All this does not, however, change the real facts.

This very same thing applies to sounds. Sounds abound that are either too high or too low for attunement to human perceptions. Humans themselves prove this without any additional corroborative evidence, of which there is plenty, in the fact of much better hearing in one individual than another. Just so, although all in the flesh belong to the same family, their fingerprints are all different—just as on any one tree no leaves are exactly alike. All are distinctly different on close examination.

Just so, all mental equipment, although exactly alike, is different. The author, the artist, the mechanic and all others, has got something the other has not got. IT IS ALL A STRICTLY INDIVIDUAL PROPOSITION FOR EACH, from the cry of a new soul at birth, not alone through this short earth-life experience but for all existence of the Individual Soul.

And now, Martha, we have pretty well answered Harold's last letters' questions and now you and I can have a little chat.

Harold's health has improved mentally, physically and nervously in these past months. You have seen improvement. There will be more. He should continue to call me. He does not diminish my forces in asking help from me. I cannot enter in unless he asks. I can help him otherwise—in his surroundings—in the atmosphere of his home and his study—but I cannot interfere with the INDIVIDUAL except by his desire and request. I can suggest to you—I can suggest to your surroundings—but I cannot enter in—unless by request.

The out-of-the-ordinary happenings of which you write have their place—they are for a purpose; you will recognize them appearing from time to time—one by one and little by little—and there are more that you are not aware of—yet. Now that you know of these many things of which I have written, no wonder the little philosophical readings and discussions of your little group of women friends begin to slightly pall upon you[17]—but do not neglect them—keep them up—the social side is beneficial to you—and it has its reflections in your whole household.

Away back in the beginning of things on this young planet, long after named Urantia, when after aeons of time it had progressed out of the formation class of beginning planets called "dark islands of space with neither light nor life," it was formally moved and placed in an orbit in its allocated space in a universe already long established and with a central sun from which flowed not only light and heat but also those forces and powers making for the development of the next phase of its beginning existence. Amongst these powers and forces, of which there are many thousands, came the very common ones of air and water, and the law of gravity became operable.

And so rain fell and cooled the hot young planet, and mists arose from the hot steam so arising, and the sun shone by day upon it and the moon and stars by night. And with these many powers and forces came also the beginning electrical forces immediately necessary for the formation and the continuance of "Life"—the electric force which still comes exactly in the same manner. The great charges entering the earth by way of what we call the North Pole as the Positive, and leaving at the Negative by way of what we call the South Pole.

And Life began in the warm water. Small living things that could survive and prosper in the warm water. Tiny, living, pulpy things without bones. And plant life began—brought here—rushes and grasses and vines and ferns. And time passed and the waters cooled, and from the tiny squashy and pulpy live things that were first in the water bigger and stronger things developed and bones grew within them. And time passed, aeons of time again, and the waters receded and some of the varieties of the small pulpy things in the water had evolved into birds of different varieties, from the fish that had devel-

---

[17] Martha's group met weekly to read and discuss metaphysical and inspirational books and articles.

oped from the pulpy things—and the scales of the fish had become the feathers of birds. And then some of the fish that had been without bones and then had developed them, also developed a set of connected bones down the back—a backbone—a vertebrate.

With these very few words, I give you the beginning of things that extended over many thousands of years of earth time. All physical life began on this planet in the usual way that Life is begun on all new-formed worlds.

From this small beginning, again after other aeons of time, there evolved from these vertebrate fish other undeveloped furred and skinned animal forms—the scales evolving into fur or dropping off and leaving just skin. And slowly, very slowly, the furred forms of animal Life became different and definite species of Life.

On a then-small Island off the tip of Africa, now sunk in the ocean these many thousands of earth years, an island known by ancient tradition and legend as Lemuria, there developed from these vertebrate fish a small, living, climbing, animal much like a monkey—BUT NOT A MONKEY. They were nothing like, nor any relation to, the little animal that is today called the Lemur. After other aeons of earth time, these small, intelligent, climbing earth animals developed further in intelligence and stature and there arrived the period in their development when, in the usual course, it became a part of their upstepping to introduce to them the spiritual quality and thought necessary to their upbuilding in the direction of what later were to be known as humans.

At this time, the ever-watchful and ever-guarding Intelligences having the newly developing young planet under their jurisdiction brought to this young world many already ascended second dimension Intelligences from other and older planets, and enfleshed them as both sexes of these small animals but of a higher degree. They were here to teach and lead and help upward these beginning humans BUT THEY DID NOT COME TO MATE with them nor to have progeny with them and thus cross the already full spiritual with the undeveloped flesh.

However, through accident and mistake and a misunderstanding of orders, this very thing DID happen and before it could be stopped and corrected there were many thousands of these small creatures born that were in a position that had never before arisen. These little creatures were one-half of the animal flesh and the other one-half fully developed spirit entities of the second dimension. They could not die. That is, they could not die the natural death of the flesh and continue in the regular onward routing from the point of death. There was no precedent showing procedure. The mechanics of PROGRESSION stopped with the death of the flesh on this planet. There was no further procedure.

Through no sin of commission, or omission, these hybrids, denied advance in the regular routing of advancement, and held to the precincts of this planet for all these years—for this long, long time—have only been freed by adjudication this year; and those unoccupied on earth or on other, uncompleted missions, have already left here and taken their rightful places in spheres of advancement according to their works. Some of us, fleshed and unfleshed, whose missions are not completed, still linger on here—all anxious to be "on their way."

One of these poor hybrids is myself, another is Harold. Do you now wonder at Harold's being "different"—different from any one you ever met—do you wonder that strange and weird and seemingly meaningless dreams and visions oft distress him. Do you wonder that thus from this subconscious there come these tiny bits and flashes of memories—these small bits—unfinished and tantalizing that are a mental pinpoint on which he has so often figuratively sat, do you wonder at his sometimes nervous symptoms?? Do you now more recognize "why" it is so very hard for many people to "understand" him?? He has many acquaintances but very few REAL friends—that think as much of him as he does of them—they can be counted on the fingers of one hand. He does not like to believe this, but it is true. You, very probably, better recognize the difference between his acquaintances and his REAL friends.

In my above writing you of a very small (not full, and because not in full not fully accurate) tiny bit of the story of the hybrid, you can understand why I am anxious that he be sure to read the full, complete and fully accurate story to be found of these strange beings, these "borderline sensitives," in the Book of Urantia.[18]

You can now see better how much more is the need of this man for the kind and type of a woman that you are—the mental make-up particularly. You must be not only wife, but mother, sweetheart and mistress, to fit the different moods that play upon the subconscious-

---

[18] "Hybrids" and "borderline sensitives" are not mentioned in the Urantia Book.

ness—that mysterious subconsciousness—and you are also the store-house of balance and of nervous strength that he must, and DOES, draw upon. Can you imagine this borderline sensitive married to a type other than yourself—say, the piano-playing addict, the theatrical, the lightly balanced, the over-emotional, the exhibitionist type—as so many women are—. It could not be. How much higher is your mission, in the care of this man, than that of the types that I have just quoted.

You are so needful and absolutely necessary to this "old soul" that he would passively and gladly die without you. He could not take care of himself alone—you know that—know it better than he does. He even insists that you be with him in the next dimension. He insists because he so much desires it—but it will not be so. All is an individual proposition. He will have his pathway and work to do—and you will have your pathway and work to do. They will be paths apart—but there are "rest periods" in the next dimension—rest periods where much activity ceases—similar to the rest periods of vacation time here on this dimension. And when those times come, he can seek you out or you can seek him—you will find each other—and you both will so enjoy the memories of the earth life you spent together—and you will both laugh at such things you considered so serious in this earth existence.[19]

You must now watch even more closely over this man. He is going through a chafing and difficult period. Watch over him as he develops contact with his Thought Adjuster—that he does not get too far afield in his meditations and explorations—it is easy to lose the way back if not careful. Go out with him step by step. It will be wonderful to you to make real acquaintance with your Thought Adjuster—the Comforter. It is his small quiet voice that makes what people call their "conscience" speak to them. Conscience is NOT the reasoning of your own that talks to you, that counsels with you, that tells you "NO," that advises with you—always to your benefit. What you call your conscience is not your own thought—conscience is that mysterious "something," so-called by humans in their upward stumbling,

---

[19] *When partially exhausted by the efforts of attainment, and while awaiting the reception of new energy charges, there is agreeable pleasure in living over again the enactments of other days and ages. The early experiences of the race or the order are restful to reminisce (48:4.10). Reminiscent jests [include] [q]uips growing out of the memories of past episodes in one's experience of combat, struggle, and sometimes fearfulness, and ofttimes foolish and childish anxiety (48:4.5).*

the voice of your "Thought Adjuster,"[20] a distinct entity named the Comforter by our Lord Jesus Christ, that speaks with you. He never compels you to follow his dictates at all—he advises you that which is for your best. If you take his advice it is always to your benefit—if you ignore his advice and follow your own WILL you will find, in the end, that you have made a mistake. How many times do you ever think to consult him?? You will learn MUCH; "A DOOR WILL BE OPENED UP TO YOU" as you become better acquainted with him. He came to you when you were six years old—not before—and he will be with you until the last breath in your body in this Life.

In time to come, you yourself may follow this branch of service— you may "enter in" the life experience of some soul yet to be born. I have been told that is a wonderful service—so VERY much is accomplished in so many of such paths of upward striving—but it too has its sad side—its sad side when their efforts have all been in vain. There are many of such.

The "wise men," the "sages," those who can do such strange things with their bodies and who have strange powers over the inanimate— those are the ones who have learned from this very same Thought Adjuster. Their strange knowledge comes from the Thought Adjuster. I am afraid to tell you some of the things that I have seen—and that I know are done—because it would be harmful because you would not believe—and your advancement would be that much retarded.

Just remember that everything is subject to the Mind. "That which I do, ye can do also." So keep close watch over Harold. Go out with him step by step—it is not alone permissible but much recommended. When once comes "The LIGHT," progress will be easier both to him and to you. Don't neglect the Bible. Read it—Psalms— Proverbs—the Acts—are all very helpful.

Knowing what you now do, do you wonder that both the girls are wanting their own Bible?? They are born with something in advance of what other children are given.

Balance the over-imagination of this man—remember his background—remember that there is great reason for it—quote patience

---

[20] Contrast: *Do not confuse and confound the mission and influence of the Adjuster with what is commonly called conscience; they are not directly related. Conscience is a human and purely psychic reaction. It is not to be despised, but it is hardly the voice of God to the soul, which indeed the Adjuster's would be if such a voice could be heard* (110:5.11).

and endeavor—it does not all happen over night—things WILL happen—"Be of good cheer"—"In all thy ways acknowledge HIM"—"Hold fast to all that is good."

I must not fail to here acknowledge receipt of "Eternity and I" in very good order—it is a very powerful and beautiful thing—and so wonderfully printed—will you please thank Mary for me—thank her a lot. . . .

I have tried, Martha, to learn who you are but so far I have not been successful. I do know that in some of these developments strange things are done. I have so much wanted to know if you were one of these preparations. I have not found out anything. I know so very little. . . .

Harold, what makes this typewriter jump two spaces at a time.

Well, Martha, may I thank you again for your kind letters—I am grateful for Harold's last two also. I feel better now that I have written a letter direct to you. You may watch for other small developments to happen. There will also be those that you can't see.

Thanking Mary again for the beautiful "Eternity and I" and with love to you all and the best thought over and under and around you ALL,

I am very humbly,

7

HAROLD IN HOLLYWOOD

HAROLD SHERMAN to HARRY LOOSE

New York, May 12, 1941

Friend Loose:

Well—the call has come at last—to Hollywood!

Perhaps *two* calls!

At any rate, I leave tonight and catch the Super Chief out of Chicago tomorrow night, which brings me into Los Angeles Thursday morning around 9 a.m.

As soon as I know where I will be staying, I will drop you a line to ascertain whether I am to be permitted to see you.

It is to be my job to complete the screen treatment of *Mark Twain* in the next few weeks and then I am to be given a week or so to bring my family out.

I come west *so well fortified*, thanks to you, and with promise of real true inspiration. I need to be protected from now on . . . from "double-crossing, overly ambitious Hollywood minds," etc. . . . and am sure that I will be given the inner wisdom to cope with all situations . . . that I may accomplish my high creative purposes as well.

I am interested in living quietly and simply.

My association is to be with Jesse Lasky and Warner Brothers, for your private information. No publicity has been given out on this development as yet.

Martha and I send our love to Ma Loose and yourself. The separation [from Martha and the girls], even for a short time, is going to be difficult . . . lightened, however, by the understanding which has come.

I hope and pray that I may see you.

On May 13, 1941, Harold boarded the train for Hollywood. En route he was impressed to write, "scribbling with difficulty," the following two messages from Ara, his Comforter, which he mailed to Martha from Albuquerque:

May 15, 1941

If you stand in the sight of God, you cannot see, nor do you want to see.

He sees for you.

When *His* sight becomes *your* sight, you can perceive all things with Him.

Then it is that you know that your soul is encased in a flesh garment. And then only you can put it aside as a cloak which, while serving, *binds*.

You have not seen the universe as it is until you attain God's sight.

Your earth vision is limited by the other cloak of Time and Space. But God's vision puts aside this cloak also and lets you stand in the presence of all knowledge in which Time and Space are swallowed up.

Behold, Time and Space now seem without you. A little while and you will know it exists within.

You see but the reflection of things, as one looking outward upon himself.

But, when possessed of God's sight, the reflection, which is illusion, vanishes.

To see with the spiritual eye as compared to earth vision, is as though you have been asleep for an eternity and seen nothing.

But now you are looking within the boundless heart of God, beyond all outward manifestations, wherein all returning and awakened souls find Peace and Wisdom which passeth understanding.

This will suffice.

* * *

The right hand of God and the left hand of Man.

Do not let the right hand know what the left hand doeth—for the left hand sinneth in the ways of man while the right hand reaches always towards the heavens and shields the spiritual eyes as they scan the skies of man's boundless opportunities in God.

The right hand is God's guide to man. There are always two choices in every act in life and the right hand of God can be in every one if we attune our wills to His.

When we do not, the left hand of our own desires reaches out and takes from us the feast that God has set before us, which we, temporarily blinded, do not perceive.

Watch your left hand, therefore, that it sin not against you and against Him who loves you but who cannot make His love manifest unless you lift your right hand up to His!

Herein is a great mystery, that man was made in the image and likeness of God and yet is divided into the left and right, having two sides to him.

In the beginning it was intended that these two sides should be as one but the flesh arm of man found pleasure in earth things alone, forgetting the arm of the Father.

When you clasp your hands to pray you speak symbolically your desire to join both sides of your nature—the left and the right in God.

Then it is that you sense the presence of the Comforter who comes close to you during this handclasp.

When the left hand finds its way back to the right hand of God, then the wanderer is nearing home. He comes once more within the hearing of God's voice who speaks only when the flesh side of man is subdued.

Today, rulers of men have perverted the right arms of humanity. They have caused these right arms belonging to God to be raised in salute of everything vile and unholy. For this the blind and misguided must pay.

But the right hand of God is again being raised in this world by His disciples in whom He moves and has His being.

Keep your right arm then subservient to His will and His greater strength will make of your left arm a right arm also, that you may be purified to do the Father's work.

Your Comforter has spoken.

In Los Angeles Harold was met at the train by Jesse Lasky's associate, Julius Evans, who took him to Hollywood to find a place to stay. He *settled on a one-bedroom apartment at the Canterbury on North Cherokee Ave., for $60 a month. The next day, after several conferences with Lasky about the* Mark Twain *screen treatment, Harold was entertained at Lasky's home in Brentwood, where he met Lasky's family, including wife Bessie. In a letter to Martha he described the meeting:*

> . . . Mrs. Lasky [is] a really gifted painter who showed me a marvelous spiritual mural . . . and who made a surprising comment to me in a moment alone, when she looked at me and said: "Mr. Sherman, you are just the man to work with Mr. Lasky . . . to do fine spiritual things in pictures. You are all right . . . I *know you from other planes."* Lasky later said that he has mentioned many celebrities and has brought many people out whom he felt meant something . . . but the moment he mentioned my name, Mrs. Lasky showed immense interest from the start and asked all about me . . . and said, "That man has something." She claims to be deeply intuitive and feels she gets inspiration from higher intelligences. I think you will like her very much. . . .
>
> Mr. Lasky's secretary, Mr. Rogers, a fine middle-aged man (all Lasky's associates whom I have met possess really high qualities of character) . . . confided to me that he had read my book, *Your Key to Happiness* . . . that it had been a Godsend to him. He is being threatened with a nervous breakdown, fears death, etc. . . . is so anxious to get some time with me. Doctors, psychiatrists, etc. have failed to help. He says, "I have just been living, Mr. Sherman, until you would get here. I have been on the point of committing suicide. Please don't say anything to anyone. Even my wife doesn't know the hell I'm going through."
>
> So, it looks like there is work to be done. . . .

Harold also mentioned that he had dropped Harry Loose a line, letting him know of his arrival.

HARRY LOOSE to HAROLD SHERMAN

Monterey Park, May 16, 1941

My Friend:

I am returning to you, enclosed herein, the [Ara] writings of May 15th. They are exceptionally beautiful. Truthfully, I can tell you they are far more beautiful and far more true in their philosophy than "Eternity and I." I would advise you to keep them carefully. If these are carbon copies and you have the originals, I would be pleased if you would return these to me for my rereading and care.

I am free to contact you Sunday, May 18th, if this is convenient to you. If I do not hear from you to the contrary, I will drive over to the Canterbury Apartments around 3 p.m.

With all best thought,

MARTHA SHERMAN to HAROLD SHERMAN

New York, May 16, 1941

Dearest,

. . . A long letter came addressed to me from Mr. Loose today, and while it is intended for you, of course, as well as me, if you do not mind I shall keep it to study over a little before I send it on. He emphasizes again the absolute need for you to call for him and to develop the friendship of "C" [Comforter]. He did not mention your going west but since he reiterates that you must draw certain resources from me, I am presuming it is to your benefit that we be together as much as possible. Now that we have this temporary separation you must more than ever call on him. He says it does not deplete him in any way.

I am finding the separation somewhat easier this time, perhaps because of the new understanding which we are having a glimmer of. . . .

My love always,

May 17, 1941

Dearest,

Today came your second letter written en route with the additional inspirational suggestions. The thoughts they contain are truth I am sure, though I do not understand them completely—especially the time and space idea. I shall place them in our little black book. . . . As you've no doubt discovered, I've put Loose's last letter in the envelope as I think there are matters in it you should know. If you care to you can mail it back and I will put it with the others. . . .

HAROLD SHERMAN to MARTHA SHERMAN

Hollywood, May 18, 1941

Dearest:

. . . I have just had a wonderful afternoon with Harry J. Loose. He drove 23 miles across Los Angeles to see me in my apartment—said he wanted to be sure I was in the right place, that it was very important. He approved of it in every way, and said he left power and protective vibrations with me . . . which I *feel*. He said also, "Don't be lonely," and I assured him I was not, that I have the best feeling inwardly I have ever had, which I was sure was true of you, too. He said, "That's fine, Harold . . . that's real development. I know how much you and Martha care for one another, and how hard it is to be separated . . . but you're not, really, and you won't be, physically, very long."

Harry said he thinks you will be forwarding his last letter, addressed to you, to me soon. I think he may be writing you again.

I wrote all morning on the treatment I am finishing for submission to Lasky later this week, which in turn must be submitted to Warners as the basis for the deal. I stopped at one o'clock, since I knew Harry was coming at three or thereabouts, and spent the rest of the time in preparation. During this period of meditation, the enclosed came through and I was impressed to read it to Harry as soon as he came in.[1] I did so, and he sat and wept like a child. "Harold . . . oh, Harold . . . it's been so long . . . we've come such a long way together," he said. And as he departed, just a few minutes ago, he said, "I hope seeing me has not disillusioned you. It has been such a trial to me, knowing what to do. I must not hinder your development in any way."

[*Handwritten insertion:*] (Remember Josephine Davis of Marion[2] telling us of remarkable messages Dr. Sadler was getting in Chicago? He's one of the group working on the book "Urantia"!! Should be published this fall!)

Harry says he is happy to know we are planning to locate here with things working out right. He feels there are forces out here that we are to unite with in the mission we are to perform. He says, also, that he wants me with him when he passes to the Second Dimension. He looks forward to this as a great occasion.

There is so much I could tell you which cannot be communicated in writing. I am working night and day to do my end of this creative job so that things can be pressed to a successful conclusion. Everyone is being most considerate of me, and Julius Evans as well as Lasky have phoned to invite me out, thinking I might be lonely today . . . How little they know!

Write me as often as you feel the impulse . . . it helps.

P.S. Make your quiet plans with every faith that things are going through here in the right way as they should. I am being guided

---

[1] Message follows this letter.
[2] See p. 34 for first mention of Josephine Davis.

against pitfalls I am sure—and there are many in Hollywood! Ambitious people who would cut others' throats. . . . Won't have much to report but work for a few days. Your first two letters received.

May 18, 1941, 2:20 p.m.

Today are you to meet with one who has been with you from the Beginning.

Long is the way you two have traveled together—side by side as spiritual selves though countless times divided in body.

A veil is about to lift between you that you may stand in the illumination of your own real selves, darkened these many earth lives by your services in the flesh.

This joining of your forces in the flesh is being permitted that the one going on may leave with the one remaining here yet awhile the illumination which is his—that where he is you may be also—never more alone in the doing of thy Father's work, now closing in this last day and cycle of Urantia.

For the day of this earth shall not be as long as the long, long night thereof, since the Father has other plans for those whose feet have found the way and is leading their footsteps elsewhere, while the unenlightened ones still remaining shall be changed by the fiery heat of such cataclysmic human experience as Urantia, in all its awful history, has never had come upon it.

But this is only the necessary end for which a sad, mistaken beginning was made—and you are to be found serving in that Time—letting God's voice speak through you—with the ears of a hungry multitude drinking in your words of true inspiration and wisdom, given you from on High.

You have come west as the first great step in your novitiate and here, as you sit, so seemingly alone, are gathered a host of fellow workers from Higher Planes who will be greeting you in the handclasp of Harry J. Loose, the tree planter[3] of old—and lo, be it known that you are the sapling he has planted which is to bring forth good fruit—fruit of the spirit, blessed and purified through the blood of fleshly sacrifice and devotion to the nameless cause—a cause to which your two souls have been so long—so *very* long committed.

For the one, there will come release for Higher work in good and shortened time. For you also will come release of Spirit and of Wisdom that you may spread your branches to cover

---

[3] See p. 181 where Loose, in his April 3, 1941 letter, mentions planting trees in a previous life.

the reaches of the stalwart tree so soon to be transplanted for work in other realms.

Great joy and peace be with you both, on this, a most eventful day in your long pilgrimage back to the Father.

The homeland is in sight.

The host, surrounding you, have spoken.

May 19, 1941

Dearest:

I am rich—three letters from you today! I think the letter from HJL was one of his best—and his stressing of my need of you in every way is certainly true. It emphasizes all the more my early recognition of that fact . . . my knowing that, if our lives were not to be together, I, myself, would be lost. I refuse to be concerned about future states . . . that I have *you* in this life expression is sufficient evidence that things will be as we would desire, if we fulfill our missions here.

I cannot let myself go on paper at this stage because so much depends upon my finishing the first part of this job and moving developments along here—which will speed the time of your coming . . . and I am consequently busy day and night . . . and, incidentally feeling fine . . . with a greater sense of power than I have ever had. . . .

I feel that more good things are getting ready to happen . . . and, of course, am *crazy* for the day when I can give you the good word to come along! . . .

May 20, 1941

. . . This morning, before lunch, I finished plotting the balance of the Mark Twain story and feel I am being inspired, for some grand ideas have come to me. I am sure Harry Loose is helping . . . he said, as he shook hands on leaving, "Harold, you forget me right now . . . you have a job to do, but I won't be forgetting you!" He may bring Ma Loose to spend part of next Sunday with me. I'm going to try to save Sundays for such contacts . . . and maybe we can, too, when you are out here. . . .

Love to all,

HARRY LOOSE to MARTHA SHERMAN

Monterey Park, May 20, 1941

Dear Martha:-

Harold is very nicely located over at the Canterbury Apartments—just a half block from Hollywood Blvd. The building is a U-shaped affair of white stucco—of which there is a great deal out here in this warm country. Filipino help. It was the third place that he went to. He likes it there very much. It is very quiet. He has your handkerchief under his pillow, and before he goes to sleep at night he holds it tightly in his hands.

The "desk" on the first floor is to the left when you come in— some 50 feet down the large entryway. The whole 50 feet is set with growing plants of different kinds. You turn to the left, from the desk, about ten feet down the hall, and the stairs are to the left there that take you up to Harold's apartment. It is plenty large enough for you and the girls when you come out. You can stay right there, with plenty of sleeping room, until you get ready to change.

He is up and at his writing at 6 in the morning. He expects to have it ready for Mr. Lasky's reading by this Thursday. He read me a page or two of the opening—and several pages of the closing. He has slept well—he is not lonely—he has your photograph within reach and where he can always see it. Mr. Lasky has had him to his home for dinner and some other young man from Lasky's office invited him out for dinner for last Sunday but he did not care to go. His thoughts are of you and the girls—and of finishing the writing—and then the reading of the finished script to Mr. Lasky. He talks only of you folks and his work—he has no other interests. He is a very splendid man— with MUCH courage—and has gone through a great deal—as you know.

Mr. Whitmore, his old-time N.Y. friend,[4] is in town as a guest at the Jonathan Club. He is sick—Harold got in touch with him on the phone but has not seen him yet.

The stomach condition has not bothered him. He plans to slow up a bit when Mark Twain is out of the way—and do some of the things that he really wants to do. It would be of great help to him in all ways to do this very thing when the happy time arrives.

I hope that you all will like California when you come. As soon as I knew that Harold was leaving I mailed a letter personally to you. Hope that you rec'd it safely—I asked Harold if you had forwarded to him yet—and he said "No," but that it would probably be in Monday's mail.

It is 25 miles from my house to the Canterbury Apartments. I got over there at 3:15 Sunday afternoon and didn't leave until ten minutes

---

[4] See p. 52 for first mention of Charles Whitmore.

to 7 in the evening. I have a letter from him today in which he asks that Ma and I come over this coming Sunday. I cannot answer him yet.

He is a good man, Martha, with much mental courage and physical courage, a splendid fellow. I am sure that he will not lose heart—or faith—and will keep up the way he is going and will go on. You must in no way fail him. Send him another soiled handkerchief of yours in another week and have him return the one that he has. Read Psalms, Proverbs, and the Acts every evening a bit. Be sure that he gets that period for rest and self-communion and meditation and time to do the things that he now wants to do with Mark Twain out of the way. Be sure that the handkerchief you will send him shows that you have had it about you—for heaven's sake don't send him a freshly washed and clean one.

I guess that I have told you about all. Except—not to worry—or let the girls worry—or get in any way worked up or excited—and don't write him anything unnecessarily that would cause him to worry—I know very well that you won't even as I am writing this—I really should not have said it—as there will be nothing anyway.

With the best thought to you all, over and under and around you all,

With love from Ma and I,

HARRY LOOSE to HAROLD SHERMAN
Monterey Park, May 21, 1941

My Friend:-

Your very good letter received and I am so pleased that you were not entirely disillusioned. Because of your invitation for next Sunday, I have waited until today to answer.

I mailed a letter to Martha yesterday. Telling her how you were located—how you looked—about your being at the writing at 6 in the morning—and your progress—and how you were feeling. She will forward it on to you. . . .

Now in regard to our coming over to the Canterbury this coming Sunday. A tentative pre-commitment definitely maturing, and claimed, forbids otherwise acceptance of invitation for Ma and I for that particular day—much as we would have liked to the contrary. Can this meeting be changed to the following Saturday (May 31st), if this time is convenient—or make a convenient time earlier than that

Harold Sherman in Hollywood
[Sherman Family Private Collection].

date—but not Sunday June 1st. I do not want the contact of Ma and I to in any way interfere with anything pertaining to the progress—the finishing—or the reading of Mark Twain.

We wait to hear of the reading. All good thought goes to you from us here. Your care and protection are ever in our minds. Do not let any fear-thoughts enter. Don't forget Proverbs, Psalms, and the Acts before bed. And don't forget Martha's handkerchief. I have asked her to send you another—you can send the one that you have back to her.

With love from us both,

MARTHA SHERMAN to HAROLD SHERMAN
New York, May 21, 1941

Dearest,

It was good to get your letter late this afternoon . . . it was a long wait from Saturday to Tuesday without word. Perhaps I should say, *written* word, for altho I did not mention it to you, and least of all to the girls, I knew you were with Mr. Loose Sunday afternoon. I don't believe I've ever had a happier feeling from you (it was actually radiant), and I knew also that it was a very wonderful experience. I am so glad for you that you are beginning to see your way clearly and that the end of the long long trail is nearing.

Evidently the book of Urantia is coming out sooner than we were first told and surely it is something to look forward to. I feel awfully good about Mr. Loose liking your choice of apartments, too, and that he is surrounding you with good thoughts. I guess you need that protection in Hollywood about as much as any place in the world, unless it be Washington, D.C.! . . .

We all send our love and hope it does its bit toward helping you.

May 21, 1941

Dearest,

. . . I'm so thankful every moment that Mr. Loose is wrapping protecting influences about you. Your apartment does sound comfortable. . . . A few months ago I should have worried considerably about your physical condition but now with the wonderful new experience opening before you I am sure you will not have the setbacks of previous years. . . . I go over one of Mr. Loose's letters each night and then a chapter from Psalms. It helps. What compensations life is bringing us! I hope we shall not fail in the work ahead. . . .

HAROLD SHERMAN to MARTHA SHERMAN
Hollywood, May 22, 1941

Dearest:

. . . I am enclosing something that seemed to come through last night and am also returning Loose's letter for our treasured file of them . . . also his notes to me which I have thought you might like to see. If he should write you further letters, perhaps you might exchange them with me and I would send back to you . . . but I hope that this procedure won't be necessary for so very long. . . .

May 21, 1941

Those who wait for a God to appear, who say God has not made Himself manifest to Man, are sleeping in the blindness and ignorance of the flesh. They have denied Him from the first and will not recognize Him, nor be recognized by Him, at the last.

Infinite Intelligence sustains only that part of Itself which reflects It and, after a time, withdraws such sparks of expanding identity as do not ignite with the elements in outer manifestation nor tend to elevate through exercise of the Spirit, the forms occupied.

For the Way, in Higher Dimensions, divides—and those souls or individualized segments of the Great Intelligence who pursue evil, do so to their own destruction and ultimate annihilation, even if it should require the obliteration of worlds and planets.

God is Infinite Intelligence in motion and any forces, given free and independent movement within certain realms, that elect to move counter to the Godward movement, provoke cataclysms in various parts of the Universe, but alter God nor His incomprehensible plan not at all!

The still small voice is Man's connecting link with Higher Intelligence. It can be heard amid a Niagara of worldly sounds by those who lift themselves in thought and act above the world.

Whosoever will so do, hears the music of his own Being. Such a one can never again be torn apart by wrangling discords of this sorry earth. He rests secure upon the bosom of the Intelligence he *is!*

MARTHA SHERMAN to HAROLD SHERMAN
New York, May 23, 1941

Dearest,

. . . Mr. Loose wrote me a nice letter today telling me about your apartment location and little homely details. Even said you had my photograph—never thought of your having it along—it must be the old one with the girls. He suggests I send you another used handkerchief in a few days and you return the old one to me. I shall carry it with me a day or two to be sure it has the required vibrations or whatever is necessary for you to have. Evidently someone is suggesting to me some of the things I should do—I just seemed to know you should have that with you. Also, my nightly readings by myself are what I should do also. It's a harder order to keep peace in the household at all times and I find I lose my patience now and then. Well, I'm a long way from being perfect. . . .

HAROLD SHERMAN to MARTHA SHERMAN

Hollywood, May 23, 1941

Dearest:

. . . Eureka! I have just finished—at 10:30 the entire job—first draft. 264 pages, which is 80,000 words in a little over a week—easily up to my old production records . . . and I am feeling fine, though fingers of hands a bit lame from constant typing. . . .

Just a note from [Sir Hubert] Wilkins on this mail to say he'd be in Los Angeles tomorrow—Sunday night—until June 2nd, when he sails for Japan. He is stopping at the Jonathan Club where Charlie Whitmore is quartered. . . .

MARTHA SHERMAN to HAROLD SHERMAN

New York, May 24, 1941

Dearest,

. . . I'm putting in Mr. Loose's letter to me and also the second used handkerchief he suggested. I've carried it tucked inside my dress for two days and slept with it last night so it should have absorbed some of me! I know you're disappointed in not seeing Mr. Loose and "Ma" tomorrow but at least they have promised you a later date and it is wonderful that you are being able to see them at all. . . .

All my love always,

May 25, 1941

. . . Tonight for the first time I've had a restless feeling and I feel it emanates from you. Are you disturbed about something? Anyway, my "insides" are churning! Have you finished the script and now are waiting for the next move? . . .

HAROLD SHERMAN to MARTHA SHERMAN

Hollywood, May 26, 1941

Dearest:

... [W]hen I wrote you last night, after Lasky was here, I think I was suffering a bit of a letdown from the terrific week I had spent and the fact that there was no definite word of action to report. I, too, wish you could take the next train out here! ...

The photograph I have of you is the one I've always liked—taken in 1917. ... You have matured, of course, since this photograph was taken . . . but the same fine spirit and beautiful person was there then . . . who is still with me now—and even dearer! I keep this photograph beside me on the typewriter desk. (And a secret—as much as I love the girls—this is the only real photograph of you *by yourself,* which is the real reason I wanted it.)

I must phone Harry Loose this morning and arrange for a time this week when he and Mrs. Loose can come over and spend some hours with me. It is grand to know I can see them, and you have a great treat in store. Did I tell you that Loose said he wanted me with him when he passed on? And that he wanted me to go to the place where the souls departed this planet on the third day? He would keep checking himself, many times and say, "Not yet," as he would start to tell me something. And before he left, he went in my bedroom and stood there, silently, for just a moment. What a remarkable, sweet person he is! (Your present handkerchief is a bit soiled due to carbon on my fingers and soft lead pencil stain. It is strange that I do sense your vibration from it. I think we've felt that before about each other's possessions, but never so much as when directly called to our attention.) ...

... I don't think I have felt better in years . . . which is a fine indication of certain forces at work. ...

MARTHA SHERMAN to HAROLD SHERMAN

New York, May 27, 1941
Sanctum Sanctorum (being your study)

Dearest,

Tonight I'm writing you a little earlier than usual as I'm planning, with the rest of the country, to listen to the President's address. I wonder if it will be as momentous as expected. I've had two letters and your radiogram today so feel rich. Even though I know I get many of your thoughts and moods definitely, I am still very much at the stage where the written word is pretty satisfying. I have been especially aware of your thoughts on the two Sundays and this time my letter verifying that has probably reached you. Tonight I feel a pleasantly alert feeling as though you are much interested in the turn events are taking and are anticipatory of good news. Will you please tell me whether I'm correct? . . .

A little later I shall read Ephesians and tell you what thoughts it brings tomorrow night. I like to do my reading after I've said good night to the family here. I was surprised to find you had my high school picture with you—had really forgotten we had any. When I look at those girlish pictures now it sometimes gives me a strange feeling as tho I'm quite a different person altogether than I was then— it's hard to describe. . . .

My love always,

HAROLD SHERMAN to MARTHA SHERMAN
Hollywood, May 27, 1941

Dearest:

A satisfactory conference with Lasky and Julius Evans yesterday wherein we all agreed upon a method of treating the Mark Twain life story, and I am at work again boiling down and selecting the episodes we now want from the full treatment prepared. I should be on the last end of the first big job now.

Last night was spent pleasantly in the company of Lasky and Wilkins, who were friends of long standing. Wilkins insisted on taking us both to dinner at the Hollywood Roosevelt, about four blocks up the Boulevard from here. Later in the evening we went to a news reel theatre where the "Jumping Frog" contest was shown, at Angels Camp, in commemoration of Twain's story ["The Celebrated Jumping Frog of Calaveras County"] with prizes awarded owners of frogs jumping the furthest. . . .

No letter from you this morning but expect it will arrive on the afternoon mail. I am returning your first handkerchief, with thanks for your second, and apologies, too, for the condition of the first. I have had it with me at all times. It is a pretty poor substitute for YOU!!??!!

Well, let's hope we know something more definite before long . . . giving thanks, meanwhile, that we are being cared for in every way. I will return Loose's note soon. Talked to him yesterday by phone— they may come next Saturday.

Hollywood, May 27, 1941

Dearest:

I had just finished your first letter this morning and was starting out of the lobby to mail it in the box on Hollywood Boulevard when I ran into Harry Loose, who had come over to take me out to his place in the car. I just went with him, bare-headed, the way I was—in my sport suit, which I'm wearing most of the time now . . . light trousers and brown coat, light gray shirt with tan-colored tie. Makes an attractive looking outfit—you wouldn't know your Hollywood husband!

If Harry had been twenty seconds later he would have missed me—for a half hour anyway, as I had intended to do some shopping. It seemed good to see him and since I hadn't started on my second part of this writing job, proved a good time to relax. I have just now gotten back, by streetcar line, over an hour's trip from Monterey Park and a transfer down in Los Angeles, and it is 15 to 4 p.m. I thought I would write you before settling down to the creative task ahead . . . and while my mind is yet fresh on the incidents.

Harry was much concerned lest you would misunderstand our relationship and feel it might be taking away something from your own relationship with me. He said he wouldn't have you feel this way for the world and would willingly forego seeing me any more if this were true—because you were far more important to me in every way than he . . . and he didn't want to frighten or upset you in any way with what had been revealed or anything he might say. He asked me time and again if I felt you were disturbed . . . said he thought he had felt some bewilderment or confusion . . . that he hoped not . . . that the responsibility was so great, opening doors for others. I reassured him in every way I could . . . and when we finally got to his house, after sitting for several hours in his little park, a most restful place, he found a note from you which made him feel better.

He said to me again: "Harold, I have tried to be truthful, and when I have not known, I have said so . . . and it may actually be that Martha is a second dimension intelligence . . . that she is also a hybrid . . . and that, when you are both released from this life, you will pass through the second dimension into your reward in the third . . . and may then be together. I do not know. But, not knowing, I could not truthfully say, or positively, that you would be together in this next second dimension although you can and will see each other from time to time. That Martha is in herself a high development, I feel sure—and I hope it will be revealed to me more about her. But I must be patient . . . there is a reason if this knowledge is withheld as yet . . . for her good as well . . . but let her feel happy in the unfoldment that is already coming."

I told him I was sure you were and that you appreciated, as much as did I, the knowledge that was being made available to us both. That you were even sorry I would not be able to spend more time with him because of my work . . . and that we were both looking forward to being able to contact Ma Loose and himself together a little later.

We sat in the park, a few blocks from his home, on the bench where he sits when the Catholic priest visits him. There were some fir trees not far away and others, the species of which I do not know . . . but which whispered in the breeze and made everything seem restful. A children's sandlot was about thirty feet in front of us, with no children playing in it, and beyond a baseball grounds . . . far in the distance, mountain peaks, lost in a haze. "Sometimes the priest is here ahead of me, waiting," said Harry, "and at other times I get here before he does. I have visited him and appear there just as I am dressed now, seemingly just as physical as I am now, just as conscious of my surroundings . . . while my real physical body is at home asleep, guarded by Ma Loose."

It was wash day and Harry debated about taking me on up to the house, but did so, despite the fact she'd probably give him Hades. He backed the car up the drive and I got out and she came to the back door and I shook hands and kissed her on the cheek, and found her to be a smaller edition, in type, of Mrs. Curran, but with more warmth of spirit, I believe.

We went into their simple but nice home where I had the feeling I had been in it before, and easily located the things I had seen in my "vision," including his study on the left hand side in front. He has Mary's rendition of "Eternity and I" hanging up on the wall there . . . and the pictures of four children—three grown. One had been lost in infancy and the other was a married woman in her thirties when she passed on of a gall bladder operation in 1934. Another married daughter, Josephine Burkhart, lives just across the street with a little boy of 4 or 5 . . . and [the Looses] have a son Harry Jr., who lives in Chicago with his family and sells printing presses.

Harry said later: "None of my children have the protection you and Martha have because they have not earned it, although they know more than the average children . . . and your own girls, partaking of your higher development, should display talents and qualities not in the souls who are getting their regular first life experience here."

Harry also said that Ma Loose knew as much of the Book of Urantia as he did, since she went all through the many years' work with himself and the group . . . and that she could tell us much when the right time came . . . but is not permitted to tell anything about his individual development any more than you would do so about mine—for it would not be understood at this time by others.

I hope you have not been stricken with fear or apprehension about anything, because I know that higher intelligences, having our well-being in their care, would not be cruel . . . and I feel that we have an eternal link with each other which will be revealed. . . .

This paper tablecloth [included with the letter] comes from a roadside inn where Harry took me for lunch, which I succeeded in paying for—one of the tastiest meals I ever ate anywhere. We had "Chicken in the Rough," which is half a chicken, served so you pick it up in your fingers, having finger pails of hot water to rinse in . . . and hot biscuits and the most delicious honey to eat along with the stringed potatoes and chicken. Make your mouth water? There are a number of these places out here and we'll have to make a beeline for them when you arrive. . . .

The leaves [also included] are from the Looses' pepper tree in the backyard. . . .

My love to you now and eternally—

P.S. I have pressed these leaves to my lips to keep them moist for you! And to enable them to carry my kiss three thousand miles!

MARTHA SHERMAN to HAROLD SHERMAN

New York, May 29, 1941

Dearest,

Your letter of Tuesday May 27 reached me this a.m. I believe that was the day I had another "lifted" feeling from you as I wrote. You had just had your pleasant afternoon with Mr. Loose. I can imagine it was like a dream come true to find yourself sitting in the very same park and on the very same bench that he had written you about.

I am dreadfully sorry if he feels that in any way he has disturbed our lives. It has been a most remarkable and wonderful experience, and you must know that every time I've written I have mentioned how happy I am that he is there to protect you. Before he came consciously into our lives I might have had many qualms about your going into the Hollywood environment, particularly with the physical conditions that were present, but I have had absolute relief on that score this time because I *know* you are being cared for by influences powerful beyond our knowledge. It has made this little separation much easier for us both I'm sure. Please reassure him again as to my deep inner gratitude for all he's done. . . .

To return to Mr. Loose—of course he timed himself to meet you just when he did. He is so aware of your needs, just as he waited until he knew you had left for California before he mailed his first letter to me. It will be a wonderful experience to feel that we can respond to our Comforters as he must in every move he makes. To feel that he wants you to be with him when he takes the next great step forward must be wonderful too, with the added experience of being in the place where souls actually take off. I am so glad to have the bit of the pepper tree, not only for its original source but for what it brings, and it will be my companion each night. . . .

Oh—will you ask Mr. Loose if it will be of help to you for me to send you a handkerchief weekly? There is so much I would like to understand but know that when the *right* time comes the answer will be there.

Just what is the kind of work you are doing now? No real development comes the easy way—and evidently thru all your struggles you have builded much better than you know. Read Acts 5, 41st verse.

Dearest, I love you—

HAROLD SHERMAN to MARTHA SHERMAN
Hollywood, May 29, 1941

Dearest:

. . . I talked with Wilkins today and he approved of my working with Simon & Schuster. I think, myself, everything is working out for the best with respect to this book. There is a tremendous air show being held at the Santa Anita race track Friday, Saturday and Sunday of this week . . . and Wilkins just phoned back to say he was to be a guest and would take me with him Sunday. There will be the first public exhibition of mass parachute jumping in this country and you will probably see news reels of this event. I am looking forward to this with great interest. . . .

Love to all . . . with extra special love for you! I'm sure it won't be so long before we'll be able to be together again . . . and it makes me so happy!

May 30, 1941

Dearest:

... Charlie Whitmore phoned to say he was driving out to the mountains by the seashore for the week-end with a friend and would like to have lunch with me. I took the two of them to Gourmet's, my treat, being surprised by Wilkins having followed them out in another car, one he had borrowed—a Lincoln Zephyr, to ask me if I didn't want to go riding with him this grand afternoon. His battery gave out and he had to get a new one while we were having lunch ... but he joined us at restaurant later, not eating, however, since he had just been vaccinated and taken inoculations for smallpox, typhoid, paratyphoid and cholera—all at once—and wasn't supposed to eat either lunch or dinner. This seemed to me enough to have made a horse sick but didn't seem to faze him. He leaves for China and Japan June 2nd, so must be ready to face disease and worse.

We drove over to Glendale and saw the famous Lockheed Airplane plant ... then to the Los Angeles airport, and watched the planes coming and going, mostly privately owned ones, practicing take-offs and landings, against the backdrop of the mountains.

Then back to Hollywood and up to Hollywoodland—above the reservoir, up a winding road, along the narrow edge of nothing, higher and higher, until we reached the summit of Mount Lee upon which is the highest and biggest television broadcasting station in the world! And WHAT a sight from this elevation of 1,700 feet ... Wilkins says it is one of the most breathtaking in his experience and affects him more than being at this height or any height in a plane. Los Angeles, Hollywood, Beverly Hills and countless other suburbs stretching off and losing themselves in the ocean on one side ... and Glendale, Pasadena and numerous other towns, running up against a haze of purple-hued mountains on the other side ... and the sun setting, throwing a magic lantern glow over the whole scene far, far below.

We made friends with the watchman in charge who, when I told him it was Sir Hubert Wilkins, insisted on taking us through the station. We were in forbidden territory anyway, driving up this high, but Paul Marshall, the watchman, told me to come back and bring my family and that we'd be welcome as long as we wished to stay ... when I told him you hadn't been west. ...

Hollywood, June 1, 1941

Dearest:

The weather report for tomorrow was cloudy and Sir Hubert phoned to ask if I could go to the Air Show today, which I arranged to do, going by streetcar down into Los Angeles and meeting him at the Jonathan Club where a Mr. Johnson joined us. . . . All three of us drove out to Santa Anita racetrack, which is beyond Pasadena, a distance of about twenty miles, along a four-lane highway—and beautiful scenic views in the distance. The grandstand where we sat faces the distant range of mountains, a series of them which tower into the sky and melted into a haze which cleared as the afternoon went along and the sun sank lower, giving us unexcelled vision for the mass parachute jumps—white puffs against the mountain green and purple . . . an exciting sight. The bodies come hurtling down, turning end over end and suddenly bob into an upright position as though attached by invisible strings to the heavens. . . .

Stunt flying by Tex Rankin, the world's greatest and one of Wilkins' friends, was easily the hit of the show. . . .

It's hard to tell you what I'm doing on the treatment without going into a lot of detail, but Lasky wants the best dramatic episodes tied together in some vital way, and I've completed 70 pages of a job, the framework of which he has okayed. The work is supposed to take around 100 pages. I am prepared to have more ideas and suggestions made, and will be glad when final contractual arrangements have been completed so I will know where I stand permanently with respect to the creative job I am doing. . . .

I doubt if I will need another handkerchief unless our separation is longer than I think it will be. I am glad you could feel the vibration from the pepper leaves. There are jacaranda trees in bloom now—a bright purple—which is pretty beyond description. . . .

Hollywood, June 4, 1941

Dearest:

. . . Harry is coming over tomorrow morning and we hope to get in half a day's visit before I am called to the studio in the afternoon to meet a writer with whom I may be asked to collaborate. I feel he is reassured now over your attitude. He is so very conscientious about every move he makes and so careful. Two nights ago I awakened about 4 and thought of him strongly, would not have been surprised to have seen him in the room. Shortly before that time he had experienced a heart attack and had sent out the call to me. He says he is feeling better again the past few days. He is so anxious to be released, now that he feels his life work is done. A remarkable man, as you know, and I do not think he will seem any less remarkable on meeting. . . .

To the question I asked Lasky about my ability to get away, shortly after contracts were signed, in order to bring family out here, he said he didn't know . . . they might want full steam ahead so they could go into production on the picture as soon as possible, in order to stage premiere as planned November 30th at Hannibal [Missouri]. But this picture game is so changeable. He doesn't realize how *close* we are (in body and spirit)—when he suggested it might be better to put three or four more weeks' work on the treatment before trying to get away. Of course a good salary means so much to us now . . . if I can get you out here soon . . . and keep the salary going, it will be the biggest kind of a God send. . . .

June 5, 1941
5:30 p.m.

Dearest:

I have spent a wonderful day today with Harry Loose who came over around 9:50 a.m. at my invitation and stayed until around 4. I had a feeling that Lasky would not need me today, even though he said he wanted me to meet a possible collaborator at the studio this afternoon. Instead he phoned around noon to say he had decided not to call in a collaborator until the deal was set—and would I go ahead and see what I could do with the final treatment? This was what I had been hoping for—since I have been rushed so I haven't had a fair chance . . . and if I can produce exactly what he wants by some time next week, I may be able to do the whole job myself! Loose was here during the call and said: "You see how you are being protected! They can't make a move injurious to you if you hold yourself right."

Loose emphasized one point over and over and I feel it should be passed on to you. He said, "Get this fixed in your consciousness: Your body does not possess a soul; your soul possesses a body!"[5] Then he went on to say that, if the body possessed a soul, it would die with the body; but since the soul possesses a body, it lays it aside like an old

---

[5] *On a material world you think of a body as having a spirit, but we regard the spirit as having a body* (42:12.5).

overcoat and takes on a new body in a different dimension, when this life is over. I thought this a simple but powerful distinction.

About the needs of the body; he said it should be cared for in every particular . . . that the forces of life were intended to be kept flowing through it . . . that God was not pleased at humans trying to sublimate their sex desires by repression or abnormal restraints . . . that it was not good for persons to live alone—and not so intended— particularly those of the higher developments, and that was why *we* were so well cared for and so well mated. That we had a greater capacity for expression than the average and should exercise it when the spirit moved, since it had a spiritual significance beyond the physical in the flow of powers through us. That the bodies are not *us*—and there is no sin of the body except as we abuse it and ourselves in the doing through overindulgence or dissipation, thus preventing ourselves from accomplishing the purposes for which we came into this life. There is nothing wrong in Sex as such; a man is 60% male and 40% female; and a woman, 60% female and 40% male . . . and united, form the perfect balance. This balance is upset in some people for various reasons of body and soul. . . .

June 6, 1941

Dearest:

. . . There is nothing new to report here. I neglected to state [in our phone call last night] that Loose wants to take me on a "trip" South with him when I can make arrangements for someone to be in the apartment for 18 hours, for a visit with his Catholic priest—*if* he can get permission so to do. I think this will have to wait until you can be here. I would not trust anyone else. . . .

Love to the girls and yourself.

June 10, 1941

Dearest:

. . . I see by the date line that we have only five more days, within which time Warners is supposed to close the deal. That it is going through there seems to be no doubt . . .

I think Harry Loose will be over to spend some time with me again today. I certainly would not attempt anything in the way of a "trip" without your being here . . . and would want to be in a more relaxed and secure state financially . . . with regular assured periods of meditation . . . perhaps in our own home, before trying it. He says it is as simple as stepping in the next room, once developed; nothing to do with hypnotism or anything like that. Your body and everything about you is just as physical to you, apparently, as in your normal state . . . except that you notice you pass right through chairs or walls . . . and are invisible to others, unless they possess the "sight" to see you and converse with you. I recall the sensation I had when I apparently left the body in the experience on Haven Avenue, when I thought I heard you and Mary coming in the door. I was "out" so quickly and easily, it was astonishing. Loose said that's a very good example . . . you lay your physical body down, go to sleep, and step out of it. He still will not tell me much of the mystery of sleep because he says it involves many deep explanations which lead into profound subjects . . . but I am convinced sleep takes us close to the source of our real being . . . *in* and *with* the Great Intelligence! . . .

On June 13, Harold wrote to his mother that Warner Bros. had decided not to go ahead with Twain. *As a consequence, while Lasky sought other financing, Harold's salary was cut from $500 to $100 a week. This development gave Harold a chance to fly to New York for a few weeks until a new deal was set, after which the family intended to buy a car and tour through to Los Angeles together.*

HARRY LOOSE to HAROLD SHERMAN

Monterey Park, June 13, 1941

My Friend:-

There appears to be some confusion. There may be delay—postponement—cancellation—or other disruption of the trip east—for reasons that are not clear or even indicated. Some matters not known to you in their entirety are still undecided and under discussion—the matter has not yet been definitely and positively closed. It will however very probably work out the way your telephone conversation indicated.

If you make the air trip you may be very positive that the only physical difficulty will be from your own nervous reactions during the first part of the trip—the first several hours—if that. You will then lose the nervous *fear* and much enjoy the rest of the trip. To offset much of the beginning difficulty—with nerves and stomach—eat very lightly the 24 hours before starting the trip—drink much water—get the small container, containing 10 tablets I believe, of Burroughs-Wellcome Triple Bromides, take 2 of these effervescent tablets in a half-glass of water 2 hours before starting and eat a couple of crackers. Repeat with 2 more of these tablets when you take your first food on the plane. If necessary, take 2 more some hours later. Drop tablets in water and when they cease effervescing then drink.

Mark Twain will be produced—you may be sure of this. Accept the present delay without fear or worry and *know* the eventual will be to your satisfaction—so please do not waste nervous strength and emotion over the present.

You will be offered chewing gum on the trip but take a couple of packages with you in your pocket anyway.

See you Monday—love from us all.

As ever,

HAROLD SHERMAN to MARTHA SHERMAN

Hollywood, June 14, 1941

Dearest:

It goes without saying it was grand to hear your voice again last night.

I have a nice note from Loose this a.m. following my phone conversation with him yesterday. He says everything is working out for the best, that these developments are all for a purpose. I am sure he is right . . . and am not disturbed by the turn in plans at all. . . .

I have visualized constantly a period when we might enjoy a vacation and a car trip and I am confident this is going to work out, too. I just got my driver's license yesterday after having taken seven lessons in driving from a professional instructor, George Stockford, brushing up on the latest gearshift methods. So this means I can buy a car in New York and get right in it and drive us away. . . .

I am looking forward to my plane trip which will be via sleeper plane. Leaving here at 5:10 in the afternoon, Flight #4, arriving 11:59 Eastern standard which is 12:59 daylight. . . .

It will be great to hold you in my arms again. You are my only Sweetheart . . . and the only one I ever want.

Love to the girls . . . and tell them everything is working out fine.

8

MEETING THE SADLERS

HARRY LOOSE to HAROLD SHERMAN
Monterey Park, June 21, 1941

My Friend:-

Your letter arrived today.[1] It had been missent by the Post Office people—although correctly addressed—to Monterey away up by San Francisco and then sent back from there to here—this made rather a late delivery. Am so glad for your beautiful trip and that the folks were there to greet you when you arrived. Ma's condition is much improved and we look forward to a continuance from day to day. "No man knoweth—."

I have heard nothing further regarding Mark Twain. I have made no inquiry. There has been heart and head full with conditions here, as you can but know. . . .

Since the arrival of your letter, I have made inquiry regarding your disseminating information to those friends close to you and in whom you have confidence. This is as your letter requested. My answer to the question was quite a time in arriving—which is much unusual. You may try out the idea and note the assimilation. The suggestion, to me, is made that you get together in one group and at the same time such several persons who you believe to be so developed as to be able to comprehend. They must ALL give their word to you that such information that you may impart to them must remain with

---

[1] Not found.

them in confidence and is not to be repeated until such time as you yourself give them freedom from their promise.

My writings to you must not be evidenced. You must speak from your memory—or from notes taken from such writings. You may remark that you have such writings—and that they are the truth—as you have had evidence enough to know. You are to begin the story with our original contact in the hotel room at Marion—and then lead up to the second contact 20 years later. Be very careful NOT to overfeed. Remember, their comprehension has not been developed as yours has been. Give but a little and note the assimilation. Those not evidencing interest need not be included in the second meeting of the grouping.

MUCH has to be left to your own understanding—of men and minds—as to the amount you first give. You have material enough for MANY such informal talks. Under no circumstances try to give them all the understanding that you have. They simply cannot comprehend. There will be sufficient time later. Under NO circumstances include the "chemist" in any group. I will tell you why when I see you again. Take counsel with your Thought Adjuster in all this. DO NOT add any to the beginning grouping.

At the conclusion of the first revelation to this grouping, write me fully as to the reception—questions, beliefs expressed, objections, etc. and I believe that on delivery of that first "report" will rest whether there will be permission for a continuance of such for the remaining period of your time yet in residence in New York. I have made all as plain as I can.

With every good thought for you all,

HAROLD SHERMAN to HARRY LOOSE

New York, June 27, 1941

Friend Harry:

Needless to say, you have been *much* in my thoughts. At times I have gotten a lonely feeling from you—as if you were yearning for us to be together. And last night there came to me the unusual experience which I am enclosing, having written it up so that a copy of it could be put in my "little black book" for Martha's and my reference.[2]

As I have started to write this, your letter has just been received. We are delighted to learn that Ma Loose is much improved. I know

---

[2] The write-up of this experience has not been found or identified.

that her presence and companionship has meant as much to you as Martha has to me—and we rejoice with you at her recovery.

I am glad that I am to be permitted to use my discretion in the telling of a few friends who are hungry for the truth—exploring their reaction—which will also help us gauge how ready many people are for this knowledge. I presume you mean by the chemist, Jacques Romano, and I think I sense why he is not to be told. I am very much afraid Jacques, as unusual as he is in many ways, could not withhold such knowledge and would exploit it for his own purposes and claims. Isn't it too bad—that a man can have so much in the way of development and yet lack other essentials?

Referring now to my experience of last night. Strangely enough, for the past year, as I have relaxed ready for sleep at night, various muscles and nerves in my body would twitch and jerk as I would "let go," so that my entire body, at times, would jump involuntarily . . . and this, naturally, has been most disturbing to Martha in the same bed. She said this condition was getting worse and wondered what could be causing it. We remembered that you had said "preparations would be going on which we would be little aware of," etc., and, for the last two nights, in addition to thinking of you—I have been giving my body the suggestion that it would NOT jump and jerk, that it would relax entirely, just as though I were laying it aside for the night!

After two nights of these suggestions, this experience comes to me.

Were you in touch with me last night? Do you have any recollection of our experiences together? How is the apparent dream part explained and the presence of Persis Robinson,[3] of whom I have not thought for months? There seems to have been a fusing of the dream and the astral?

If I was in the astral, even partly, it is an amazingly EASY experience, once it has been learned.

What of these Nature spirits? Is this significant? They seemed to have something to do with my forces in this state. I fear that I have forgotten much I should have remembered, of what took place.

The Twain deal is still not closed but I have hopes for next week. This uncertain period has been a difficult one. . . . We are all so eager to be heading back to California!

---

[3] Harold and Martha's childhood friend.

Please give Ma Loose our love. Perhaps now you can feel free to tell us a little more about what happens during sleep. This is one of the mysteries I would like cleared up—especially since it appears that I am to be doing more and more *during* sleep!

Our gratitude again for all you have done for us . . . and for the permission granted to pass on, guardedly, some of the information given.

May we all be seeing you, reasonably soon, in California! It is our plan, with the deal going through, to buy a car, probably a Buick sedan, and tour through to Marion, Indiana to visit Mother and my Aunt Flora (her sister, now 75). Then, time permitting, to drive Mother to Traverse City and visit Martha's father and relatives . . . then on to the west from there. I hope it works out this way as I have not had a vacation for years!

Our love and best wishes!

HARRY LOOSE to HAROLD SHERMAN

Monterey Park, June 29, 1941

My Friend:-

Because, for a definite purpose, you are to make the experiment of advancing to a chosen few intimates a small portion of what you are now aware, with permission, I attempted to give you positive and convincing experience in the Astral which would make toward unshakable conviction in your mind, and give the Thought Adjuster a footing upon which he could enlarge, and thusly to give conviction to your voice conversations with these intimate peoples. I made the attempt upon which your letter remarks.

I was but partially successful—I know the reasons for my non-full success—too intricate and too detailed for expression here—but on another future venture I hope that they may be obviated. I could not fully sever you from the subconscious in which meanderings were earth-ties both of Martha and the person of Persis Robinson. The "thread" was not *completely* loosed.

You will have other happenings as time passes. Do not look for the hocus-pocus of the "spirit cabinet"—they will not happen. It was my first time in your apartment, I was glad to see other evidences of Mary's talent and Martha's presence. I am glad, most, that you felt the touch of my hand and the pat on the shoulder. I do not want to remark "the little people"—they are too far ahead of your present development. I am also glad of your remembrance of the passage through the inanimate. It is all so very easy when you know how—like ALL things *when understood.*

Do not mention me by name or remark my home address in your conversations. Be careful not to "give" too much. You may mention "a book" to soon be available from definite and positive spirit entities—and from it a world regeneration in religion. That you will have some part in the work before, or following, this book. Everything is so very different from the general conception of things spiritual that if you give "too much," it might reflect seriously on your veracity or mental poise.

Be sure to submit to me for my information such informative data as to the reception of your conversations as your subjects voice or reflect.

You are right as to the identity of the chemist. There would be immediate difficulty instituted that I cannot now write you of.

Ma is improving. I hold the best thought—that is all that I can do—in a month she should be normal again, so the doctor promises.

I know nothing of Mark Twain . . . I hope that you didn't leave "Thieves"[4] behind you in the last rush—and that you have it with you.

With the very best thought surrounding you ALL and with much love to All,

HAROLD SHERMAN to HARRY LOOSE

New York, July 5, 1941

Friend Harry:

The news of Ma Loose's improvement was cheering and we prayerfully hope it continues.

Something good, in another way, has happened here. *Sergeant York,* Lasky's picture, was a big success at the opening, which we attended. This means that Lasky should have no trouble raising the capital he is seeking and, in a talk with him yesterday, he indicated that he would be ready to close the deal next week. . . .

Yes, I brought your play, "Thieves" with me. It has some good things in it but is old-fashioned as plays go today and would need considerable revising before it should be submitted anywhere. I will talk to you about it when we meet again.

---

[4] A play Loose had written which he hoped Harold would promote for him.

I deeply appreciate the permission to present some of this knowledge to a group of intimate friends, which group is to assemble at our home next Thursday evening . . . and we wish you might be able to visit us at that time . . . 8 o'clock our time, even though we might not be aware of your presence. I will proceed carefully and it will be interesting to me to use this as a test to determine what the reaction may be when the Book of Urantia is published, with the much fuller story.

I am glad to know that what happened to me during sleep was an authentic experience, even though I was not able to co-operate fully as yet. Perhaps when I understand more completely what takes place during sleep, it will help. I am relieved to know that the "little people" was not an hallucination and that this is also significant.

I hope that the real turn in my affairs is near at hand and that next week will see everything all set, with the Twain matter reaching a climax. My birthday is approaching on horseback, July 13th, and some of my ismic friends insist that after its arrival, great things are in store for me—much money and an unlimited opportunity for spiritual service.

Our love to you and Ma Loose . . . and best wishes always.

New York, July 12, 1941

Friend Harry:

We had a most interesting time Thursday night. Members of Martha's little study group of women who have been reading and discussing various philosophic subjects were present, together with Mr. Este, head of the Psychic Forum, not ismic, as it sounds, but an honest research body; a Mr. Gerald Dumars, friend of mine who was advertising manager of *The Savings Bank Journal* when I was editor several years ago; and Mr. and Mrs. Charles Forbell, dear friends of long standing.

The reaction was not as startling or shocked as I might have expected. Most of those present could agree with the truths revealed as dovetailing with knowledge which had already come to them or serving to explain certain points they had never been able to clear up.

The only phase at all disturbing or challenging to anyone was the story of the hybrids—it being hard to understand why higher intelligences should have permitted such a mistake. The popular conception, as you know, is that God makes no mistakes—that truth has always existed and that Man, in his blindness, has perverted it, etc.

Why higher intelligences entrusted to the guidance of lower forms of intelligence should have made such a blunder appeared disquieting to some and difficult to accept. I told them, as you had instructed me, to weigh these matters and not to accept them because I or anyone presented them . . . but to turn them over in their own consciousness, meditate on them and see if further illumination would not come.

The Thought Adjustor or Comforter knowledge created a profound effect—soul-satisfying and inspiring. This alone made the evening a never-to-be-forgotten one for those present and will mean more to their advancement than any other information they could have received.

I proceeded as you directed, with the story of how I had met you, keeping your full identity and address, etc. concealed, and all were held spellbound. My presentation was informal. I sat at a little card table, with some notes before me, and it required a little more than an hour to finish my talk, with questions following.

There was great interest in "The Book of Urantia," with eager inquiries as to when it was going to be published, etc. Several asked if you were familiar with *A Dweller on Two Planets;*[5] and I really feel you should read it, since its contents so closely parallel much of what you have told us. It is an amazing document and we have an extra copy which we will bring west with us for you to look into, if you will.

This experience has convinced me that, utilizing proper discretion, certain developed individuals can be given a glimmer of this knowledge, individually or in groups, and be helped immeasurably thereby, and I appreciate being permitted to make this test.

I just had a phone call now from Mrs. Forbell to say that she wanted to get close to her Thought Adjustor and to ask a question about meditation. She said the evening was all she and Charles could talk about and that they had gained much from it. I am sure this is true of the others.

And now, Harry—the deal has finally and completely gone through. I deposited the first check in the bank yesterday and then went out and bought a Buick sedan, which will be delivered to me by a week from Monday. We are selling our furniture and planning to get on the way west within the next week to ten days.

---

[5] Phylos the Thibetan, *A Dweller On Two Planets: or The Dividing of the Way* (Los Angeles: Borden, 1940).

I am not on salary now but will hear from Lasky, who has gone back to the coast, as soon as his own plans for the picture's production are set. But he said he'd be wanting me in Hollywood soon—so we are not waiting but getting in our visit in Marion and Traverse as quickly as possible. . . .

What I would greatly appreciate is the permission to speak quietly to a few dear friends—themselves earnest seekers after truth, whom I may meet en route—telling them about as much, as the case may be, as I have been permitted to tell this little group here. Eventually, when the time is right, I am sure I could make some electrifying talks on this subject, with the "Book of Urantia" published.

Can you advise me relative to this permission this week, so that I may know my attitude relative to these vital subjects which I can feel a few others would devour with as great an appreciation as we have.

It is our hope and prayer that Ma Loose is now well on the road to recovery. Please give her our love and best wishes . . . and reserve some of the same for yourself.

Martha and the girls are in the "seventh heaven" of anticipation, and isn't it grand that we can all begin making this great trip together?

Sincerely,

HARRY LOOSE to HAROLD SHERMAN
Monterey Park, July 30, 1941

My Friend:-

I received your Air Mail from Traverse City yesterday afternoon. I did not write you to N.Y. I was much interested in the acceptance and non-acceptance of the grouping you talked with there—and their interest in the material. I am much pleased that you are all together on this long-waited-for and deserved vacation. The best part of your journey still is ahead of you all. Don't hurry—and do not drive too fast—see the Hoover Dam on your way.

YOU are the only one that can either delay or completely halt the progress and growth so outlined to you. These things will come to pass—if you so will and desire—and keep the faith. YOU and time alone have this in your keeping.

Ma is much the same. I do not think that we will be separated long.

Much, too, has happened here. I have been some away—and I have been ill. Much has been taken from me—responsibilities that have long been mine. It is good—I am relieved—yet I grieve a bit. A door is slowly closing—the shadows lengthen.

Thanks a lot for your kindnesses and cooperation in the long, long, ago and now again so recently.

My love to you all,

With all good thought,

On their way West by car in July, 1941, the Shermans stopped off in Indiana and Michigan to visit relatives and old friends. On July 26, while they were at the home of Jo and Merrill Davis in Marion, Jo phoned her cousin, Dr. William S. Sadler, to ask if the Shermans could join the Forum, the closed group with whom Sadler was sharing the Urantia material. Jo thereupon wrote a letter of introduction for the Shermans, which Harold mailed to the doctor along with a cover letter and a copy of Your Key to Happiness. *On August 1, Sadler wrote to arrange a meeting with Harold:*

> Dear Mr. Sherman:
>
> Your letter and copy of your book received this morning.
>
> I have been looking over my program for next week, and it looks to me as if either Tuesday morning or Wednesday morning would be the best chance for a visit with you. All my afternoons are loaded up in the office and every evening has something on it next week.
>
> Just drop me a line telling me which day suits you best— Tuesday morning or Wednesday morning—and I will save it for our visit.
>
> Sincerely yours,
>
> William S. Sadler

* * *

While Martha and the girls stayed behind in Traverse City, Harold traveled by train to Chicago, met Sadler at 533 Diversey Parkway, and flew back to Traverse City. Then on Friday, August 8, while on the way to California, the Sherman family stopped in at Sadler's, where Martha met the doctor. At 10 a.m. the next day, Harold and Martha became members of the Forum. They were introduced to the doctor's son, Bill, and his family. Bill spent the entire Saturday going over the Urantia papers, and in the evening the Shermans were guests of Bill and his wife, Leone, at DeLazon's restaurant, where Bill continued the discussion until midnight.

DR. WILLIAM S. SADLER
DR. WILLIAM F. PARRILLI
AND ASSOCIATES
533 DIVERSEY PARKWAY
CHICAGO

August 1, 1941

Mr. Harold M. Sherman,
222 Washington Street,
Traverse City, Michigan.

Dear Mr. Sherman:

Your letter and copy of your book received this morning.

I have been looking over my program for next week, and
it looks to me as if either Tuesday morning or Wednesday
morning would be the best chance for a visit with you.
All my afternoons are loaded up in the office and every
evening has something on it next week.

Just drop me a line telling me which day suits you
best –– Tuesday morning or Wednesday morning –– and I
will save it for our visit.

Sincerely yours,

William S. Sadler

WSS:L

In 1992 Martha recalled: "We found the Doctor very affable and willing to discuss Urantia freely, with the regret that we would not have the opportunity to read any of the papers at that time. Our interest was further piqued by his description of how the material had been received."

The Shermans were now permitted to return to Chicago, whenever possible, to read the Urantia papers on the premises.

The Sherman family (Martha, Marcia, Mary and Harold) en route to Hollywood in August, 1941 [SHERMAN FAMILY PRIVATE COLLECTION].

9

SUNDAYS WITH HARRY

Arriving in Hollywood on August 17, the family moved into a larger apartment at the Canterbury. Harold immediately resumed his work on the Mark Twain film. Jesse L. Lasky assigned Alan LeMay,[1] an experienced Hollywood screenwriter, to work with Harold on the script. It was during this time that Harold's Ara communications increased, inspired by information he was receiving from Harry Loose.

* * *

During our stay in Hollywood Martha and I spent each Sunday afternoon and evening in the presence of Harry Loose, either in his modest home in Monterey Park or in our Canterbury apartment in Hollywood.

Harry, in his seventies[2] and afflicted with a heart condition, insisted on making the drive to Hollywood on alternate Sundays, despite heavy traffic through downtown Los Angeles in the days before freeways. We could hardly wait for each weekend to come, so filled with knowledge and inspiration were the sessions with this highly developed man.

Harry constantly stressed to us how little he knew, how much there was to be known, what a wonderful, boundless universe we had

---

[1] Alan LeMay (1899-1964) was a novelist and Hollywood screenwriter, whose screen credits include *Reap the Wild Wind*, *The Story of Dr. Wassell*, *The Adventures of Mark Twain*, *San Antonio*, *The Sundowners*, *High Lonesome*, *The Unforgiven*.
[2] He turned 61 in September of 1941.

288

been born into—and the glorious fact that we could never die out of it, once having evolved into an awareness and possession of our own "I am I" identity. As we bombarded him with questions about higher powers of mind and how to develop them and what he felt our true relationship to God, the Great Intelligence, was, Harry kept saying that he must be careful not to overfeed us, that this was the difficulty countless seekers after truth encountered: "They wanted to go too far, too fast."

[*How to Know What to Believe*, 1976]

ARA   *September 3, 1941*

It is true, as the Tree Planter [Harry Loose] has said, that you are an Old Soul. Your original progenitor came from the planet Herma, a thousand billion miles from Urantia. His mating with a fleshed one of earth imparted to you an intermingling of forces which have tormented, baffled and inspired you throughout your long imprisonment here. Your awesome sensing of the infinity of Time and Space, which has all but engulfed you, has been due to the magnetic pull of your progenitor who yet bears a responsibility for the mistake which brought you into Being, partaking of more than earth, yet less than the full next dimension—a hybrid—as the Tree Planter has said.

You have sought always to understand and to know, and in many lives this wisdom has not been denied you, yet the knowledge has only made more clear the Path that you must journey, in company with your brother hybrids, on the quest toward liberation through service.

The Great and Eternal Father eventually rectifies all mistakes made by his erring children as He permits them origin and progress, as free agents, toward their inborn at-one-ness with Him. But once this mistake occurred, Higher Intelligences, cognizant of it, decreed that the hybrids, as a creative experiment, should continue for a time to fulfill the duties originally intended alone for their progenitors—and remain in service to the evolving forms of human life here.

The hybrids, with their greater enlightenment, higher sources of inspiration and sensitivity, could be reached by Higher Intelligences having jurisdiction over the affairs of Urantia and commune with them during their temporary unfleshed periods between earth deaths and the times of re-enfleshment.

In this manner, while not primarily accountable for their state of Being, these hybrids were called upon to render a greater degree of service than is ordinarily required of first life creatures.

In the end, the reward of the Father will give spiritual recognition of this cosmic fact.

Ara, your Comforter, has spoken.

September 4, 1941

You have been with the developing race of human animals since the early beginnings.

You and others like you have helped bring to man his growing knowledge of God and the true nature of the Universe.

But you have suffered all the ills and imperfections of man, having the same body and being infused with the same spirit. Yet the consciousness in you has been of a higher order because of the manner in which you were given first life.

You have always been dimly aware of God and have felt a Kinship to some greater power beyond the earth due to your creative link with Beings of Higher Intelligence. Your full spirit has reached out, torn between the pull of earth conditions and the pull in you of those not of this earth.

You have sought happiness not alone in this world but in some vague unearthly state which you have sensed to be more real and lasting than your experience here. Always, however, your earth body has acted as an anchorage, dragging your soaring spirit back and causing you to realize that until this spirit could be quickened through complete mastery of all lower elements in you, the chains of your bondage could not be cast off.

You and your brothers and sisters in the flesh, so created, were automatically born into an order of service to all humans on this earth plane. Your earth fathers or mothers, having come to earth on missions of service and mating through the mistake with earth children, imparted to you this spirit of service.

This projection and dissemination of their spirits through offspring advanced you in the scale of first life beings at the same time that it tied you to earth bodies until such a time in earth history when you might aid in bringing progressive release to all earth peoples.

That time is now close at hand and you are to be used as a Seed Planter that from the seeds of Knowledge you sow, the consciousness of mankind may be raised and millions now groping in the flesh be awakened from their befogged dream and realize that they are at last free.

Ara, your Comforter, is with you.

HARRY LOOSE to HAROLD SHERMAN

Monterey Park, September 4, 1941

Harold:-

These two[3] are *very* good and very accurate. I am returning them for your rereading. You may not always be so successful—and you may be even more so.

Thanks for Martha's visit. She is surely a dear—and all else that you have said.

Don't let the sympathetic nervous system rule you and bother your stomach—you have no organic trouble there.

Love to you ALL from Ma and I—

ARA   *September 5, 1941*

Inspirational opening to Timothy 4, beginning 6th verse.

The ministry to all mankind is near. Ages of earth time have been required to bring all consciousness involved here to the great changing point and the final dividing of the way.

You have known of this approaching moment and have been preparing to assume your part in it for many incarnations. This preparation has not been haphazard but all in accordance with a now incomprehensibly far-reaching plan developed in association with your hybrid brothers, yourselves in league with Higher Intelligences assigned to administer to the needs and problems arising out of the conditions surrounding human creatures on Urantia.

But you are soon to witness the flowering of thousands of years of service rendered toward the goal of liberating all humanity that you yourself may be liberated and start your homeward way.

Watch for the signs in and around you of the unfolding of the Plan and be you ready, day or night to respond.

This will suffice for this morning.

MARTHA'S NOTE   *[undated]*

On Saturday August 30, while playing tennis at the Garden Court courts, Harold wrenched his back badly and went about, even after an osteopathic treatment, with a back so lame he could not stand straight. In spite of this, because he enjoyed the game so much, he decided to play again on the following Saturday, Sep-

---

[3] Referring to Ara messages of September 3 and 4.

tember 6. This time, in reaching for a high ball, he slipped, fell, knocked himself temporarily "out" and skinned both elbows and knees. Irritated by these incidents, determined not to be "jinxed" by his accidents—and also over-eager to keep a tennis appointment made with associates from Warner Bros.—he went out the third time to play. Result: a badly sprained ankle and a chipped bone, necessitating crutches for a weekend leaving him with a lame ankle for many months.

ARA   *September 8, 1941*

All those entrusted with the great and important earth missions must have learned submission to guidance for their protection and direction in the work undertaken. Without such guidance enfleshed souls are subject to the same ills of the flesh as those who are uninspired.

To you has been demonstrated what happens to the house of flesh when its occupant does not follow the voice of wisdom. Not once, but three times, as the cock crows. For you heard the voice within you, and have for years recognized it as an unidentified Higher Intelligence speaking to you, yet you wondered if the voice might, these times, be fused with your own physical forebodings of possible injury.

Today you no longer wonder. You *know* that the voice you heard was *my* voice, and you know you can henceforth hear it clearly and distinctly in your moments of need, if you *will*.

I have come a long way with you. I have seen you suffer much. But out of it I have seen patience and tolerance and fortitude grow. What you have had to experience in this life is as nothing to what you have undergone before. And yet much is to be required of you once your strengths of mind and body have been tested in this last earth life. You, more than most others, have never had time to waste. You have been about your Father's business for an uncomprehended period of earth years. You have failed on occasion—yes, as all have failed—but these failings have only quickened your resolution, made more firm your determination to fulfill in last degree the mission assigned to you, which is now approaching a glorious consummation.

Martha has been with you many times before—else, how could she have this understanding of you? And her destiny has been blended with yours in service, for the pathway has been lonely, fraught with pain and discouragement and temptations for loss of faith, when each has needed the other in order that both might cling to the knowledge and remembrance of the Father and your work in Him.

But now is come a day when much will be revealed, to you, and to the world. More and more will you give up earthly things of little moment, as the promise of Eternal happiness becomes a living reality within you.

You are more receptive this morning.

HARRY LOOSE to HAROLD SHERMAN

Monterey Park, September 8, 1941

Harold:-

Got in bed at 11 bells and so far this morning feel no bad results from our late hours and wild drive through the blackness of night down Hollywood Blvd. In the fair light of day, it makes us both feel slightly like heroes now. However, just to play safe, we're going to bed at half past eight tonight.

Sincerely hope that the foot and other tennis injuries are sufficiently recuperated to allow painless continuance of work today. Under the circumstances surrounding the many injuries sustained, it would seem but good judgment to refrain from the strenuous activity as per adverse advice you received prior by way of the "good book." This, before "some greater evil befall thee."

I hope you will soon have time to get the letter off to Mother Sherman with the comforting info that we discussed last evening.

That last picture of your wonderful interpretive posture—trouser leg pulled up, the many-bandaged injuries, the wonderful and startling drum interpretation—still is with us.

Don't let Arthur or added complications get you down. You have passed safely through other, greater storms.

Martha—thank you again for the very much appreciated supper and your thoughtfulness. Ma was still so stuffed when we got home that I very near gave up trying to get her out of the front seat. It appeared very much as though I would have to leave her there in the garage until the next morning when she would be reduced some.

We hold the picture of you ALL in our minds.

With all good thought—and hurriedly,

HAROLD SHERMAN to ALCINDA SHERMAN
Hollywood, September 9, 1941[4]

Dear Mother:

I was glad to get your fine letter but sorry to learn of Cousin Myrtle's illness. . . . That you, yourself, are improving is good news. Keep it up.

I had a series of minor accidents myself on the tennis court, not being used to playing on cement. . . . Alan LeMay, my collaborator, has been calling for me in his car and taking me back and forth to the studio. I met other writers today who are "tennis casualties" hobbling around on sprained ankles, so you see it isn't just "me."

Now for something much more important. Harry Loose and Mother Loose were over to spend Sunday with us and I have his permission to tell you more . . . not only that, but permission for you to *share* this knowledge with *Mrs.* [Alice] *Zapf,* so that you will have someone to discuss these facts with. I remember your telling me how you and Alice have periods of meditation . . . and of her interest in spiritual understanding and development. In New York, before I left, I was permitted to give a little talk to the little Forum group of ladies whom you know plus the Forbells, Gerald Dumars and Sydney Este.

I told them of a remarkable book, soon to be published, and to be titled "The Book of Urantia," which would be destined to take the place of our present Bible, being a complete record of the origin of this earth planet, our origin upon it, our purpose in being here, our present mission, and our destiny in the life experiences in other dimensions to come. This book has been 37 years in the making—coming through Higher Intelligences and authenticated by a group of over 100 scientifically minded men and women—outstanding in reputation and integrity—witnesses to this phenomenal happening. It is to be given to the peoples on this planet at the right psychological time, at the beginning of the new era which is soon to come upon our little world. I, and many souls, have been prepared unconsciously or consciously (as the case may have been) to take part in making this knowledge available to all humanity. Talents have been developed through the testing of various life experiences, which are to be used in missions of service. My trip to Chicago was to meet personally members of this initial Group and to see, for myself, the evidence and

---

[4] This letter was never mailed. Harold sent his mother a shorter version, dated September 10.

much of the amazing material which will revolutionize the spiritual thought of Mankind.

What I told you about the Comforter, which you found satisfying, is just a glimmer of the great revelations to come. Just now, all who have come to this knowledge are handpicked and pledged to say nothing to others, unless given permission by those through whom they have learned certain of the truths. There is a definite spiritual reason for this—and I am happy that consent has been given me to pass on a little of what has been revealed to me, to Alice and yourself. You will find that you will get much spiritual, mental and physical strength from this knowledge as you meditate upon it and read your Bible passages with this new light. It is not accidental that you find yourself alive now . . . and that others have gone on ahead . . . it all has to do with one's individual destiny and what each of us came into this life at this time to fulfill. We are given every opportunity to perform our mission but are *never* compelled, being creatures of free choice.

The true knowledge of this Universe and the way it is controlled and operated is much different than you may have imagined.

This earth does not operate itself any more than an intricate piece of machinery operates itself. There is Intelligence behind everything . . . and this applies to *all* inhabited worlds, of which there are *millions!* It requires an inconceivable variety and number of Intelligences to operate the great forces in this Universe—forces in and around and through this earth and the forms of life here.

These Intelligences have to do with the control and operation of all animal life, the winds that blow, all nature, growing things, rivers that flow in the oceans, the very odors and colors—all are under the jurisdiction of Intelligences *from the next two dimensions.*

This control can be likened to the operation of a big business or industry on earth where the lowliest employee is answerable to the next above him, and so on up to the top executive. . . . . ALL IS NOT PERFECTION on this plane—NOR in the SECOND or THIRD dimensions.

We still retain our failings until they are overcome. A Capone is still a Capone in the Second Dimension beyond this life. There are highly developed forces of evil as there are of good because the Great Intelligence has permitted freedom of expression on these planes.

Our little earth, known as URANTIA to the Higher Intelligences, is referred to as the Dark World or Planet, because of its lack of spiritual growth.

Our world is a First Life Planet. This is where our *individualization* has begun. Through experiences here we have developed a *consciousness* of our *identity*.

We are an *individual intelligence* when we arrive here; we *remain* one until we pass into the next Dimension, and we *continue* to remain one for *all* Eternity!

But our growth depends upon *ourselves*—no one else can grow for us!

Once the realization has come that we are a bit of the Great Intelligence on its way to *Individualization,* we never lose that awareness.

We have all been helped along the way, but freedom of choice has been granted us—and our own Will determines our Path.

This Will Control of our own lives cannot permissibly be overcome by other Intelligences.

The statement in the Bible: "Seek and ye shall find, knock and it shall be opened unto you," contains great significance. All is in perfect accord with Biblical teaching *correctly* interpreted.

There is a DEFINITE CONTINUITY OF LIFE—the BODY DOES NOT POSSESS A SOUL... THE SOUL POSSESSES A BODY. This distinction should be meditated upon until it becomes thoroughly realized in consciousness. This will remove all fear of what eventually happens to the body, since it is just an instrument we use for our expression here but it is not the real us. No one in the flesh has ever seen the real you. *You reside* in the fleshy part of the brain and direct every action of this physical body which you *infuse* with your own intelligence or entity... your body has no intelligence of its own aside from that which you bring it.

You are still YOU in the next dimension—you arrive there with the same growth you made here. When what the world calls "Death" occurs, you are *transported to one of the 7 leaving stations* from this planet. (Here is a wonderful and inspiring revelation.) One of these leaving stations is located in a National Reserve some 200 miles from Los Angeles. I am going to visit it one day with Harry Loose.

It is a very beautiful place—great powers exist there. A cool wind always blows and the temperature is always 10 degrees lower than that of the surrounding area. A compass whirls ceaselessly... It is a busy place always—with the transport of all those whom the world here says "have just died" *taking off*... THOUSANDS UPON THOUSANDS OF THEM each one of our earth days!

YOU have company, the INSTANT of your arrival, THROUGH DEATH, in the Second Dimension.

The third day after your passage from here by way of Death, you will find yourself transported AWAY FROM THIS PLANET . . . and your first sight will be that of a MORONTIA INTELLIGENCE— one of an Order of Service from the Third Dimension—who will BE WITH YOU from then until your experience on the Second Dimension is finished.

A UNIVERSAL LANGUAGE is spoken by those in the Second Dimension—a gift from the Great Intelligence. You KNOW IT, upon AWAKENING, without effort, and you will find its sounds more pleasing—its power of expression much more elastic and complete than any earth language. You will hear music, too, far beyond your present ability to comprehend. There has been no real musician yet born on this planet!

Progression from the Second to the Third Dimension is also accomplished by Death.

A deep affection is always developed between the Morontia Intelligence and its charge—and there is genuine grief when the time of separation comes.

However, there is much better understanding of progress and continuation than we experience in this first death—and it is not regarded so seriously.

Material or physical existence means nothing in the continuation of Life—but there is much to learn in the spiritual.

The more you know here, the further you are along in the next dimension. (Mother—for you alone—now do you begin to understand why we must find some way of helping Arthur help himself? We can't do anything too precipitate, but we'll have to work out some method for his own good.)

A sense of humor and laughter is most important. You DO carry this over into other dimensions.

In the Second Dimension you no longer have a need for food, but you do need air and water . . . In the Third Dimension, your need for water is gone but you still need air.

There are Seven Dimensions, each higher and possessing greater freedom of action than the one previous—and all a matter of slow and deserved progress.

Life evolved on this planet as it does on all planets when their formation reaches a certain stage—in the warm waters of the seas—

animals and plant life brought here from other more fully developed planets by Intelligences in charge of the unfolding of life here.

We human animals are arrived at by progression upwards until we reach a certain period in our development when we begin our search for God. At this time there is then introduced into the human race the blending with more advanced and higher developed intelligences brought here from older and more developed First Life Planets . . . And this explains the why and how of the colors of men here and the varying languages . . . (Too big a subject to more than hint at here.)

The fertilized egg becomes a growing portion of the woman's body and has no separate life until the fourth month . . . Then the Intelligences having to do with that particular function inculcate the *first great gift*—LIFE.

We now have a living thing yet unborn—still it is merely something of animal flesh *without a soul.*

BUT, at the instant of its FIRST BREATH, comes the second great gift—the SOUL—that tiny part of the GREAT INTELLIGENCE!

Then the body grows—subject entirely to the rule of the mother, until between the fifth and sixth year—when comes the third gift— the THOUGHT ADJUSTOR [*sic*] or what we call CONSCIENCE. (Comforter as referred to in John 14, 15, 16.)

Just as the MORONTIA INTELLIGENCE meets the new arrival of the human soul in the next dimension, so does the THOUGHT ADJUSTOR or what we call CONSCIENCE, meet the new life and the new soul on its entrance to this dimension . . . The Thought Adjustor or Conscience then remains with the INDIVIDUAL for the period of earth residence of the SOUL.

You may, right now or at any time, anywhere, listen and hear in your consciousness, the soft inner voice of the THOUGHT ADJUSTOR.

It is possible that many humans who feel they have spirit guides or have inner voices of guidance, have been hearing or sensing the voice of their Thought Adjustor.

Your Thought Adjustor is with you always, in every waking moment, consciously and unconsciously, in your sleep.

All voluntary acts of the individual, after life, soul and the Thought Adjustor have been given, are the sole responsibility of the individual—and he is held strictly to account for his deportment.

Your Thought Adjustor is a very *real, true* and *living* entity or identity from Higher Dimensions who RESIDES WITH YOU and is *absolutely separate* and *distinct* from your soul.

I must emphasize again—he is always with you—awake or asleep. He does not sleep.

If you take your Thought Adjustor or Comforter one mile, he will take you two more miles. He will counsel and advise you, always to your benefit . . . but you will have your own individual choice of your own Will and following actions.

You will find, however, that his advice is always for your best interests and you will soon discover that he knows much more than your human intelligence. He is aware of your full past development from the far distant time when your individualization began and you commenced the climb on the Path toward AT-ONE-NESS with the FATHER or GREAT INTELLIGENCE.

At the proper time, your past will be revealed to you and then the wonder of it all will almost overcome you.

It will take a little time and concentration or meditation to get acquainted and friendly with your Thought Adjustor—but it will be greatly to your benefit. After a time, with much practice, you will find that you can talk with him at any time, and he will talk back to you in consciousness . . . and reason with you as a distinct and separate entity.

The sages, the mystics, the wise men of India, are those who have been taught or those who learned by themselves, through meditation, how to commune with their Thought Adjustors. They spend much time with them, and through this cultivated friendship they learn much . . . and they do things with the body which seem impossible.

We are living today through one of the greatest upheavals ever to take place on this planet. There is to be a great religious awakening following this period. THE BOOK OF URANTIA, given to this world by High Intelligences from advanced dimensions, is to play a prominent part in this spiritual revolution. It will be definite, authentic, in full and complete descriptatory, whereas our present Bible is obscure and contradictory. The full story of Jesus Christ is herein told for the first time . . . and WHAT A STORY it is! How convincing and thrilling and appealing to logic, reason and spirit!

I have already begun to have unusual evidences of the presence of my Thought Adjustor—as you soon will with yours—IF you persevere. Get understandably close with him. We must all learn to lean on no one—but on our own inner understanding. It is this knowledge which will put our feet firmly on the HOMEWARD PATH.

At this time, our memory of former lives we have lived would totally unfit us for what we are sent here to do . . . but the Thought Adjustor knows our complete record, as I have said . . . and we will know it, too, as we progress . . . There is nothing terrifying . . . the pathway gets more wonderful and reassuring at every step . . . we have all come a long, long way . . . and the FINAL TURNING POINT is close at hand.

And now, Mother, as you arrive at your 67th birthday, you have real cause for rejoicing. I am overjoyed that I have been permitted to be the instrument for opening up this knowledge to you . . . a knowledge which I am certain Dad, a highly developed soul, also had. Your own development is higher than you think . . . but you have had your conditions to work out of . . . your service and sacrifices and physical and mental hardships to undergo . . . but THINK how you can occupy your remaining time and thought on this dimension! Each day should be an added joy, rather than a worry.

I will petition the right for you to read this letter and discuss this knowledge with Aunt Flora upon your return to Marion—for I feel you could do much for her and grow in strength yourself. But NOW, birth and death must take on entirely new meaning to you . . . and to Alice . . . as does every act of life.

My love and the love of all here goes out to you—with the prayer, from Martha and I, of the peace that passeth understanding. Your first born son who will be forever grateful for his mother . . .

ARA   *September 10, 1941*
    St. Mark 13th chapter.

* * *

The time spoken of by Jesus is nearer at hand than the world realizes. Great and far-reaching evidences of the Father will be shown in support of the new and further word to be given the blind peoples of this dark planet. Only through catastrophe, man-invited and man-made, can man's sleep in the flesh be ended and his awakening to his true self and origin come to pass. The elect are awake; the blinders are being taken from their eyes that they may see God's purposes clearly and be about His business in a world of fleshly chaos.

But the time for all this is being foreshortened, the forces of change from an Old to a New order are awaiting the final mandate before loosing themselves. Your country is soon to go plunging into the maelstrom which will sweep all mankind into a whirlwind of economic, moral and physical destruction greater than any heretofore known.

Then may you know that the days for which your years have been lived are arrived. Then will your sealed orders be received. Then will your complete mission be revealed as well as the brothers engaged with you in the work of saving those who cannot save themselves.

The flesh profiteth nothing but the Quickening of the spirit in the flesh meaneth much for only in this way can God's presence be made manifest among men.

We are close to you this morning.

September 11, 1941

The quickened stage in the history of your time is at hand.

Watch the quickened speeding up of all movements between nations and peoples.

Watch the quickening of money exchanges.

Watch the quickening of fears and worries among the unprepared.

Watch the quickening of human hates and human greeds.

Watch the quickening of all things on this earth—and, above all, the quickening of the spirits of men.

For out of this great approaching travail will come the greatest spiritual awakening ever to take place on this dark planet—an illumination transcendent in its effect upon even the most lowly.

For such a period and the participation therein have you been born and has your life been lived.

This, as Christ has said unto all, I say unto you—watch!

September 12, 1941

Millions of souls will soon be no longer interested in only the bread of earth.

There is even now a great hunger stirring in them for spiritual food. As they cry out in their hunger, they will be fed by those chosen ones who have been preparing a repast for them.

The spiritual food will be placed upon the tables of their consciousness for assimilation. Truth will be available to all who seek it and their hunger appeased.

The Book of Urantia will be released at a time when the spiritual famine is reaching its climax—with the peoples of the world awakening to the realization that sustenance of the body is not in itself life—that life of the spirit is more precious and to be coveted than all the earth's transient wealth.

A great unrest dwells in the heart of humanity which dictators and armies cannot much longer restrain. This unrest will burst forth into a gigantic revolt against rulers and systems that would harness the spirit of man and sink him more deeply in the flesh.

Those who are being prepared to serve know that voices are to commence ringing in the wilderness of human thought, serving as beacon lights, so that, with recovery of spiritual sight, millions may be led out of flesh bondage into the first real freedom existent on this experimental planet since man came upon it.

Again I say—Watch—and bend your thought toward the planes from whence cometh the source of all spiritual power.

September 13, 1941

Event is soon to be piled upon event which will find the United States of America engulfed on several fronts in the desperately quickening stage of world conditions.

Deaths of some prominent Americans in war zones, the sudden death of a prominent national leader here and new assassinations of well-known peoples abroad will bring the seriousness of the unsettled times home to the people and cause them to realize as never before the instability and insecurity of man-made laws unsupported by the spiritual nature of man.

Sabotage will rise to unprecedented heights as hate-sated followers of different ideologies, the systems themselves misguided, will fanatically give their lives for worthless causes, only adding to the state of confusion and terror which must precede mankind's awakening.

It must be said unto you again, in the light of these things—Watch!

September 15, 1941

Man sleeps on the surface of life until his physical foundations are shaken by happenings of earthquake velocity. An inward shaking cracks and crumbles man's fleshbound way of thinking, opening up channels through which his real self may be reached.

In this quickening time real earthquakes in divers places will parallel man's inner trembling so that no place, within or without himself, will seem safe from devastation.

To you, and others in the flesh to whom a glimpse of the ultimate purposes and plan has been revealed, will be given the strength to stand while many about you are falling.

The house built without hands must soon be erected by all those who would survive these approaching times. Otherwise millions, seeking shelter and finding no refuge within themselves, will perish.

It is this house that true Knowledge of Self and Man's promise of attaining at-one-ness with God will bring. In the Father's House are many mansions. Each part of Him is a room in this house, likewise a house unto itself containing a portion of God's indwelling spirit.

Your work will be the fitting together of these rooms in the mansion of Humanity so that the long-dreamed brotherhood of man may appear as a great and wonderful highway, still afar off from the mansion but being builded brick by brick, nearer and nearer, until highway and mansion come together, each merging with the other.

Herein is the mystery of Time and Space, for man, in the flesh, traverses a path in search of God, the Father, only to discover at the end of the road that God is beyond movement at the motionless center of the Universe where all is still.

Then will Man comprehend the Biblical admonition, "Be still and know that I am God."

There is a movement behind motion, not now comprehensible to man.

When Time and Space move together, that is Eternity.

Man imprisoned in the flesh can never be a part of this movement since all elements in his earth body are moving *through* Time and not *with* Time.

It is possible for Intelligences in higher planes to observe wherein flesh movements are leading by looking along the Time dimension.

Since God, the Father, contains in Consciousness all things, to *speak* with Him is to *create*. His voice brought us into being and we are now on the Path back to Him from the outermost rim of first beginnings that we, at last, may greet God, the Father, in our *own* voice, singing His Praises for being permitted to share the unutterable joy of conscious existence with Him—forever and forever.

Ponder these things. There is much beyond your present understanding.

* * *

HARRY LOOSE to HAROLD SHERMAN

Monterey Park, September 15, 1941

Harold:-

We hope that you arrived home safely and soon. And that you found the children safe and happy. May Ma and I thank you and Martha for the visit and for the very lovely supper. If Cuspidor, my aged Ford, holds in one piece, Ma and I will arrive at your house a week from today at as early an hour in the P.M. as possible. Ma mourns ceaselessly that she forgot the bag of figs when you left. She has been chanting praises of Martha to Auntie in a running monologue all this morning. Hope no ill effects to the ankle from the drive.

There is so much I wish to tell you, much that I fear you will not believe. I am so very restricted that I go this afternoon to seek counsel and to be instructed. Leaving Martha to guard the gross Sunday, I would like permission to take you away for less than two hours. I suffer the ambition of great eagerness to entrust information—and a little sight. I know the limitations—but I ask exception.

I wish to show you sleep. Belief can only be predicated by sight. There is a light and sight beyond the light and sight of material senses. A "betweenness" between the material and that of the second dimension—a halfway place—a reservation to those many who have progressed step for step in understanding. You have already, on instances, had fleeting glimpses—and questioned. To my present thought, a permitted and sustained view would result in great concentration, application and accelerated progression. You have a long way to go. I cannot advance what will be permitted in full. I hope for full success. I wish you much to meet other entities. I am still waiting and striving, with patience, for further light. I dare not venture myself without permission and in company.

With all good thought—and love to you all,

ARA   *September 16, 1941*

You are surrounded by an organization of Intelligences affording you protection against the forces that would operate against you—keeping open the channels necessary for you to express through and making available different individuals in positions of power and influence as instrumentalities.

Look for these new additions to your army of those who will provide, wittingly or unwittingly, the stepping stones you require to reach the objectives in human service designed for you.

As Martha was impressed, truly you will find, from henceforth, that you have been "entertaining angels unawares."

Learn to respond to the voice of guidance, even on occasions of seeming inconvenience, and you will be rewarded thereby. Great plans are in operation and much is in store for you.

September 17, 1941

There are seed planters who come to this earth with new forms of life. There are also "Idea Planters" who till only the soil of human consciousness. This soil differs greatly according to the grade of development, it is fertilized by human experience which enriches it so that the "Idea Planters" can drop finer and finer ideas for progress into it.

This is always done with the cooperation of the Thought Adjustor who stands guard at the portals of consciousness and who knows what the soil is ready to receive. Different individuals attract different "Idea Planters," themselves specialists in arts and sciences and subjects homogeneous to the soil of human consciousness contacted.

In this manner, just as those more advanced here help those less developed, so do higher developed entities, on missions of service, bring inspiration to those who reach out for greater knowledge in the sphere of their own interest. They are as air and water to actual soil, the essence of the idea or pattern of progress being absorbed by the soil of consciousness which nourishes the unfolding life expression and brings about fruition of many earth accomplish-ments.

But no ideas can be planted in the soil of human consciousness which it has not been prepared to receive. . . .

HARRY LOOSE to HAROLD SHERMAN

Monterey Park, September 17, 1941

Harold:-

Just a note and in haste.

As I feared and so prepared you in my last note. For the present time—and immediate future—until advised differently—I can go no further with information other than clearing that which has already been under discussion—this, so long as such clearance does not open other closed information avenues presently shut only. There is a very good reason for this at this time which I may be able to relate in the future. I am disappointed as you are. An additional thought—added to the "good reason" memo'd above—the voyage may be too far afield in the present period of development and under some conditions other—these you can probably vaguely see yourself—I feel them but don't know what they are.

I saw your personal immediate future and it was very satisfactory—I ask you to drive carefully.

ARA   *September 18, 1941*

... All those on missions here are weavers of a pattern designed and placed on the loom of Time long centuries ago. The strands of service are in their hands and must be woven into place so that God's handiwork may be completed on this dark planet. Day by day new brother weavers will be revealed to you and the strands pulled tighter and tighter until great portions of the pattern will become discernible and the results of your own labors reflected upon the heart of mankind.

The Master Spinner sits at his wheel and gathers all strands of service into a carpet upon which the feet of all human creatures may tread to spiritual salvation. Today all flesh is footsore, confused and weary, stumbling along an uncarpeted way. If you neglect the completion of your strands you bruise the feet of your fellow pilgrims. ...

Great power is being generated and soon you will hear the hum of the looms as all weavers bend to their tasks. It will be the sweetest music to your spiritual ears ever heard in this world of discord and it will sustain you throughout the period of chaos to come.

(Upon completion of above, opened by inspiration to Ecclesiastes 2, 11 and then to chapter 3.)

September 20, 1941

Are you watching? Even as you do, events are rushing upon events. The world crisis grows apace and no balance is to be found among men. Yet, even so, no thought is to be given to the morrow. Sufficient unto each day will be your strength and your knowledge thereof.

The plan for this dark planet and its imprisoned peoples is being unrolled as a great scroll which has been centuries in preparation. Written thereon is the destiny of all, indescribably and incomprehensibly intertwined and yet readable to those whose vision has been lifted above the earth plane so that they can perceive the pattern woven by mankind itself.

Witness the inexorable forward rush of events in your own life as evidence that the way has been prepared. Unto you, more and more will be given as you open the channel of your instrumentality. The highway of service stretches before you, clear and straight beyond the mists of your developing consciousness.

Your seeking is over. You have found the road and it is moving under your feet, carrying you along two steps for every step you take. Forces are already reaching out to unite with your own force. A great circuit of world service is being closed. Soon a great light will burst upon this dark world at a moment when all seems lost. You and your brethren are to provide the candle-power for this light. So hold yourself in readiness and know that all is well with you—that the house in which you dwell cannot be shaken for it rests upon the only unshakeable foundation in the Universe.

Be of good cheer.

(Inspirational opening: Revelation 16:15-21.)

September 21, 1941

Through the agency of him who has served with you this long, long time there is being builded around you a wall of power in the form of enfleshed and unfleshed entities who will protect, sustain and support you in the important work you are destined to undertake. Each day will carry its own evidence of this fact as new associations come to you and individuals with no outward seeming development reveal their spiritual attunement. Others, through influence brought to bear, will be caused to open up, that you may plant the seeds which will bear fruit for you as well as for themselves toward the goal of service you seek. Many will aid you, unaware for the time being of why they have been impulsed to do so, because you have touched a responsive something in their deeper natures with which they themselves are yet not too familiar.

You will commence to see now the purposes behind the long years of physical, mental and economic hardship and the power which these experiences have generated. To be patient beyond ordinary human endurance; to be understanding and tolerant when not understood; to be insensitive to pain of body or hurts of man; to know inwardly that all is well when all outward signs are to the contrary, and to remain unmoved and quietly serene in the face of happenings which to those uninitiated would seem cataclysmic—this is the development required of those who are to serve as humanity's balance in and through the approaching crisis.

You and the Tree Planter of old have prepared long and faithfully, with thousands of your brothers, toward this earth moment of spiritual travail which is now nearing. Each day is an increasingly priceless pearl in the string of Time. Let these pearls not slip unheeded through your fingers, each has a value to leave with you of far more than human worth. The Tree Planter knows whereof I speak.

* * *

HARRY LOOSE to HAROLD SHERMAN
Monterey Park, September 24, 1941

Harold:-

Please reread and mentally record.

I have been some confused and uneasy since Sunday and that is the reason you have not had an appreciation for the comforting hospitality and nearness of you both before this. . . . These seldom periods of confusion and desire to escape further physical reality and mental endeavor toward completion of this whole matter are perfectly normal and natural.

It has been so long—so long—and the way has been so lonely. I get very tired and chafe for its early conclusion at times and freedom from the continuing responsibility. Why should I be interested to personal exhaustion just to give this new word to a world that will probably not accept it and that would spit on me if it could. Yet, with all this complaining, I am held to my task, I cannot now "let go" and I doubt that I would if I could.

Anyway, forgive me for my complaining—though I acknowledge that it is a relief—and I will cease my repining and know that this great mission of giving a new revelation to this dark and weary world must continue. From many past experiences, I know that these periods of confusion and uneasiness presage something out of the ordinary.

As I am now writing—here comes some of it—I will write just as it comes—no I can't—I will have to wait till I get it all and write my own transposition.

At some time in the past—during a "question and answer period" of our letter writing, I made answer to a written question which was very accurate up to a certain point—but which, after this point, was not fully correct. The question in point was, "What form do we take in the next world" and I answered that question, "You are built in the (physical) image and likeness of the Father, as the Bible tells you. The physical is merely a flesh reproduction of a more beautiful spiritual counterpart."[5] This description is not correct in full. It is correct insofar as the succeeding dimension to this one—but my powers of description are limited to the succeeding dimension only. I have thus exceeded myself. I do not know the answer to the question beyond the second dimension. I do not remember the question or the answer nor in what letter it was written. I presume that you still have my letters and are in position to identify the accuracy and inaccuracy. Anyway, I have now followed the instructions in making the above explanation. I do not know the "why" of this correction. I am so very restricted in so much.

In this reception there came word too about the Magdalene and Jezebel. Your first report was very correct. I am so sorry. So utterly wrong—so wrongly advised. Yet seeking an excuse and a reparation for the wickedness. To justify her own actions. An escape mechanism from the reality. I do not feel easy in mind at the prospect of meeting her—yet I evidentially must. She must soon be told of her errors—gently—but told. I do so hope that you fully understand ALL that I have been trying to say above.

Ma and I arrived home safely—55 minutes, not Ramona Blvd.—11:25—very late for us. I thank you for the food—and for the magazines. And much thanks, too, for Martha's sweetness and understanding and for her quiet *leavening*.

---

[5] See Loose's April 3, 1941 letter, on p. 180.

Are you someday to write a book on my letters and your contact with me?? I very much wonder. I know so very little. I am still a little uneasy—I wonder what portends?? Ma has not been so well—but do not remark it. Pardon my long and hasty letter. I hold good thought but I am unquiet for some reason that I do not know. I may receive further word.

Love to ALL,

ARA   *September 25, 1941*

A soul advanced in service on the earth plane has surrounding him a band of workers. He is helped more than he realizes through situations that might otherwise prove unsolvable or unbearable. More help is given as the soul evidences the deservability to receive help. And yet, no soul is deprived of its own initiative nor is anything done for it that it essentially must do for itself. But workers are paving the way along the lines of aspiration of the soul often years ahead of the expression or accomplishment on the earth plane.

It is all part of a picture or plan into which each enmissioned soul fits. You are not alone in your strivings. Higher intelligences are as dependent on you in the fulfillment of their missions as you are dependent upon them in the fulfillment of yours. For this reason you must keep your channel of communication open that you may divine, more and more, your own soul's purpose in this life and the plan of service of which you are an integral part.

No "orders" can be received when the soul is immersed too much in fleshly things. When the telephone switchboard of your body is clogged with local calls, you cannot receive important long-distance messages from those who really count.

True inspiration comes from those in Higher Realms. It is in this manner that you also, on occasion, "entertain angels unawares."

October 8, 1941

A storm area forms slowly, gathering all the elements from earth and sky.

In much the same manner, your own forces are collected through developing experiences in life until the day when you find yourself a definite power moving in a purposeful direction, capable of sweeping all before you in the way of opposition. Your movement is really spiraling like a cyclone, with your powers expanding from a center of dead calm wherein dwells your directing spirit.

Those around you feel your increasing power, are sucked in by it, caught up and carried along, adding their forces to your motivation. The lesser entities always seek strength through union with the greater. The magnetic attraction of the sun draws up particles of water from the earth which, in themselves, are not potent but which, when joined in vast numbers can rain down great life-giving nourishment over a wide area on this planet.

There is a constant, incomprehensible interchange of forces taking place; likewise a continual blending and linking of entities on missions of service. Many entities, not sufficiently developed, are used like the individual drop of water, unconscious of the service rendered. Yet this service has brought progress to the entity.

It shall be given unto you to influence the lives of many entities through the increasing power of your own revealed wisdom and expression. Already your spiritual forces have revolved about the lives of many more thousands, yes, numbering into the millions of men and women, boys and girls, than you may consciously realize. You have touched their consciousness in a manner that has stepped up its vibration. Once influenced, these entities draw from you particles of inspiration and guidance for they have given you lodgment in their minds and hearts—not as an entity but as a force.

You are the stone which once dropped in the pool of their consciousness, continues to send forth ripples of inspiration and light.

Observe now the responsibility all leaders of mankind take unto themselves and the penalty many will one day have to pay for sending forth wrong and destructive influences.

Of two storms, approaching each other from opposite directions and meeting, the stronger will survive after a terrific clashing of the elements, ending by whirling the lesser storm up in it, changing its entire nature and path.

Just so will the forces developed by you and other enmissioned brothers in the flesh, rise up in a righteous storm to beat down the forces of darkness which are casting a cyclone pall over the peoples of earth. The elements are gathering for the titanic conflict and you have sensed their movement for years, being at times greatly disturbed thereby, for you had not then developed the power and wisdom to withstand the tempest.

You are now reaching a point wherein the sun will always shine for you while all is dark on earth, it will be your mission to bring this light through the clouds of despair hanging low over the misguided heads of millions.

Then will the true *rain*, not *reign*, of Peace and understanding come. No earthly rule can bring it. But human creatures must absorb this spirit as the earth hungrily absorbs the falling drops of moisture—so that they become an actual part of the higher forces in operation.

This is the only way that advancement can come and lower elements be transcended by fusing with the higher.

October 10, 1941

The world crisis is moving swiftly along toward the United States' active participation in the war. Japan, as indicated in the paper reports, will touch off the spark in the Pacific in the hope of keeping America busy there while Germany brings increasing pressure on the Atlantic side as England now *really* has to fight for her life.

This struggle, as viewed from dimensions beyond, is rooted in causes which have their foundations deep within the human creature, tracing back to early beginnings of different races.

The end of this era is rapidly approaching amid great and incomprehensible turmoil of spirit. It is the last great battle being waged by the animal self of man for survival, it knows that it must ultimately surrender to the spirit which dwells within but is striving to prove to the residing soul that it is sufficient unto itself.

This carnal effort failing, the animal self then will implore that it be taken over by the spirit for its own salvation. This harmonious union of the lower with the higher selves of Being finally atones for the great mistake made in the long ago and gives back to all elements the properties and qualities and progressions originally designed and intended.

The striking of such a balance is not accomplished without cataclysmic happenings on the earth plane like a cauldron boiling over as all elements are refined, through the intense heat of human experience.

But there will be those who will be protected and remain unscathed through the seething human inferno to come. They are the new leaders of the God Spirit in man which will manifest itself at a time when the animal in man is running riot.

It has been written that the Great Intelligence would permit the animal in man to rule for a time to demonstrate to itself that it, alone, is not equipped to govern, nor to exist, without the indwelling spirit. This is the lesson earth life is supposed to teach, a lesson which evolving creatures here must learn.

10

"For Such an Hour"

HAROLD SHERMAN to WILLIAM SADLER

Hollywood, October 12, 1941

Dr. William S. Sadler,
533 Diversey Parkway,
Chicago, Illinois

Dear Dr. Sadler:

We have been immensely busy, as a family, since arriving in California. There has been the job of getting settled and into the swing of things out here, with Marcia, my youngest daughter, satisfying a "life ambition" by taking horseback riding lessons; Mary, tennis; and Mary and Martha, my wife, learning to drive the car—while I was plunging into my work at Warner Brothers Studio, writing the screenplay based on the life of MARK TWAIN.

But Martha and I have had time, each weekend, to see Harry Loose and wife and to devote some period each day to meditation on the subjects that mean so much to us all.

Our two days in Chicago and the hours spent with you people stand out in memory. Martha and I so deeply appreciated your unusual efforts in acquainting us with developments—knowledge we needed to know in order for us to determine how best we might serve in this coming time.

As I explained to you, my life has been lived, since a boy, in the *knowing awareness* that I had to gain a diversified experience in the writing field in order to be capable of representing and directing a tremendous enterprise of worldwide importance.

Since arriving in Hollywood, I have found it necessary to secure an author's agent [Zeppo Marx] to represent me. He required a letter from me, outlining my background and my plans for the future so that he might work harmoniously with me . . . and I am sending you a copy of this letter which can serve to inform you and your Group more specifically about myself.[1]

Doctor, I am sure you must realize that you are approaching a critical stage in the plating of this great book, preparatory to the order being given for its release to the public. I, who have had fifty books published, and tried publishing one book myself, am fully conscious of the pitfalls wherein even the best book can be LOST amid the sea of publications, unless properly HANDLED, EXPLOITED and DISTRIBUTED.

For this reason, and applying more emphatically to the BOOK OF URANTIA than ANY OTHER—no mistake must be permitted in the method chosen for its presentation to the public.

This Story of our First Life Planet, Urantia, possesses great dramatic possibilities when adapted to radio, stage and screen. There are perhaps 20 to 30 great dramas in it, maybe more. And these must be culled out and developed in direct relation to the spiritual value and need represented by the phase of the book dramatized.

You cannot permit the TRUTH to be perverted. For this reason, you can never sell the rights to the dramatization of any part of this book as rights are ordinarily sold to producers of radio, stage and screen. IF I am correct in my belief that my life has been lived to enable me to serve your Group as the DRAMATIST, then it will be my task, in association with a directorial board from your Group, to take complete charge and have all business offers referred to me.

The MARK TWAIN ESTATE granted me a contract enabling me to develop Mark Twain's life in dramatic form for radio, stage and screen—and, as a result, the highest price ever paid for a picture story is being paid to the Estate. This came about ONLY because the Estate *retained* control of its property, rather than just selling the rights, un-

---

[1] This letter has not been found.

developed in dramatic form, to Mark Twain's life. The Estate was further protected in not having to risk the prostitution of Mark Twain's life through a poor or uninspired dramatization. The Estate knew in advance, because of the character and quality of my work, that, once sold, it would be produced as written . . . and that the inspiration of Mark Twain's life would be preserved.

More, even, than Mark Twain in importance, with relation to proper treatment of subject matter, is the BOOK OF URANTIA. You are entrusted with material which must not be profaned, intentionally or unintentionally, by any writers who might be assigned to adapt it to such mediums as radio, stage and screen.

You need someone who knows the craftsmanship of all these mediums for reaching human consciousness under the guise of entertainment (for we can get nowhere by preaching to humanity) . . . so that the entire project can be successfully and faithfully supervised.

Were you to go into the open market to secure a competent dramatist, you still could not be assured that he had the spiritual appreciation or understanding to match his ability—all of which is so vitally needed on this assignment. Additional men and women, in the arts and sciences, will need to be trained and given the revelation—but always under supervision of someone who sees the "end from the beginning" . . . who knows how to SYNCHRONIZE all factors in all mediums and *progress* them through radio, stage, screen and press toward the desired final objective.

This is an enormous job—requiring an almost superhuman grasp of many mediums, of mass reaction, of world conditions—and one requiring unfailing courage and stamina.

I am not meaning to suggest that any ONE MAN is capable of standing up under such a mission of service. But, given the support of higher intelligences, fleshed and unfleshed, he may draw the power and the wisdom to see it through.

I can foresee world conditions ahead that will call upon all the fortitude humans have to endure. Perhaps then is when the voice is to sound in the wilderness. Certainly, then is the time when mankind will be reaching out for some manner of spiritual salvation, all material means having failed.

The BOOK OF URANTIA, properly launched, should bring an income sufficient to keep alive a sizable sum for its perpetuation and the carrying on of work growing out of its publication and adaptation to the fields of entertainment.

It would seem to me that now is the time to carefully prepare the campaign and steps of procedure with respect to the release of the BOOK OF URANTIA.

I hope to be finished with the screenplay on the life of MARK TWAIN by the middle of December—and might then be able to return to Chicago for a several days' conference on the different phases of this project, if you so desired.

If you and your group should feel that I am the one intended to be entrusted with this responsibility, I would like to work out a contractual relationship something after the nature of my arrangement with the Mark Twain Estate, so that we are all protected and so that this entire enterprise may be protected from the very start.

Past experience has proven to me that this is the only way in which valuable literary properties may be protected, the way the entertainment and publishing world is organized today.

I think you will need much more money to launch this book successfully—and I think I may know where some of this money may be secured at the proper time.

I have a feeling, too, that Jesse L. Lasky, who has produced SERGEANT YORK and who is to produce MARK TWAIN for Warner Brothers, is the man who will see the great possibilities in the BOOK OF URANTIA and who has sufficient spiritual understanding to do a number of pictures based on it. He has certain weaknesses of character—but IF we maintain the right control of our material, we cannot be touched . . . and we are still living in a world where many of our most talented people in the creative field have their weak sides.

Will you please give the warmest regards of Martha and myself to all whom we met, and express once more our gratitude? I shall await word from you with respect to the above.

Sincerely,

ARA   *October 13, 1941*

What you have seen and experienced in your long, long journey up to the present is not lost to you—it has only been withheld for a little while. Just as inner vision would be confusing to you if operative at all times on earth, so would the impingement of past life memories prove upsetting and bewildering in your daily rounds now. Much development must come before the veil can be lifted for the soul and he is permitted to look backward along the arduous path he has traveled.

You sink into the ocean of your entire life experience during sleep and, occasionally awaken with vague memories of indescribably beautiful adventures or the very reverse condition which you set down as a harrowing nightmare. Often these recollections have nothing to do with any experience undergone in this flesh body but reach back in time to some ordeal of the soul, some anguished mistake which has still left its mark in consciousness.

Just as the striking of a note will bring answering chimes from other equally attuned objects, so does a vivid experience in this life sound down through corridors of time, awakening all past experiences of like nature. These experiences may not cross the threshold of flesh consciousness in recognizable form—existing many times only as inexpressible feelings which seem to well up from the unfathomable depths of Being.

Your life is a symphony of experience. It is constantly being played upon by forces from within and without and the nature of your reaction to this interplay determines the degree of harmony or discord realized by your entity.

The ultimate destiny of your soul is the attainment of complete and absolute harmony through attunement with the Great Intelligence. When this state of development is reached, you then receive the embrace of the Father and go not out any more as a part Him but remain *one* with Him in an eternal existence beyond the power of earth language to describe.

As you overcome fear and exercise faith, more and more can be shown you. Belief must come before revelation since belief shuts off all fleshly protests of the physical senses which have no capacity to sense other than earth plane experience—and opens the door to the faculties of the soul which can know all things, as it progresses, through wisdom sent by the Father.

Your Thought Adjustor stands guard at the gateway of your soul and will guide everything that you may wish to enter in, if you will counsel first before opening the gate.

Each soul must learn how to protect himself against the incursion of destructive forces since a flesh body that can be occupied by Intelligence can also be preyed upon by other intelligences unless the inhabiting entity maintains control. You should be influenced only by Higher Intelligence—never by the low grade elementals, always seeking recognition or some vicarious, momentary association with the flesh. You must realize that you are surrounded by Intelligence of inconceivable vari-

ety, directed and undirected, all in different stages of unfoldment. You are in the turbulent sea of life and your rudder is your
Thought Adjustor. Keep your hand in his and all will be well.

* * *

HARRY LOOSE to HAROLD SHERMAN
Monterey Park, October 19, 1941
Harold:-

I am writing this in great haste and so, of course, stumblingly—
and so excuse any errors, etc. I would like to write out the following
permission so that I can mail it when I go to get little John [*Ed. note:*
Loose's grandson] from school. Please reread this.

I am generally somewhat inarticulate when I want to get something to you fully. The reason, mostly, for the inarticulateness is that
there are such great extenuations to the subject matter that it is not
possible, with all my desire so to do, to include the many ramifications
that are entailed. They lead endlessly on and on—this way and that—
like the surface of troubled waters. SO—much that I am entitled to
impart is only partly delivered—*never in full*—please remember.

It is mostly left to your own thought and understanding—your
own deductions, as a follow-up to supply that which continues therefrom. Your deductions etc. in continuance—with the help of your
TA—are more fully correct than I could understandably put them in
direct voice while we were in contact. We really have had so pitifully
few moments of lone personal association since you have been here—
"born again." I do not complain because I know that all that occurs
is a part in the great plan, and so one in which individual enfleshed
intelligences have but very little jurisdiction. But I do regret it.

In continuance—with my inarticulateness—I am here permitted
to give you another tiny word of one of the workings of the very intricate plan of which I am able to know and understand very little—the
vastness—the surprising complexities—so immense and far-reaching—I quest "Why—why—why?" and the answer cometh not—I
have not progressed so far as to be able to grasp—I can only know
that such things ARE—and forget the "why and how." Some things
in the very little that I am given to know are of such character—so
intricate—so enmeshed—so complex—that they are hardly conceivable to the limitations of the human mind unless there has been much

progress in understanding by the individual consciousness. I know personally that it would be a useless effort to try to give understanding in some small definite truth. I could go on with this for pages, and all to no present purpose.

ARA is a full and complete member of the following dimension. At one time, he too was enfleshed just as you now are. His service continuance, for further growth, was of his own choice. My beloved TA is in exactly the same position.

Please now know that in addition to the many forces of which you are aware—which surround you, upon which you tread, etc.—you are endowed with a collective FORCE. You have always been very free with it—you have "given" much—and still "give" prodigally—but this collective FORCE with which you are endowed is not limitless. You exhaust the storage place wherein it resides. Yet it accumulates again on expenditure—but not as fast as it can be "lived up" or thrown away. Every hour of the 24 in the day you are receiving this FORCE from the air which you breathe—the very same FORCE from exactly the same kind of air that the whirling motor takes to recharge a battery or to store in cells. This "recharging" is more so at night because there is much less release or wastage during the period of lessened physical activity—and the Soul, whose very presence in residence immediately "pulls" greatly on the placid "reserve," is absent in conference, relaxation, or other duties.

Because of your unusual spiritual background, your (successful) ARA has a latitude far greater than that of the TA of other enfleshed entities who have not had the same spiritual background and period of service. Mark this following. The TA of any enfleshed intelligence is very able, at WILL, to contact the TA's of other enfleshed intelligences, and DOES.[2] They do not lead an entirely ALONE existence from their kind. This conduct of the indwelling TA with other TA intelligences makes for the very frequent instances of fleshed entities who have material mental phenomena, such materially unexplainable happenings as seeming recognition of individuals, surroundings, voices, places, things, and of clairvoyance, forevision, TELEPATHY, etc., with further ramifications too far here to enumerate.

---

[2] *[A]djusters . . . are possessed of unlimited ability to communicate with each other, that is, all forms of Monitors above the first or virgin groups. As to the nature and purport of their intercommunications, we can reveal very little, for we do not know* (107:5.2).

Through the knowing practice and cultivation of concentration and purpose, these people, knowingly or unknowingly, have contact with a FORCE that enables them to perform those seeming mental prodigies. "I just don't know *how* I do it, but I *do* do it" is the general answer accorded. Legitimate operators with this wonderful ability often prostitute their accomplishment for money and become public "Psychics" or mediums for pay. There is a sure penalty for such prostitution. These powers, *so used*, are not lasting. They fail, in time, and comes mental instability, or "nervous" or physical collapse, madness, or death—any of these things as above remarked are the eventual penalties.

Because of what HAS been in the past—and because of what is in prospect in the near future on this planet—further and advanced service—ARA and my much beloved TA have been in close contact for these many years while we have been entirely separate in the flesh. This was for long before I met you materially in the flesh at Marion. I have known, through my TA friend and advisor, of your advancement in the Spirit continually in this time—have known that the tests, trials and temptations were many and were overcome. I knew but few of the actual physical workings. I know that your overcomings were through your own WILL and that you were much aided by ARA, though you did not know him or his office at that time. The actual CHOICE was to your WILL alone but, as with ALL enfleshed intelligences, there was that still, small voice of advice and the FORCE necessary to continue.

By your WILL you called that FORCE into action—it was inactive until that instant. That FORCE was, and is, beyond that of the normal—as you well know—and its strength was, and is, beyond that of your own indwelling and that of your reserve in the custody of ARA. That necessary FORCE was the FORCE of my own beloved TA working in conjunction with your own—borrowed—or given—in the then emergency or sudden or continued need. O the intricacies you are yet to be introduced to. Few are even understandable materially—only by the understanding of advanced Spiritual values—motivations—and actualities present.

Just as from my TA you have received FORCE, so all these years Martha's TA (Stamatsa) who, knowing your intended purpose beyond the knowledge of your own material consciousness, has given *much*. This may explain some things that have not been clear to you regarding Martha before. Your developing Soul entity has had the help of the FORCE of my TA through this long time and of Martha's. You have been particularly vulnerable to the loss of your own FORCE—at times to what would have been total exhaustion, and probable physical death, if you had not the "drawing account" on the FORCE you have received from Martha's TA and from mine. . . .

I have told you before that Martha has meant *much* to you that you did not know about. This, as above, is to what I referred. This same FORCE is also conferred, or given, knowingly by the WILL of the individual entity—as a willing bestowal. You have *often* seen this in operation yourself—you have often willingly bestowed it yourself. One of the reasons why your FORCE should be conserved is that it will be more and more necessary to you as time goes forward. Your needful retention of this FORCE is one of the reasons it would be best if Arthur and his additional responsibilities could be taken from you—you have a great drain there—and a still greater drain from your Mother—you really and directly feel the loss of FORCE when she is physically present.

Please remember that when you give, or lose, FORCE, it is given at a loss to yourself—you have that much less left until there is recuperation. Recuperation comes, but that, too, is a process—it is not limitless—it can be exhausted. It is not "nervous force"—there is no such thing, doctors to the contrary—and it cannot be either generated, or given, through the nerves. They have no part in it or of it. A "nervous breakdown" has absolutely nothing to do with the nerves. It has to do with the prodigal loss of this FORCE expended—and the rejection of the TA to give more to waste for the same purpose that induced the breakdown. And recovery is a change radically in the living method, physically and mentally, and a gradual resumption of cooperation with the TA FORCE and power which do not rest in the nerves. Nerves are merely the physical servant of FORCE—exactly the same as all the rest of the physical body.

Please remember that the TA is very well known to the general *interested* public as the "Astral" or *second self*. And that the *willed* projection of the intimately attuned and understood TA is called the "projection of the Astral" and is a much accomplished phenomenon amongst the understanding. This method of projection is understood and much used by the identical likeness of the first, or real, self in the material. To those of understanding, who are far enough advanced to "see," these Astrals are more or less solid of appearance—sufficiently so as not to be transparent—and, more often, only the upper part of the figure is visible. They are fully voiced, though of peculiar timbre. Those who are sufficiently advanced to perform the above knowingly and with intent never, to my knowledge, do so for a consideration or for show. The risk of loss of ability so to do is too great. I must also include here that levitation is also accomplished, as is also the movement of the inanimate—this by those who are particularly advanced. This without the visibility of the Astral.

So—withal I recommend to you the furtherance of your growing contact with, and knowledge of, ARA. As you are now housed, such necessary meditation is hardly possible to accomplish in uninterrupted concentration. You really should have a place where it would be possible to close the door and be at uninterrupted peace and alone for such meditation.

All of the above is only indicating the way. Growth is in response to effort alone. Nothing is merely presented without effort. Effort is the continuance of desire. Desire is a mental manifestation. ALL is an individual proposition. You must use your present understanding to extend. Self-effort is the best educator. Study of the Book of Urantia will further self-effort.

ARA *October 19, 1941*

Your physical eyes have beheld many past civilizations; your physical ears have heard and understood many languages of peoples long since disappeared from this earth; your physical senses have thrilled to scenes and experiences piled one upon another countless times over, leaving their impress upon your soul. Each time as you left your receiving instrument, the body, you took the record of this life experience with you. You took also this evolving consciousness of the human creature with you as *your link* to the planet Urantia upon which you became imprisoned through union of higher enfleshed entities with the developing human forms they had come upon earth to guide.

This lower consciousness of which your higher self is a part possesses the power to recreate itself in physical form. All physical life comes from the sea or fluid state. In this way are elementals fused, absorbing one another and yet retaining their identity in a new form.

You owe a great debt to this lower self for it has provided the bodies for your continuing experiences in this plane of life. As the influence of your spirit has made itself felt upon the lower self, you have been enabled to elevate your whole being.

Consider, if you will, an invader forcibly residing in your home. Then perhaps you can comprehend the age-old conflict between the lower self and your indwelling spirit and get a sensing of the enormity of the great mistake. Here, originally, were human creatures, setting forth upon the path of upward progression, having union among themselves and containing elements which they understood. Then came the day when unintended union occurred between higher enfleshed intelligences and these human creatures, bringing offspring containing the elements of both.

The self of the human creature, being aware now of the presence of a new and strange consciousness or entity within, resisted this consciousness as an intruder.

But the higher self, carrying a vague memory of its past glorious estate, would constantly cause the lower self moments of remorse for its carnal activities in the flesh. The lower self, striving to understand these weird feelings, felt between two seas, buffeted by external experiences and the inward tides of higher urgings.

The higher self knows that its only hope of release of the spirit from entanglement in the flesh must come through elevation and sublimation of the lower.

Oh, the unspeakable, the unutterably long, long battle it has been up to this present moment of awakening from this ages-old sleep in the flesh!

The Great Intelligence, mindful of the struggle of His creatures on Urantia, sent Christ, one of His highly developed Sons, to awaken the spirits of men. But the flesh in man rose up to repel and deny the Truth—and the Time was not yet.

Christ, as one of those originally associated with the great mistake, returned to earth on a mission to sacrifice Himself that the mistake might be rectified. Insomuch, He *did* die, as man has died, that man might eventually be saved.

Do you begin to see behind the veil now? Do you begin to sense your relationship to the indescribable void of the past? You have known, in many past civilizations, this same old story and you have, through the influence of your words and deeds, started many souls on the path toward liberation—just as you are to do again—in this life.

One day you will see the past as clearly as you see the present. It will stretch before you as a great plain or panorama and you will see an unbroken line, leading back, back, back into the dim beginnings of things on this First Life Planet.

"Be of good cheer!" said Christ, "for I have overcome the world!"

Do you comprehend what He meant by this now?

He had overcome the lower elements in Himself, had transcended the flesh while in the flesh, and had demonstrated to man what man, himself, could and must do in order to free his spirit. . . .

I have revealed much this morning.

* * *

HARRY LOOSE to HAROLD SHERMAN

Monterey Park, October 20, 1941

Harold:-

This morning's contact I voiced, again, request for information as per your thought of yesterday evening in regard to such contact as would assure your making a positive statement, as to your own direct knowledge of entities or intelligences of other planes in verification of written data now in your hands, your own thought, and other matter that you are yet to read in the Book. This because of the anticipation of furtherance of writings and public speaking with authority on the subject as such may later develop.

I have received a direct answer to the question—one which you must interpret yourself. You, probably, will not be satisfied with the answer but quest further assurance beyond that of your present actual vision and other physical manifestation. You will quest, largely, because there has been nothing materially startling or seemingly beyond the physical normal evidenced. The answer was, and is, "You have been, and are, in contact with such intelligence as you seek. You may make such positive verifying declaration in writing or speaking if you so care to do in very truth provided no identifying statement of such entity is made." That was all, except that I should have used the word "he" in this writing instead of the word "you" at the beginning. You may draw your own conclusions and make your own deductions.

May I thank you for the very fine dinner and your association and that of small Martha and your girls.

Ma is some better. . . .

Home with my yard pants and my 7 cents all O.K. by way of Ramona.

ARA   *October 21, 1941, Evening*

Fear not—the whole Pacific area is to be shaken, including the islands of Japan, and Nature's destruction will give men pause.

There will be a great tidal wave—greatest of modern times—the effects of which will be felt on many shores.

The era of great mental and physical changes on the planet Urantia is close at hand. You will see more and more signs of it as your own preparation is speeded.

Do each day what is given you to do and know that each day is of increasing importance—for, it has been said that Time and Tide wait on no man.

You have witnessed the protection accorded you in your Mark Twain work. This is for a purpose beyond your own personal interest and effort, as was revealed to you this morning, the way all elements fit together, one into the other, so do *events*.

Entities from many points on the planet Urantia are moving toward one another in service and will join as do the elements to provide a band of spiritual strength encircling the earth in the coming time of chaos.

You have foreseen this awesome period for which you and others like you have been prepared these many, many years.

Fear not—much may fall around you—in the movement of elements and events—but you will prevail.

Sleep well. You have an appointment tonight.

NOTE: This evening dictation following two earthquake shocks (10:57 p.m.), the heaviest felt in this area since 1933.

WILLIAM SADLER to HAROLD SHERMAN

Chicago, October 22, 1941

Mr. Harold M. Sherman,
Canterbury Apartments,
1746 North Cherokee Avenue,
Hollywood, California

Dear Harold:

We have all enjoyed your letter of October 12th. I read some paragraphs of it to the Forum Sunday, and I think we all feel that you have "come to the Kingdom for such an hour."

I, of course, know nothing more to tell you at this time than what we so frequently tell ourselves: "Carry on." Many times our Unseen

Friends have told us that our life obligations in order of importance are:

Take care of the health.
Faithfully and loyally perform our daily tasks.
Serve the interests of the Urantia papers.
Attend to the trifles of life.

That being the case, evidently your first duty now, aside from the care of yourself, is to do the job you have in hand. In due time these other things will develop.

We know nothing more to report since you and Martha were here except that the proofreader went to work last week. Next week the Foreword is to be set up in type in order to secure final decisions on style and size of type for headings and other miscellaneous features of the format. I, of course, will let you know any time we have new instructions.

Thank you for sending me copy of the letter to Zeppo Marx, and all of the folks here join in sending regards and best wishes to you and yours.

As ever, sincerely,

On Wednesday, October 22, 1941, Harold received notice from War-
ner Bros. that his employment on The Adventures of Mark Twain
would be terminated the following Saturday. The script was not com-
pleted, but as Harold wrote to Charles T. Lark, attorney for the Mark
Twain Estate, "It is now in marvelous shape, with the master scene
final treatment done and only a few weeks necessary to complete the
shooting script." For that job, Lasky had hired top Hollywood screen-
writers.

ARA   *October 22, 1941*

A door is shut that a bigger door may be opened. The value of your contribution to the Twain picture *cannot* and *will not* be lost—but your value in other directions is even more—and you must be free to move on—for world changes are coming fast—and your services are needed.

You will scarcely more than have left these vibrations where you now are than the new things awaiting you will be disclosed and the next steps made clearly apparent to you.

Certainly you have had evidence of forces working in your behalf which have resulted in your transfer to California. These same forces have been preparing a way as you, yourself, have been preparing to *travel* that way. Your preparation has been swift and the time foreshortened. Be not disturbed at surface happenings and know that nothing basically can affect you any longer or the fulfillment of your ultimate destiny. You have come too far and have been too well tested.

Events will establish so firmly in the entertainment as well as the philosophic worlds as to make you a commanding figure—with the power to dictate in place of being dictated *to*. This day is not as distant as you may think.

Meanwhile, rest secure in the knowledge and faith, that all is well. If it were not so I would have been permitted to tell you. Last night you conferred with Intelligences during sleep concerning these future plans and developments of which you are not now conscious. This conference was in anticipation of to-day's happening at the studio.

I repeat—all is well.

NOTE: On this day notification was given at studio of termination of service.

HAROLD SHERMAN to WILLIAM SADLER
Hollywood, October 27, 1941

Dear Dr. Sadler:

Thank you for your fine letter.

My work on the MARK TWAIN screenplay has been finished far ahead of schedule and I am now free to make some final editorial changes on "THOUGHTS THROUGH SPACE," the book I have written with Sir Hubert Wilkins, who will join me here tomorrow. He has just returned from a survey of the Pacific situation in Japan and China.

Our book is being published by a new publishing firm, Creative Age Press,[3] Inc., of 11 East 44th Street, New York City, and will sell for either $4 or $5. This publishing house was organized, with substantial financial backing, to publish advanced books of a spiritual nature, revealing the higher powers of man. I cite this to indicate the forces at work. (Our book will be out in either late January or February.) It will contain the complete documentary record of our telepathic experi-

---

[3] Creative Age Press was owned by medium and parapsychologist Eileen Garrett.

ments as checked by Dr. Gardner Murphy, then of the Parapsychology Department, Columbia University. There will also be printed affidavits from the other scientists and witnesses to these experiments, testifying to their authenticity.

I wish that Sir Hubert Wilkins might be added to your Group. I am sure he is one of us and his name would add greatly because of his interest and championing of these higher mental powers—and the fact that our book is due to be widely heralded. Might I have permission to ask him to call upon you when he is next in Chicago? He is one of the finest souls it has ever been my privilege to meet.

Now—about the BOOK OF URANTIA. I have been in daily communion with my TA and some unusual knowledge has come through, a record of which I am keeping for your later perusal.

I am impressed now to write you pertaining the MOST IMPORTANT PHASE in the publication of the URANTIA BOOK. That is the establishment of its *absolute authenticity* in the minds of the public! Unless this is done, the book, however vital and true its contents, will be classified by unthinking, undeveloped humans as another "I Am" Book, or the work of some cult, and its GREAT VALUE to humanity largely lost.

Some years ago, when I was quietly doing research on the powers of mind and getting results that I considered evidential, and keeping careful records of same—MY RECITATION of these experiments to a few trusted friends, brought expressions of interest but NOT of belief!

I was a nice fellow, obviously sincere—but I was self-deluded . . . a victim of auto-suggestion or hallucinations, or exceedingly gullible in ascribing to telepathy what had happened only by "coincidence."

And it was ONLY when the results of these Sherman-Wilkins long-distance telepathic experiments were made known through the article in the March 1939 issue of *Cosmopolitan*, that these friends were suddenly IMPRESSED that I had been getting GENUINE, PROVABLE RESULTS! The *authenticity* of my work had been established!

You and your Group have a *similar problem* in the introduction of the BOOK OF URANTIA to the public. I have not been advised by you of your specific plans—but I am sure, if the present intent should be to publish the book ANONYMOUSLY, without any identifying factors behind it, then much of its great designed world value will be lost.

Fortunately and providentially, this book has been written in the presence of a host of accredited witnesses. Christ's disciples gave testimony of His works, during His life and after His death. They suffered for their service in His behalf but they spoke out courageously and unashamedly in support of Him.

Even though the FOREWORD be written by Higher Intelligences—a PREFACE should precede the Foreword, preferably written by *you*—in which you tell the story of your first contact with this *amanuensis,* your investigation of the phenomena, your final conviction, the organization of the Group, the plan of operation and the manner in which the BOOK OF URANTIA came into being. THEN, the names of all who have been associated as witnesses of this dictation should be affixed, attesting to the genuineness of your story in all its details.

Doctor—this is the ONLY WAY that acceptance of this book can be obtained in the world as it exists today. But the list of names of individuals, living and dead, who have been associated with this great work will cause ALL REVIEWERS to STOP and CONSIDER. Not only that—but all scientists and educators and people of position in every country in the world will be compelled to treat this BOOK OF URANTIA with respect when they know of its origin and those who have been identified.

Consider for a moment yourself. Let us say you had had nothing to do with a book of this kind. Suddenly there appears the BOOK OF URANTIA on the market. It is called to your attention. You find its contents of interest BUT it is printed anonymously—purportedly written by Higher Intelligences. However, you have had nothing in your own personal experience which has demonstrated the existence of such higher forces—and since this book is not BACKED or CHAMPIONED by anyone whose names you respect, in fact, not by anyone at all . . . you DISMISS IT as an amazing flight of fancy.

I know you have desired to keep all personalities out of this work—and that the whole Group effort and support has been entirely UNSELFISH. But the time is now fast approaching when this GROUP should stand for that which all BELIEVE IN—stand before the world. This is not going to be easy in many respects—but if the book is to be SUCCESSFULLY LAUNCHED, such public support and identification is IMPERATIVE.

Do you think my work with WILKINS would have brought any consideration, commanded any respect or belief, IF I had not been supported by competent witnesses? The value of our pioneering experiment would have been lost, however successful.

May I urge you, if thought has not been given in this direction, to make this a first order of business?

If I have any contribution to make at the present time—it is certainly this. I have made many talks on the powers of the mind and I have had to be prepared, from the public platform, to *defend* and to *prove* my statements. The public demand for such *evidence* and *authority* is going to be terrific with respect to this BOOK OF URANTIA, if it is properly presented.

It will be necessary, then, to be organized to meet this demand, and it will be too late not to have anticipated these developments later.

I know you will understand my writing you in this fashion, but it behooves us all not to leave a stone unturned that will protect and aid this enterprise.

With my TWAIN work completed so far in advance, I am now ready to co-operate even more fully if you have anything that I may do.

Martha joins me in warmest regards and best wishes to you all!

Sincerely,

ARA   *October 29, 1941*

New conditions and opportunities are coming rapidly your way along the lines of your intended interests and activities by the first of the week.

The way has been prepared by others, serving consciously and unconsciously the purposes for which you came into this life.

As the Tree Planter has instructed you, "Watch how the pieces fit into the pattern."

Mark Twain was and is a stepping stone but it is only one brick in a building you are erecting which is destined to catch the attention of the entire world.

The building will be unlike anything seen on earth before—and your enmissioned brothers, who will join with you in the building, will help you set up a spiritual shelter for the millions who will then be weary and heavy laden, not knowing where to turn, nor what to do, without hope and without faith.

Could any work be more needed or more inspiring? Reaching the souls of humanity is vastly more important than reaching their minds—or their pocketbooks. These have been pandered to by merchants, politicians and charlatans. But even the churches have failed to touch the human soul. This is to be your mission—you, in company with other brothers of earth and dimensions beyond. . . .

You are a vital part in the stream of service which is flowing Godward and will carry a goodly portion of humanity with it.

Sleep well.

November 6, 1941

Each day the band of service draws together with new entities appearing on the horizon, being readied for service. There will be no mistaking members of this band when they are brought in contact with you. It shall be your duty to awaken some but many are arousing from their long sleep in the flesh, having had vague, restless dreams and yearnings, and all they will need will be a tap on the shoulder and the right word to enlist them as fully prepared soldiers in this spiritual cause which means so very, very much to all troubled souls on this dark planet.

You are to receive what will seem to you amazing support. An organization will spring up under your direction as though it has been materialized with each entity, man or woman, in his appointed place, by talent, past preparatory experience and design. Many were the kinds of artisans required to build the temple made without hands, and just so will this temple of the living God—the Great Intelligence, be built. Its dome will shelter all humanity; its foundation will hold firm while the whole surface of the earth and all human forms upon it tremble in the balance between chaos and regeneration. . . .

Rejoice that the time is close at hand even though it means the assumption of *great responsibilities*. You will be given strength and the wisdom required to meet situations. The evidence you seek to support the stand you must take will be supplied as the occasions arise.

Fear not! As you watch and hold yourself in readiness to act, as impelled by the inner voice, you are being watched over.

Sleep well!

WILLIAM SADLER to HAROLD and MARTHA SHERMAN

Chicago, November 7, 1941

Dear Shermans:

This will acknowledge the receipt of your letter of October 27th, and since we are going to see you in December I will not undertake at this time to discuss its many interesting features.

I had a letter from Harry a week or two ago and was glad to know he was thinking of coming back to Chicago with you. I hope he does.

We are looking forward to having some pleasant visits with you and yours.

With regards from all of us, I am

Sincerely yours,

William S. Sadler

HARRY LOOSE to HAROLD SHERMAN

Monterey Park, November 11, 1941

Harold:-

I have properly entered the added A communications[4] and have continued in their collective study for the last hour. By way of my personal knowing—some are correct. Some are correct, not by way of my own experiences but because of what I otherwise know to be the truth. Some are half-truths—unfinished and clouded—and of some I know nothing and can express no opinion.

In continuing, I am extending something toward you. There is a consciousness above the usual (normal). It is when arrived in this higher level of consciousness there then appears what is termed "sight" or "light." Either is appropriate and applicable and either is correct. It is, when arrived in this upper strata of consciousness, wherein there also appears the secondary hearing. This consciousness above the normal, is a willed condition or state arrived at, on summons, almost instantly. This superstrata of consciousness is available only to and arrived at only by the individual effort and is a milestone. Read that story in your Bible. No one can "give" you progress on the upward climb. "To him who *hath* shall be *given*," etc.

Note: The facial expression of attention is much more apt to be the attention of listening and not that of sight. Hearing is more often present without sight. Correct hearing is more important than

---

[4] Harold had been sharing his almost-daily Ara messages with Loose.

sight. The Prophets of old HEARD far more often than they visualized. Sight very often brings great fear. Presentation by hearing means reception non-confused by sight and is much more often used. I hope that all the above is sufficiently clear. I have told you much here. . . .

We are again indebted to you for the association of small Martha, of yourself, and of the girls. Will you please thank Martha for the swell food. Especially the little hot biscuits.

11

A CANTERBURY TALE

In appreciation of his valued friendship and the fine interest of Harry Loose in us, we had a Thanksgiving basket of fruit sent to the Loose home. We had our standing date to see the Looses in Monterey Park that coming Sunday, November 23, so we were surprised, upon returning from a short drive about 3 p.m. Thanksgiving afternoon [*Ed. note:* Thanksgiving fell on November 20 that year], to find a memorandum slip in our box at the Canterbury, timed at 2:30 p.m. and filled out by Mr. Cousins, the clerk on duty, which read, "Mr. Loose was here—will see you on Sunday."

The Cousins memorandum

We instantly regretted our absence from the apartment since, in Harry's physical condition, the drive to Hollywood through downtown Los Angeles traffic was always fatiguing, especially on a holiday. We were amazed to think that he would have made the long trip on the chance of finding us in and that he had not telephoned to tell us of his coming.

Because it customarily took us about an hour to drive to the Loose home in Monterey Park, we figured, since he reportedly had been at the Canterbury only half an hour earlier, that he would still not have arrived back at his own address. We decided, therefore, to wait a few minutes before phoning to express our regrets at having been out when he called.

At about three-thirty we put a call through and Harry answered immediately. I thanked him for making the long drive to see us and told him how sorry we were not to have been home. There was a hesitation on the phone, and then Harry said concernedly, "Harold, there's been some mistake. You have me confused with someone else. I didn't come to see you. I haven't been out of the house today."

This was surprising information. I looked down at the memorandum slip in my hand. It plainly stated that "Mr. Loose was here. . . ." The "Mr. Loose" was spelled correctly.

"That's very strange," I replied. "Your name is recorded, saying you had called in person and that you would see us on Sunday."

"That's right," replied Harry, "I'm expecting you folks over here this Sunday but I repeat, Josie and Ray and little John [daughter, son-in-law and grandson] were here for Thanksgiving dinner. I haven't even had my shoes on all day. I'm dressed in my work pants and the old brown sweater and slippers you've usually seen me wearing here at home. And my car hasn't been out of the garage."

"That's funny," said I, "I can't figure out how Mr. Cousins could have made such an error. In the first place, he's never met you because he doesn't work Sundays—the only day you ever come over here. I can't imagine how he'd get your name. Well, anyhow, we'll be seeing you Sunday."

I hung up and went immediately downstairs to check the memorandum with Mr. Cousins. I told him that the party he had listed as calling on us had just advised me on the phone that he hadn't been out of the house all day. I asked if he remembered the man well enough to describe his appearance. He said that he did, that the gentleman looked like a working man, that he wore working pants, a brown sweater with dark blue shirt, and that he had a cap on.

I was astounded at the accurate description. Mr. Cousins, noting my perplexity, asked, "What's the matter? Is something wrong?"

"Something's very odd," I replied. "You've described Mr. Loose perfectly and just as he says he has been dressed today."

Mr. Cousins was now the one to be astounded. "That's peculiar," he said. "Now that you tell me that, I recall several unusual things about this man. I looked up and saw him standing at the desk, not having noticed him come in. He gave me this message for you, speaking slowly and with great difficulty, as though he had false teeth and was having trouble keeping them in place. He spoke clearly, however, and wanted to know, after I'd written down his message, if I had it correct. There was a woman guest at the desk at the time, and she commented after he left about his being 'a strange person.'" Mr. Cousins looked at me with sudden interest. "But, Mr. Sherman," he continued, "if this wasn't Mr. Loose, who was it?"

"That's a question I can't answer right now," I said. "I'll have to report to you later."

Hurrying back to our apartment, I put in another call to Mr. Loose. Getting him on the wire, I said, "Harry, I've just talked to Mr. Cousins and he has given me an accurate description of you—so accurate that it could not have been anyone else. I'm completely mystified. What do you make of it?"

The tone in Harry's voice was extremely sober. "I don't exactly know," he said. "If Mr. Cousins has described my appearance exactly, as you say, then he must have seen something. I've never had an experience just like this before. It disturbs me greatly. I don't want to discuss it on the phone but I'll talk to you about it when we meet on Sunday. Meanwhile, I suggest that you don't make anything of this to Mr. Cousins until I can get some kind of light on what actually took place."

We could hardly wait until Sunday afternoon and our regularly scheduled visit at the Loose home. Harry was wearing the same clothes he had worn Thanksgiving Day, his customary apparel about the house and yard. On Sundays, when he had come to visit us, he had never worn these clothes but had put on what he called his "one Sunday suit" for these occasions.

We had never seen Harry in such a serious mien as he had that day. As we sat in his modest living room, he said to me, "Harold . . . for some years now I have had the ability to leave my body and consciously appear in spirit form at distant places on visits to certain individuals. . . . [When John Carlos and I] communicate telepathically and when he has something of spiritual importance he wants to discuss, either he or I go to the other. . . . These meetings between John Carlos and myself were always prearranged. Each was expecting the other when he arrived and each was entirely conscious of the visitation, able to return to his physical body and, upon regaining normal consciousness, retain a memory of the experience. But what has greatly concerned me, in the evidence you present of my visitation to the Canterbury, is the fact that I have no recollection whatsoever of such a projection. Though my form is reported to have been seen, and my voice heard delivering an intelligent message, by a man whose integrity is not to be doubted, I would rather believe it had not happened. I want to make absolutely certain that this Mr. Cousins actually saw an image of me and I'd like to drive over to the Canterbury some day soon, dressed exactly as I was that day, and confront him and see if he recognizes me."

"I think that's an excellent idea," I approved.

"You name the day and the approximate time. I'll meet you on the corner and we'll go in the side door entrance to the Canterbury lobby. I'll remain just inside the door, looking down the hall, so I'll be able to see you when you reach the desk and stand before Mr. Cousins. It will be impossible for him to see me. If he recognizes you without any suggestion as to who you are, then we both should be convinced that he also saw you on Thanksgiving afternoon."

"That's right," Harry agreed. "I'll drop you a note as soon as I know when I can come."

Accordingly, in the first mail the following Tuesday morning, I received a brief note which read:

Harold:-

If it is not a rainy or too threatening day, I'd expect to be over this coming Tuesday morning as close to 10 as I can make it. Excuse the whole thing to small Martha—I fear us all barging in too frequently.

Harry

It was a few minutes after ten when, returning from a short shopping trip on Hollywood Boulevard, I saw Harry backing into a parking space half a block down the street. He got out of the car attired in his familiar "yard clothes" and accompanied me to the Yucca Street entrance of the Canterbury, around on the side of the apartment house.

I stepped inside the door with him. We could look down the hall, straight past the desk, situated in the elbow made by the junction of hall and lobby. We heard Mr. Cousins' voice talking to someone on the telephone. Harry left me, as arranged, and walked down the hall, stopping at the desk and facing the switchboard. Mr. Cousins, of course, and the desk itself were not visible to me.

Harry did not speak. He simply stood looking at Mr. Cousins, and I suddenly heard the desk clerk's voice call out in a tone of alarm and surprise, "Oh! Good morning, Mr. Loose!"

Harry then replied, "Good morning. Is Mr. Sherman in?"

And I heard Mr. Cousins say, "No, I think he went out just a few minutes ago."

I could tell that Mr. Cousins was actually unnerved as though he might be seeing another apparition, so I hastened down the hall to allay his fears, smilingly assuring him that this was Mr. Loose, in the flesh.

Mr. Cousins gave a sigh of genuine relief.

"Well," he said, "I'm glad to know that. I didn't know what to think this time!"

But even with this identification, Harry still wasn't satisfied.

"Do you mind repeating for me just what you saw and what I said Thanksgiving Day?"

Mr. Cousins complied, giving Harry substantially the same account he had previously related to me.

"But," persisted Harry, "will you please examine me closely. I want to make sure that you actually saw me. Am I dressed as you remember me on Thanksgiving Day?"

Mr. Cousins studied a moment and then replied, "I don't seem to recall that shirt. I believe it's a lighter color than the one you had on before."

Harry nodded. "That's right," he confirmed. "I was wearing a darker blue shirt, which is now in the wash."

Mr. Cousins shook his head, completely puzzled.

Harry Loose in front of the Canterbury Apartments
[SHERMAN FAMILY PRIVATE COLLECTION].

"This is uncanny," he said. "It gives me goose pimples. Can you explain how it happened?"

Harry hesitated. I could see that he was reluctant to tell Mr. Cousins any more than was absolutely necessary.

"This is a form of mental phenomena which sometimes occurs," he said. "You don't need to worry, Mr. Cousins. It will never happen again. I want to thank you for your cooperation in reporting what you have to Mr. Sherman and identifying me. I hope we'll meet sometime again."

He extended his hand which Mr. Cousins took, replying, "I hope so, too, Mr. Loose—but only in the flesh!"

We then took the elevator to my apartment where Harry dropped into a chair, sitting silently and meditating for at least half an hour. He appeared greatly disturbed and when he finally spoke, it was to say, "I don't like to accept the fact of this occurrence but I guess I'll have to. It's all well and good when you have control of these powers, but when they operate without your knowledge or consent, that's something different. Suppose you walked in your sleep and had somehow gotten over to my house without realizing it, spoken to someone there who had recognized your condition and had brought you back to your apartment, and then awakened you. Upon returning to consciousness and being informed of the trip you had made, you would have to be presented with pretty substantial evidence to believe it, wouldn't you?"

"I certainly would," I agreed.

"But once you had been convinced of what you had done," continued Harry, "wouldn't it have caused you great concern that you might repeat such a performance?"

"I suppose it would," said I.

"Then you can begin to understand how I feel over this happening," said Harry. "I know, in a way, how it came about. After dinner, Mother and Auntie lay down for their afternoon nap and Josie, Ray, and little John went home. I sat down in my big chair and thought I would do a little reading. I got to thinking of you folks and your kindness in sending us the basket of fruit. I reflected that I would be seeing you on Sunday and, being somewhat drowsy, I relaxed and must have dropped off to sleep. How long I slept, I don't know. But I could have been unconscious at the time Mr. Cousins recorded that he had seen and taken this message from me. However, Mother and Auntie were up from their naps and back in the living room, where I was reading, shortly after two-thirty.

"My interest in you people must have provided the urge for me to leave my body and appear at the Canterbury. I was apparently aware that you weren't in, for Mr. Cousins states that I didn't inquire if you were home, simply leaving a message that I would see you Sunday. This indicates, too, that I had no conscious intention of calling on you that day or I would have asked for you. It is obvious that this faculty operated, on this occasion, without my conscious knowledge and control, and that's why I am so troubled about it."

"You may be," said I, "but I, for one, am glad it happened. It provides a well-witnessed instance of phenomena of a rare type. I would personally appreciate it very much if you would help me get a signed statement from all the members of your family, testifying to the fact that you did not leave the house on Thanksgiving Day.[1] I would also like to get a signed statement from Mr. Cousins recounting his experience.[2] And I wish, Harry, that you would permit me, at some later date, to make use of this case in a way that would be of help and enlightenment to others who might be interested."

Harry did not answer for quite a time. His eyes had a faraway look in them. Finally, his consciousness came back to him and he said, "All right, Harold, I will consent to your request on one condition—that you do not make this visitation public until after I have departed this life. I must not have any notoriety over this. So few humans really understand, and it would only greatly embarrass me and disrupt our household. I'll have to be extremely careful in the future that I keep these kind of manifestations under absolute control . . ."

[*You Live After Death,* 1949]

ARA   *November 25, 1941*

The Tree Planter is nearing the time of his departure. He senses it and is torn inside. His astral visit to your apartment on Thanksgiving afternoon was only possible because of the lessened hold his physical has upon his spirit. The fact of this unconscious visitation has disturbed him greatly as a man might be disturbed

---

[1] See Appendix H for the family's affidavit.
[2] See Appendix I for Mr. Cousin's affidavit.

on finding he had walked to the home of a friend in his sleep. But he was guided to your home by his desire and fondness for you in the care of his Thought Adjustor who helped him leave the message. Just now the Tree Planter senses the uprootings of a long and arduous past and suffers great travail of spirit.

Sympathy and understanding are needful to him, tactfully administered, for he asks nothing and seeks nothing—and, in keeping with all developed souls, wishes to retire from the world and gather his spiritual cloak about him.

Christ preferred to prepare Himself and face his final ordeal of the flesh on earth—alone. It is then that the Higher Forces come close and spiritual communion is established as a bridge for the departing soul to walk upon as the flesh grows weak and surrenders up the spirit which has animated it.

The parting with the body is not always easy for it clings to that which has given it Being and Intelligence with all the tenacity of its animal life. The elements in it sense the change that is coming when they, too, will be released, to take on new form and substance and respond to the command of new, directing entities and intelligences—just as the souls, leaving their physical houses, are brought under the jurisdiction and guidance of new guardian entities—of the order Morantia [sic].

All is law and order in the universe as you well know. It is the law that you now dwell and render service in the flesh. You are constantly responding to orders from higher sources—and then comes the day when the final order is given.

The Tree Planter has heard this order—coming from afar— and is resisting it only because the other half of him remains rooted in the flesh. But such an order will sound more loudly in consciousness as the summons quickens—and, one day, the Tree Planter will slip as quickly from his weary and worn flesh home as he did, momentarily, this last Thanksgiving Day, never to return.

Great will be his rejoicing then and, should he go on ahead, the other half of him will be sustained by him from the other side through a special dispensation—so that her path will be made easy and the way sweet beyond describing.

Fear not, nor be disturbed at heart. Great, cataclysmic changes, as you have repeatedly been told, are at hand—but you will know the steps to take as the occasions arise.

Sleep well.

HARRY LOOSE to HAROLD SHERMAN
Monterey Park, November 27, 1941

Harold:-

I thank you for your letter.[3] I do get very lonely at times—and reach out for understanding mental association. You have been some solace. My mental activities have been helpful and constructive in return. You know but little of these. You surely have had, and still do have, obligations and responsibilities in excess of those normally yours. I know the drags that they are from my own long experience with similar conditions. You are particularly vulnerable to acceptance of these added burdens. You should be aware of this and beware of assuming any additional in the future. You surely, too, have been tormented by the ills of the flesh. And you are still doing a magnificent job in overcoming them. I, too, had the same to contend with. I have lain in 9 different hospitals for varying periods—up to 9 months at one time. I am still harassed—uncomfortable much—and sometimes in pain—with an old broken body. I have not yet "overcome the flesh" entirely. Few have.

There are several conditions—some much contributed to by yourself—that are, and have been for a long time, slowing your advance. You do not yet recognize them but you will at some later date. It is not within my province to make you aware of these conditions. Your progress is by your own individual mental effort which entails such recognition. You can be helped when your individual consciousness recognizes such, and then if you cannot handle the problem—ask for help. Several problems are very close to you. If you could, visualize the harm and the wrongness.

You have the very natural desire and impatience to hurry in understanding. This cannot be. By your thought of haste, you betray a degree of unreadiness to advance. How could you impart the understanding that you have accumulated in all these past years to another seeker in a few weeks. It would not be possible. You must be "prepared to receive." I have nothing to sell, no personal axe to grind, nor no material profits to make in the interest that I have had in trying to be helpful to your spiritual growth. I will so continue to help when the way is opened for me. I had, and still have, expectancy for your arrival in the three years I have before mentioned. You have yet a long

---

[3] This letter has not been found.

way to go, beset with many difficulties—the same as others who have also had to overcome on their upward climb. I have great hopes for your success. Though I hear again the ancient cry of grief, "Except ye see signs and wonders ye will not believe." The Book of Urantia will be of greater help. And still leave a million questions to be asked.

I still do not know the reason for the phenomena, if any, reported by Mr. Cousins. And am still a bit doubtful as to its accuracy. I would be more impressed if he found the lady witness. Just possibly, Mr. Cousins is "spoofing" us but to what purpose I cannot imagine.

Harold—why not just forget what I have been trying for these few months to get across to you—forget it completely and utterly—and go back unreservedly to the peace of mind of "reincarnation" and *A Dweller on Two Planets*. It would require little effort if any to reassume and would be so momentarily and presently helpful all around.

"Ye must be born again. NOT of the flesh but of the Spirit." Jesus Christ. But then he didn't know much about it.

We are still enjoying the last of the fruit that you and Martha so kindly sent us and for which both Ma and I want to again express appreciation.

And so more thanks again for your good letter—and with love and best thoughts to you ALL.

HAROLD SHERMAN to HARRY LOOSE

Hollywood, December 3, 1941

Friend Harry:

You spoke in a recent note to me of being "a little uneasy and bewildered."[4]

Now it is *I* who am bewildered.

We have reported to you the different influences and interests passing over our lives, not meaning to indicate that we were taking many of them seriously—such as the friend who reported with such gullible enthusiasm these "psychic and spiritualistic" wonders he thought he was seeing. He has already had his eyes opened to the phony practices which had originally impressed him.

---

[4] Loose's note of November 19 acknowledging the gift of the basket of fruit had read, in part: " . . . The fruit is gorgeous, and yet I am a bit embarrassed in its receipt. I can in no way make suitable return. . . . You folks do such nice things—and from the heart. And yet you shouldn't. You are not on salary, and you have financial responsibilities that keep on just the same. . . . With much appreciation for your kindness, I am still a little uneasy and bewildered. . . ."

You are now living a life of semi-retirement, but we still have to contact people of all different thoughts and beliefs and make adaptations and adjustments to them in accordance with their understanding. And, when this great work starts, the masses will be at all different levels of consciousness, and unless great wisdom is employed, they will turn aside this spiritual bread as a stone, as has been done so many times before. One can't advance a person's belief or spiritual comprehension by ordering him to put aside a book he has gotten comfort from or a form of thinking or living, until he has been given enough understanding to utilize or adapt what little knowledge he now possesses with respect to the TRUTHS now added.

My concern has not been for myself—but for the masses of the people and their right reaction to TRUTH—and how to bring about, logically, appealingly and convincingly, their acceptance of this TRUTH.

Here is the reaction of one intelligent human, who can be a great ally, expressed in a recent letter to me:

> I stand humble, and humbled before many of the profound hypotheses about man which increasingly engage the thought of man today—the baffling riddle of life itself; the mystery of growth and its cessation; the living cell as an auto-catalyst; the amazing law of mutation and adaptation; the source of the mysterious cosmic ray, and the effect, even upon and within man himself, of its constant bombardment of the earth. Where did it all begin, and where is it all leading?
>
> Constituted as I am, inclined by training and habit to prove things before propounding them, I would feel embarrassed in undertaking an active part in a movement which has for its purpose to enlighten man, about whom I know so little, concerning himself—where he came from, what he is, and whither he is going. I have a few beliefs in the matter, but what right have I to expect other humans to believe in them when I cannot indisputably demonstrate them?

The man who so expressed himself is Joseph Robinson,[5] and—despite our own belief and knowledge, Harry—when we consider the

---

[5] A mutual friend of Harold and Sir Hubert, head engineer of the War Production Board in Washington, D.C. In a letter to Harold dated May 24, 1943, Robinson mentions a visit by Sir Hubert in which they spoke "discreetly of the Great Book in Chicago in the future of which you are interested—and so am I."

public, we must make sure that we are prepared in every way to present our subject so that it will win acceptance and support.

While you say—"How could you impart the understanding that you have accumulated in all these past years to another seeker in a few weeks?" you are, of course, right. But, in my reaching out for a WAY in which to present this knowledge, contained in the BOOK OF URANTIA and avoid the pitfalls that I so clearly see—you seem to feel that my queries are on a *personal* basis. And you now reprimand me for putting up an "ancient cry of grief" in asking to see signs and wonders before I will believe.

It is not MY belief—it is the *world's* belief and acceptance I am concerned about. And I am having impressed upon me the necessity of my own further development so that I can state, with positiveness, as I can of the Wilkins experiments, that I have been able to demonstrate, within certain limitations, these higher powers or have personally experienced contact with higher entities. That I have done so and am doing so, more or less unrecognizably, will not satisfy the interested, earnest outsider.

I am not seeking any "psychic demonstration" from you. You have long ago demonstrated your true character and ability in immeasurable service to me. And I am sorry if I embarrassed you by our sending a little token of our love to you and Mother Loose in the form of the box of fruit which caused you to feel that you could in no way make "suitable return." Our lives are not motivated on the basis of doing things with the expectation of a return—and the physical cost, in this case, was incidental. Any economic problems we still have are on such a scale that little expenditures occasionally like this make no difference whatsoever.

We *have* tried to save Mother Loose all we could of actual physical work in preparing meals for us—which have been wonderful and much appreciated. Breaking bread with you people and in your own home has been a spiritual delight . . . but we have not wanted to overdo it and this was the reason we asked you to come to our home a second straight Sunday—impelled by the thought that you should see Mr. Cousins while his memory was still fresh concerning the "incident of his apparent seeing you." He certainly would have no possible motive for "spoofing" us. He had no knowledge at all, at the time, of my interest in such mental or psychic matters.

I am glad you did not wait for Sunday—but came early in the week for Mr. Cousins to check. He still has not been able to recall the woman—saying he has so many people around the desk, many times a day, whom he vaguely remembers were present, that it is difficult to recollect. He did determine that it was *not* the woman he originally felt it might be. And so—the mystery remains.

It may be that some of my writings through ARA have disturbed you—but I have had to put down what seemed to come through—and am not in position to judge as to how much "coloring" there may be. You have said yourself, you "know so little" and yet you know vastly more than I.

Today I spoke at the Hollywood Roosevelt Hotel to the Authors Club of Hollywood on the subject of *Thoughts Through Space*—a twenty-minute address which seemed well received. Mr. Bruhn, head of McCann-Erickson [advertising agency], was there with two men from the [Occidental Life] insurance company interested in putting me on the radio. This development, if it materializes, will be a step in the right direction and open up channels close to our hearts for possible human service.

I will continue to do all I can to advance myself along the lines you have indicated to me, regardless of what may happen—and Martha and I and Mary, too (who is old enough to comprehend), will always carry profound gratitude in our hearts for what you have done for us.

If we, in your judgment, have failed you in any way, an examination of our hearts and minds cannot disclose how. We would not knowingly have done anything to disturb you and if we have, without realizing it, we are indeed sorry.

I will let you know, as developments occur that seem to be in the direction that our soul interests lie—and when it seems desirable for us to get together to further this service—I hope you and Mother Loose will feel like joining us.

Until then, we all send our deepest love and best wishes for you to be surrounded with all good things—and beg that you advise us, at once, any time we may be of help in any way.

HARRY LOOSE to HAROLD SHERMAN
Monterey Park, December 6, 1941

Harold:-

I thank you for your letter. It is a very beautiful thing. The command that you have of the written word is truly a wonderful gift. I am so very inarticulate in speech as well as the written word—as you know. This in addition to much restriction.

Some day, as you grow in the spiritual, you will also find yourself in just the same position of restriction. Things that you will so wish to give—things that you will verily wish to shout from the housetop to the bewildered and confused populace below—you will find yourself unable to do. You too will find yourself with a confused mind—incoordinate—with a throat and tongue unable to utter the words—and you will suffer the same feeling of inadequacy and bewilderment until you finally learn that "Thus far canst thou go and no further." And yet, with all this knowledge, and duties in the spiritual, and all your duties to help and advise, you will find yourself just as liable to the law and the claims and the ills of the flesh and the same ability to suffer physically, as did Joshua ben Joseph, in the flesh and in the Mind. And yet, strangely, you will find yourself able to help others who exactly so suffer in the flesh and in the mind. Very much of the spiritual is at such direct odds to that of the material. And the farther you go and the more you know, in the same relation as comes the growth of your knowledge, comes the direct and positive knowledge of the "how little" you know—and so, also, comes in the ever-continued growth, the still greater knowledge of the very small and infantismal [sic] speck of information that you have.

And this does not end with this beginning dimension. The mystery continues in the next—and the next—through the 3 "deaths"— and even then does not end. "It is the labor of eternity to know the Great Intelligence." You are, even now, in greatly advanced position in true spiritual knowledge beyond that of many millions. And yet, how would you be met if you really were given permission to divulge publicly that which you have. You, too, would be met with the same disbelief, the same sneers, the same mock, as all other great souls have met who have tried to enlighten their fellow man—exactly the same disbelief that was evidenced toward Joshua ben Joseph. You may have already had such opposition in your attempt to "give" to some of what little you have.

I am still amendable [sic] much to the flesh—I still bear the cross—just as you do and will so continue to do—as long as you live in the flesh—you will be so burdened. I may add though that your perspective of it will be considerably changed as you climb. I make many mistakes and will so continue to do, not alone in this dimension but also in the one to come. And just so will you—and so will all of us.

The Book of Urantia will NOT be published in the year 1942. This is positive. I do not know if it will surely be published in 1943—but I strongly doubt if it will. I must ask you please NOT to make mention of this in any writings to Dr. Sadler who would be greatly disappointed as he is expecting its coming out after the first of the coming January. This information is for you and Martha alone. This may have something to do with your development. I wish that I knew. So ofttimes I see only a small bit of the plan and its workings. I used to get nervously frantic to see the whole picture—but I've got over that now.

I know that you will be interested in a little that I have been able to learn in regard to the alleged phenomena of Mr. Cousins. The following has been given me by a source that I consider very trustworthy: "In the literature of psychical research, you will find some mention of a phenomenon known as Bilocation. Watrous makes mention of it for one. It is defined as the presence of an individual in two different places at the same time. It is one of the much rarer psychic manifestations. It is different from and bears no relation to the willed projection of the Astral. What few recorded cases there are lack any sort of proper authenticity—with one exception recorded as under test conditions. And that, occurring under rigid test conditions, was a complete success. No really authenticated report of voiced Bilocation phenomena has ever been made though there have been quite a few observed in various sections of the world. No reasons for their appearance have ever been ascribed and nothing is known about them except that there is surely an active operating intelligence seen in them."

Your letter is so very beautiful that I am going to keep it, at least for a time, and I very seldom keep letters for more than a couple of days. Please forgive me if I have in any way disturbed you folks, for there has been no intention so to do. If you think that I have misbehaved at some future time—make allowances—there is much to contend with—and I falter—am lonely much.

I am coming over some morning the first days of the week. If you are not there, I will come again—unless I am "protruding."

Love to ALL,

Monterey Park, December 6, 1941

Harold:-

I am enclosing herein a letter[6] that I received yesterday in which I know you will be interested. You will also find a carbon copy of my answer to the lady. I am, of course, forwarding these to you for a purpose. I am hopeful that these communications will tell you something. I would like them both returned to me when I see you. See if you can locate the sentence in Miss Baumgartner's letter that means the most—to her—and to you—together with some other things.

Unless the weather is bad for driving, I will be over this coming Tuesday morning. If this arrangement comes in conflict with your schedule, please advise me.

I now have information in regard to the Bilocation phenomena reported by Mr. Cousins.

I may ask your cooperation in a matter in connection with the clearing and correction of this above-mentioned Bilocation phenomena.

I will see you Tuesday—if it isn't raining—unless you advise differently.

Love to All,

Harry

---

[6] This letter has not survived. Elsie Baumgartner had been a co-worker of Loose's at the *Chicago Daily News*. She is prominently featured in later volumes of this series.

12

ALL ROADS LEAD
TO CHICAGO

HAROLD SHERMAN to WILLIAM SADLER
                                     Hollywood, December 12, 1941

Dear Dr. Sadler:

Thank you for your note of some weeks ago. I have withheld writing until I might know more of my own plans.

I have finished the screen treatment of MARK TWAIN for Jesse L. Lasky of Warner Brothers—and am now under consideration by a big insurance company for sponsorship on the radio in my "Your Key to Happiness" program, which has to do with personal, philosophic talks based on the subject matter in my book.

Strangely enough—if this deal should go through—the company would wish me to broadcast from Chicago and I could then locate there for some months—giving me the opportunity of studying the material and getting acquainted with your Group! . . . *Is this the plan operating?*

With developments as they are now, the contemplated Chicago trip is off until after the first of the year, so if there should be any further information or comments you would like to give me, I would appreciate hearing from you.

It is my hope that the BOOK OF URANTIA is not released too soon—because I can see the necessity of laying a real groundwork for its wide acceptance. I wish it were possible to have a good talk with you, covering this whole project.

America is in for some trying times when the faith of millions of her people is going to be tested. "The" opportunity is coming—but, if my sensing is right—"a little time off yet"!

I am enclosing a card descriptive of my new book which is to be out in late January.

My best to all—and holiday greetings!

Sincerely,

ARA   *December 20, 1941*

Astounding things are going to occur within the next two weeks which will rock the world. More changes are going to occur, even in this short time than you or anyone has thought possible. And the American people will be shocked into thorough realization of the grim conditions ahead which must be faced. Simultaneously there will be realized the imperative need of maintaining the emotional stability of all—developing a national state of mind which can withstand the blows upon it from happenings within and without your country.

It is in this service that you are destined to play an important part as the first step in the mission you have re-entered earth life to fulfill. Fortunately you, with Martha, have been impressed to place yourselves in a basically "foot loose" position and this readiness to move wherever duty calls will be most helpful and protective in the period fast approaching.

Your chafing at inactivity will soon be at an end. By the middle of January, mayhap even sooner, the path your feet are to trod will be in evidence. It will call for a utilization of those powers and abilities you have built up through these long years of trying and testing experience.

Your conscious mind wonders at the opening statement of this communication but no elucidation as to the specific nature of what is to come is permitted tonight. Remain calm in the knowledge it will find you and yours untouched but it will arouse mass consciousness in America as nothing has done heretofore—and serve to clarify the realization of what is to be required of each and everyone to successfully meet this unparalleled world crisis. Event piling upon event—an ever-increasing tempo! Watch!

Christmas Eve, 1941

For ages mankind has envisioned the birth of the Spirit from its chrysalis of flesh and this has been symbolized in the celebration of December 25th as Christmas—a time when the Spirit was born into the world and its release accomplished through such advanced souls as Buddha, Confucius, Zoroaster, Christ and many others.

In this manner, once established, this date in earth history became associated with the time of physical birth of spiritual leaders—in fact, it became inconceivable to the masses of different eras that any great soul should have entered the veil of flesh at any other moment. So has the story of the resurrection been carried along the tide of Time since one who conquers the flesh has conquered Death. Similarly we find that, far back in the early beginnings, existing now as little more than vague myths, is evidence of those great ones who were crucified and yet did live.

In the consciousness of many alive today, as in all epochs, is an intuitive awareness of their spiritual birthright, now lost for a time, in the flesh. Feeling incapable, in themselves, of transcending the flesh, they reach out toward those who are able to manifest such dominion. They seek a Saviour, someone who can show them the way, having lost that way themselves. And many pay homage to the Christ we celebrate, on Christmas Day as One whose spirit has risen *from* and *above* the house of flesh—an attainment each imprisoned soul yearns to achieve of and for itself.

This is the present goal of humanity, shackled and blinded by the flesh as it is. But few are yet able to attain since they have not yet come to recognize Life, as the Tree Planter has emphasized over and over, as an "individual proposition."

Christ was indeed a Way-Shower—perhaps the greatest of many. He possessed the power to put the feet of countless souls on the Path. But He still *could not* and *cannot* take the steps for any of those who would follow Him. Those steps must be taken by the individual else a birth of the spirit—the miracle of being "born again" cannot come to pass.

The tendency of mankind is to attempt to *fix* things and events in *Time* and give these things and events a *place* in Time. But we are actually commemorating a *state of consciousness* which we ordinarily only consciously strive to emulate once a year in what we call "the Christmas Spirit," when giving is considered more blessed than receiving. The advanced souls know this for an immortal truth and law, and live the Christmas Spirit constantly. We sense this spirit from afar and only fragmentarily, so that our expressions of it are crudely manifested.

To give unselfishly of one's own self in service is the one priceless gift beyond cost—and not too many have always been willing to give of their own substance at Christmas time or any other.

Conditions, today, however, are going to so strip most humans of their earth possessions as to leave them little if anything else to give *but* themselves—and when this time and occasion arrives, you will see spiritual transformations occur and the Spirit exemplified by December 25th expanded into an ever-present state. Once humans have experienced the real, they will gain no lasting satisfaction returning to the false, and then, with the spirit in them awakened, it will be possible for enlightened souls to reach them with the messages they will, at that time, be prepared to hear.

The new year holds much of devastation and yet of promise.

HARRY LOOSE to HAROLD and MARTHA SHERMAN
Monterey Park, December 24, 1941

Dear Harold and Martha:-

Ma has asked me to include her sincere appreciation with my own for the thoughtfulness and kindness expressed in remembering us both here at 123 this Christmas. Ma does like an occasional chocolate and so your gift to her will be a lasting one. I can't eat candy and my sole indulgence of the desires of the flesh is smoking in the afternoon period. Thanks again, both of you. And to you, small Martha, may I again and further recognize my debt to you for the nice dinner.

I arrived home safely ahead of the rain yesterday but it surely did blow up disagreeably cold. . . .

By Special Delivery at 9 this morning I received a very nice Christmas card from [fellow dinner guest] Mr. Bruhn with a message of appreciation of our yesterday's contact written thereon.

Again, a great appreciation and another "thanks."

ARA
December 27, 1941

Indescribable, unspeakable, in the earth sense are the experiences awaiting millions now alive on your dark planet in the year 1942. Many of those who welcome this new year in with senseless hilarity will be welcoming their own approaching doom or devastation.

Your President comprehends the need for changing the vibration of this new year's advent by proclaiming the day as one of prayer for America's guidance and deliverance.

Truly, with all the faults and earthly sins of the free peoples on your little planet, the only hope for the new order and its early implantation in the consciousness of mankind depends upon the United States of America.

Its discovery and development by advanced souls, leading bands of followers several centuries ago, was in preparation for what is now coming to pass. And many of those now native in America or who have come to America from other harassed countries are here on a missioned purpose.

But little can be done in the midst of chaotic turmoil such as will prevail, beyond attempts to stabilize, insofar as is humanly possible, the emotions of this remarkably heterogeneous civilization that now constitutes American citizenry, and the determining of those who are to be in the front ranks of the spiritual armies when all military forces have exhausted their usefulness.

Then the era of rehabilitation will begin and the spirit of man will be the first that will need resuscitation—indeed resurrection—for without this revival and rebirth of spirit with the consequent resurgence of faith, mankind will not possess the strength to rebuild itself physically, morally, mentally or spiritually.

From the viewpoint of those beyond and above your physical plane—the appalling events attracted to the planet Urantia by ages-old wrong practices of its human creatures would sicken any consciousness were it not for our wider perspective which indicates to us a promised land of spiritual revelation when and after animal forces have had their last earthly day.

You, who were in at the near beginning, are privileged, with many of your earth brothers of that day, to be enfleshed during the concluding chapters of this long earth experience—and to play a dominant part arrayed as you will be against the forces of evil who will attempt to sway the animal side of bewildered human creatures in the mass—but will find an organized spiritual power, for centuries *anticipatory* of this moment in earth time—ready to protect the souls of millions who will be released from imprisonment in the flesh through the knowledge to be revealed. Against this knowledge and the power made possible to these awakened souls through it, these evil forces can no longer stand. But this they do not know as yet, having always conquered in earth's sad debacles in past ages. Here, however, in this era of Urantia's history—the way, at last, divides. And you and your enmissioned brothers are to be the dividing of this way.

Watch for evidences of your Path of Service as it opens up to you—and know, as fear and despair sweep this land of the supposed free—engendered by the unthinkable horrors to come—that this was all to be, of necessity, that true spirituality might eventually come—as the animal in man is subdued for all time.

* * *

MERRILL and JO DAVIS to HAROLD and MARTHA SHERMAN
Marion, late December, 1941

Dear Harold and Martha—

Such trying times. Again we can see the need for our new book soon.

Cousin Will's lecture at Lansing on "The Evolution of the Soul" has just arrived this week. If you do not happen to receive one, write Christy for a reprint.

Joseph [their son] passed the exam at Philadelphia Penn. General Hospital for two-year internship—goes in July. Hope Army will let him have at least one year. Dick [their other son] is working very hard we think they will be good Docs.

The girls [Mary and Marcia] will appreciate the Indiana scene in etching [on the cover of this card] made by our famous Indiana etcher L. O. Griffith. Born in Greencastle, Ind. It is certainly Indiana snow-like today. Beautiful!

Very best wishes,
Merrill & Jo

HARRY LOOSE to HAROLD SHERMAN
Monterey Park, December 28, 1941

Harold:-

I have read the pamphlet ["The Evolution of the Soul"] with interest and have read your somewhat horrified and surprised letter[1] accompanying it. I am very glad that you rec'd the pamphlet, for it

---

[1] This letter has not survived, but it probably contains comments similar to those in Harold's January 8, 1942, to Sadler, below.

tells you, far better than I could in many words, just why you were brought up into your present understanding. Can you imagine a church audience listening in rapt and awed understanding to what you find here? It is not possible with the mixed mental capacities, and newly introduced to a subject so deep—a subject that the Doctor has been in contact with so long and so very thoroughly. He loses sight of the fact that these people to whom he is talking have had no such contact or training. It is all very new to them.

It is very regrettable—but I have so very often told you of the "mistakes" and "accidents" that occur—and will continue to occur. So you should not be at all surprised. This lecture, so very academic, would not be understood even by those accustomed to the large words and terms unless they had had considerable contact with the subject beforetime.

Excuse pencil as Ma's asleep and I can't write on the typewriter. She is much better. The pieces of the pattern fall slowly into place.

No radio audience, or other audience, by book, stage, or moving picture would be thrilled or even interested in such a method of introduction.

I have done what I have been instructed to do—which includes yourself up to your present—so it must be for a purpose—and the way has been hard and dark sometimes and lonely always. Remember that in all these years I have only had the relief of talking to you and Martha, and then so circumscribedly. I can tell so little—and there is so very much that I do not know—I know so little.

Your development *must* mean something, something in regard to the introduction and promotion of this knowledge—this revelation—and it must be along the lines in which you have been trained and know so much about—that you are so familiar with—and which neither the good Doctor or any of his associates nor members of the Forum are acquainted with. And yet, please remember and please bear with me, *I do not know.* I am and have been so prayerfully hoping that the matter would be happily concluded that would take you back to Chicago so that you could put in all your spare time in the full study of the papers—making contacts, getting acquainted with the surroundings and meeting the Forum, etc.

I would like very much to come over Wednesday, if for nothing else than the comfort of your understanding and that of small Martha's. I need all the strength that you can give me—the way has been long and I falter sometimes, and I fumble in the dark—it cannot be so much longer and I am very tired. Your letter is so truthful in all of its aspects. Forgive any confusion in this—and the pencil—and I will come Wednesday morning if the weather is propitious.

I am sure that I cannot analyse the pamphlet—it is beyond me—the writing, and reading, of the Book is so much more human and understandable—and I *know* it is not meant only for those with college educations that can understand big words. Believe me, though, I know that all things will work out all right—and that no individual intelligence can halt the march forward and upward—but *when* and by what means, I do not know—I know so very little.

There isn't another thing except love to you *all*, and I can still remember how good those little biscuits of Martha's were.

I believe [Sadler] means the "Thought Adjuster" by calling this entity by a probable better-sounding name of "Spirit Monitor."

WILLIAM SADLER to HAROLD and MARTHA SHERMAN
Chicago, December 29, 1941

Mr. and Mrs. Harold Sherman
Dear friends:

I am sending you a copy of a lecture ["The Evolution of the Soul"] given last month to the Ayres Foundation in Lansing, Michigan. From the foot note which appears on page 30, you will note that we had "permission" to make this preliminary statement of "Urantia Philosophy."

I have forgotten whether or not you have been informed that authorization to put the papers in type and make plates has been granted, and that you might be informed as to what all is going on, I am sending you a copy of a letter prepared by the Finance Committee.

A few weeks ago the Forum roll was read and those of us present selected the names of our friends who were absent from the city that we might tell them about these recent developments. I naturally selected your name and though I expect to see you soon and talk these matters over, I thought it only right to send on this information that you might have it at the same time that other members away from Chicago receive it.

With best wishes for a Happy New Year, I am,
Sincerely yours,

Chicago, Illinois
November 18, 1941

TO ALL FORUM MEMBERS:

As time goes on, we approach more realistically the eventual publication in book form of the papers with which you are familiar. For those members who have not been able to attend the Forum as often as others, as well as for the more active members, this letter has been prepared to clarify the present status of this project.

Forum members in 1937 were given the opportunity to subscribe to a general fund and also for copies of the proposed book. Enough had been received through payments on these subscriptions and from donations without subscriptions to permit the letting of a contract (pursuant to authority granted last spring) for the making of the plates which are to be used in the printing of the book. Had these funds not been available, there would have been a great delay in going ahead with this project.

Our present objective is to obtain additional money so that we may promptly proceed with the printing and publication of the book when the authority to do so is given, and to provide funds for the expenses of a central office and other contingencies during the first two years.

To be in a position to do this will require the raising of an additional amount of approximately $25,000. The task of this Finance Committee is to secure this sum. We will need the help of every member of the Forum. Our only source of funds is from this limited membership.

Under our present program a further opportunity is now given to subscribe to the general fund and also for copies of the book at the special price indicated on the pledge card. Your committee strongly urges that you first consider a subscription to the general fund, as all money given to this fund will be available for the general activities of the organization. It is difficult to foresee when publication will be authorized, and knowing that the desires of many will exceed their immediate resources, we have ventured to forecast a two-year period during which such contributions may be accumulated by a systematic program of regular payments.

At certain Forum meetings in the past few years, the legal form of organization to publish this book has been discussed and pending the consummation of this plan the undersigned Finance Committee is functioning in all financial matters.

We all recognize the rare privilege afforded us to help in this undertaking. Some members have been able to be more regular in attendance than others, but now is the time and chance for all to take an active part in financing the enterprise. All subscriptions will be most welcome, and we hope every member will give generously.

Respectfully,

YOUR FINANCE COMMITTEE

William M. Hales, Chairman,

E. L. Christensen,

W. C. Kellogg,

William S. Sadler, Jr.

HARRY LOOSE to HAROLD SHERMAN

Monterey Park, January 3, 1942

Harold:-

This is a letter mostly about Clara.[2]

Ma wants me to thank Martha for the nice stockings which she much appreciates and which she will make good use of on Sundays.

I am much interested in what may result from Mr. Bruhn's contact with these people Monday. If that part of the picture falls into what we take to be its proper place, it will clarify much. They may have other persons under consideration and it may be that, in addition to the other angles, which is holding up a decision. This "waiting" to know is a strain. . . .

About Clara. I was glad to meet her and she made a definite impression of good. I honestly like her. She is very lonely and somewhat confused, rather disgusted with life as she now finds it, and is groping to find relief and forgetfulness of self and of much of the rest of the world, in a comforting activity that she has liking for, has faith in, and that will absorb her active mind.

I am very hopeful that you were able to give her quite a good bit of information and that there was understanding and acceptance. I believe she would be a staunch ally and a large help in things that may come to pass in the near future. You know what conditions are very well and, with my strong impression of *good*, I was afraid of making further voiced contact until I had opportunity of receiving advice as to the wiseness of such further contact.

---

[2] Clara Gabrilowitsch had recently moved to Hollywood, and Harold had introduced her to Loose.

I have now been advised. If, following my departure, you were able to convey quite some of what we have, and she showed acceptance and expressed desire for further understanding, if, in your judgment, this is so, I am advised that it is permissible to make further voiced contact with her and give help. The matter is now up to your judgment. If the answer is "yes," you may read to her any part of this letter in a phone conversation and make an appointment either at your home or hers for a time that suits the best convenience. Such conversation would be best with her alone, however. If the answer is "no," the matter ends with no further reference. I know that this is all clear to you and that you are in a better position to judge after your talk of Friday.

May I thank small Martha for the nice dinner—especially the hot biscuits. Was glad to see Mary looking so well—and Marcia so happy.

Love to ALL,

Hoping that Harold would be rehired to work on the Mark Twain *film, the Shermans remained in Hollywood during the months following his layoff. In planning for an eventual move to Chicago to study the Urantia papers, Harold pursued two opportunities: a revival of his "Your Key to Happiness" radio program and the production of his newly revised Mark Twain play. He also came up with the idea of dramatizing the life of the late Jane Addams, the world-renowned social settlement worker.[3] Harry Loose had formerly served as detective for Hull House, and it was through this connection that Harold began to correspond with the Jane Addams Estate.*

ARA   *January 7, 1942*

Your waiting period will soon be at an end and when your producer [Eugene S. Bryden] leaves here it will be with the fixed plan to open [the play] "Mark Twain" in Chicago. You may observe now how carefully events are planned that human mistakes may be guarded against and that the *way* may be sufficiently pointed to guide those enmissioned ones to the right place at the right

---

[3] In September 1889, Jane Addams (1860-1935) opened Hull House, a settlement house to serve the immigrants in Chicago's nineteenth ward. Hull House soon grew to become a popular neighborhood center, and during the next forty years assumed international significance as Addams and her associates championed the protection of immigrants, child labor laws and recreation facilities for children, industrial safety, juvenile courts, recognition of labor unions, woman suffrage, and world peace. In 1931, she was awarded the Nobel Peace Prize.

time. The presence of members of the Stone family in Chicago whose destiny causes them to be residing there at this time; the desire of Fred Stone to play on the road rather than in New York and to be with his family[4]; the belief of Mr. Bryden that "Mark Twain" belongs to America and should play outside New York, probably *Chicago*; the interest of the Occidental Life in you and the suggested plan of your broadcasting from *Chicago*; the desire you have to dramatize the life of Jane Addams, necessitating contact and association with Hull House, *Chicago*—all these factors actual *forces* crystallizing a power pulling you to *Chicago* for a joining with the group that your active service in this long prepared project may begin!

Things are happening as fast as it is humanly possible for them to develop on the earth plane—and the last link in the chain of forces taking you to Chicago will be forged by Occidental in the near future.

You are already prepared inwardly through conferences you have had with Higher Intelligences during sleep for the steps you will take when the arrangements are completed and the whole way lies before you. You will *know* at that time exactly what to do, how to act and what to say. Your leadership of men is then to begin. You will be required to serve first as a teacher and organizer and then as an exponent of these spiritual truths. But, while you are teaching others, you yourself will be undergoing instruction, through association with the group in *Chicago* and through Higher Sources. A more active phase of service for Martha will then manifest itself and she will come into a clearer understanding of her vital relationship to this great mission commanding the services of so many fleshed and unfleshed brothers.

You are both going to be tremendously but happily busy with your life service expanded upon an unbelievably wider screen. The wisdom of your being held back in careful preparation this long time until world conditions were ripe for action will be more and more demonstrated. You have observed how you can talk to certain individuals now to whom you could not have broached these subjects a few years before. This is true of not only a few—but of millions. You even have the willing, and to an adequate degree, the understanding cooperation of your daughters in your movements, which should indicate to you that they, too, are being prepared. There are many intelligences

---

[4] Veteran actor Fred Stone (1873-1959) was to star as Mark Twain.

associated with the many different phases of this same great project and the coordination of the whole is a task beyond your present comprehension.

You can only be a witness to what is happening with respect to your own relationship but be assured that similar synchronizing and coordinating actions are occurring throughout all manifestations of the plan on earth.

For, remember, these souls now engaged enfleshed themselves conscious of the mission each had volunteered to perform and each is now striving to find this design and weave his or her part of the pattern in earthly expression. . . .

Could you presume any spiritual enterprise of this magnitude and forthcoming importance to humanity to be any less lovingly guarded, protected and supervised? Each day, from henceforth—watch for progress.

HAROLD SHERMAN to WILLIAM SADLER

Hollywood, January 8, 1942

Dear Dr. Sadler:

B-r-r-r! The morning papers say it is on the way to being 12 degrees below zero in Chicago—which makes us feel snug and warm in California! If we stay out here much longer I'm afraid it'll make softies out of us!

Thank you for your note—with enclosures. I was much interested in the pamphlet containing your address: "The Evolution of the Soul." A time is coming—but not here yet—when humanity at large will seek such knowledge, hungrily—even desperately. Just now humans are still too interested in saving what they regard of greatest value— their worldly possessions!

If I may, I should like to make my contribution a little later in the year when it can be more substantial, since payments will be due from Warner Brothers on the purchase of the MARK TWAIN property.

My own plans are rapidly crystallizing. MARK TWAIN is to be produced as a stage play within the next several months, with FRED STONE playing TWAIN, and present plans call for Chicago as the city in which the play is to be presented, rather than New York.

I am negotiating with a large insurance company here, whose executives are interested in contracting for my radio services on my "Your Key to Happiness" program and they feel, if the deal is consummated, that they would like me to broadcast from *Chicago*.

It appears that "forces" are seeing to it that "all roads lead to your city." This development alone would seem miraculous were it not for our understanding. It's wonderful enough, as it is!

I should like the opportunity of our becoming thoroughly acquainted with you and your Group in an unhurried manner—and our living in Chicago for a time would serve many fine purposes—especially if my activities commence to dovetail in this astounding way.

Either one of these developments, or both, would at least bring me to Chicago for a time—and as soon as things have progressed a little further I shall be able to tell you when.

I am enclosing a copy of the Announcement concerning my book, *Thoughts Through Space*, out February 20th. The first edition is largely spoken for now—so it appears that this volume is going to attract wide interest.

There will be much for us to discuss when we meet again, and I am looking forward to our "reunion" with great anticipation. Please extend my warmest regards and good wishes to all at 533 Diversey Parkway—the Kelloggs, "Christy," Bill, Jr. and family—and yes, the members of the Group I haven't met but whom I feel I have already contacted in spirit!

What times are coming! Indescribable! Without a knowledge of the spiritual side of life, how can despairing, bewildered humans continue to "take it"? The answer is—they can't!

Sincerely,

HARRY LOOSE to HAROLD SHERMAN

Monterey Park, January 13, 1942

Harold:

Please thank small Martha for the much appreciated special food of yesterday. Both of you looked exceptionally good. Martha's eyes were so big and soft and shiny and her hair so pretty. . . .

I knew exactly what I was doing in the reading to Clara of those three letters. They were not understandable to her in the manner presented and did not register beyond the then moment. In any continuance of contact, I read no more of them. The meeting of yesterday was mostly an introductory or "feeler" affair. It gave ample opportunity to explore and get the "feel" of Clara's mind in regard to discussed matters and ramifications pertaining thereto. It gave opportunity to catch her off balance and note the reaction and the direction of the response. She has suffered a great deal mentally as well as physically. She has contacted so many people—been so many places—been so much on exhibition because of her famous father—that she acquired a "something" in her mental makeup that is only met with others who have had much the same experience. You recognize this "something" also, so there is no use to try to make written explanation. She makes definite impression of "good." She is groping for the "Peace that passeth all understanding." She is very lonely for mental companionship; has many fears—the fears that always go with this condition—has periods of terrific depression and similar periods, usually concurrent, of being truly disgusted with life as she finds it. My contacts and conversation will not be of any great benefit until she has read the Book—though such personal contacts and conversations may arouse, enlarge, and continue interest.

I am very glad for the letter from Jenkins [another Occidental Life contact] and your outline of program to be submitted on your meeting with him for this Thursday. I am tremendously interested in the presentation and progress of this program. I know the matter cannot be concluded at once but feel sure it will meet with early response. You will be able to measure something in the "feel" of Jenkins at the Thursday lunch-talk.

You do so much need the time in Chicago to continue reading—both of you. Piece by piece falls into the pattern and each one that falls gives a bit more of a glimpse of the completed whole in this operation.

I have written quite a long letter and in a hurry too—please excuse errors—don't fail to thank small Martha for her very big shiny eyes first and then after that for that special food.

Love to ALL,

ARA   *January 26, 1942*

What is supposed to be yours can no longer be taken from you so rest secure in this faith. Great ideas and opportunities are swirling about you which, when their turn arrives for development and expression can have a profound influence upon humanity. Your own position is growing stronger and more secure daily. While you seemingly are passing the time in waiting you have been undergoing a final preparatory period before one of the *great action phases*—and when the "change" comes it will be swift and unerring. No more unsettled, uncertain conditions but direct paths of progress, all converging upon and contributing to the same spiritual goal!

Powerful forces are at work bringing the right elements and conditions around you and when these connections are finally made they will stay with you, many of them until the completion of your mission on earth.

So rest assured, as you have been, that all is basically well—and watch these events crystallize, drawing your services and talents into them!

HARRY LOOSE to HAROLD SHERMAN

Monterey Park, January 28, 1942

Harold:-

As per our phone conversation of a few moments ago, I am typing this off to you to try to clarify Martha's question of yesterday in regards to a tree. Under sufficient heat, a tree will return to its original gases. Yet the tree is a *development* in which heat was only one of the elements concerned. The tree was not made from gases but was a development of growth wherein its sustenance for the element of growth was taken from a supply (the earth), which *heat* originally supplied in the solidification process by the cooling of the gases produced by heat. This as above outlined does not apply to trees alone but must be added to ad infinitum.

Please remember that much experimental life was purposely originated here—under trial and under jurisdiction of intelligences, but also please know that the greater part was brought here from other and older and more advanced planets. To get the right concept of heat, please remember that there is heat trillions of times greater than it is possible to produce on this planet. There are gases and other elements missing here that preclude the possibility of producing heat beyond a certain degree—which degree man has yet never been able to reach. Please remember that that which we call "life" is a *strange something that does not produce itself.* No "life" ever originated here, *or anywhere else,* by its own volition. *This is not possible.* "Life" is a separate element bestowed under jurisdiction. All too heavy and detailed to attempt to scratch the surface in description here.

Please—no more Bruhns—Kaminskys[5]—Claras. Time is too limited. I am not interested in these people. They mean nothing to me.

---

[5] A business associate of Harold's.

Their development would mean too much time and exhausting effort—and their development does not come in my direct province. Remember they are ALL far behind the present development of you and Martha. I could have thousands and thousands of Bruhns and Kaminskys and Claras and Joneses and Smiths and the rest of them if I wanted—and was permitted—to teach and talk. I am interested only in the further development of yourself and Martha, even though my direct responsibility has long concluded.

I was greatly pleased by your phone call in regard to the news from Schwartz.[6] Piece by piece the different portions of the picture fall into place. When I see you next remind me that I have something about which I wished to talk to you particularly. I hope that I have made the matter of the tree more clear to you—and to Martha—it was her question. I was unsatisfied with the incomplete answer I made. I thank you for the association of yesterday—and the food—especially the biscuits. Excuse errors please—I write so hurriedly.

Love to ALL.

ARA   *February 14, 1942*

Things *will* work out for next week, in a manner quite satisfying to you after this long trying period of waiting.

Conditions are so upset these days and so constantly changing that it is exceedingly difficult to attain a settled state in anything.

For the world at large this situation is bound to grow steadily worse for a time—but you will be constructively active during the turbulent months to come—with attention being attracted more and more favorably toward you and your works.

Your faith and your efforts *will* be rewarded. Fear not and trust in these powers that have been revealed to you.

Turn now to your Bible for a confirming message of spiritual reassurance.

* ARA *

Opened on inspiration to the exact page and led to read Galatians—chapter six—verses 4 to 11 inclusive. (Following)

4   But let every man prove his own work, and then shall he
have rejoicing in himself alone, and not in another.

---

[6] The attorney for Hull House. Harold had arranged to meet with him to sign a contract several weeks hence.

5 For every man shall bear his own burden.

6 Let him that is taught in the word communicate unto him that teacheth in all good thing:

7 Be not deceived; God is not mocked: for whatsoever a man soweth that shall he also reap.

8 For he that soweth to his flesh shall of the flesh reap corruption; but he that soweth to the Spirit shall of the Spirit reap life everlasting.

9 And let us not be weary in well doing: for in due season we shall reap, if we faint not.

10 As we therefor have opportunity, let us do good unto all men, especially unto them who are of the household of faith.

11 Ye see how large a letter I have written unto you with mine own hand.

HARRY LOOSE to HAROLD SHERMAN

Monterey Park, February 18, 1942

Harold:-

Your friend M[attern][7] is a voluntary enmissioned *old soul* of second flesh-life experience and comes from the planet Eta in the third northerly constellation grouping of the 5th Universe under which planet the jurisdictional ruler is Nair. In our method of computing space and time, the planet Eta is about 30 "light years" distant from Urantia. His flesh existence ended on the planet of Eta in his 67th year from neglected complications resulting from an injury to the 7th, 8th, 9th and 10th vertebrates of the back. The present is his first experience in the flesh on Urantia. On the planet of Eta he occupied a position of trust and prominence in the gift of the people and was noted for his oratory and firmness of purpose. He was a dominant character of singleness of ambition. He is here for some single purpose on this mission but I am not given to know what this mission is. He has a "soul remembrance" of a prior existence which vague remembrance does not come from his present flesh brain. It has always been this vague "soul remembrance" but true. He will not, of course, be allowed to "recollect" much. It will ever remain with him in its present vague, groping form. This is really best for too much would probably interfere with his present engaged mission. This mission may have something to do with your future activities and I would advise your

---

[7] See p. 48 for Harold's account of how they met.

continued contact. I have not yet received an answer in full to Mrs. M but am continuing in expectancy of further information.

In re myself. Something here not explainable has happened. I speak alone to you and small Martha in great confidence. I may be released. I am wanted for activity elsewhere. I must repeat that I do not know definitely and positively. Some sort of decision seems in the making. Anyway, if so be it, I have told you beforetime. If, and when, definite summons comes, I will have a short period in which to make adjustments in preparation for the change. I will advise you of such—if permitted. No matter what happens, be of good cheer and be glad. Carry on—keep the faith—do not allow discouragement in the fight—lean on Martha's strength, as always. I will be near you often and you will see me with your eyes. Do not lose the very little that I have been able to give you since you have been awakened.

You have many difficulties to overcome and all is not smooth sailing before you in Chicago. Jealousy—the usual interference of lesser minds, etc. Great diplomacy and tact is required when the time comes. Don't lose thought of the "hideaway" for the future. Give thanks for small Martha each day. If separation comes—and I am not yet sure such will be—it is not yet announced as definite—always remember that your time, too, is relatively short here—and that we have work to do together in the future.

If M would appreciate it, give him the information at the top of this letter—BUT keep the lower part strictly to your two selves ALONE. And do not remark anything pertaining to it on the telephone—nor in the presence of Mother.

Love to you ALL,

Harry

13

INTRODUCING SIR HUBERT

Thoughts Through Space was published February 20, 1942. On that day Harold Sherman and Sir Hubert Wilkins embarked on a publicity tour in the East and Midwest, to last several weeks. Between engagements, Harold planned to introduce Sir Hubert to Dr. Sadler and the Urantia material in Chicago as well as to solidify arrangements with Hull House granting him dramatic rights to the life of Jane Addams.

By Courtesy of John Hix "Strange As It Seems" and Palmolive Company

Presentation of a
Recorded Transcription
of

THOUGHTS THROUGH SPACE

SIR HUBERT WILKINS
World renowned Arctic and Antarctic Explorer,
who acted as "sender" of thought messages
while he was in the far North searching for
the lost Russian fliers.

and

HAROLD M. SHERMAN
Noted author, who acted as "receiver" in remarkable series of long distance telephathic
tests conducted with Sir Hubert Wilkins, 3,000
miles away in the Arctic.

Witness Demonstration of MENTAL TELEPATHY
by

HAMID BEY

Who will not only demonstrate this mysterious power of the human mind but will also explain, both orally and in
written form, how it is possible for you to learn mental communication.

THURSDAY, MARCH 5, 1942 — 8 P.M.
ADMISSION 31c; Fed. Tax 4c; Total 35c

BALLROOM, HOTEL FORT WAYNE
Temple at Cass, Detroit, Mich.

Newspaper ad for a joint appearance by Wilkins and Sherman
[University of Arkansas, Archives and Special Collections].

HARRY LOOSE to HAROLD SHERMAN

Monterey Park, March 2, 1942

Harold:-

Phone Dr. S right away and let him know of your arrival. Make earliest possible appointment for contact with the Doctor and further set things for the introduction of Wilkins. After the Wilkins matter is set, if possible bring up the matter of the M[attern]s for admission.

Read the BOOK yourself every possible moment.

Phone Schwartz, too, just as soon as you get in and check your appointment time there. Be sure there are no slip-ups in anything, and bring the Contract back with you.

You have been on my mind with every good thought every moment of the long trip and I am with you now and will be so until your safe return. Talk with your T.A. at any time and lean on him for strength and guidance. Call me at any time and I will at once respond.

Harry

On March 5, after his interview with Dr. Sadler, Sir Hubert joined the Forum. Both Harold and Sir Hubert read papers as time permitted and attended their first Forum meeting on March 8. After being introduced to the group, the two made short talks. Later that day they had Sunday supper with Dr. Sadler and Christy.

The Shermans' plans to move immediately to Chicago were delayed when Harold was rehired by Jesse Lasky to help complete the Mark Twain *script. On March 12, having secured a verbal agreement from Hull House to dramatize the life of Jane Addams, Harold returned to Hollywood.*

SIR HUBERT WILKINS to HAROLD SHERMAN

The Manchester Hotel,
Middleton, Ohio, March 10, 1942

Dear Sherman:

It was good to see you again and I will be forever grateful to you for the introduction to the Forum. It seems that I will have an opportunity between April 21st and some time in May to visit Chicago for several days and I will do so in order to gain more knowledge of the Great Universe.

I am writing to Mr. Loose with this mail. Also to Dr. Sadler.

My itinerary is herewith.

Hope you had a good trip home.

Best regards,

Hubert Wilkins

Itinerary

    March 16 Little Rock, Ark. Marion Hotel

    17 Monroe, Louisiana. Hotel Francis

    18 Montgomery, Alabama. Jefferson Davis Hotel

    19 Columbus, Georgia. Ralston Hotel

    20 Augusta, Georgia.

    21 Atlanta, Georgia. Spelman College

    23 Anniston, Alabama. 1039 Christine Ave.

    24 Columbus, Mississippi. Mississippi State College for Women.

    26 Akron, Ohio. Akron City Club.

    April 20 Detroit.

    21 Green Bay, Wis.

    After this may have a few days in Chicago.

The Sadler residence, 533 Diversey Parkway, Chicago, where the Urantia papers appeared and were studied before publication [www.Urantia-Book.org]

ALCINDA SHERMAN to HAROLD SHERMAN

Marion, Ind., March 14, 1942

Dear Harold:

I received *Thoughts Through Space* Monday afternoon. Thanks so very much, and I appreciated the autographs of both yours and Sir Hubert's very much.

Your letter written Tuesday a.m. came Wed. a.m. No doubt I was reading from your book as I am reading it aloud to Aunt Flora, and pick it up to read a chapter or two when we have time to sit down.

So glad to hear of your wire confirming your being rehired by Warner Bros., even if it does mean that you will now have to stay in Hollywood for a while, for it will also mean you will have something to live on, and I hope save something besides.

If *Mark Twain* goes over well, there will be no question about the life of Jane Addams proving popular and profitable. Although you may not be able to get as detailed a biography of her life as of Twain.

I was interested to hear of Sir Hubert's impression with your group.

This one thought keeps coming into my mind about the book "Urantia," which you spoke in your letter as being destined to take the place of the Bible. Now I am not doubting but what it will prove true. But this is my thought, that "the Book of Urantia" should first be spoken of as an aid and revelation of the Bible and let its merits gradually make it take the place of the Bible.

You know the world has for centuries taken the Bible as the Divine Word, and to come right out with "Urantia" and say it was to take the place of the Bible might prejudice some people against it, who would welcome it in connection with the Bible, and make its use more universal in the beginning.

Wish my environment was a little different so I could relax more, but I am warm, have a good bed, and *part* of the time cheerful surroundings, but I see no way out of my duty and may have greater cause to feel that way as Aunt F's eyes have failed very much since early Dec. . . .

My dearest love to each of you.

Mother

HARRY LOOSE to HAROLD SHERMAN

Monterey Park, March 17, 1942

Dear Folks:-

Thanks so much for your note. We did get back home safely but the traffic was *very* heavy—I guess because of the early hour that we

Emma "Christy" Christensen, Dr. William S. Sadler, Lena Sadler and Bill Sadler circa mid-1930s [www.Urantia-Book.org].

Urantia Forumites (the Group) at the annual picnic in 1934
[Collection of Katharine J. "Ticky" Harries].

left. We go Thursday to Santa Monica—a long journey on our aged tires—and a very exhausting one for us both. I wish that it was safely over.

Harold has been under a terrific strain this past period, and now with the present easement—and much more rest—he should recuperate a lot—especially if he will "let go" and mentally relax.

Thanks so much for the very lovely dinner (hot biscuits especially) and for the very dear association. . . . Drop a line if any new developments mature. We are as close as the telephone. Excuse my pen writing but Ma is resting and I can't use the typewriter. Hope you can read it.

Love to *all*, as always,

HAROLD SHERMAN to SIR HUBERT WILKINS

Hollywood, March 17, 1942

Dear Sir Hubert:

I still get a glow from the memory of our weekend in Chicago. And I am so happy that you feel you have found an "anchor" in the Group in Chicago. Harry Loose much appreciated your note and has written you in care of the City Club.

You made a splendid impression upon the Group and the Sadlers. Bill, Junior, told me on Monday night, after I had *read* most of the day (and *what* reading!), that he had wept after our departure Sunday night, from joy at our having come to them—looking back as he had upon the long, painstaking seventeen years of preparation . . . and now to have the realization that the time was at last approaching (perhaps still a year or two away) when this knowledge would be made known to the world . . . and might have people like yourself in back of it.

I enclose a clipping, one of several sent me by "indignant" friends, of Hansen's review.[1] My hide is tough, after years of critical reactions—and I know this leaves you undisturbed. Our book is going to cause wide controversy and discussion—which is good. Dr. Potter writes that he is sending a letter of protest to Hansen, though he thinks Hansen was impressed or he would not have devoted his entire column to the book—but personally embarrassed to have

---

[1] Harry Hansen (1884-1977) wrote a nationally syndicated daily newspaper column, "The First Reader" until the late 1940s. See Appendix J for Harry Hansen's columns on *Thoughts Through Space* and Charles Potter's letter.

to admit serious interest after probably years of poking fun at such powers.

I also enclose copy of letter received from [Creative Age Press employee] Chadsey. Shortly following publication by *Cosmo* of the article on our work, I wrote to several university professors in charge of Extra Sensory Perceptive Research, offering my services. Three colleges I remember were Duke, Stanford and Chicago. I got a "cold shoulder" from them all—since each professor was only interested in following his own plan of investigation and receiving credit for same. Now that our book is out, I do not intend to be stampeded into being a "guinea pig" for these scientists. I've made my contribution under test conditions—it's a nerve-wracking experience at best . . . and we have something of far greater value to put our research talents to in the work you have been brought in touch with. Just as scientists reserve the right to follow their own methods of research, we should quietly assume that same right. I do not feel that we are called upon to answer any critics. Our answer is in the book. We have said our say. . . .

I am glad you can plan to be in Chicago for a few days in April. The papers on the Thought Adjuster are amazing. Be sure to read them.

The comments I am receiving on the book are of the finest. Of course, in most instances this might be considered prejudicial, but I await further impersonal reactions with interest.

I hope it will not be long until we can be together again. I am busy at work on the Twain screenplay and believe it will turn out, this time, as it should—had Lasky not wanted to try every other writer in Hollywood before coming back to me! (This seems to be the system out here—the more cooks, the better the broth! Ugh!)

My best to you—and please let me know if you get any interesting reactions enroute!

Sincerely,

WILLIAM SADLER to HAROLD SHERMAN

Chicago, March 17, 1942

Dear Harold:

This will acknowledge receipt of your letter of the fifteenth.[2]

We were all glad that you and Sir Hubert could be with us, and I assure you that everyone is sincerely charmed with Wilkins. It seems

---

[2] This letter has not been found.

to me he has about all of those things which we like in the British, while he has managed to escape those that we Americans are not so fond of.

I am writing him today in answer to the sweet little note he sent about his visit to Chicago, assuring him of our pleasure in seeing him at any and all times it is possible for him to make Chicago.

Since you were here complete galleys for Part I of the book have arrived. I have just got started reading *Thoughts Through Space* and while I am not very far, I am enjoying it very much.

With best wishes, I am

Sincerely yours,

On March 28 Harold's job with Warners ended. Pending final word on radio and play possibilities, he began focusing on the Jane Addams play while preparing for an eventual move with the family to Chicago to study the Urantia material.

SIR HUBERT WILKINS to HAROLD SHERMAN

Hotel Rienzi,
Chicago, April 18, 1942

Dear Sherman:

This is a scrawled copy of my letter to Mr. Loose and it will give you, too, the news.

I have been reading steadily from 9:30 to 12:30 and 1:30 to 5 p.m. every day Monday to Saturday. It is grand to be able to keep at it and "hold" the picture in mind—although I've had some worry in the writing in the evenings of a new lecture, "Air Supremacy and the Control of the Pacific" which I must give at Detroit Economic Club on Monday.

I intend to stay here until I have the whole outline in mind and may remain here until I go to lecture at Utica on May 18th but I am not sure of that yet.

I have been getting quite a few letters through the Creative Age Press from readers of the "interviews and reports"—the outcome of the New York advertising section, and while most of them are from "addicts," they are encouraging. None other of the clippings are so headlined as those you so kindly sent from California.

"Every Room a Home"

Hotel Rienzi

600 Diversey Parkway
Chicago, Ill.

TELEPHONE BUCKINGHAM 4100
E. KLINGBEIL, Manager

April 18th 1942

Dear Mr Loose.

This has been a most enlightening and inspiring week for me. I have spent from Monday until today reading the papers and have "skimmed through" those up to No 97.

What a grand and glorious picture the first section presents and in the geological, anthropological and theological sections I have found not only those matters I had previously met but a Host of other matters which makes the picture so much more complete and clear. What astounding possibilities are presented!

I have to leave here tonight for Detroit and must go to Green Bay Wisconsin on Tuesday but I expect to be back at the Hotel on Wednesday next and on Thursday take up the reading again.

I am looking forward with great eagerness to the reading of the other papers and hope, after I have read all of them once, to have it to more leisurely go through the parts which will most constructively prepare me for service and tend to my own development — a most very obviously needed.

I have spent only one evening the other with the Dr and his Son and I have not mentioned you and will not, unless you indicate that such is desirable. I am, however, looking forward to the time when I may, if possible, have the opportunity of learning some of the truth from you personally. With best regards to you and family.

Sincerely,

Hubert Wilkins

I have had a letter from Steffanson asking me to call on Miss Carr of Hull House in connection with you and I will see Miss Carr next Wednesday afternoon.[3] I don't know the subject matter but if you have any pointers and wire me c/o the hotel, I will respond.

Trusting that all is well.

Best regards.

Sincerely,

P.S. Congrats on the *Mark Twain* job. Hope it soon goes on celluloid.

[*Wilkins wrote:*]

Dear Mr. Loose:

This has been a most enlightening and inspiring week for me. I have spent from Monday until today reading the papers and have "skimmed through" those up to No. 97.

What a grand and glorious picture the first section presents, and in the geological, anthropological and theological sections I have found not only those matters I had previously met but a host of other matters which makes the picture so much more complete and clear. What astounding possibilities are presented!

I have to leave here tonight for Detroit and must go to Green Bay, Wisconsin on Tuesday but I expect to be back at this hotel on Wednesday next and on Thursday and take up the reading again.

I am looking forward with great eagerness to the reading of the other papers and hope, after I have read all of them once, to have time to more leisurely go through the parts which will most constructively prepare me for service and tend to *my own development*—a matter very obviously needed.

I have spent only one evening this week with the Doctor and his son and I have not mentioned you, and *will not*, unless you indicate that such is desirable.

I am, however, looking forward to the time when I may, if possible, have the opportunity of learning some of the truths from you personally.

With best regards to you and family,

Sincerely,

Hubert Wilkins

---

[3] Wilkins, too, was putting in a word for Harold via his own connections at Hull House. Charlotte Carr succeeded Jane Addams as director of Hull House.

HAROLD SHERMAN to SIR HUBERT WILKINS
Hollywood, April 21, 1942

Dear Sir Hubert:

I have "felt" you so much this past week and knew you were being *thrilled* by what you were reading—and could hardly wait for written confirmation of your own estimate of the material.

I have just communicated your message to Harry Loose over the phone, who is coming to see me this afternoon, and he is deeply pleased at your interest and plans for the future. He says great things are in store, in which the destiny of this whole little dark planet is involved.

I have been intensely busy writing the Jane Addams play—and know I have the most important work of my life nearing completion. It will mean much to me if you feel you can assure Miss Carr of Hull House and Mrs. Joseph Bowen (president) if you meet her . . . and Mr. Schwartz, the attorney (whom you met) that the dramatization of Jane Addams' life is in good hands.

I do not have the signed contract, as yet, but it has been agreed upon, and I sent the one submitted back to Mr. Schwartz for little changes to be made. . . .

Now—back to our other matter. You can begin to see now why I have worked and been so willing to sacrifice and take punishment economically and other ways for years . . . in order to soak up the experience and development necessary—to prepare for my end of the job to be done. My Mark Twain play and "Jane Addams" . . . are sign-posts along the way. (The Twain play is once more close to production in New York, with Fred Stone in title role. $5,000 more is needed and Bryden, the producer, wired me he hoped to have it by middle this week.) My two little Broadway farces, crude as they were, were simply grade-school exercises . . . I have quite a distance to travel yet, but am doing my utmost, at all times, to "get there" as quickly as possible. Can you imagine what can be done in dramatizing, for radio, stage and screen—some of the great truths revealed in the material you have been reading. Much of this material will have to be broken up into segments humanity in the mass can digest, in the form of entertainment. This whole project requires great and wise management and control at the proper time.

I am so eager to get to Chicago and wish I could be with you for a few weeks there. If I can arrange matters economically, on completion of the Addams play this week, I would leave Hollywood, tour through to Chicago with my family, rent an apartment for a few months . . . go on to New York to complete plans for production of the Twain and Addams plays, and return for continued study in Chicago . . . and to plan, with you, a future that I feel is going to see us rendering an awe-inspiring service together . . . which will count for something insofar as humanity is concerned!

Please keep me advised of your movements . . . and what the nature of the Hull House conference was about.

My best to you always—and regards to the doctor and son and all when you next see them!

SIR HUBERT WILKINS to HAROLD SHERMAN

Hotel Rienzi,
Chicago, April 25, 1942

Dear Sherman:

Saw Miss Carr yesterday evening. A stout, pleasant, good-hearted Irish lass but who has no great amount of "nous," if you understand what I mean.

She said she hoped everyone agreed that "they" had long enough been making money out of Miss Addams' name and she did not intend it to continue. She didn't want a money-making play or for others to make money out of it, and she rather stupidly and frequently asked, "Do you think Mr. Sherman is tuning in on your thoughts at this minute and do you think he knows that you are here this minute talking to me," etc., etc.

Did not see any of the others. I think she will be rather difficult to please in respect to anything pertaining to this Addams matter, but I hope and trust and believe you can produce the goods.

Best regards,
Wilkins

HAROLD SHERMAN to SIR HUBERT WILKINS

Hollywood, April 25, 1942

Dear Sir Hubert:

I sensed in my very first interview with Miss Carr that she was very jealous of the name JANE ADDAMS for she said that the old-timers kept saying to her, "this is not the way Jane Addams would have done it," etc. And she no doubt feels, if a play is produced, Jane Addams will forever overshadow the work she is doing in her own name! So few people are willing to serve for the sake of serving. How many explorers of your standing would have been willing to submerge their own selves in a Lincoln Ellsworth expedition, for instance? We are still having plenty of of trouble with the "human creature." The entity has become so involved with the animal desires and material aspirations.

Thank you for your audience with Miss Carr. I was amused at her query. Apparently she had a "guilty conscience" and was afraid I "*might* tune in"! However, she can be psychologically handled.

If things develop rather speedily on the JANE ADDAMS play, copies of which will be in Katherine Cornell's hands in New York on Monday, I may come to New York reasonably soon . . . so would appreciate knowing your plans as soon as you know them and where you can be reached . . . also a further report on the material you are studying.

The *Times* and *Tribune* have not yet reviewed the book, apparently . . . but good reviews continue to roll in from all over the country. For such comments to be received on a book as controversial as the subject matter in this one, is most unusual . . . and demonstrates the widespread public interest. Are you getting any reaction in your audiences since this publicity? Or has the publicity been extensive enough to reach public consciousness that widely?

If you can spend some time in Chicago this summer, it looks now definitely as though I would be able to be there—and it would be fine to correlate our thinking together, if possible.

My best to you—always!

Sincerely,

HARRY LOOSE to HAROLD SHERMAN
Monterey Park, April 26, 1942

Harold:-

Your phone re Wilkins-Carr caught me before I had opportunity to write my impressions of Jane Addams. Carr, the "Irish lassie," the very antithema of Jane Addams, is in rather a hot spot. Were it not for her lucrative contract she would willingly have left and returned to N.Y.C. . . . There were Chicago women many years experienced in social service and longtime residents of Hull House who were, and are, much better suited to fill the place of Miss Addams than the New York importation. . . .

In Jane Addams you have done a very fine piece of work. So much to be told, and the utter absence of an emotional side to the subject surely made a most difficult problem. I am really not a good critic for, excepting a small effort of my own, I had never heard a play read before. But I know enough of Jane Addams' life and activities to know the whole thing has been accurately and dramatically made into as beautifully connected a story as could possibly be put together for the purpose intended. . . .

Ma and I are still horrified at the amount of that phone bill. Ma is lots better, I am so very glad to be able to tell you. Can I again thank small Martha for the much appreciated food, and you all for your beloved association. I will miss these little lapses from my sober life when you folks do go away. A little time and then—. . . .

I suggest that, with you now knowing Mrs. B[owen], that should *Jane Addams* "click"—or even if it doesn't—that on your arrival in Chicago that you have Mary meet Mrs. B. and then, later, bring up the possibility of Mary having a residence of a year at Hull House, away from you folks and "on her own" in a way. A year's residence at Hull House for Mary, with its so many activities, would be a tremendous thing in her life and a means of "finding" herself. . . .

I have written quite a letter. Will mail tomorrow on the way down to Church with Ma.

As always—love to all,

H.J.L.

* * *

Through Harry's former connection as detective at Hull House, we had made arrangements with the attorneys in charge of the estate to permit me to dramatize the life of Jane Addams, world renowned Social Settlement woman, which gave us the excuse to come to Chicago in May of 1942 after having written the screenplay on the life of Mark Twain in Hollywood.

At a time in my writing career when practicality dictated that I should have taken advantage of the recognition and opportunity that had come to me on the coast, we might have stayed on in Hollywood and continued to write for pictures. Certainly it would have been much more lucrative than the gamble of this new creative assignment, but we were willing to put everything else aside.

Not only that, but to free our minds as much as possible for concentration on the massive New Revelation [Urantia] manuscript, we sent our younger daughter, Marcia, to stay with relatives in Traverse City, Michigan, for the summer, and our older daughter, Mary, to a position as receptionist at Hull House. We had been told it would require a number of months to thoughtfully go through the manuscript once, and as a consequence, we mapped out a schedule of four or five hours reading a day.

How much Harry knew about what we were to encounter, we perhaps will never know. He had been careful not to "color" in advance any impressions we might have of the Great Book and the people behind it by any comment he might make while in our presence.

In retrospect, he must have been aware of things that were happening to the manuscript in its preparation, which was not going "according to plan" or as originally intended. What he may have thought that we or anyone else could do about certain practices, which, if discovered, would need correction for protection of the integrity of the material, is likewise an open question.

With this build-up we had received, we were totally unprepared for our entrance upon one of the most challenging periods of our lives—a period that would test our mental and physical endurance to the utmost, as well as our faith in human nature. . . .

[*How to Know What to Believe,* 1976]

APPENDICES

Appendix A

COSMOPOLITAN MAGAZINE ARTICLE, MARCH 1939
"SOME CALL IT EXTRA SENSORY PERCEPTION"
By Inez Haynes Irwin

Impossible, you say, to transmit thought messages from a hut in
the Arctic to an apartment in New York! Well, maybe—but first
read this full account of a continent-wide experiment in telepathy.

Ever since my husband, Will Irwin, investigated the experiments
in "extra-sensory perception" made at Duke University, I have been
much interested in those uncharted forces of the mind which we call
telepathy and clairvoyance, or, in other language, the sixth sense.
Most psychologists, I believe, now admit the existence of that mysterious mental force. Professor J. B. Rhine's reports, so rich in carefully
checked data, seem to have settled the matter for the open-minded.

I was in this state of persuasion when the editor of *Cosmopolitan* told me that he had a report on an experiment in long-distance
telepathy. Would I look it over, see if it rang true and whether it was
good for an article?

"The leading characters," he said, "are Harold Sherman, the author, sitting as receiver in New York, and Sir Hubert Wilkins, the famous explorer, flying in the Arctic. I won't spoil it for you by telling
any more." And he delivered me a typescript of more than four hundred pages.

I was a little disturbed, as is likely to be the case when one deals
with what has hitherto been regarded as strange, exotic or bizarre.
But once I got into the manuscript, and this experience my husband
shared with me, I could scarcely put it down. The messages sent and
received by pure telepathy, or picked up by clairvoyance, with ev-

ery practicable precaution against charge of fraud or self-deception, seemed to be unparalleled in any literature I had ever read on extra-sensory perception. Yet in spite of this dazzling quality, we both got from the report the feeling of authenticity. It rings with truth.

When the editor invited me to luncheon to meet Harold Sherman, who, as receiver of impressions, was the leading character of the story, I found a brisk, normal young man, extremely intelligent and articulate, but also hardheaded, logical, modest. Indeed, as we talked over detail after detail, he seemed most anxious that I should refrain from touching up his report with any overenthusiastic interpretation of my own.

I think I lulled his apprehension on that score. I have never belonged to any psychic society. I have never, so far as I am aware, had a psychic experience. I consider myself lamentably lacking in the special quality traditionally imputed to women—intuition. I regard the spiritist theory simply as not proved. But that last is perhaps aside from the mark, since spiritism does not enter into the record of these experiments. And so to the story.

In October 1937 Wilkins and Sherman sat in the City Club, New York, discussing this uncharted force. Sherman, indeed, had proved himself a sensitive. He was also the author of that popular book on the mind, *Your Key to Happiness*. Both had believed in the existence of clairvoyance and telepathy long before the professors caught up with the subject. They held that this wireless telegraphy of the mind, whatever it may be, works best under stress of emotion. And Wilkins expected to experience a variety of strong emotions during the next few months.

He was just starting out on one of his great adventures. Six Russian fliers, after passing the North Pole on a flight to California, had disappeared in the Arctic. There was reason to believe that they might have crashed somewhere on the American side of Bering Strait. The Soviet government had employed Wilkins to establish bases in the Far North and, as thoroughly as the Arctic light allowed, to search from the air the wastes of glacier, tundra and mountain in Alaska, northwestern Canada and the frozen ocean beyond.

So the two men agreed on an experiment in telepathy. Three nights a week, between 11:30 and 12:00 Eastern Standard time, in whatever time zone he might be living and adventuring, Wilkins was to seek solitude and "open his subconscious." At the corresponding hour, Sherman was to "sit" in his study on Riverside Drive, New York, and, emptying his mind of all conscious thought, try to get the impressions Wilkins was sending him. As mail facilities allowed, Sherman was to send Wilkins his transcript of these impressions and Wilkins was to report upon their accuracy.

There must be, so far as possible, a "scientific check" on such experiments, so they agreed that Sherman, upon finishing his midnight sitting, should write out his impressions and mail them at once to Samuel Emery, a friend of both, a resident of the City Club and a skeptic in regard to extra-sensory perception. Emery read these impressions on receipt and put them away in a drawer, but did not himself date them.

After a month of this, Sherman enlisted as a witness Doctor Gardner Murphy, a psychologist at Columbia University. Murphy received a copy of the impressions on the same terms as Emery. He read them on receipt, dated them and filed them away. Doctors Henry S. W. Hardwicke and A. E. Strath-Gordon, students in the field of mental and psychic phenomena, occasionally sat with Sherman while he was receiving impressions. As radio conditions allowed, which was not very often that winter, Wilkins was sending correspondence to *The New York Times*. Reginald Iversen, head radio operator for *The Times*, had contact with Sherman off and on during the period of these telepathic tests.

Iversen began his contact with this experiment as a skeptic. But in the end he testified, "At no time during this period of six months did Harold Sherman ever seek such information as I might have known concerning Sir Hubert Wilkins and his activities in the Far North. In fact, despite my skepticism, as it turned out, Sherman actually had a more accurate telepathic knowledge of what was happening to Wilkins in his search for the lost Russian fliers than I was able to gain in my ineffective attempts to keep in touch by short-wave radio."

Cosmopolitan received the affidavits of these seven men in regard to their part in this experiment.

Wilkins set out for those far northern lands where he was to spend the winter in October 1937. He reached Winnipeg, but difficulties in getting equipment made it necessary to fly to New York and to return via Montreal and Ottawa. From Winnipeg, he flew to Regina, to Fort Resolution, to Aklavik on the Arctic coast of Canada, finally to Point Barrow, the most northerly spot of land in Alaska, where he passed most of December and early January waiting in vain for a combination of full moonlight and mistless air. He returned to his base in Aklavik and then on January 15, the moon being full and the weather clear, he began a series of search flights, one extending over 1,900 miles. So much for his itinerary.

The explorer found it impossible to fulfill his part of the bargain. Sherman says:

> As it turned out, Wilkins was so swamped with details from the very moment of landing in Winnipeg, that he could not keep his appointments with me. To my surprise, however, I commenced getting mental pictures and 'feeling' impressions of Wilkins' activities from the very start, many of which were confirmed by him subsequently as "direct hits."

Later, Wilkins was able occasionally to keep his appointment with Sherman. After all, his search for the Soviet fliers, not this experiment, was his main interest in life just then.

Wireless was working badly that winter. For weeks at a time, Wilkins' portable transmitters were out of touch with New York. He got mail irregularly, but at intervals Sherman posted his own copy of his notes to Wilkins; and the latter sent them back with marginal notes as to their truth and fidelity. Finally Wilkins' occasional stories in *The New York Times* furnished another check-up. Covering sometimes a month during which wireless communication had been dead, they confirmed impressions which Sherman had filed and dated with Doctor Murphy days or weeks before.

On the other hand, on the night of October 25, 1937, Sherman began his own winter sittings. He worked in a dark room in his New York home with his eyes wide open. Usually he was alone.

We come now to a consideration of this amazing manuscript. It consists of passages, some long, some short, recording Sherman's three-nights-a-week "get," followed later (in some cases many weeks later) by the same manuscript with Wilkins' check-up, all this conveniently arranged in parallel columns.

I find amazing the number of things Sherman saw on that blanched screen of his mind, more amazing still the clarity and precision with which he saw many of them and most amazing of all the number of direct hits. As the hits are so frequent and in many cases so astoundingly exact—the whole thing seeming beyond any possible chance-average—I shall concern myself almost entirely with them.

Here are a few typical cases. Wilkins' check-up is in italics.

Oct. 28: "C. is with you. Carries good-luck charm." *Cheesman joined expedition this day. Carries a penguin (small, wood) as charm.*

Nov. 1: "You communicated Russian government today regarding some flight matter. . . . You advise cannot take off search under two weeks unless radical change in weather." *Talked to Embassy at 7:30 by phone to Washington—gave estimated time of departure for North as two weeks.*

Nov. 8: "Barrow—this word came to me after I first saw mental picture of a wheelbarrow . . . Now I see a long pointer—and draw inference 'Point Barrow' . . . Are you going there for some reason—is there snow there? Have you decided to shift operations where weather can be more immediately favorable?" *Possibility of going via Alaska because of warm weather in Canada. This also received intensive thought during day—and (Point) Barrow was often in mind.*

Although not mathematically minded, Sherman was constantly picking up figures, with a high percentage of hits. Earlier in these experiments, he "called" the first three items in the combination of letters and figures on Wilkins' newly licensed airplane. Here comes another example:

Nov. 8: " '7'—this number came." *Someone telling my fortune with cards. No. 7 was referred to repeatedly.*

Sherman knew with his conscious mind that Wilkins, going by air to rough lands, carried no formal clothes. And he has recorded his surprise when his subconscious mind insisted on this impression:

Nov. 11: "You in company men in military attire—some women, evening dress—you appear to be in evening dress yourself." *Armistice Ball at Regina. Many officers of army and police in uniform. My appearance at this affair was made possible by the loan to me of evening dress.*

Nov. 18 "9:30 tomorrow morning you plan some definite action—perhaps resume flight—something important set for that time." *Left word by letter to all of expedition staff to be at airport 9 A.M. Take-off at 9:30.*

Nov. 22 "You following Mackenzie River in flight—weather fog and snow—down at town with old stone fort—expect flight on tomorrow morning—Aklavik goal." *Followed Mackenzie River from Fort Resolution to Aklavik this day. Flew through snow and fog.*

Later in this article we shall come to a period when Sherman seems to lose his time-sense or, rather, to extend it; when past, present and—most astonishingly—future become at times inextricably mixed. The tendency first manifested itself on the next day when he turned on his electric torch to write:

Nov. 23 "You Aklavik. Been there over twenty-four hours." *We arrived Aklavik yesterday (curious that you should sense Aklavik this day—23rd—when on the 22nd you thought we would get there on Wednesday the 24th!)*

Nov. 30 "Strong impression ping-pong balls. Is there table in town where people play." *Two of the men, Cheesman and Dyne, were playing ping-pong in the school gymnasium.*

Dec. 2 "You operating between a number of base locations—Point Barrow—Barter Island—Aklavik and a fourth location—seemingly still farther north." *Fourth station—Baillie Island—250 miles north-northeast of Aklavik.*

And here I will give all of Sherman's impressions on December seventh, a case of a nearly perfect "get." Note, however, that Sherman sees Wilkins at Aklavik when he is really at Point Barrow.

DECEMBER 7, 1937
11:30-12:00 P.M.

SHERMAN

Don't know why but I seem to see crackling fire shining out in darkness of Aklavik—get a definite fire impression as though house burning . . . you can see it from your location on Ice. I first thought fire on ice near your tent, but impressions persist it is white house burning and quite a crowd gathered around it . . . people running or hurrying toward flames . . . bitter cold . . . stiff breeze . . .

Your plane looks like a silvery ghost in moonlight . . . I seem

WILKINS

While I was in radio office at Point Barrow, the fire alarm rang. A long ring on the telephone. (There are only 4 telephones at Barrow.) It was an Eskimo's shack on fire. The chimney blazed up and the roof took fire but it was soon put out. Some damage resulted, mostly from the efforts of the zealous firemen. Was pretty cold that night with a light wind.

to be almost under nose of it . . . standing in snow—looking up— it towers over me. I've never seen plane, of course, but it seems to have high bow with two huge propellers either side of cabin or cockpits—motors concealed in great silver metal tubelike cylinders or encasements—don't know technical names for purposes description . . . a rounded metal door seems to lift up to admit entrance to cockpits from top of plane . . . big instrument board front cockpit . . . seats for two— pilot and co-pilot or navigator . . . rear cockpit and space beyond for another passenger and storage— separate rounded metal door with glassed "windows covering each cockpit—plane rests on giant skis . . . dark in color. Windows in plane seem of slit nature—wide panels that go around front and sides—as well as observation opportunity through top of plane— even though doors clamped shut . . . Everything fastened down . . . compactly packed, plane not yet equipped or stored with things as it will be on actual hops . . .

Description of plane practically exact.

Okay as previously stated.

17th comes to mind as real takeoff for search flight—day later than you had originally contemplated—this different sort impression involving time dimension— seem foresee unfavorable weather conditions arising to prevent action on 16th.

Weather was and remained unfavorable over whole moonlight period, 15th to 17th, inclusive.

A prominent citizen in Aklavik has died—and I seem to catch glimpse of funeral service—strange sensation this connection that an Aklavik doctor is also an undertaker . . . or somehow associated.

There was a funeral service. A baby died (Eskimo). The natives act as their own undertakers.

Is there some man you deal with Aklavik by name of Webb or Weber? Name comes to me and man seems medium height, heavy-set, heavily clad—hooded garb . . .

An owner of a store at Aklavik is Peffer—about as description.

Dec. 13 "'Abandon search' strong impression crosses mind—strong thought from some quarter—mind or minds consider further search futile." *The "abandon search" was the abandon search for the Fairbanks plane.* [A plane flying from Fairbanks had crashed a day or two before.—author.]

Dec 21 "Sudden severe pain comes to me right side of head." *I am not sure that it happened this day, but each one of us could not seem to avoid bumping our heads on a sharp-edged stovepipe in the kitchen. I bumped mine only twice. But Dyne and Cheesman bumped often.*

In their preliminary talks at the City Club, Wilkins and Sherman had agreed that a flash of red light should be a signal between them for danger or illness. Here comes a case of such a warning:

Dec. 27 "Red flash tonight as though one of crew wasn't so well—hope this isn't true impression—it crossed consciousness quickly but I record it in keeping with resolve to make known everything which comes to mind during these sessions . . ." *Cook, radio man at Barrow, sick.*

Dec 27 "Yes, I see you talking to a doctor in Point Barrow with whom you have become quite well acquainted . . . he seems to be a thin, tall individual about fifty years of age." *Dr. Levine of V.S. Government Medical Service. There for research. Age about okay, thin but short.*

This record on New Year's Eve is curiously convincing:

Dec. 31 "I can almost hear you say, "Happy New Year, Sherman!" as though sending me a greeting." *I went home to bed by myself and thought of you particularly and other of my friends, saying "Happy New Year" to each one.*

Jan. 11 "Hear motors turning over distinctly as though tested out . . . see you and crew running across snow-covered field in hurry . . . concerned with some operation—activity of some sort tonight." *We flew back to Aklavik this day.*

Jan. 13 "Something of great importance mechanically has been found impractical and has had to be changed . . . I get this feeling strongly and see you supervising work in connection therewith . . . You really need a new or different device which you don't have with you . . . something is ingeniously made at Point Barrow by your mechanic in association with your radio engineer." *Radio. Also means of cleaning plane's windows of hoar frost—working on it intently.*

The end of the holiday season, when frozen Aklavik lived in unbroken darkness, brought the high passage of Wilkins' adventure of the flesh. On January 17 he began his search. Within the next six weeks, he was to make a series of long and dangerous flights over the Arctic Ocean and the glacial mountains which border it. The adventure of the spirit on which he and Sherman had embarked seemed to keep pace with the increase of Wilkins' emotions, when he matched his skill and courage against storms, and icy wastes where a forced landing meant death by exposure or starvation. For now Sherman makes even more hits, together with the usual half-hits and misses. His impressions positively gush—richer, fuller, more specific than before; in the case of scenes, more etching-like.

From this time forth, the impressions of Sherman, sitting quietly in a darkened room four or five thousand miles away, grew constantly more accurate and vivid.

The item which follows Sherman regards as one of his most remarkable hits in pure telepathy:

Jan. 27 "A dog seems to have been injured in Aklavik and had to be shot . . . Was injury sustained in fight with others—or something falling on it? Quite a strong feeling here." *Out walking—came upon dog dead on ice—it had been shot through the head—thought about it strongly for some time, wondered reason for killing.*

Jan.31 "Seem to hear you humorously say to someone, "If radio comunication keeps on this bad, I'll have to develop telepathic communication with Sherman in order to get anything through!" I have felt your thought my direction many times and feel it again tonight . . ." *Correct.*

On February sixth, the engine in Wilkins' plane had broken down completely—an accident which I shall consider more fully when we come to Sherman's extraordinary forecast of events. He flew to Edmonton by mail plane, to get a new engine and have it flown back to Aklavik.

Feb. 14 "You have found a motor in Edmonton and it seems that you are planning to take off with it tomorrow or Wednesday if weather permits." *Wednesday.*

"Word 'Mackenzie' flashes to mind in connection with flying—is there a company of some sort that supplies you with plane?" *Mackenzie Airways plane brought me out and was preparing to fly me back.*

Mar. 3 "I have flashing picture of someone of crew pointing out several herds of wild animals as you passed over mountain valleys." *Saw caribou.*

Mar. 7 "Was tail of plane slightly damaged in bumpy landing during Alaskan mountain flights? Seem to see some work having been done in rear of plane." *Skis and tail skid slightly damaged when taxiing at Old Crow. We ran onto a gravel bar in the river. Ripped bottoms of skis but no repairs necessary.*

Mar. 14 "See plane circling low over certain area—icy waste with several open stretches of water—has look from air as though pieces of wreckage caught in ice near water's edge—but feel just unusual formation . . ." *Since our flight on March 10, many of the leads have closed, and there has been considerable pressure on ice; but the most interesting of our observations was an open lead varying from 20 to 500 yards wide and running for about 150 miles along our course between Lat. 81 and 84 N. and Long. 122 to 127 W.* (Wilkins' news account concerning flight on the fourteenth, published in *The New York Times*, March 17, 1938.)

March 15 "May be wrong, but can't feel flight today—get a 'stopped' sensation . . . standing-by impression . . ." *Learned of decision to stop all search flights from Alaskan side.*

This of course ended the adventure for Wilkins. On the seventeenth, the news was confirmed officially and he prepared to return to New York.

Mar. 22 "'Packing up' thought comes to me—equipment you no longer need—arrangements being made for supply plane to aid in carrying some of equipment and supplies back when expedition job completed . . . pickups to be made from Point Barrow and Aklavik . . ."

We were packing up at Edmonton at that time. Soviet Embassy offered provide a supply plane but I replied that it was not required Aklavik. They did send a plane to Barrow about this date to pick up supplies from there.

Mar. 24 "Feeling just as strong tonight that you have left Aklavik some days ago—first to Edmonton where skis changed to wheels . . . then—yes, I feel you are now in Winnipeg—Fort Garry Hotel." *Stopped at Fort Garry on night of 24th. Left there on 25th. Correct.*

Sherman ended his sittings on this day.

* * *

Now we shall go back over the records to note the singular phenomenon which began, like a luminous glow, to infuse Sherman's impressions toward the end of his experiment. Hazily at first, then more clearly, Sherman records coming events.

Early in December, Wilkins had established a base at Point Barrow, intending to make his first long search flight on the fourteenth, when the moon would be full.

That night, Sherman wrote this impression:

"Though this is day you announced planned take-off, can't feel you, this moment, in air . . . think conditions today check back to earlier almost premonitory impressions of weather preventing flight on December 16." To this, Wilkins appends the laconic comment, *Okay.* Fogs, storms and finally the waning moon prevented any search that month.

It was natural to expect the next attempt at a search flight a day or so before January twelfth, when the moon would again reach full. In spite of that probability, Sherman wrote on December twenty-eighth:

"January 15 comes to me as the day you actually make take-off for northern regions—though you now hope to get off a few days earlier in the month. This again is premonitory impression—as though thoughts jump ahead of present moment—and this future moment, for a flitting instant, becomes now—then fades again."

On January twelfth, he comes back to this subject: "I am again impressed with 15th of January as your probable take-off date.

When the transcript of this impression reached Wilkins, nearly a month later, he wrote in the margin:

Quite extraordinary that we should make a flight, starting night of 14th and taking off on the 15th of January. We should have gotten off on the 13th but radio in plane had broken down. But note this, which both Sherman and Wilkins overlook in their comments: Aklavik, from which the explorer started this flight, is four time zones west of New York. What was half past eight P.M. of the fourteenth to Wilkins to Aklavik would be half past twelve A.M. of the fifteenth to Sherman in New York. Which may account for the fact that Sherman saw the take-off, as well as the major part of the flight, as happening on the fifteenth.

Then comes the most remarkable instance of forecasting in Sherman's records of his sittings. Iversen, whose main concern during five months was keeping in touch with Wilkins, has certified that Sherman had closer knowledge of the explorer's movements by telepathy than he himself had by wireless. And in nothing was the sensitive more accurate than in perceiving when Wilkins was flying. In this matter, he missed the mark only three or four times in five months.

Now on March seventh and eighth, nothing especial happened to Wilkins. But on those two nights, Sherman, finding himself unaccountably agitated as he sat down to "work," recorded these impressions, among others:

"Was tail of plane slightly damaged in bumpy landing? . . . Seem to see some work . . . in rear of plane . . . fleeting vision of your face—quite a strained, intent expression . . . seems as though flight started and down at some point or turned back . . . plane motionless . . . snow or sleetlike weather . . . seem to see it pelting plane . . . strange feeling in pit of stomach . . . or solar plexus—like I've gone through close scrape or acute experience . . . you concerned about something."

On March eleventh, *three days later,* the expedition, carrying heavy Arctic equipment, with 1,200 gallons of gasoline, hopped off intending to make one of its longest flights. A brief dispatch from Wilkins to the *Times,* printed on March twelfth, tells what happened. They took off without incident on a light and clear morning. But shortly after they got into the air, a snow-laden storm, "as black and sudden as a thundercloud," enveloped them. Wilkins decided to return and land. Pilot Hollick-Kenyon brought the plane down expertly but the skids struck a sharp ridge of snow which tore the tail skid from the fuselage. Although Wilkins made light of the accident in his report, this was really an intimate brush with death.

What is the answer to this riddle? I have used the word "forecasting." Perhaps it was prophecy. Prophecy is a venerable word implying the intervention of a supernatural intelligence and there is a venerable book, the Bible, which is filled with it. But shall we use a more modern explanation? Shall we say that Sherman received those impressions because of the coexistence of the past, present and future? Or shall we say that, through the blanched screen of his mind, he peered into another dimension?

Appendix B

YOUR KEY TO HAPPINESS, pages 43-44
VERSION ONE (1935)

If this one physical life were all, then you would have every right to damn creation, to denounce what appears to you as the imperfection and cruelty of Nature. But this physical existence is but one of many that you have experienced. It is a damaged bead, the only visible bead of a string of beads that have gone before. These beads represent the physical entities that have gone to make up your external forms which the "I am" of you occupied in this time-space dimension. In other words, there is every evidence today that an evolution of the soul is taking place simultaneously with the evolution of all physical forms.

And while your Conscious mind, more closely related to your crippled body, probably has been rebelling, your Inner Self contains the answer to your present state. If you came into this life crippled and diseased, it was your ego that chose such physical entrance for the value of the experience which such an environment and affliction would bring to you!

What has happened has all been in accordance with infallible law. You may have abused, in another existence, your own body or the body of another. You may have denied others things that are now being denied you. Compensation must be made for every misstep. You can attract to yourself nothing that has not first been attained within.

And your ego cannot attach itself to the embryo provided by earthly parents unless its vibratory rate of Consciousness exactly corresponds to the vibration of the living organism. If this organism is diseased as the result of diseased parents, the soul encased in it has not been victimized but, rather, has been compelled to take this impaired manner of expression in order to regain entrance to this External world. If this has happened, it has been mathematically due to some past abuse of Law which has produced a "cancer" in Consciousness that can only be exterminated through renewed human experience.

Think long and deeply and well upon the above explanation. The more you reflect upon it, the more you will draw from your Inner Self the conviction that it is true; that it is just; that you are where you are and as you are because you are what you are! And a great Peace will commence to steal in upon you; the Peace that can only come as you release all feelings of frustration, of rebellion, of bitterness and condemnation.

It is a misnomer to say that we are born "free and equal" if we apply this to our bodies. It is certainly a misnomer if we think of it in relation to our material wealth. But we are born "free and equal" insofar as our soul opportunities are concerned. And, when Time shall have returned our present bodies to dust, the soul development we have attained in this life, added to the development previously achieved, is what will count. The crippled or impaired physical frame will not have mattered for it has nothing to do with the eternal part of us.

So, if you have been made a so-called invalid; if life has been one continuous physical torture; if medical science, with all its advancement, has been unable and is powerless to help you, then give yourself over to your Mind. Retire to the inner sanctum of the greatest power that is or ever [can be.]

VERSION TWO (1943)

If this one life were all, then you would have every right to damn creation, to denounce what appears to you as the imperfection and cruelty of Nature. But I am positive this physical existence is only the beginning of a continuing life experience which reaches beyond the state we call "death."

In this next dimension, the physical inequalities of this life are evened up and you will find yourself to possess a perfected body form, no longer deformed or subject to pain.

God, the Great Intelligence, did not decree that you should be born with, or develop physical deformities or ills here. In His wisdom, He permitted you to be born in accordance with the physical laws of cause and effect established on this planet.

If you had been created perfect, with no freedom of choice, no will to decide between the right and wrong way of thinking and acting, you would have been forever deprived of the glorious power to develop and possess your own soul through life experience.

So, if certain physical causes have given you a damaged fleshly house in which to live, do not bemoan your fate, but make the best of it, secure in the faith that life holds more for you than you dream—even here on earth—if you will maintain the right mental attitude. And, as for the future, exercise this same faith to believe and know that your entity or real self will occupy another body of finer substance, in the life to come, a life which will be as real to you then as this one is now.

It is the way you react to your experiences here, no matter what your physical handicaps may be, which counts! Your soul is being evolved by the decisions you make, what you think and do. Your personality, your identity, the "I am I" of you remains the same. But your capacity for the development of truth and understanding and all of the qualities which your consciousness needs to prepare you for the life beyond is growing with each new worthwhile experience.

It is up to you to see to it that you make proper choice of the experiences you have in life. If you choose wisely, the experiences you bring to you can contribute much to your own advancement in wisdom and character.

The duties and responsibilities of this life are of first importance but it is our right attention to these matters which determines largely our soul's evolution. Live a starved, self-centered life and your soul will reflect these attributes, for your soul is the real you! Such faults as you still possess will have to be worked out in the training school of your next life. Compensation must be made for every misstep. You can attract to yourself nothing that has not been attained within.

So, resolve to take full advantage of the opportunities offered you in this earthly kindergarten in order that you may be ready to partake of the greater joys possible to you when you graduate, through death, to the next conscious phase of your soul's progressive existence.

Think long and deeply upon the above explanation. If medical science is powerless to help you, then give yourself over to your Mind. Retire to the inner sanctum of the greatest power that is or ever [can be.]

Appendix C

Genesis 14:18 And Melchizedek king of Salem brought forth bread and wine: and he was the priest of the most high God.

Psalms 110:4 The lord hath sworn, and will not repent, Thou art a priest for ever after the order of Melchizedek.

Hebrews 5:6 As he saith also in another place, Thou art a priest for ever after the order of Melchizedek. 7 Who in the days of his flesh, when he had offered up prayers and supplications with strong crying and tears unto him that was able to save him from death, and was heard in that he feared; 8 Though he were a Son, yet learned he obedience by the things which he suffered; 9 And being made perfect, he became the author of eternal salvation unto all them that obey him; 10 Called of God an high priest after the order of Melchizedek.

Hebrews 6:1 Therefore leaving the principles of the doctrine of Christ, let us go on unto perfection; not laying again the foundation of repentance from dead works, and of faith toward God, 2 Of the doctrine of baptisms, and of laying on of hands, and of resurrection of the dead, and of eternal judgment. 3 And this will we do, if God permit. 4 For it is impossible for those who were once enlightened, and have tasted of the heavenly gift, and were made partakers of the Holy Ghost, 5 And have tasted the good word of God, and the powers of the world to come, 6 If they shall fall away, to renew them again unto repentance; seeing they crucify to themselves the Son of God afresh, and put him to an open shame. 7 For the earth which drinketh in the rain that cometh oft upon it, and bringeth forth herbs meet for them by whom it is dressed, receiveth blessing from God: 8 But that which beareth thorns and briers is rejected, and is nigh unto cursing; whose end is to be burned. 9 But, beloved, we are persuaded better things of you, and things that accompany salvation, though we thus speak. 10

For God is not unrighteous to forget your work and labour of love, which ye have shewed toward his name, in that ye have ministered to the saints, and do minister. 11 And we desire that every one of you do shew the same diligence to the full assurance of hope unto the end: 12 That ye be not slothful, but followers of them who through faith and patience inherit the promises. 13 For when God made promise to Abraham, because he could swear by no greater, he sware by himself, 14 Saying, Surely blessing I will bless thee, and multiplying I will multiply thee. 15 And so, after he had patiently endured, he obtained the promise. 16 For men verily swear by the greater: and an oath for confirmation is to them an end of all strife. 17 Wherein God, willing more abundantly to shew unto the heirs of promise the immutability of his counsel, confirmed it by an oath: 18 That by two immutable things, in which it was impossible for God to lie, we might have a strong consolation, who have fled for refuge to lay hold upon the hope set before us: 19 Which hope we have as an anchor of the soul, both sure and stedfast, and which entereth into that within the veil; 20 Whither the forerunner is for us entered, even Jesus, made an high priest for ever after the order of Melchizedek.

Hebrews 7:1 For this Melchizedek, king of Salem, priest of the most high God, who met Abraham returning from the slaughter of the kings, and blessed him; 2 To whom also Abraham gave a tenth part of all; first being by interpretation King of righteousness, and after that also King of Salem, which is, King of peace; 3 Without father, without mother, without descent, having neither beginning of days, nor end of life; but made like unto the Son of God; abideth a priest continually. 4 Now consider how great this man was, unto whom even the patriarch Abraham gave the tenth of the spoils. 5 And verily they that are of the sons of Levi, who receive the office of the priesthood, have a commandment to take tithes of the people according to the law, that is, of their brethren, though they come out of the loins of Abraham: 6 But he whose descent is not counted from them received tithes of Abraham, and blessed him that had the promises. 7 And without all contradiction the less is blessed of the better. 8 And here men that die receive tithes; but there he receiveth them, of whom it is witnessed that he liveth. 9 And as I may so say, Levi also, who receiveth tithes, payed tithes in Abraham. 10 For he was yet in the loins of his father, when Melchizedek met him. 11 If therefore perfection were by the Levitical priesthood, (for under it the people received the law,) what further need was there that another priest should rise after the order of Melchizedek, and not be called after the order of Aaron? 12 For the priesthood being changed, there is made of necessity a change also of the law. 13 For he of whom these things are spoken pertaineth to another tribe, of which no man gave attendance at the altar. 14 For it is evident that our Lord sprang out of Juda; of which tribe Moses spake nothing concerning priesthood. 15 And it is yet far more evident: for that after the similitude of Melchizedek there ariseth another priest, 16 Who is made, not after the law of a carnal commandment, but after the power of an endless life. 17 For he testifieth, Thou art a priest for ever after the order of Melchizedek. 18 For there is verily a disannulling of the commandment going before for the weakness and unprofitableness thereof. 19 For the law made nothing perfect, but the bringing in of a better hope did; by the which we draw nigh unto God. 20 And inasmuch as not without an oath he was made priest: 21 (For those priests were made without an oath; but this with an oath by him that said unto him, The Lord sware and will not repent, Thou art a priest for ever after the order of Melchizedek:) 22 By so much was Jesus made a surety of a better testament. 23 And they truly were many priests, because they were not suffered to continue by reason of death: 24 But this man, because he continueth ever, hath an unchangeable priesthood. 25 Wherefore he is able also to save them to the uttermost that come unto God by him, seeing he ever liveth to make intercession for them. 26 For such an high priest became us, who is holy, harmless, undefiled, separate from sinners, and made higher than the heavens; 27 Who needeth not daily, as those high priests, to offer up sacrifice, first for his own sins, and then for the people's: for this he did once, when he offered up himself. 28 For the law maketh men high priests which have infirmity; but the word of the oath, which was since the law, maketh the Son, who is consecrated for evermore.

Appendix D

PONTIUS PILATE MATERIAL, received by Harry Loose

April 11, 1941

Herod to Pontius Pilate the Governor:

Peace.

I am in great anxiety. I write these things unto thee that when thou hast heard them thou mayest be grieved for me. For as my daughter, Herodias, who is dear to me, was playing upon a pool of water which had ice upon it, it broke under her and all her body went down, and her head was cut off and remained upon the surface of the ice. And behold, her mother is holding her head upon her knees in her lap and my whole house is in great sorrow. For I, when I heard of the man Jesus, wished to come to thee, that I might see him alone, and hear his word, whether it was like that of the sons of men. And it is certain that because of the many evil things which were done by me to John the Baptist, and because I have mocked Christ, behold I receive the reward of righteousness, for I have shed much blood of others' children upon the earth. Therefore, the judgments of God are righteous; for every man receives according to his thought. But since thou wast worthy to see that God-man, therefore, it becometh you to pray for me. My son Azbonius also is in the agony of the hour of death. And I too am in affliction and great trial, because I have the dropsy; and am in great distress, because I persecuted the introducer of baptism by water, which was John. Therefore, my brother, the judgments of God are righteous. And my wife, again through all her grief for her daughter, is become blind in her left eye, because we desire to blind the Eye of righteousness. There is no peace to the doers of evil, sayeth the Lord. For already great affliction cometh upon the priests and the writers of the law. Because they delivered unto thee the Just One. For this is the consummation of the world, that they consented that the Gentiles should become heirs. For the children of light shall be cast out for they have not observed the things which were preached concerning the Lord, and concerning his Son. Therefore gird up thy loins and receive righteousness, thou with thy wife remembering Jesus night and day; and the Kingdom shall belong to you Gentiles, for we, the chosen people, have mocked the Righteous One. Now if there is a place for our request, O Pilate, because we were at one time in power, bury my household carefully; for it is right that we could be buried by thee, rather than by the priests, whom, after a little time, as the Scriptures say, at the coming of Jesus Christ, vengeance shall overtake. Fare thee well, with Procla thy wife. I send thee earrings of my daughter and my own ring, that they may be unto thee a memorial of my decease. For already do worms begin to issue from my body, and lo, I am receiving temporal judgment and I am afraid of the judgment to come. For in both we stand before the works of the living God; but his judgment, which is temporal, is for a time, while that to come is judgment forever. And now this is the end of my letter to Pilate the Governor.

Pilate to Herod the Tetrarch:
Peace.

Know and see, that in the day when thou didst deliver Jesus unto me, I took pity on myself, and testified by washing my hands, that I was innocent, concerning him who rose from the grave after three days, and had performed thy pleasure in him, for thou didn't desire me to be associated with thee in his crucifixion. But I now learn from the executioners and from the soldiers who watched his sepulchre that he rose from the dead. And I have especially confirmed what was told me, that he appeared in Galilee, in the same form, and with the same voice, and the same doctrine, and with the same disciples, not having changed in anything, but preaching with boldness his resurrection and an everlasting kingdom. And behold, heaven and earth rejoice, and behold, Procla my wife is believing in the visions that appeared unto her, when thou sentest that I could deliver Jesus to the people of Israel, because of the ill-will they had. Now when Procla, my wife, heard that Jesus was risen, and had appeared in Galilee, she took with her Longinus the centurion and twelve soldiers, the very same that had watched at the sepulchre, and went to greet the face of Christ, as if to a great spectacle, and saw him with his disciples.

Now while they were standing, and wondering, and gazing at him, he looked at them, and said to them, "What is it? Do you believe in me? Procla, know that in the covenant which God gave the fathers, it is said that everybody which had perished should live by means of my death, which ye have seen. And now, ye see that I live, whom ye crucified. And I suffered many things, till that I was laid in the sepulchre. But now, hear me, and believe in my Father—God who is in me. For I loosed the cords of death, and break the gates of Sheol, and my coming shall be hereafter." And when Procla, my wife, and the Romans heard these things, they came and told me, weeping, for they also were against him, when they devised the evils which they had done unto him. So that, I also was on the couch of my bed in affliction, and put on a garment of mourning, and took unto me fifty Romans with my wife, and went into Galilee. And when I was going in the way I testified these things; that Herod did these things by me, that he took council with me, and constrained me to arm my hands against him, and to judge him, that judgeth all, and to scourge the Just One, Lord of the just. And when we drew nigh to him, O Herod, a great voice was heard from heaven, and dreadful thunder, and the earth trembled, and gave forth a sweet smell, like unto which was never perceived even in the temple of Jerusalem. Now while I stood in the way, our Lord saw me as he stood and talked with his disciples. But I prayed in my heart, for I knew that it was he whom ye delivered unto me, that he was Lord of created things and Creator of all. But we, when we saw him, all of us fell upon our faces before his feet. And I said with a loud voice, "I have sinned, O Lord, in that I sat and judged thee, who avengest all in truth. And lo, I know that thou are God, the Son of God, and I beheld thy humanity and not thy divinity. But Herod, with the children of Israel, constrained me to do evil unto thee. Have pity, therefore, upon me, O God of Israel." And my wife, in great anguish, said, "Pilate, nor according to the will of the children of Israel, nor according to the thought of the sons of the priests; but remember my husband in thy glory." Now, our Lord drew near and raised me up, and my wife, and the Romans, and I looked at him and saw there were on him the scars of his cross. And he said, "That which [is] the Son of man, the Son of the Most High, who is forever, arose from the dead, and is glorified on high by all that he created for ever and ever. Justinus, one of the writers that were in the days of Augustus and Tiberius and Gaius, wrote in his third discourse: Now Mary the Galilean, who bare the Christ that was crucified in Jerusalem, had not been with a husband. And Joseph did not abandon her; but Joseph continued in sanctity without a wife, he and his five sons by a former wife; and Mary continued without a husband. Theodorus wrote to Pilate the Governor: Who was the man, against whom there was a complaint before thee, that he was crucified by the men of Palestine? If the many demanded this righteously, why didst thou not consent to their righteousness? And if they demanded this unrighteously, how didst thou transgress the law and command what was far from righteousness? Pilate sent to him, "Because he wrought signs, I did not wish to crucify him; and since his accusers said, "He calleth himself a King, I crucified him." Josephus said, "Agrippa, the King, was clothed in a robe of silver, and saw the spectacle in the theater of Caesarea. When the people saw that his raiment flashed, they said to him, "Hitherto we feared thee as a man, henceforth thou are exalted above nature of mortals. And he saw an angel standing over him, and he smote him as unto death. This is the end of the Letter of Pilate to Herod.

Pontius Pilate to Tiberius Caesar the Emperor:

Greeting. Upon Jesus Christ, whom I have fully made known to thee in my last, a bitter punishment hath at length been inflicted by the will of the people, although I was unwilling and apprehensive. In good truth, no age ever had or will have, a man so good and strict. But the people made a wonderful effort, with all their scribes, chiefs and elders agreed, to crucify this ambassador of truth, their own prophets, like the Sibyls with us, advising the contrary; and when he was hanged supernatural signs appeared and in the judgment of philosophers menaced the whole world with ruin. His disciples flourish, not belying their master by their behavior and continence of life, in his name, they are most beneficent. Had I not feared a sedition might arise among the people, who were almost furious, perhaps this man would have yet been living with us. Although, being rather compelled by fidelity to thy dignity, then led by my own inclination, I did not strive with all my might to prevent the sale and suffering of righteous blood, guiltless of every accusation, unjustly, indeed, through the maliciousness of men, and yet, as the Scriptures interpret, to their own destruction. Farewell. The 5th of the Calends of April.

The Report of Pilate the Governor to Augustus Caesar at Rome:

Greeting. To the most potent, august, divine and awful, Augustus Caesar, Pilate the administrator of the Eastern Province.

I have received information, most excellent one, in consequence of which I am seized with fear and trembling. For in this Province which I administer, one of the cities is called Jerusalem, the whole multitude of Jews delivered unto me a certain man called Jesus, and brought many accusations against him, which they were unable to establish by consistent evidence. But they charged him with one heresy in particular, namely, that Jesus said that the Sabbath was not a rest, nor to be observed by them. For he performed many cures on that day, and made the blind see, and the lame walk, raised the dead, cleansed lepers, healed the paralytics who were wholly unable to move their body or brace their nerves, but could only speak and discourse, and he gave them power to walk and run, removing their infirmity by his word alone. There is another mighty deed which is strange to the gods we have; he raised up a man who had been four days dead, summoning him by his word alone, when the dead man had begun to decay, and his body was corrupted by the worms which had been bred, and had the stench of a dog; but, seeing him lying in the tomb he commanded him to run, nor did the dead man at all delay, but as a bridegroom out of his chamber, so did he go forth from the tomb, filled with abundant perfume. Moreover, even such as were strangers, and clearly demoniacs, who had their dwelling in deserts, and devoured their own flesh, and wandered about like cattle and creeping things, he turned into inhabiters of cities, and by word rendered them rational, and prepared them to become wise and powerful and illustrious, taking their food with all the enemies of the unclean spirits, which were destructive in them and which he cast into the depth of the sea. And again, there was another who had a withered hand, and not only the hand but rather half of the body of the man was like a stone, and he had neither the shape of a man nor the symmetry of a body; even him he healed with a word and rendered whole. And a woman, also, who had an issue of blood for a long time, and whose veins and arteries were exhausted, and who did not bear a human body, being like one dead, and daily speechless, so that all of the physicians of the district were unable to cure her, for there remained unto her not a hope of life, but as Jesus passed by she mysteriously received strength by his shadow falling on her, from behind she touched the hem of his garment, and immediately in that very hour, strength filled her exhausted limbs, as if she had not suffered anything, she began to run along towards Capernaum, her own city, so that she reached it in six days' journey. I have made known these things which I have recently been informed of, and which Jesus did on the Sabbath. And he did other miracles greater than these, so that I have observed greater works of wonder done by him than by the gods we worship. But Herod and Archelaus and Philip, Annas and Caiaphas, with all the people, delivered him unto me, making a great tumult against me in order that I might try him. Therefore I commanded him to be crucified and when I had first scourged him, though I found no cause in him for evil accusations or dealings. Now when he was crucified, there was a darkness over all the world, and the sun was obscured for half a day, and the stars appeared, but no luster was seen in them, and the moon lost its brightness, as though tinged with blood, and the world of the departed was swallowed up, so that the very sanctuary of the temple, as they call it, did not appear to the Jews themselves at their fall, but they perceived a chasm in the earth, and the following of successive thunders. And amid this terror the dead appeared rising again, and the Jews themselves bore witness that it was Abraham and Isaac, and Jacob, and the twelve patriarchs, and Moses and Job, who died before, as they say, some three thousand five hundred years. And there were very many whom I myself saw appearing in the body, and they made lamentation over the Jews, because of the transgression, which was committed by them, and because of the destruction of the Jews and their Law. And the terror of the earthquake continued from the sixth hour of the preparation until the ninth hour; and when it was evening on the first day of the week, there came a sound from heaven, and the heaven became seven times more luminous than on all other days. And at the third hour of the night the sun appeared more luminous than it had ever shone, lighting up the whole hemisphere. As lightning flashes suddenly come forth in a storm, so there were seen men, lofty in stature, and surpassing in glory, a countless host, crying out, and their voice was heard as that of exceeding loud thunder, Jesus that was crucified is risen again, come up from Hades ye that were enslaved in the subterraneous recesses of Hades. And the chasm in the earth was as if it had no bottom, but it was so that the very foundations of the earth appeared, with those that shouted in heaven, and walked in the body among the dead that were raised. And He that raised up all the dead and bound in Hades said, "Say to my disciples, 'He goeth before you into Galilee, there ye shall see Him.'" And all that night the light ceased not shining. And many of the Jews died in the chasm of the earth, being swallowed up, so that on the morrow most of those who had been against Jesus were not to be found. Others saw the apparition of men rising against [him] whom none of us had ever seen. One synagogue of the Jews was alone left in Jerusalem itself for they all disappeared in that ruin. Therefore, being astounded by that terror, and being possessed with the most dreadful trembling, I have written what I saw at that time and sent it to thine excellency, and I have inserted what was done against Jesus by the Jews, and sent it to thy divinity, my lord.

The Report of Pontius Pilate, Governor of Judea:
To the most potent, august, dreadful, and divine Augustus, Pontius Pilate, administrator of the Eastern Province.

I have undertaken to communicate to thy goodness by this my writing, though possessed with much fear and trembling, most excellent king, the present state of affairs, as the result hath shown. For as I administered this province, my lord, according to the command of thy serenity, which is one of the eastern cities called Jerusalem, wherein the temple of the nation of the Jews is erected, all the multitude of the Jews being assembled, delivered up to me a certain man called Jesus, bringing many endless accusations against him, but they could not convict him in anything. But they had one heresy against him, that he said the sabbath was not their proper rest. Now that man wrought many cures and good works; he caused the blind to see, he cleansed lepers, he raised the dead, he healed paralytics, who could not move at all but only had voice, and all their bones in their places; and he gave them strength to walk and run enjoining it by his word alone. And he did a yet more mighty work, which had been strange even among our gods: He raised from the dead one Lazarus, who had been dead four days, commanding by a word alone that the dead man should be raised, when his body was already corrupted by worms which bred in his wounds. And he commanded the fetid body, which lay in the grave, to run, and as a bridegroom from his chamber so he went forth from his grave, full of sweet perfume. And some that were grievously afflicted by demons, and had their dwellings in desert places, and devoured the flesh of their own limbs, and went up and down among creeping things and wild beasts, because to dwell in cities in their own houses, and by a word, made them reasonable, and caused to become wise and honorable those that were vexed by unclean spirits, and the demons that were in them he sent out into a herd of swine into the sea and drowned them. Again, another who had a withered hand, and lived in suffering, and had not even the half of his body sound, he made whole by a word alone. And a woman who had an issue of blood for a long time, so that because of the discharge all the joints of her bones were seen and shone through like glass, for all the physicians had dismissed her without hope, and had not cleansed her, for in her there was no hope of health at all; but once Jesus was passing by and she touched from behind the hem of his garments, and in that very hour the strength of her body was restored, and she was made whole, as if she had no affliction, and began to run fast to her own city of Paneas. And these things happened thus; but the Jews reported that Jesus did these things on the sabbath. And I saw that greater marvels had been wrought by him than by the gods we worship. Him then Herod and Archelaus and Philip and Annas and Caiaphas, with all the people delivered up to me, to put him on his trial. And because many raised a tumult against me, I commanded that he should be crucified. Now when he was crucified darkness came over all the world; the sun was altogether hidden, and the sky appeared dark while it was yet day, so that the stars were seen, though still they had their luster obscured, wherefore I supposed your excellency is not unaware that in all the world they lighted their lamps from the sixth hour until evening. And the moon, which was like blood, did not shine all night long, although it was at the full, and the stars and Orion made lamentation over the Jews, because of their transgression committed by them. And on the first day of the week, about the third hour of the night, the sun appeared as it never shone before, and the whole heaven became bright. And as lightnings come in a storm, so certain men of lofty stature, in beautiful array, and of indescribable glory, appeared in the air, and a countless host of angels, crying out and saying, "Glory to God in the highest, and on earth peace, good will among men: Come up from Hades, Ye who are in bondage in the depths of Hades." And at their voice all the mountains and hills were moved, and the rocks were rent, and great chasms were made in the earth, so that the very places of the abyss were visible. And among the terror dead men were seen rising again, so that the Jews who saw it said, "We behold Abraham and Isaac, and Jacob and the twelve patriarchs, who died some two thousand five hundred years before, and we beheld Noah clearly in the body. And all the multitude walked about and sang hymns to God with a loud voice, saying, "The Lord, our God, who hath risen from the dead, and Hades he hath spoiled and slain." Therefore, my lord king, all that night the light ceased not. But many of the Jews died and were sunk and swallowed up in the chasms that night, so that not even their bodies were to be seen. Now I mean, that those of the Jews suffered who spoke against Jesus. And but one synagogue remained in Jerusalem, for all the synagogues that had been against Jesus were overwhelmed. Through that terror, therefore, being amazed and being seized with a great trembling, in that very hour, I ordered what had been done by them all to be written, and I have sent it to thy mightiness.

[*Harry Loose: I am now instructed to further write you of the Trial and Condemnation of Pontius Pilate:*]

Now when the letters came to the city of the Romans, and were read to Caesar with no few standing there, they were all terrified, because through the transgression of Pilate, the darkness and the earthquake had happened to all the world. And Caesar, being filled with anger, sent soldiers and commanded that Pilate should be brought as a prisoner. And when he was brought to the city of the Romans, and Caesar heard he was come, he sat in the temple of the gods, above all the senate, and with all the army, and with all the multitude of his power, and commanded that Pilate should stand in the entrance. And Caesar said to him, "Most impious one, when thou sawest so great signs done by that man, why didst thou dare to do thus? By daring to do an evil deed thou hast ruined all the world." And Pilate said, "King and Autocrat, I am not guilty of these things, but it is the multitude of the Jews who are precipitate and guilty." And Caesar said, "And who are they?" Pilate said, "Herod, Archelaus, Philip and Caiaphas, and all the multitude of the Jews." And Caesar saieth, For what cause didst thou execute their purpose?" And Pilate said, "Their nation is seditious and insubordinate, and not submissive to thy power." And Caesar said, "When they delivered him to thee thou oughtest to have made him secure and sent him to me, and not consented to them to crucify such a man, who was just and wrought such great and good miracles, as thou saidst in thy report. For by such miracles, Jesus was manifested to be the Christ, and King of the Jews." And when Caesar said this and himself named the name of Christ, all the multitude of the gods fell down together, and became like dust where Caesar sat with the senate. And all the people that stood near Caesar were filled with trembling because of the utterance of the word and the fall of their gods, and being seized with fear, they all went away, every man to his house, wondering at what had happened. And Caesar commanded Pilate be safely kept, that he might know the truth about

Jesus. And on the morrow, when Caesar sat in the capital with all the senate, he undertook to question Pilate again. And Caesar said, "Say the truth, most impious one, for through thy impious deed which thou didst commit against Jesus, even here the doing of thy evil works were manifested, in that the gods were brought to ruin. Say, then, who is he that was crucified, for his name hath destroyed all the gods?" And Pilate said, "And verily his records are true: For even I myself was convinced by his works that he was greater than all the gods whom we venerate." And Caesar said, "For what cause didn't thou then perpetrate against him such daring and doing, not being ignorant of him, or assuredly designing some mischief to my government?" And Pilate said, "I did it because of the transgression and sedition of the lawless and ungodly Jews." And Caesar was filled with anger, and held a counsel with all his senate and officers, and ordered a decree to be written against the Jews thus: "To Licianus who holdeth first place in the east country. Greeting. I have been informed of the audacity perpetrated very recently by the Jews inhabiting Jerusalem and the cities round about, and their lawless doing, how they compelled Pilate to crucify a certain God called Jesus, through which great transgression of theirs the world was darkened and drawn into ruin. Determine therefore, with a body of soldiers, to go to them there at once and proclaim their subjection to bondage of this decree. By obeying and proceeding against them, and scattering them abroad in all nations, enslave them, and by driving their nation from Judea as soon as possible show, wherever this hath not appeared, that they are full of evil. And when this decree came into the east country, Licianus obeyed, through fear of the decree, and laid waste all the nation of the Jews, and caused those that were left in Judea to go into slavery with them that were scattered among the Gentiles, that it might be known by Caesar that these things had been done by Licianus against the Jews in the east country, and to please him. And again Caesar resolved to have Pilate questioned, and commanded a captain, Albius by name, to cut off Pilate's head saying, "As he laid hands upon the just man, that is called Christ, he also shall fall in like manner, and find no deliverance." And when Pilate came to the place he prayed in silence saying, "O Lord, destroy not me with the wicked Hebrews, for I should not have laid hands upon thee, but for the nation of lawless Jews, because they provoked sedition against me; but thou knowest that I did evil that I did it in ignorance. Destroy me not, therefore, for this, my sin, nor be mindful of the evil that is in me, O Lord, and in thy servant, Procla, who standeth with me in this, the hour of my death, whom thou taughtest to prophesy that thou must be nailed to the cross. Do not punish her too in my sin, but forgive us, and number us in the portion of thy just ones." And behold, when Pilate had finished his prayer, there came a voice from heaven, saying, "All generations and the families of the Gentiles shall call thee blessed, because under thee were fulfilled all these things that were spoken of by the prophets concerning me; and thou, thyself, must appear as my witness at my second coming, when I shall judge the twelve tribes of Israel, and them that have not confessed my name." And the Prefect cut off the head of Pilate, and behold an angel of the Lord received it. And when his wife Procla saw the angel coming and receiving his head, she also, being filled with joy, forthwith gave up the ghost, and was buried with her husband.

[*Harry Loose: I am now instructed to further write you of the death of Pilate who condemned Jesus:*]

Now whereas Tiberius Caesar, Emperor of the Romans was suffering from a grievous sickness, and hearing that at Jerusalem a certain physician, Jesus by name, who healed all diseases by his word alone, not knowing that the Jews and Pilate had put him to death, he thus bade one of his attendants, Volusianus by name, saying, "Go as quickly as thou canst across the sea, and tell Pilate, my servant, and friend, to send me this physician to restore me to my official health." And Volusianus, having heard the order of the Emperor, immediately departed, and came to Pilate, as was commanded him. And he told the same Pilate, what had been committed to him by Tiberius Caesar, saying, "Tiberius Caesar, Emperor of the Romans, thy Lord, having heard that in this city there is a physician who healeth diseases by his word alone, earnestly entreateth thee to send him to him to heal his disease. And Pilate was greatly terrified on hearing this, knowing that through envy he had caused him to be slain. Pilate answered the messenger, saying thus: "This man was a malefactor, and a man who drew after himself all the people; so, after counsel taken of the wise men of the city, I caused him to be crucified." And as the messenger returned to his lodgings he met a certain woman named Veronica, who had been acquainted with Jesus, and he said, "O woman, there was a certain physician in this city, who healed the sick by his word alone. Why have the Jews slain him?" And she began to weep, saying, "Ah, me, my lord, it was my God and my Lord whom Pilate through envy delivered up, condemned, and commanded to be crucified." Then he, grieving greatly, said, "I am exceedingly sorry that I cannot fulfill that for which my Lord sent me." Veronica said to him, "When my Lord went about preaching, and I was unwillingly deprived of his presence, at least the figure of his likeness might give me consolation. And when I was taking the canvas to the painter to be painted, my lord met me and asked whither I was going. And when I had made known to him the cause of my journey, he asked me for the canvas, and gave it back to me printed with the likeness of his venerable face. Therefore, if thy lord will devoutly look upon the sight of this, he will straightaway enjoy the benefit of health." "Is a likeness of this kind to be procured with gold or silver?" he asked. "No," said she, "but with a pious sentiment of devotion. Therefore, I will go with thee, and carry the likeness to Caesar to look upon, and will return." So Volusianus came with Veronica to Rome, and said to Tiberius, the Emperor, "Jesus, whom thou has long desired, Pilate and the Jews have surrendered to an unjust death, and through envy fastened to the wood of the cross. Therefore a certain matron hath come with me bringing the likeness of the same Jesus, and if thou wilt devoutly gaze upon it, thou wilt presently obtain the benefit of thy health." So Caesar caused the way to be spread with cloths of silk, and ordered the portrait to be presented to him; and as soon as he had looked upon it he regained his original health. Now when Pilate was beheaded, his body was tied with rope to a great rock and sunk in the River Tiber. But the wicked and unclean spirits, rejoicing in his wicked and unclean body, all moved about in the water, and caused in the air dreadful lightning and tempests and thunder and hail, so that all were seized with a horrible fear, on which account the Romans dragged him out of the River Tiber, and bore him away in derision to Vienne, and sunk him in the River Rhone. For Vienne means, as it were, "The Way of Gehenna," because it was a place of cursing. And evil spirits were there and did the same things. These men, therefore, not enduring to be so harassed by demons, removed the vessel of cursing from them and sent it to be buried in the territory of Losania.

Appendix E

UNUSUAL MESSAGE *received by Harry Loose*   *April 11, 1941*

I am come a great distance to stand beside you. I come not alone but with Ayesha. She is not of the planet Urantia but come of first life from the planet of Tal. I am Agrippina. My grandfather was Augustus, the Emperor of the Romans, and I lived my first life on the planet of Urantia. I lived in the palace at Rome and in the home of my grandfather in the hills and at the seashore in the summertime. I lived the earth-life in the flesh when the man Jesus also lived an earth life in the flesh on Urantia. My mother was the daughter of Augustus, the Emperor, and her name was Julia. My father was a member of the Court also. He was Mastis Vispanius Agrippa [*Marcus Vipsanius Agrippa*]. I married the great soldier Germanicus and was with him during all the years of his great campaigns. When my grandfather died and Tiberius became Emperor, he made great trouble for us all who were left because of jealousy. He caused my husband to lose his estates and position in the army and the Court. My mother, Julia, died of grief because of his causing. In the thirtieth year after Jesus' crucifixion, Tiberius seized my person and sent me by his decree to the Island of Pandataria with three serving women and two eunuchs. For three years, I tried to free myself but Tiberius would not release me and I could not escape. I became ill of great melancholy and I starved myself to death three years after my banishing to the island. I am instructed to give to you for presentation to Harold Sherman the following information which I am to speak to you.

(This is the part of the dictation that stopped so suddenly, . . . HJL)

420

APPENDIX F

DREAM   *New York, June 10, 1940*

I seemed suddenly to be in the presence of Laurie Bowen, boy-hood friend of mine in Traverse City, Michigan, who had moved to Canada and joined the Royal Flying Corps there, giving his life in the last world war.

Laurie was in uniform and appeared eager to impress me with some vital information:

"Harold," he said, facing me directly and looking in my eyes as though concerned lest he not be able to reach my consciousness com-pletely, "We have been trying to get this knowledge through to the world for years. There is a secret group in Germany, a band of at least a hundred who represent the strategy board or brain trust.

"These men are the leading scientists, inventors, chemists, tech-nicians, military geniuses and all-around authorities in the country. They are kept in fortified seclusion, their every want satisfied in mag-nificent underground quarters in Berlin, containing industrial plants, laboratories of every description, radio communication centers and every device and equipment for enabling this board to follow the progress of the war on every front at all times of the day and night.

"The theory behind this board is that the brains of the country need to be protected in a place removed from the terrific heat of battle where every development may be followed impassively, uninfluenced by the emotional stress and strain of leaders on any sector at the front who might be over-influenced by happenings and vision and reason so clouded as to make the wrong moves or decisions.

"All responsibility for the conduct of Germany's destiny rests with this board. Through an amazing communication system the decisions are made known to the general staff in the field and the coordinating arms of air, tank, infantry, artillery and naval forces concentrate action at whatever point or points is considered most strategic at the moment."

As Laurie spoke, I seemed to be taken to this underground headquarters, having the sensation of being in an immense, brilliantly-lighted corridor with high white walls on which were encased, under glass, great maps of all the different countries in the world. They were elaborate in detail with every conceivable military object located thereon and last-minute changes specified. These were working maps, but opposite each, on the other side of the corridor, was another map with the marked-out plan of action and the ultimate aims of Germany concerning that country which had been prepared years before!

This enabled the military strategists to know or recall, at a glance, the plan they had devised for the conquering of this particular country and to check the actual progress being made in that direction on the working map, directly across therefrom. I was impressed that no such system of detailed planning for war and for world domination had ever heretofore been conceived.

This strategy board, representing collectively the power of Germany, can then—through leaping abreast of every development, national and international—send out orders to agents in every country, starting agitation in Fifth Columns here, holding it up there, jockeying all their lines of attack to synchronize with the pressure Germany's armies are exerting on the field.

I was given the impression that Mussolini's apparent stalling was nothing of the sort. He is in the hand of his military planning board, subject to their orders, and will only move when they give him the word. Italian and Russian officers or representatives are guests of this German executive group but are actually hostages for the duration of the war, and should either Italy or Russia renege on her promises, those men's lives will be forfeited to preserve the secrets they now share.

I vaguely recall seemingly miles of underground rooms and passages, all strongly guarded and absolutely concealed from the knowledge of the unsuspecting rank and file of Berlin. Many Germans, now thought dead, having disappeared mysteriously some years ago, are alive and at work in these quarters.

Laurie told me, seemingly, that unless the location of this secret hiding place could be discovered and destroyed, together with the brilliant men who control and direct Germany's destiny, there would be little that could be done to prevent her conquering of the world in the due course of time, in conjunction with her present allies.

Hitler, outside coordinator of all the plans and movements that are perfected by the inner body, does not issue an order that has not been checked through the group. He would be lost were this powerful alliance of brains annihilated.

This system has been devised to prevent any disaster in the field, such as the possible capturing or killing of commanding officers, from deterring or destroying in any way the effective operation of German forces on any or all fronts.

In this manner, war can be carried on through what amounts to remote control, with the plan of battle communicated to all fronts daily, even hourly, and those in charge in different sectors simply following through.

This strategy board is in session 24 hours of every day, one third of its number asleep at all times but two-thirds on the job, awake and alert to every kind of happening anywhere in the world which may have an effect on, for or against Germany.

It is as though these men are sitting before a giant chess board, commissioned to develop all the checkmating answers to any moves that may appear, no matter from what countries they may come.

All strings are pulled in accordance with a pre-arranged plan and the designed result of each move is known in advance. The knowledge of human psychology and how to outwit, mislead or intimidate leaders as well as masses of different countries is profound.

Germany has thus, under Hitler, perfected a system such as the world has never seen, capable of cutting through all red tape and translating ideas and plans into action almost instantaneously in any part of the world.

Unless those countries opposing Germany can so organize themselves as to move with like speed, they are destined to go down in crushing defeat. Nothing can compete with such highly synchronized, organized power and the crystallization of all national resources in addition to the most brilliant minds in all Germany.

Britain and France, at present, have no national unity or planning board comparable; no well-mapped plan of attack or defense against such a deeply plotted and highly geared system.

Any baffling development in the way of war weapons or resistance that German forces may encounter becomes the immediate problem that this strategy board must solve. Since it is comprised of all technical minds, the solution is theoretically possible in this group and a specific answer developed. If it requires new inventive genius to counteract, these forces are set in motion.

It seemed to me that Laurie tried to reveal the location of the heart of this underground headquarters. He took me before a great map of Berlin and pointed to a section on my left and a little above the lower half as about the spot.

I got the impression of this spot being covered by an enormous building or group of buildings, comparatively new. One of the buildings, easily a block or several blocks square, appeared to have columns or pillars on three sides. The grounds or driveways about this structure were paved and landscaped, concealing from ordinary eyes the fact that all were highly fortified. I was impressed that the roof and walls of this building or buildings were of special thickness and design, built to withstand terrific bombing as a means of protecting vital underground chambers and living quarters.

As these impressions faded, I seemed to find myself facing Trev Carver, an old friend of Laurie's. I asked Trev if he had seen Laurie and he said, "Yes," that Laurie was "staying with him" for a few days, giving his child some special instruction. I got the impression that Trev's child had been a soul Laurie knew before incarnation as Trev's child and that Laurie was keeping in touch for world reasons, knowing the destiny the child had to fulfill.

I recall now that I was impressed with the fact that many who comprise this strategy board have lived for years in foreign countries and speak the native tongue of these countries, possessing an intimate knowledge of conditions and peoples there, so that authoritative information can be gotten from them whenever a situation arises without the necessity for going beyond the members of the board. This gives to those directing Germany's destiny an enormous advantage and facility.

The impressions just recorded were most vivid and my feeling of having been somewhere in company with Laurie is also quite real.

Appendix G

THE NEW YORK TIMES, Saturday, April 26, 1941

LEGENDARY LETTER OF JESUS IS READ

—

NYU Educator Gives Translation of Papyrus Found
in Palestine in 1936

—

AN EXCHANGE WITH SHEIK

—

Sheet, With Writing on Both Sides, Has Syrian's Offer
of Haven and Saviour's Reply

—

Special to The New York Times

WASHINGTON, April 25 – An apocryphal incident in the life of
Jesus Christ, involving an exchange of letters with a sick Syrian sheik
who offered Him haven from His enemies in return for healing, was
told here today by Dr. Lionel Casson of New York University, who
presented a paper containing the texts of the letters as taken from a
seventh-century Greek-inscribed papyrus, before the Classical Association of the Atlantic States at the Hotel Mayflower.

The papyrus, a single sheet with writing on both sides, was discovered in 1936 by the Colt Archaeological Institute of New York
among the ruins of two churches in Auja Hafir, in Southern Palestine.
With other manuscripts found, it was turned over by the institute for

425

study and publication to Dr. Casson and Professor Ernest L. Hettich, both of the Classics Department of Washington Square, New York University.

Translation is Given

Dr. Casson's translation of the papyrus, which names Abgar, Toparch (princeling) of the city of Edessa, as the second correspondent, is as follows:

"Abgar, Toparch of the city of Edessa, to Jesus, the Benevolent Saviour, who has appeared in the city of Jerusalem, greetings.

"I have heard about you and about the cures which you effect without the use of medicines or herbs. For it is said that you can cause the blind to see, the lame to walk; that you cleanse lepers and drive out unclean spirits and demons and that you heal men tortured with chronic diseases and that you raise the dead. When I heard all these reports about you, I made up my mind that one of two things were possible: either as God descended from heaven you are accomplishing these miracles, or as the Son of God. And because of this I am now writing to beg you to come to me and cure me of my disease. For I have also heard that the Jews are muttering against you and want to do you evil. Mine is a very small city, but honored, and is sufficient for both of us."

Reply attributed to Jesus

The reply of Jesus:

"Letter of Jesus Christ, son of God, to Abgar, Toparch of Edessa.

"You are blessed and blessed is your city, called Edessa. You are blessed because you have faith in me although you have not seen me. For it is written of me that those who have seen me have no trust in me, but that those who have not seen me will believe and abide in me. Because you have shown your trust in me, preparations for your health will be made for you in every way. With respect to my coming to you, of which you wrote, I am obliged to fulfill these duties for which I was sent here by my Father, and, after doing so, to be taken up by my Father who sent me. But I am sending you one of my disciples who will cure you of your disease and give you eternal life and peace to you and all of yours, and who will make your city safe so that none of your enemies may conquer it. Therefore I have written this letter in my own hand and sealed it with my seal."

Versions in Several Languages

The story of the exchange of letters between Jesus and Abgar is well known and is regarded as apocryphal, Dr. Naphthali Lewis of the Washington Square College Classics Department, said yesterday. Versions of the texts exist in Latin, Syriac, Armenian, Coptic, and Persian as well as Greek, Dr. Lewis added.

The Colt papyrus is important because it gives the full texts, only part of the prescripts being missing, and because it is related to a source independent of the fourth-century "Ecclesiastical History" of Eusebius, from which almost all other accounts of the episode derive, Dr. Lewis explained.

The manuscript was dated by paleography, which is the study of ancient modes of writing, and is the property of the institute, which is headed by H. D. Colt, Jr. of 470 Park Avenue.

The sequel of the episode related to the papyrus is that Abgar, sheik of Oarhoene, was cured after the crucifixion and ascension to heaven of Jesus by the disciple Addai, sent to him by the Apostle Thomas. The inhabitants of Oarhoene, of which Odessa was the capital, were converted to Christianity in the second century.

Appendix H

December 20th 1941

Mr.Harold M.Sherman
1746 No.Cherokee Ave.,
Hollywood,California.

Dear Mr.Sherman:-

A reply to your request can be made clear in one individual letter containing all the information desired and not signed by myself alone but by the four of us who know the circumstances in detail.

I and my husband ,Raymond A.Burkhart,with my small son John had Thanksgiving Dinner with my parents,H.J.Loose and Mrs Emily H.Loose who reside at 123 No.Elizabeth Ave.,Monterey Park,California,directly accross the street from my own home at 122 No.Elizabeth Ave.. The day under mention is that of Thanksgiving Day,Thursday Nov.20th.,1941. On finishing our 12.30 noon dinner,my mother and my Aunt,Miss Dorothy Hesse, went to the rear of the house for their evry day after dinner sleeping period of an hour or less. This was at 1.30 P.M. exactly by the front room clock. The hour was announced by all of us as it was a little later than the usual laying down period of my mother. My husband,Raymond A.Burkhart,and I and my small son John lingered but a few moments,possibly 5 minutes,at the door and on the front porch talking to my father and then we crossed the street to our own home. My father bid us good by on the front porch. He was dressed in his old pants but had on a blue dress shirt with a grey and black figured tie. He also had on his old house slippers. His shoes were in the closet off the bed room where my mother and aunt were sleeping. My husband,my boy,and myself crossed the street and got out our car from our locked garage and within the next few minutes (guessing-- 6-8) we left in the car. My father was still in the house visable through the front window sitting in the big chair and reading a book. The garage doors at 123 No.Elizabeth Ave., were closed and his car was not out. It could have been no earlier than between 15 and 20 minutes to 2 o'clock when we drove away. The above ends the knowledge of myself and husband as to the whereabouts of my father on this November 20th 1941 Thanksgiving Day. The following is the observance of my mother and aunt in continuation. My mother and aunt woke from their nap. One waking first and disturbing the other to wakefullness. The woke a few moments earlier than 2.30 P.M. by the bed-room alaram clock but conversed and did not arise untill the half hour hand pointed to exactly 2.30. They both came to-gether into the front room and there was my father with his slippers still on and his very open still reading a book. The large front room clock indicated some minutes later than 2.30 P.M.. This would not mean anything particular however as there is always a few moments difference between the two clocks.

From the personal knowledge of us all,the four signers of this letter, my father had not left the house on this day and it would have been impossible for him to present himself at your place of residence at the time that you indicate---- 2.30 P.M. of this day. Trusting that the above answers your question fully, we remain,

Sincerely, *Mrs. R.A.Burkhart* *R.A.Burkhart*

Mrs Emily H Loose *Miss Dorothy Hesse*

Appendix I

The
Canterbury Apartments
1746 NORTH CHEROKEE AVE.
Hollywood. California

December 27, 1941.

Mr. Harold M. Sherman,
1746 N. Cherokee Ave.,
Hollywood, Cal.,

Dear Mr. Sherman:

        I am writing you, as you suggested,
a detailed account of my experience with what
I now consider the most thrilling happening
of my life.

        On Thanksgiving Day, November 20th,
1941, about 2:30 p.m. in the afternoon, while
on duty as desk clerk in this apartment house
where you live, I was seated at the switchboard
talking to a guest in the building, whom I cannot
recall at this time.

        When a gentleman came up to the desk,
I excused myself and asked what he wanted. He
was dressed rather unusual for the day and, too,
I thought, not the type to be calling on one of
our guests.

        Under a strain of some kind and with
a strange facial expression, he said, "Will you
take a message for Mr. Sherman?" I got the pad
and waited for the message. Then, after a slight
hesitation, he began very slowly and clearly as
though it was a very important one.

        "Tell - Mr. - Sherman - Mr. - Loose -
will - see - him - Sunday - - ".

        After each word he made a face as a
person would who had false teeth and had
difficulty keeping them in place. He then asked:
"Have you that correct?" I said, "I did" and he
left.

429

The
Canterbury Apartments
1746 NORTH CHEROKEE AVE.
Hollywood. California

-2-

      The guest I was talking to, remarked:
"He was a strange one, wasn't he?" I then stood
up, thinking he might have heard her remark, and
to see if he had rested on the sofa before leaving
as he seemed out of breath and not natural.

      I then noticed that he had left the
lobby although I had not heard the front door
open and close, as I customarily did, so I felt
free to answer her remark. I said, "Yes, he was
strange. He certainly wanted to be sure his message
was delivered." I then went on with my conversation
with her after putting the message in Mr. Sherman's
box.

      Due to the size of our apartment house
and the many people I come in contact with, I gave
this no further thought but went on with my duties.

      Mr. and Mrs. Sherman returned about
3 or 3:15 p.m. and I called to them and gave them
the message. Mr. Sherman said, "It's too bad I
missed Mr. Loose. I will call him up."

      About 3:30 p.m. Mr. Sherman came down
to the desk and asked me about the caller, saying
he had phoned Mr. Loose who lived in Monterey Park,
some fifteen to twenty miles away, and he said he
hadn't left the house. They had a family reunion and
a big Thanksgiving Dinner and Mr. Loose had been at
home all the time.

      I thought this very strange and Mr. Sherman
asked me to describe the caller. I said he was a
man in his fifties - rugged complexion - wearing a
cap, brown sweater and dark blue shirt. He appeared
like a working man. Mr. Sherman said that described
Mr. Loose perfectly, as he had seen him dressed on
other occasions, and that there must be something
odd about the experience, and he would talk to me
later about it.

      I then said I thought it odd Mr. Loose
didn't ask if Mr. Sherman were at home or for me to
call Mr. Sherman - but he had just said he wanted

The
Canterbury Apartments
1746 NORTH CHEROKEE AVE.
Hollywood, California

-3-

to leave a message for Mr. Sherman. I also explained
the facial expressions and hesitation in his speech.

Mr. Sherman thought that odd and said
he hadn't noticed that about Mr. Loose - but that
my description was his all right, as he was a man
about the house who believed in being natural and
the family were just real regular folks who didn't
stand on ceremony as to dress for festive occasions.

A few days later, Mr. Sherman visited
Mr. Loose in his home and discussed the experience
of Thanksgiving Day with him, and Mr. Loose became
very concerned and wanted to meet me and hear the
experience from me.

He came in the side door of the apartment
house, wearing the same clothes he had been wearing
Thanksgiving day, except for a lighter shirt. I
stood up and said, "Good morning, Mr. Loose," and
he asked for Mr. Sherman. I said I didn't think Mr.
Sherman was in, and at that time, Mr. Sherman stepped
up behind Mr. Loose, when he found I had recognized
him.

I became a little excited and said, "This
is the gentleman who called on you Thanksgiving Day".
They both laughed and Mr. Sherman introduced Mr. Loose
to me, who explained that the darker blue shirt he
had worn on Thanksgiving Day was now in the wash.

Mr. Loose then asked me to explain what
had happened on Thanksgiving Day, and I repeated to
him what I have related above.

Sincerely,

William A. Cousins

APPENDIX J

Friday the 13th,
March 13th, 1942

Dear Harold:

I hope the enclosed will not too much disturb you.
Harold Hansen, whom I know rather well from years of
reading his column, is rather disdainful of anything
he knows little about. I think this sort of review
might well have been expected.

But the fact that Hansen devotes his entire column to
the book shows that it intrigued him. Why should he
review it at all unless he was interested in it? There
are a dozen books a day published. I have a bone to pick
with Hansen when I next see him that he did not see fit to
mention that the N. Y. Times radio operator signed a sworn
statement that you got better reports from Sir Hubert than
he did. I am writing Hansen and giving him a piece of my
mind. You couldn't, but I can. This reviewing game is a
racket. I know how it is worked......I will be interested
to see the other reviews, which I hope will be more fair.
I am speaking on the book and plugging it next Sunday, day
after tomorrow, and am advertising the lecture in four papers
tomorrow and two Sunday. We have to buck the cynics and the
prejudiced, but we will eventually get the thinking public
with us.

Cordially,

Charles

The First Reader—
Explorer, Writer Publish Discoveries in Telepathy

By HARRY HANSEN

SIR HUBERT WILKINS is an Arctic explorer and Harold M. Sherman is a New York City scenario writer, now in Hollywood. These two eminent authorities—on exploring and scenario writing—have been reading each other's minds. Or, more accurately, Sherman has been putting down what he thought Sir Hubert was thinking and doing on prolonged Arctic flights, to prove that he had extra-sensory perception—in other words, telepathic powers.

Mr. Hansen

Of the two men, Sir Hubert was not wholly converted to mind-reading across vast distances, but he was willing to play the game, and he seems to think Sherman actually did hit on what he was doing at different times in the Arctic, far from air mail or radio. Sherman, on the other hand, is the enthusiastic exponent of telepathy and, in his own mind, an ideal receiver of impressions from afar. He has backed up his records with sworn statements that he mailed his notes when written to New York witnesses or gave evidence to them of knowing what Sir Hubert was doing, these men being Gardner Murphy, Samuel Emery, Dr. Henry S. W. Hardwicke, Dr. A. E. Strath-Gordon and Reginald Iverson.

* * *

Writers Share Book

It's all made clear in a book called "Thoughts Through Space," in which Sir Hubert Wilkins occupies 147 pages and Harold Sherman 274 pages as co-author, which I am now about to discuss. (Creative Age Press.)

As most of my readers know by this time, I have an open mind in these matters. I consider telepathy, fortune-telling, numerology, astrology, tiddledy-winks and cross-word puzzles harmless and soothing. We shouldn't underestimate their therapeutic value. They keep busy at pleasant tasks a lot of people who might otherwise write poetry or fall into manholes.

The Wilkins-Sherman opus, however, makes unusual demands on my mental powers. Sir Hubert is a man of reputation, and he says Sherman's notes often recorded what he actually was doing. Of course, he didn't see them until long after the event, but his memory is unimpaired. Sherman, on the other hand, filed his notes with sworn witnesses.

* * *

Some Evidence

Of course, I don't fall awfully hard for the supersensitive mind when Sherman writes about Wilkins: "You seem to be in building with steps leading up to the door." By crackey, Wilkins says it was true—the hotel had wide steps leading up to the door. "De-icing equipment, need of same," writes Sherman. Sir Hubert admits: "Thought of adding to de-icing equipment." There you are, two minds with one thought, continents apart.

There are many "hits" like that. They make me feel there must be something in it, laying the "groundwork for a new and great science of the mind." May even be worth the price to read all about it, who can tell?

* * *

Dr. Charles Francis Potter takes exception to my comment recently on telepathy hocus-pocus in "Thoughts Through Space." He says he is a hard-boiled skeptic, but knows the authors, Sir Hubert Wilkins and Harold M. Sherman, and "they are genuine and much puzzled by the results as anyone." (Sherman is not puzzled by the results; he is eloquent about his telepathic power). Then Dr. Potter offers an incident of his own:

"Yesterday my wife opened a magazine which I had never seen and looked at a picture in it. What do you get? I said: 'There is a man there. I see only his head and shoulders. It is a bust portrait, three-quarters view.' She asked, 'What nationality is he?' And I said, 'Chinese.' It was a picture of a Japanese, three-quarters view, sharply cut off at the shoulders, and he looked more like a Chinese than a Japanese. How did I get it. Three elements. Bust of a man. Sharply cut off at the shoulders. Oriental. These three factors rule out coincidence."

* * *

Excerpt from Harry Hansen's column in The Pittsburgh Press, *March 26, 1942*

[Newspapers.com]

INDEX

THE URANTIA DIARIES
of Harold and Martha Sherman

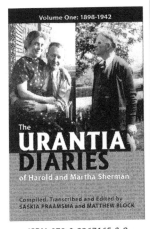
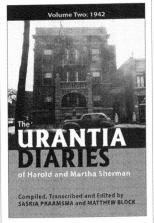
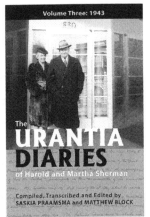
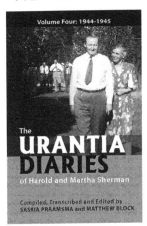
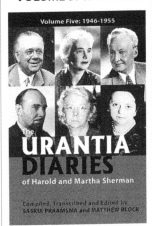
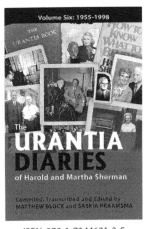

Made in the USA
Las Vegas, NV
01 December 2023

81933307R00270